SHIFTING THE PATTERNS

SHIFTING THE PATTERNS

Breaching the memetic codes of corporate performance

If Price

and

Ray Shaw

2000

Published in 1998 by Management Books 2000 Ltd,
Cowcombe House,
Cowcombe Hill,
Chalford,
Gloucestershire GL6 8HP
Tel: 01285-760722. Fax: 01285-760708
e-mail: MB2000@compuserve.com

Printed and bound in Great Britain by Biddles, Guildford

British Library Cataloguing in Publication Data is available

ISBN 1-85252-253-4

Contents

Foreword

I have had the privilege of being familiar with the thoughts in this book for several years now. I first got to know If Price from my role as the host of the Complex-M discussion list on the Internet – a group of 500 managers and academics who debate the influence of complex systems studies (or "complexity") on the management of organisations. As my relationship with If broadened, we learned that we shared many academic interests. Many hours of reading and debate later, If presented his, and his colleague Ray Shaw's, ideas to a gathering of the New England Complex Systems Institute. From that date forward, he was known as 'Dr Meme'.

Perhaps the most difficult choice a publisher faces when opting to print a particular book is determining just how many trees should be felled so that the ideas of an author can be widely distributed. The power of *Shifting the Patterns* lies in the fact that the ideas herein will be widely distributed almost regardless of what the publisher decided. And, in a self-reflective twist, from the book itself you will understand why. If's and Ray's meme of memes is too potent for any of us to ignore.

Memes are an often recognised but seldom labelled component of how each of us goes about making sense of the world. When a meme 'works' (think, for example, of the idea of DNA as the program of life) we use it as a filter or a frame. The meme calls attention to certain aspects of the situation. It forms a field of attraction that draws related 'concepts' or 'images' in to converge upon the defined 'idea'. The attraction creates added force to the meme that creates more attraction, and so on.

Re-engineering was a positively valued meme once. That meme has been replaced by one that conjures up images of layoffs, cutbacks, and employee suffering. No manager worth his salt would dare use the word 're-engineer' without the awareness of the negative images so summoned up. but re-engineering is not an isolated case. Memes surround the manager and employee in almost everything we do. What this book does is give you a sense of their influence and ubiquity. Only with awareness can you make memes work for you.

One of my favourite examples of this involves the meme that identifies DNA as the program of life. The meme originates in the coincidental timing between the development of the computer and the groundbreaking research by Watson and Crick on the double helix. As computer programming advanced in the public attention span so too did DNA research. These two scientific developments became intertwined in the mind's eye much like the double helix itself. So what, you may ask? Well, ponder this. When you hear the words 'mutant gene' what image occurs in your head? Most likely you think of some form of 'error'. Mutant genes interfere with the proper programming of our DNA, don't they?

To the biologists among us, however, 'mutant genes' are the sole source of the variation and adaptation every species needs to ensure its long-term survival. 'Adapt or die' as they sat. The mutation is not an error but a strength. But most of us are not biologists and instead fall under the heavy influence of the programming meme. To computers mutations in software are bad. And it is 'badness' that influences how we perceive the mutant gene. The political and social implications of this meme influence are huge. The debate about genetic engineering, about genetically altered food, for example, is seldom about the desirability of increased variation; instead it focuses on the 'risks' of mutation. Our debate reflects the memes of the computer programmer and the electrical engineer. Darwin and Mendel please step aside.

Now the computer meme is not the end of the story. As If and Ray tell us, 'memes compete'. Whatever you thought of the US justice system, the memes of OJ Simpson, Monica Lewinsky and Louise Woodward compete to help you form a new image – an image that will survive unscathed only until the next big case which captures attention, and an image which filters and frames your view of that justice system and perhaps even affects your behaviour.

If Price is not the first to write about memes, and he will not be the last. George Orwell was prescient and got the date wrong (*1984*'s thought control is with us but 15 years after Orwell predicted). But only If and Ray (who dares to publicise himself as a mutant meme) could capture the power of memes in language that is as accessible to the businessman as it is to the scientist. Using If's work, and Ray's inspiration, as a guide, you will learn to recognise the memes through which you categorise the world. In this era of self, the memes we use are important components of identity and determinants of action. We each have some awareness of the images we use to categorise and to communicate. Only by recognising them for the memes they are can you hope to either temper their influence on you or better to utilise them for influencing others.

Perhaps this too will be a meme.

Michael Lissack
Financier, whistleblower, entrepreneur
  and management scientist

Acknowledgements

Acknowledgements are one of the last things to do when writing a book yet one of the first items a reader might read, coming as they do at or near the beginning. So our first go to those who brought us together and, so to speak, got us going. In this, personal thanks must go to Brian Weeks. He was soon to be followed by Doug Stanford who not only offered many words of encouragement but put pen to paper himself to provide the many fables that serve to illuminate the text.

Encouragement throughout has been warmly extended by family and friends. Some have been challenged by the exploration of ideas and exchange of views. Many have also put physical, mental and emotional effort into helping this book to emerge. To both the special few and the many we extend our appreciation. Particular thanks go to Joy Batchelor and Judi Lawrence for pattern-shifting editorial challenges, and to Paul Ingrams at MB2000 for his work on the final manuscript.

As for the ideas themselves, their interconnectedness and the shared experiences that underpin many if not all of them, our thanks must go to many people and organisations, to clients, to colleagues, as well as to leading writers, consultants and explorers of our time. We have attempted to acknowledge many of the latter within the 'sources' section at the end of each chapter. The more informal contribution of many of our contacts cannot, though, go unacknowledged – for it is in the nature of these exchanges, as much as the formal, that something is triggered, built upon, sometimes contested, yet more fully digested.

We also wish to publicly acknowledge the experience and contribution of each other in the writing and emergence of this book. There is something in the experience of co-authorship, at times highly creative and great fun, at other times more stressful and hard work, that bears witness to the difference that 'difference' can make, provided one continues to value such differences. It speaks to co-creation and is but a small, very small example, of the human capacity to value difference, and at times to shift patterns, for a different emergent result.

11

The co-creation and contribution, we acknowledge, is far wider and greater than we can even begin to articulate. There are, then, here but a few small words of acknowledgement to very many people.

We also acknowledge our own patterns.While we have tried, in the general text, to be gender neutral, many examples, drawn from our business experiences, reflect cultures where a male pattern predominated.

Last but not least is to acknowledge the reader for their act of co-creation; for, reading – as with listening – is very little if not a creative act; we are partners, so to speak, in a different conversation.

Preface

The journey of a thousand miles
starts with the first step.

Ancient Chinese Proverb

The idea of this book is simple. It is that performance reflects patterns, patterns that simultaneously enable and limit levels of performance within certain boundaries or horizons. The patterns of our concern are those to do with people and companies, and the results they generate.

There is a profound connection between underlying patterns and the results that are made possible and realised with, and through, them. This idea, that performance reflects patterns, may be interpreted as so 'simple' that it is hardly enlightening, and so 'obvious' that it hardly needs expanding. How is it then, that people and companies so often seem unable to create patterns which meet their aspirations for performance in a timely manner; and how is it that we so often continue to engage in patterns which fail to generate the results we want, whether in public or private life? It may be easy to grasp the abstract connection between patterns and performance, but the bigger challenge is the actual practice of shifting patterns for major breakthroughs in performance. In this regard, we need to become effective pattern shifters and performance engineers.

Our limited capacity to shift patterns is exacerbated when we deny, and leave unacknowledged, the degree to which we are so often locked-in to patterns that limit, whether these be patterns operating at the personal, inter-personal, cultural, company or inter-company level. This simple idea of a connection between patterns and performance leads to an apparently simple conclusion: if you want to change the performance of people, or a company, then you'd better change those patterns that limit performance. Yet, all too frequently, any aspiration to improve performance is translated into simply trying harder within a familiar established pattern. As a result we tend to drive ourselves insane by pursuing the law of repeated action: "When in doubt, do what you did yesterday. If it isn't working, do it twice as hard, twice as fast and twice as carefully."

It appears then, that the practice and capability to really shift patterns are more complex than the mere grasp of the abstraction. When we make such attempts there is often frustration at the small degree to which patterns are actually changed. But just as one can point to cases where massive expenditure has achieved little effect, there are also those where limited expenditure results in a truly transformational effect. Remarkable results can be achieved from highly leveraged shifts in patterns.

What we may begin to see is that our individual and collective competence to shift patterns that limit performance is not well-developed. This question of competence is not limited to whether we can or cannot shift patterns; rather, it embraces the speed and efficacy with which we can effect shifts. For, without timely shifts, companies may become extinct – trapped in patterns appropriate to earlier times. It is easy to call for much higher levels of performance from a company, to make demands upon it (whether reasonable or unreasonable) that call for "more for less, with greater quality and faster than ever before"; but what is going to be the pattern that delivers such results within the particular circumstances and environment of a company?

Richard Pascale has suggested that our shared patterns of thinking – our paradigms – need to shift: "The ultimate, and largely ignored, task of management is one of creating and breaking paradigms . . . the trouble is that 99 per cent of managerial attention today is devoted to the techniques that squeeze more out of the existing paradigm – and it's killing us." We suggest that paradigms are but a part, albeit an important part, of any pattern. It may be better to suggest that the prime task of management is one of creating and breaking patterns, of continuously evolving higher performance patterns, and that too much time is devoted to adding yet more sophisticated techniques onto existing patterns that have either reached, or are close to, their limits.

If the idea of a connection between underlying pattern and levels of performance is so simple, how come the practice of shifting patterns is apparently so difficult to effectively execute? Part of the answer itself lies in a pattern. Our general cultural training and the urgency of the business world tend to limit inquiry and solution to the symptomatic level. As a result, we often conspire to pursue and provide superficial cures to deeply rooted limits. We fail to distinguish between surface and deep structures. Indeed, people sometimes conspire towards convenience, playing it safe by offering acceptable solutions that won't work, rather than more effective solutions that, in confronting current limits, might not be accepted. The practice of shifting patterns is also problematic because of the complex interconnections of sub-patterns within larger structures that have both generalised similarities and unique differences. Generalised solutions which ignore the unique attributes and circumstances of particular backgrounds will have limited effect. Equally, inventing unique solutions may be criticised as conduct akin to continually reinventing the wheel. What's important is to see the similarities *and* the differences.

A different way of asking why patterns are so difficult to shift is to ask why established patterns seem so easily to persist? Here we draw a parallel with the natural world, where patterns of physical form and existence appear to last pretty much unchanged over millions of years. The discovery of the evolutionary process, and of the contribution to it of genes and genetic replication, does much to explain the constancy and change of physical patterns of life forms. Genes are the fundamental building blocks upon which physical form takes shape. They are, so to speak, at the root of the biological pattern and seek to replicate themselves and their existence by continuation of their host, the particular species. But reproduction is not perfect. New species emerge by accident through random variation or mutation of genes, the resultant variation in physical form then being favoured or otherwise by the prevailing and perhaps changing environment. When favoured, the new form takes over from the old – leading to the extinction of the established species in favour of the new.

We identify a similar process in the world of human organisation; the same dynamics operating within a much more rapid timescale. Here we are talking, not about the physical form of a company, but its 'living form': how it is organised, what it does, the purposes it serves, the principles it operates from, how it interacts with its environment, and so on. In short we call this the 'living pattern' of the company. If genes shape the physical pattern of species and species variants, what shapes the living pattern of companies? Genes may be viewed as the prime unit of biological inheritance, units which form part of richer biological complexes that determine physical form. We draw and expand upon the idea of the 'meme' as an equivalent unit of cultural inheritance. It is argued that memes form part of richer complexes which, in turn, shape and determine company structure and practices. In a similar manner to the gene, an established meme is intent upon replicating itself by continuation of its host, the particular form of company. We suggest that new species or variants of companies emerge through similar evolutionary processes. Ultimately new variants of companies emerge through the variation or mutation of memes. The key difference is that this does not have to be left to accident or random variation. We can, by human intention and creative act, wilfully change the basis upon which any pattern of company is built.

What triggers such changes? Crisis often serves to shift the pattern of a company. Whether it is rapidly falling profits, declining market share, product/technology obsolescence or some other cause, the crisis operates as a pattern interrupt. The company is forced to confront its limiting pattern. The difficulty with leaving it to crisis is that crisis may come too late. Furthermore, crises place companies into adapt mode; forced to change by virtue of their environments. There is an alternative mode, generative or creative; where, given a shared intention, it is realised that the envisioned future cannot be reached using existing patterns. The fact that we can't get 'there' from 'here' is confronted. The force for change, once committed to the outcome, is then internal, rather than external circumstance.

Whatever it is that serves to operate as a pattern interrupt, and whatever patterns are interrupted, it does not mean that there is a sustainable shift in pattern. When deep structures are unaffected former patterns often reassert their dominance. Patterns are often so self-sustaining that they resume even after considerable interruption. Thus it is so often that: *'plus ça change, plus c'est la même chose'*.

Our purpose in this book is to trace a journey, a journey that explores patterns, the source and origin of patterns, the interconnectedness of patterns, and how patterns may be changed. It provides no prescription, no fixed recipe that is applicable for each and every circumstance. It does suggest a generalised process that is applicable to all. What is the point of the journey? Ultimately it is that each of us may become better pattern cultivators, that we can learn to 'see' the invisible, beneath the surface, patterns that so often serve to limit performance. Only in seeing them, and understanding their origins, can we be free of their grip and empower ourselves to shift those that limit for something else that will help us achieve the results we desire.

This book adopts a certain pattern, a pattern that is intended to provide a structure that fulfils our purpose. In summary, the logic of the book is easily captured: it is that possible results are bounded (simultaneously released and limited) by the pattern that gives rise to them. If you want a different level of result, and you are near the limit of the pattern that gives rise to that result, then you must shift some aspects of that pattern. The design and practice of a new pattern makes a new result possible. Yet familiarity often blinds us. In addition, the pattern, like the gene, is bent on replicating itself and thus avoiding extinction. Many patterns are so deep-rooted, inter-connected, and invisible, that attempts at change all-too frequently do no more than scratch the surface. To initiate a sustainable change in the amalgam and dynamic of patterns – to shift the patterns – requires an expanded capacity to break free from our cultural inheritance – the established patterns – and to breakthrough to something new.

The journey of the book takes us through a number of openings, expansions, and closures, leaving keys on the way that help us to unlock our own patterns. The book opens with *Marching to Different Drums*, an invitation to think differently about companies, their performance, and indeed, ourselves. A revolution is taking place, a revolution in thinking and perspective that is enabling some companies to create much more result than they once imagined to be possible. Shifts of thinking as profound as those of the last renaissance may be needed for companies to survive, let alone prosper. The very way that we think about organisations and companies reflects the evolution of patterns and may themselves need to change.

Where the first chapter seeks an opening, the next two inquire into the underlying limits that serve to keep people and companies stuck, or limited within certain performance boundaries. Chapter Two, *A Walk on the Dark Side*, reveals how, in practice, unspoken, unwritten rules – part of the informal organisation – influence behaviours in companies. These informal codes shape how a company really works as distinct from how it is supposed to work. Very frequently they encourage behaviour diametrically opposed to the longer term interests of the company.

Chapter Three, *Origins Within*, explores the underlying origins of such rules. It argues that most are internally sourced, less products of the conditions or circumstance 'out there' and more, much more, at an almost invisible operating level 'in here': within the complex, self-organising patterns, the paradigms, that define a company. The dominant management paradigm is exposed and the 'rules' aligned with this paradigm revealed. Deeper influences on the pattern of Western thinking are explored.

Chapter Four, *The Pattern's Eye View*, looks at organisational systems as 'living', self-organising, self-maintaining entities. The dynamics and processes of evolution in the genetically specified system open a window onto analogous processes and dynamics in a 'culturally' or 'mentally' specified system. By drawing a parallel between the gene and genetic pattern and the memetic or cultural pattern we argue that, as the organism is to the gene, so the organisation is to the pattern or meme. Both are vehicles for, respectively, the gene's or meme's replication: that is, there is an inherent tendency in self-maintaining systems to the replication of past patterns. If so, then any company, at any time, risks being no more than a reflection of its past, in a sense, no more than an extension of past patterns and formulas of success. That is all too often our experience of companies. An understanding of the dynamics of such patterns is key to breaking out, to change and changing, if such change is to be managed by human intention rather than chance or late reaction to crises.

Chapter Five, *Patterns that Prison*, traces some of the patterns that apply in the personal and interpersonal domains; and how, so often, we are as if stuck within them. Fundamental human processes are explored, ones which often serve to limit different openings or possibilities. The infection of brains by memes serves as a model for many

18

practices of human perception and offers an explanation of the beneath-the-surface, informal, processes which generate self-sealing and self-fulfilling perceptions. How can we start to breach such constraints?

Chapter Six, *Stop the World – I Want to Get On!*, examines the connection between language and the world we see and relate to. By changing the language we change the world. Ideas get created, conveyed, replicated or developed through conversation. Memes mutate through language. By freezing the way we see the world we can trap a current reality and, in doing so, shift it. Rather than unfreezing being a route for change we suggest it is sometimes necessary to freeze a current view so that people can first 'see' it; in effect, making what is 'invisible' visible, so that it can be dealt with. It often takes courage to really confront our skilled incompetence – how we participate in, and reinforce, limiting patterns.

Systems Thinking is introduced as one means for seeing the patterns. Yet 'seeing' and raising our awareness of the grip patterns exert is but one step. How do we then proceed to interrupt these patterns and to develop new ones that are more aligned with the results we wish to produce?

Chapter Seven, *Beyond the I That Beholds*, takes us beyond 'seeing'. Any one of us may 'see' but what does it take to make a difference to established patterns and what difference can be made? What is necessary to shift from being the observer and narrator to being an active player in a new game? All too often we put ourselves into the world as great narrators. The narrator's position can be comfortable. However, even when the roar of the crowd can shift the game or at least raise it, the source of real action is the commitment of the players. The openness we generate within ourselves when we move to a commitment to action is the source of new levels of results. Fundamentally, there is a dramatic shift in orientation from external cause, from seeking explanations external to ourselves, to internal source, to becoming and being agents in transformation, resourceful and purposeful in pursuit of shared visions.

Chapters Eight and Nine, *The Fifth Attribute* and *Collaborate to Compete*, look at patterns at the intra- and inter-company levels. Chapter Eight takes up the earlier theme of the dominant management paradigm and seeks ways in which we may move from 'controlled' to 'committed' enterprises. It continues to develop the means whereby companies (and people) may become not just adaptive but generative systems, creating futures and making them happen, rather than just responding to changes in the environment. Chapter Nine, in exploring the patterns between companies, challenges the holy grail of unbridled competition and develops the idea that we may well need to collaborate in order to compete. Yet, at different levels, there are many patterns that seek to replicate competition, patterns that will limit or destroy prospects for sustained collaboration. We start to see how the patterns at all the different levels – personal, interpersonal, company and intercompany – interact and, in a sense, conspire to maintain established order. What, then, provides real movement, the opportunity for real breakthroughs, from these patterns and this established order?

Chapter Ten, *When Butterflies Flap Their Wings,* plays on the oft-quoted example from Chaos theory to show the principle of sensitivity to initial conditions, and how small differences can amplify into large effects. The metaphor of the butterfly is also used to indicate the transformation between states in a company. Being cocooned in an established pattern can, at one level, be comfortable. At another, breaking out beyond those boundaries to a new state and capacity, is captured in the butterfly's ability to fly. The drama and potential of the metamorphosis is evidenced in as yet too few companies. We show something of what happens when companies release themselves from those patterns that limit what can be. When new patterning replaces old, considerable energy and resourcefulness are released.

Marginal graphics

The book offers a number of media in written form: occasional short anecdotes illustrative of particular patterns; statements of underpinning theory; short fictional essays describing journeys; extracted and profiled quotes; heightened text; visual illustrations. This range of media is intentional. It breaks up the normal pattern of traditional books and quickly signposts the reader to sections of particular relevance to his or her own circumstance. Graphic symbols serve as signposts throughout the text, as follows:

The main text.

An illustrative case.

A link to another chapter.

A short story.

Underpinning theory.

An exercise.

A chapter summary.

Primary sources.

In this way, we hope to make it easier for a reader to choose their own pattern of reading: at one extreme reading from cover to cover, at the other, focusing only on that which 'jumps' from the page. The brief glimpse of the latter may encourage further inquiry; the more rigorous reader may later want to focus on particular concerns. The book is designed to help either process as well as other patterns.

Please enjoy.

1

Marching to different drums: a new Renaissance?

"If a revolution destroys a systematic government, but the patterns of thought that produced that government are left intact, then those patterns will repeat themselves in the succeeding government."
Robert M. Pirsig

The product of patterns

main text

In most British and American corporations the accepted management dress code for men is still the business suit.

In many, the cut of that suit and even the colour and make of the shirt and tie that accompany it, has a considerable impact on one's managerial career. Image counts, right? In Norway, by contrast, the prevailing dress code often embraces an informality that the visitor finds hard to understand. On social occasions the contrast is reversed. For a dinner party our Anglo-Saxon executive is likely to dress down. 'Smart-casual' rules. His Norwegian opposite number is likely to wear a suit. Dressing up for the party is seen as a courtesy to the host.

Such harmless conventions, understood and accepted by all concerned, assist the smooth functioning of formal and informal social gatherings, whether they be 'parties' or 'companies'. They may be seen as trivial examples of what this book is about: the taken-for-granted codes or norms of behaviour which exist in all forms of human organisation. We proceed beyond the trivial to examine deep underlying patterns; how those patterns simultaneously serve to both enable and limit performance, and how a shift or shifts in such patterns can make greater performance both a possibility and a reality. But did we say "trivial examples"? In some cases, just breach the conventions and see what happens! For breaches can carry threat as well as promise.

There is often no need to be consciously aware of such patterns. Their existence enables an organisation to function. Indeed, shared 'patterns' are a prerequisite of organisation. Problems are only perceived when not everyone operates to the same norms. For example, the Anglo-Saxon executive of either gender is likely to arrive at the dinner party a short, but polite, interval after the time stated in the invitation. He or she does so to avoid the embarrassment and impoliteness of arriving too early. Applying, without thinking, such a code when first asked out to dinner by neighbours in Norway, I was embarrassed to be telephoned 15 minutes after the invited time by our host who was greatly concerned that I had misunderstood his invitation.

The point is not cultural subtleties that frustrate, or even baffle, the uninitiated. It is that such trivial examples illustrate the power of tacitly accepted norms, not only in nations and social gatherings, but in any form or scale of organisation. They enable, but simultaneously limit, the organisation. Consider, before we leave the subject of parties, the grand occasion of a formal reception. It could not live up to guest's expectations without a shared and accepted etiquette; one that works because it constrains. However, as the world changes, so too must etiquette evolve – lest the species of function it supports become a quaint anachronism. The same is true for other forms of 'company'.

The example of a party provides some insight into the operation of a company or any other form of human organisation. All organisations may be said to be a group of individuals gathered for a period to accomplish a common purpose. Without certain codes and conventions they could not function, yet they are also limited by those same codes. We are using the word 'pattern' to embrace the complex sets of interlinked codes and conventions, together with the thinking, ideas, perceptions, common presumptions, tradition, culture and shared language that underpins all organisations. Such patterns, carried in the minds and cultural artefacts of the members, define the organisation.

We assert that there is a connection between the pattern(s) of a company and its performance; and that, if we want to change performance, then the patterns which give rise to that performance must, intentionally or otherwise, shift. We can significantly expand our capacity to intentionally shift deeply entrenched patterns for wholly different levels of qualitative and quantitative result. Punctuating the equilibrium of a prevailing pattern starts to release a different level of performance in the future.

At the most general level, a new interpretation of what an organisation 'is' provides an opening for a new Renaissance. Countries, societies, markets and political structures are the creations of a multiplicity of co-evolving, interacting patterns, that serve to both enable and limit. Prevailing patterns which outlive their utility, as all patterns do, contribute to the demise of the societies or companies that carry them. A new purpose and destiny is perhaps possible in organisations and in the world, if organisations can find it easier to escape the grip of their patterns. As Paul Hawken puts it in *The Ecology of Commerce*:

"We do not know what business really is; or therefore, what it can become. We should not be surprised then that there is a deep-seated unwillingness to face the necessary reconstruction of our commercial institutions so that they function on behalf of our lives."

At lower levels, collective patterns shape organisations. For companies struggling to perform or even to survive in a more frenetic, competitive world, there is an opportunity for new levels of performance in the act of getting free with their mental processing. Self-organisation offers a new paradigm of 'control through commitment' in a world where old conceptualisations of hierarchy and stability no longer fit. The shifting, by accident or design, of patterns is a prerequisite of any transformation of an organisation.

Patterns, though operant at broader levels, are ultimately carried by individuals. People can release latent potential if they choose to see and shift their own patterns. Anyone may be able to help others if he or she can assist them to see their patterns, not simply as an abstract exercise, but as a spur to thinking and acting differently.

The momentum for change within companies comes from people being willing and able to challenge current norms, and from managers being willing to create environments in which different thinking, and different behaviours, can flourish. We are neither criticising any established patterns, nor promoting any new recipe, prescription, or set pattern for transforming performance. We are suggesting a way of thinking about companies that explains why many well-established 'recipes' often fail, and proceeding to provide a meta-level framework of action in the shifting of patterns.

We will be drawing on theories of self-organisation and evolution to argue for business, and other, worlds being the product of those patterns. Actions may be born in conscious choice and purpose, and the confluence of that choice and purpose with the choosing and purposing of others, but they are more often rooted in the blind response to the 'patterns' that govern our minds. Many have made the same point in different ways. John Locke[1] was succinct:

"The ideas and images in men's minds are the invisible powers that constantly govern them."

John Maynard Keynes[2] perhaps less so:

"The ideas of economists and political philosophers, both when they are right and when they are wrong, are more powerful than is commonly understood. Indeed the world is ruled by little else. Practical men, who believe themselves to be quite exempt from any intellectual influence, are usually the slaves of some defunct economist. Madmen in authority, who hear their voices in the air, are distilling their frenzy from some academic scribbler of a few years back. I am sure that the power of vested interests is vastly exaggerated compared with the *gradual encroachment of ideas* (emphasis added)."

Or in the words of former US National Security Adviser, Zbigniew Brzezinski:

"Ultimately it is ideas that mobilise political action and thus shape the world."

We suggest that nations, institutions, vested interest groups and commercial companies self-organise out of the inherent replication of their patterns. Without 'companies' little or nothing would be achieved and companies not founded on some set of shared patterns can be no more than the enforced subjugation of the lives of some to the ideas of others. Our concern is with the consequences, for the individual, the organisation, its wider society and even the global environment, when organisational response to change is driven by blind adherence to the prevalent pattern rather than by generative choice in the matter. To catch, and shift, the patterns of one's own thinking is to exercise choice as an individual. To interrupt, by whatever means, the pattern of a company is to enable it to learn, innovate and perform. It implies a different view of management. So what do we mean by pattern?

Patterns within patterns

Is a pattern:

☐ A national, or corporate, culture as in the example with which we started?

☐ A code – an unwritten rule – of acceptable behaviour?

☐ A particular game to play and a way of playing?

☐ A certain shared language, either a national tongue or the jargon and acronyms of a particular profession or company?

☐ A particular belief system, a shared set of assumptions and perceptions of the world, a paradigm, strategic recipe or common mental model?

☐ A set of relationships, a series of perceptions, verbalised or otherwise that influence how people feel about and act towards each other?

☐ A shared tradition of thinking?

Our answer, in every case, is: "Yes, but not only!" We are concerned more with a complex and inter-connected whole than with isolated aspects. The pattern is a symphony, a holistic mix. The sound of a symphony is the combination of the interacting sound waves generated by an orchestra of musical instruments rendering their own particular variations on the score. The oscillations and vibrations combine and echo in the concert hall to produce the wave that falls upon the listener's ear. The acoustics complicate the pattern of the symphony; so, too, do the moods, perceptions and memories, the state of listening of the individual – and that state in turn depends on surroundings, emotions, events in the recent and distant past, expectations of the future and of the concert; nationality, biochemistry and so on. The pattern is the interaction of the whole with the mind of the individual.

Many writers from various disciplines have examined one or other component; say, the influence of perception, of paradigms, of culture, of belief systems, of individual psyche and psychology, of language and nationality, of gender, of organisational surroundings or of corporate culture. The results are theories, models, recipes and language to describe and deal with one aspect or other. We seek a different perspective by asking what influences not just the components but the whole tangled, interconnected web?

If patterns have a physical expression it is in the neural pathways of a particular brain, the artefacts of a culture, and the behaviours of actors in human systems. They manifest themselves as an interconnected system of thinking, perceiving, speaking, behaving, relating, acting, communicating and believing. If each separate aspect of a pattern is considered as the score for one instrument in the orchestra, one can think of the pattern as the total symphony. This switch, from characterising parts to considering the whole, is one aspect of the shift that we invite readers to consider. The other aspect is that we are not just saying that organisations create patterns. We claim that organisations and people are not only creators of, but also *creations of* their patterns. Patterns beget people and organisations. They are the score of the organisational symphony; they succeed, the more times they can shape the playing of the orchestra.

So, what level of pattern or patterns are we seeking to expose? The individual pattern, or the aggregate? The answer is both and all, for there are many patterns which interact and interconnect to influence performance. Patterns and organisations evolve and adapt in interacting systems on all scales and levels. Later we will illustrate some of the patterns applying at the individual, interpersonal, company and inter-company levels, and we invite our readers to consider their inter-connections. To borrow an image from the science of Chaos:

Big patterns have little patterns
that ride on them and fight them.
Little patterns make bigger patterns
and so *ad infinitum.*

Co-evolving patterns

The comparison we will be making with genes and the attendant evolutionary perspective is intended. Without wishing to be diverted to the nature versus nurture debate, we observe that it is 'patterns', more than genes, that shape people and human organisations. As, for example, Jared Diamond points out in *The Third Chimpanzee*, it is a blend of culture, language, art, technology, organisation and belief systems more than any genetic differences that distinguishes our species from any close biological relatives. All have co-evolved over perhaps 40,000 years and especially through the 10,000 odd years of recorded history.

 Just one of his examples serves to demonstrate such co-evolution. Save for Finnish and Basque, all of today's European Languages from Greek and Albanian to Gaelic and Norwegian are blends and descendants of one ancestral Proto Indo-European (PIE) language which colonised Europe sometime between 3,300 and 2,500 BC. Through the last 500 years PIE's linear descendants have spread across the planet. The unravelling of their ancestor's colonisation of Europe is a fascinating study in linguistic palaeontology.

PIE was apparently spoken on the western steppes of what is now Ukraine, or southern Russia, whose inhabitants had recently learnt to domesticate the horse; a technological pattern shift that simultaneously enhanced their capacity for transport, hunting, herding, farming (with ploughs rather than digging sticks) and warfare. Significantly, one of the most recent inventions whose origins can be traced back to a PIE root, that is an invention which preceded the spread of the language, is the wheel, dating from about 3,300 BC. With the wheel in place, the economic and technological advantage of the first horsemen was complete. Archaeological evidence testifies to their rapid spread westward carrying their patterns with them. Once they reached the geographical limit of the steppes, in present day Hungary, their economy had to adapt to forests rather than grassland; but it continued to spread, as today's languages testify, merging and blending with the pre-existing pattern of metallurgy and agriculture of Europe. Peoples who ended up speaking derivatives of PIE were genetically different from its originators but linguistically colonised. PIE's subsequent derivatives contributed at least as much as physical geography, and far more than genetics, to the subsequent political and national distinctions of Europe, a continent whose nations could be said to be the creations of linguistic evolution.

Patterns, then, are carried and transmitted through language, education, and cultural imprinting. In a real and deep sense people are their patterns. Linguistic and cultural patterns are far more profound determinants of nations and 'race' than are genetic differences. The boundaries one would cross in journeying from northern Norway to southern Greece are noticeable much more by sudden shifts in language than by sudden changes in the physical characteristics of different people. Immanuel Kant expressed it two centuries ago:

> Nature employs two means to separate peoples: differences of language and of religion.

'Patterns', more than genes, create the realities of personalities and national identities and, we will argue, every scale of organisation in between. Approaches to such issues as 'management' reflect the prevailing patterns of the societies, and educational specialisms, in which they are grounded.

Pattern cultivation: managing with different drums

Over the 500 years since the Renaissance shifted the European pattern, PIE's linguistic descendants, with their associated patterns of technological and organisational thinking, have enjoyed unprecedented global success. People learnt to influence and control, to organise others, and to exploit the resources of the world around them, as never before. Patterns of control, of command, of organisation, of rational, reductionist science, and of engineering prowess enabled 'progress', the like of which no other patterns of language and beliefs have ever enjoyed. Those patterns still prevail in much action and most theory on the nature of management, treating it as a process of control and co-ordination; one in which managers set the drum-beat to which an organisation marches. The drum-beat imposes standard rhythms and processes on an inherently disorganised world, enabling, through organisation, the achievement of that which would otherwise not be possible. Inherent in this book is an invitation to the reader to explore the limits of this dominant pattern.

 Imagine that you sit on the board of Treadmill Eurasia plc, the European Division of a hugely successful multi-national corporation. Tomorrow you will be making a decision on a new investment project, upon which your advisers have, with disarming honesty, presented the following report. What will you recommend?

PROJECT 'X'

Executive Summary

"Enormous physical difficulties confront this proposal. Those who must execute it will be involved in a venture that stretches the limits of current technological competency, journeying into waters for which existing knowledge is wholly inadequate. The technology for measuring progress and completing the necessary charts is in its infancy. Two competitors, with between them 130 years of accumulated experience, dominate the trading infrastructure. Raw material supply is subject to the depredations of various groups of well-armed criminal organisations whose activities are, quite literally, piracy. Governmental regulation of the depredation is nigh on impossible. The support of the current government is luke-warm and liable to be withdrawn at any moment. To succeed, the project has to establish a niche in a market dominated by well-established, mature, trading relationships. Its products are not anticipated to appeal to those who control the source of supply, for they have commanded high premiums in your home market by virtue of their established dominance."

Well, do you invest? Do conventional management paradigms, conventional tools for strategic decision making, conventional risk-assessment, or conventional market wisdom grant it any chance? Come to that, do you actually know any group of consultants, or internal planning staff, who would risk being so definitive in their summary of a potential venture?

'Project X' became one of the longest-lasting, and richest, companies that the world has ever known. It was to change the course of world history and to be the foundation for the largest commercial empire ever assembled. Its 'take-over', not just of another company, but of a whole continent, should give even the most battle-hardened corporate raider of the 1980's pause for thought. It was a pioneer of a new form of corporate organisation and governance; one of the world's first limited stock corporations. Its legacy remains with us to this day. It was the East India Company, whose final demise coincided with the apogee of British imperial power; power that it had done much to build[3].

This is not to say that established ideas on strategy, or risk assessment, or control and organisation are 'wrong' or not useful. They have enabled, and continue to enable, many forms of human accomplishment. It is to say that they, like any other pattern, are also, and simultaneously, limiting. Today's successful organisations are not succeeding through that form of control that is born out of the passive conformity to rigid specification. Those of the future are likely to do so even less. A new form of control, and a new domain of performance, lies in understanding the emergent rhythms of different drums, different drummers and different drumming. There is, we argue, a different paradigm of managing; one that operates on the patterns that create the system. It is in its infancy in organisations, just as is genetic engineering.

It is indeed a challenge to those patterns of management which consider the organisation as an inert, engineered structure, but it is one with implications at least as profound as those of the new biotechnology. We will be arguing that influencing the collective patterns that shape how people and organisations think, act and perform, their inner drums, is a more important purpose than is detailing, and attempting to synchronise, the actual activity conducted within the organisation. Whereas the capacity of geneticists has expanded to embrace genetic engineering, we see the same or similar potential to expand the work of managers and others to pattern 'engineering'. Although both are in their infancy it may, however, remain the case that pattern engineering is more art than science. Since patterns cannot, in reality, be 'engineered', and since the term 'genetic engineering' is itself an example of an old pattern reproducing in a new context, we will henceforth talk about 'pattern cultivation'.

The organisations: national, political, economic, scholastic, religious and commercial, that arose and fell during the branching of PIE into its component parts were, inevitably, influenced by different leaders, rulers, philosophers, generals, managers, entrepreneurs, technologists and religious teachers, to name but some. They were also influenced by chance and contingency as the interplay of nature and interacting organisations played itself out. The process resembles, as we shall come back to consider, evolution through natural selection. It is a process in which some combination of fitness, luck and timing determines the relative successes of different patterns and the organisations that carry them.

Whether of an emergent or established nature, organisations develop and sustain themselves, they self-organise, around their patterns. They seek at least a transient stability. Indeed, it is the nature of patterns to seek their own replication and hence the preservation of whatever organisation and 'mind-set' sustains them. Yet as history speeds up, organisations face a need for faster and faster change. Managers and leaders seek ways of making their companies more responsive. Individuals seek ways of living within a less ordered and less predictable society.

Surviving, let alone prospering, from the old paradigm of predictability, control, continuity and order – the one that has served us so well – becomes progressively more and more challenging. There is a different form of control – or better, influence – to be gained through moving from managing by planning and specifying what happens within a company, its content or activity, to cultivating the context, the patterns and relationships, that influence the system – the company – to behave the way that it does. A different route to transformation, for individuals and organisations, lies with the inner drums through which we interpret and create our world. From outer or external control to an inner force or spirit, just how is such a shift enabled? The latter half of the book provides some keys.

If there is a 'Route 1', it is that of creating different conversations, of 'relanguaging' yourself and your organisation. Breaks of rhythm and convention in conversation – a different language – help shift prevailing patterns. A book that intends a different 'conversation' with the reader requires illustrations beyond conventional case studies. We are privileged to share a few fables starting with the tale of 'The Different Drum'.

The Different Drum – Part 1

The village of Aniko nestles comfortably in a sleepy valley. Through the valley winds a river which sparkles and chatters as it makes its way to a small harbour where the boats of the local fishermen dance and play in the sunshine. In the centre of the village is a shaded square where the villagers entertain a bustling market once a week. Anyone coming to the market would be struck, not so much by the colourful swirl of amiable bartering which characterises most markets, but by the imposing, ornate temple, which extends squat, solid and serene, along the whole northern side of the square. This is the temple of the K'ian monks, famous for the temple drums which are used by the monks in all their ceremonies. The origin of the temple is now forgotten, but the Abbot's favourite legend is that it was founded by grateful villagers after an earthquake had devastated their neighbours up and down the coast. The tale has it that the earthquake was preceded by a dreadful storm and many of the villagers took shelter under their upturned boats. To ward off the evil spirits they drummed on the boats with their paddles and they believed this action to be the reason for their salvation.

Drumming has always been a key part of the rituals. The monks believe in a path to enlightenment characterised by rising levels of meditation. At the first level the conscious mind is overloaded, in order that the unconscious mind is set free to meditate. The complexity of the drumming techniques has evolved to achieve this overwhelming of the conscious mind. Simultaneously with the rhythmic sound of the drums, particular mantras and chants are used to trigger the desired meditation. To begin to achieve the necessary skill, novice monks spend hours each day practising the elaborate rhythms and techniques. As they gain fluency the monks engage in ever more intricate and challenging patterns, able eventually to do away with the need for chanting. It is said that a master K'ian drummer, using the temple drums, can connect to each individual in a crowd simultaneously so that he or she achieves a unique state of profound meditation.

Such is the fame of the temple that people travel long distances to experience the drumming for themselves. Visitors can observe the novices training with practice drums in the temple grounds. On certain festivals they might be lucky enough to attend some of the public ceremonies when the famous temple drums themselves are used. Strangers may come prepared for festivity, but are inevitably overawed by the aura of mystical presence on these occasions. On rare instances, if visitors have an introduction to the Abbot, they may be allowed into the temple building itself. There the temple drums are stored and cared for with exquisite attention and reverence. Each drum has its own stand, richly and ornately carved and gilded. Each drum has a rank, its own history and ritual and an attendant monk solely devoted to its preservation. As these monks gain experience they graduate to the next ranking drum. The fortunate visitor witnessing this splendour will retain the memory for the rest of his life.

However, the visitor will not have seen all the temple drums; for in the Abbot's study, in the heart of the temple, is a small niche. In this niche, there is a simple, unadorned drum; such as a child might play. There is no sign to indicate how this drum comes to be there, nor what its importance might be. That it is important is without doubt, as the Abbot spends some minutes in contemplation before it at the start of every day. The only time this drum is discussed is when a novice is formally accepted as a temple drummer, thus becoming a full monk. On that day the novice is invited to the Abbot's study where he hears the story. The Abbot always begins his explanation with, "This is a different drum, my son, and ..."

To be continued...

Conversation: the real currency of companies

main text

It is often said that 'money talks' or 'finance is the language of business'. Both aphorisms grant an access to a particular, and prevalent, current pattern; one that can limit when it elevates money above its status as a medium for economic exchange. We suggest language is the medium through which a company works, that 'conversation' is the currency of organisations and companies. Language enables so much yet it also limits, for patterns of language package how people see, and relate to, their world, their companies, each other and themselves. We 'see' as well as converse through the concepts and relationships embedded in language.

Conversations need not be verbal. They include the conversations we have with ourselves and embrace what is thought and yet not said as much as what is said. Patterns can be, indeed usually are, expressed in the unspoken and unwritten. We are frequently unaware of them yet they transmit themselves in the language, verbal and non-verbal, that expresses the company. What is said, espoused, and written in vision statements, policies and procedures about a company may not be the drum that serves to define the march, or marches, actually followed. For 'drums' can be internal and informal, unsaid and yet known. The patterns in our minds shape, and can even dictate, how we see and think about the world and therefore how we react to the world. Conversation, in this sense, shapes the context for action, the action itself, and the results that flow therefrom.

We hope to enable individuals to catch, and shift, the patterns – the thinking and conversation – that shapes their actions, both as individuals and as company members. Those who expand upon this capacity will make a greater difference to themselves as well as to those around them.

To catch the patterns: the story of Tex

I was almost through completing a project assisting a company based in Texas with the development of high performance teamwork, when I was quietly approached by the head of Human Resources. He wanted to know if I would be willing to "have a word" with someone who, for the sake of this story, I will call 'Tex'. The manufacturing plant of this company was moving toward self-managed work teams. It was one of the best examples of the reality and practice of such a movement I had then witnessed. For the uninitiated, and those unaccustomed to the smooth talk of some consultants, it should be noted that the development of self-managed work teams is not plain sailing and, for many, is a revolution as well as a revelation. Self-managed work teams are not a mechanical solution. To be effective, they require a lot of pattern shifts, among 'managers' as well as 'workers'.

The head of HR was concerned that Tex was one of the most "ornery, difficult and cantankerous people they had. Why, he could hardly say 'Good morning' to you, never mind give you the time of day." The pattern of opinion appeared to be well-established on the part of HR! Their concern was legitimated on the basis of the impact of Tex's presence on the rest of the team, if not on the head of HR himself. Could something be done?

A benefit of coming from the 'outside' is that one is less victim of – less stuck with – the patterns from within. I had no shared experience and no commitment to the opinion of the HR department. It was, after all, merely their opinion, strong though it may have been. I chose to meet with Tex, if Tex chose to meet with me. At a content level I had not the least idea of what to say or do. At a context level I knew what I chose to stand for, and thus, at a deep level, what I was up to. My guess is that the head of HR also understood this.

Tex must have suffered 20 minutes of pretty undiluted waffle from me before I broke the pattern and sought to listen, and to 'see', as Tex saw. What emerged was a highly principled person who set a high store by standards, as witnessed in, and by, his ability to restore to pristine condition the classic cars of yesteryear. He was aware of the low opinion of some others and mirrored theirs with his own opinion of them. As I listened, he began to reveal through his own words his concerns about teams and teamwork.

Through what he said I discerned two significant concerns and a prediction: first, that working within a team might lead to a dilution of his own high standards; secondly, that some so-called team-mates shared nowhere near the same standards of work and contribution as he; and third that this team thing might not last; or, more accurately, only last as long as it remained a management fashion. I began to appreciate that he interpreted teams and teamwork as some collusive arrangement which, in effect, would challenge his strong belief in standards. (This and similar concerns about 'teams' are shared by many, including members of so-called 'management' teams. For example, the untold yet hardly kept secret is that many people experience compromise and settle for mediocrity in order to sustain their membership of a team. The operant rule appears to be avoidance of any possible upset or challenge to either one's peers or the 'team leader'.)

Imagine the shift in pattern when I suggested to Tex that he might be a very effective team member and, if he so chose, team leader; not by compromising but by sharing his standards with others. That what he might give and share with others as a standard-bearer might be a great gift for the whole team. The simple thing was that in talking it through Tex could see for himself the pattern that he was adopting, that to keep his belief in high standards intact, and to avoid possible dilution of those standards, he kept himself apart, perhaps in the eyes of others an "ornery, difficult and cantankerous person". From Tex's perspective the low opinion of others was, perhaps, a price worth paying for the standards that were clearly so important to him.

What completes this story as others described it to me was a "complete transformation in Tex" and "I don't know what you said but he's turned himself around 180 degrees." Yet for me, there has been no transformation in Tex. He believes in what he has always believed in. What happened was that he was able to catch himself in the patterns that constrained him, to catch himself and discover new openings to be expressed in his beliefs. Being a member of a team has become an opportunity for self-expression rather than self-denial. Tex had seen that for himself.

Yet the story may be the bigger. For there was perhaps another party 'caught', and to some extent frustrated, in their pattern; the head of Human Resources. Was he able to 'see' how a pattern of opinions can serve to constrain, particularly when one confuses opinions with reality?

 Many people are victims of, or passive slaves to, patterns with their habits and actions frozen by particular set of language and inherited beliefs. A fragment of an eighteenth century English prayer: "God keep the squire and his relations, preserve us in our proper stations", sums up a pattern that maintained an harmonious social fabric by constraining the thinking and behaviour of its inhabitants for generations. Not dissimilar patterns still prevail in many large companies where those who carry them are essentially passive vehicles, benefiting when the pattern works to preserve them from any social upheaval or undue job insecurity, but becoming victims when the society, or the company, is paralysed.

There is an option beyond that of either victimhood or reasonable compliance; it is being master of our patterns, being aware of, and free with them, using them when they empower, but being consciously ready to recognise their limitations when they do not. To choose that option, to choose to be free with some of the ideas and assumptions that infect our minds and our communities, we have to interrupt the patterns that those ideas create, to invent a different perspective.

As with individuals, so with companies. We believe there is an urgent need in the world for more organisations to march to a different drum, to a beat which releases greater human energy and purpose while contributing to the creation of a sustainable future.

But is this really germane to business? Some might argue that all that has ever been needed has been some inspiration and purpose on the part of a few at the top; a good band of compliant troops at the bottom, and all things become possible. Some might even say that greed works quite well, with the desire to acquire material goods and possessions and the position they give you in society, providing the essence of an effective system. We argue that this particular pattern is limiting. Ultimately, it is only patterns and the prevailing conventional wisdom that prevent people from creating organisations, and even societies, which are more generative, wealth creating, environmentally sensitive, socially aware and, not least, fun. We hold it to be within the gift of human power, choice and potential to create such conversations for a different future. But we get ahead of the Abbot's story...

 ## The Different Drum – Part 2

This is a different drum, my son and... "This drum is more important to us than any of the temple drums that you have seen, and now, as a temple drummer, you will begin to appreciate this for yourself. Let me tell you its story.

Imagine if you will, the village long ago with the temple established but still in the flower of its youth. It was a good time. The deities smiled on us so that the crops multiplied in the fields and the nets of the fishermen were laden with their catches. The village grew prosperous. The K'ian temple also flourished, and congratulated itself on achieving such an amicable relationship with the Gods.

Years passed and still the village prospered. People for the first time began to know wealth and the trappings it might bring. Then, and for the first time, the hearts of the villagers began to know envy. People forgot what it was like to live in mutual harmony; neighbour would try to outdo neighbour and soon they no longer spoke openly to one another. Meanwhile the temple monks of that time, secure in their success, continued to drum their message to the Gods; confidently, they thought, ensuring the continued future of the village. If the Abbot noticed that there were more harsh words and less happiness in the community he gave no sign. Villagers began to keep themselves to themselves and travellers coming to Aniko were happy to do business, but even happier to leave again.

Inevitably the wheel of fate turned. Good harvests became a thing of the past as rain and disease destroyed the crops with unseasonal severity. Fishermen returned with empty nets and it seemed as if even the fish had abandoned the sea. The village was forced to draw down the reserves put by during the good years. Neighbours blamed each other for the change in fortune. They resolved to ignore the offenders and begged their monks to help restore the village's favour with the Gods. The monks shut themselves in the temple and for days drummed their most powerful invocations. The villagers, on hearing these efforts echo through the valley, began to feel reassured. However, nothing changed and soon there were ominous mutterings that it was the monks, who had brought the misfortune upon the village. Relations between temple and village deteriorated.

One day, there appeared in the square a lean young man of unusual appearance. He was neither a proper traveller nor a beggar, but clothed in a fashion unknown in the village. Sitting down beneath the great plane tree he produced a small drum and began to tap out some melancholic rhythms. At first he was ignored, being neither good enough to merit attention nor bad enough to invite ridicule. Occasionally he would venture something a little more lively. As the days went by and the villagers grew accustomed to his presence one or two of the stallholders would give him a small portion of their own meagre food and drink. The drummer was always courteous and would give a lively flourish in acknowledgement of each offering.

After a few weeks, some of the villagers took to gathering about the drummer in the evenings and small groups would sit and converse into the night. The temple monks at first scorned this strange drummer. They made mock of his style; why, he didn't even know the most basic of K'ian techniques. However, as the drummer began to draw more people round about him in the evenings, the monks began to view him as a rival and to feel resentment. The Abbot of the time, witnessing the stranger's performance from the temple, was at a loss to understand his appeal to the villagers. For want of a better solution he resolved to do nothing for a month in the hope that the drummer would move on to another village.

Over the next month the drummer carried on as before. In the evenings, yet more of the villagers would gather and neighbours who had not been on speaking terms once more began to enjoy each others' company. Eventually, the Abbot could stand it no longer. He asked two of the monks to fetch him the drummer so that he could learn his secret. The monks returned with the drummer, bringing him to the Abbot's study.

The Abbot regarded the drummer for a while, then began by asking him what he was doing in the village. The drummer replied that he was just passing through. The Abbot then asked where he had learned his drumming and how did he achieve such a powerful effect with the villagers. The drummer appeared genuinely surprised and laughingly stated that he had taught himself to play and had not been aware of any particular impact he had on the village. The Abbot grew impatient, convinced that the drummer was hiding something and making fun of him. He insisted on knowing the drummer's secret. "Perhaps it was something to do with the drum", he speculated. "It was nothing to do with the drum", maintained the stranger. "You will discover for yourself", he said, whereupon he presented the Abbot with his drum and took his leave.

The Abbot was baffled by this behaviour and, that evening, eagerly watched to see what would happen in the square. As had become the pattern, the villagers gathered around and talked. There was no sign of the drummer, nor any indication that the crowd had even noticed his absence. The Abbot was puzzled and next day tried to track down the drummer, but he was not to be found anywhere in the village. The Abbot was desperate to find out more and that night he disguised himself and went to join the villagers in the square. He listened to the conversation around him, which had not lessened in the drummer's absence. The Abbot meditated on the mysterious stranger. Eventually, one of the last to leave the square, he returned in a troubled and deeply contemplative mood to the temple.

From that time to this, the K'ian order has conducted itself in a very different fashion and the village has again enjoyed prosperity.

At this point in the narrative the Abbot always pauses before finishing with the traditional challenge to the new monk. "So my new monk, now that you have heard the story, tell me how this drum has touched upon your life and how it may continue to do so..."

Yesterday's winners, yesterday's language, or a new Renaissance?

The world of business is changing. Writing management books that seek to prescribe a solution to the resultant challenges is a growth industry; one that often ignores the fact that there is nothing new about change. Machiavelli's observations of the process of change in Renaissance Italy are as relevant today as they were then[4].

So what is all the fuss about? Is it merely that a generation of 'Western' managers and professionals, a generation who have been granted a life of unprecedented comfort and material ease, are finding that the harsh realities of global competition are catching up with them? From many individual perspectives especially in the rest of the world that might seem to be true. Worldwide competition and the re-emergence of patterns not derived from the Proto-Indo European stock are part of the shift that is taking place; the challenge to a set of 'Western' or 'Westernised' patterns that have been evolving for five hundred years; years that saw dramatic shifts in the nature of companies and other organisations, and in technological progress. When

Machiavelli was writing it took longer to travel from Italy to England than it did in the heyday of the Roman road... Five centuries later, any amount of digitised information can be transmitted – effectively instantaneously – from one place to another.

And the communications revolution, or more accurately the data transmission revolution, is but part of the change. Other philosophies, other cultural traditions, are impacting the theory and practice of management. Global economic power balances are shifting, old industries are dying and new patterns of technology and business are emerging with unprecedented speed.

The relative balances of power between purchasers and suppliers are changing in industry after industry; sometimes, as, say, in motor vehicles or consumer products, towards the purchaser, and sometimes; as in UK retailing, towards the retailer and away from both the final consumer and the manufacturer. Elsewhere, ideas and brands can no longer be protected as they once were. The time available to capture an economic return on a new product is shrinking. Knowledge, rather than physical labour or capital, determines the value to a product or service.

New forms of business are emerging. Distributed manufacturing renders 'country of origin' less and less meaningful. Virtual companies, shifting alliances, partnerships and other forms of business interconnectedness force companies to be, simultaneously, competitors and collaborators.

Even sources of political power and legitimacy are changing. National identity is shifting with the emergence of regional economic blocks and the simultaneous rebirth of nationalism in smaller political units. Multinational corporations have turnovers that place them in the top 50 of global GNPs and, as Professor Russ Ackoff has pointed out, the ironic side-effect is that at a time of the collapse of communism and the supposed triumph of capitalism, half the world's largest economies are run, in effect, through a paradigm of centralised planning. Not that old style corporatism is succeeding. The successful and growing multi-national companies are run very differently from the centralised hierarchies of even ten years ago. Corporatism is collapsing nearly as quickly as did Communism. New and more fluid organisational forms – different patterns of organisation – are succeeding as countless management writers are pointing out.

The result is deeply unsettling, especially for many who were successful under the old patterns. One successful middle manager, in one of the world's largest and (until recently) most admired companies described to me a conversation now common among his colleagues to the effect that, unlike their parents, grand-parents and great grand-parents, they do not see the possibility of being able to offer their children the expectation of a better future that they were offered by their parents. Despite the often overwhelming evidence of accelerating change, many of us, in our companies and our private lives, cling, while we can, to what is known and comfortable; to the language, recipes, and patterns of the past; to all of that which once worked.

Yet many of those patterns, and the comfort of middle management, are a recent innovation. When the East India Company collapsed in the Indian Mutiny of 1857 it was succeeded for 90 years by British imperial rule, without any fundamental change to the administrative structure. The Indian Civil Service of those days never had more than 1,000 members (contrast over 20 million today!). The organisation was flat. In each of nine provinces a provincial political secretary had reporting to him perhaps 100 district officers. Each district officer did what was necessary to reduce racial and religious conflict and banditry, dispense justice impartially and honestly, and collect taxes. The system worked, and required the smallest of headquarters staffs and colonial administrators in London to keep it functioning. Most of the latter were clerks[5].

Some commercial companies in the last decade of the twentieth century are re-discovering the virtues of simplicity of structure, much to the horror of the layers of middle managers and specialists who have proliferated over the last half century or so. The industrial West has seen two great waves of job displacement this century, one in agriculture as mechanisation and diesel replaced muscle power between 1920 and 1950, and a second in manufacturing starting in the mid- 1970s. A third wave is still gathering momentum. Consider the following graph, whose end just predates the advent of delayering, right-sizing, re-engineering, and out-sourcing, and similar panaceas for dealing with the problem of competitive organisations in the 1990s.

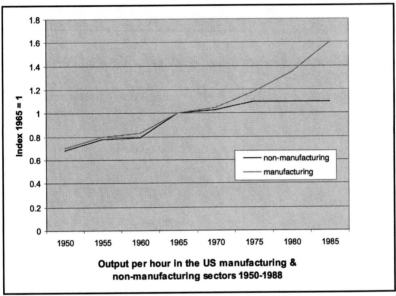

Figure 1.1

The historical background to the business challenges of the 1980's. Whereas, since the early 1970's, manufacturing productivity had been rising exponentially, non-manufacturing productivity had hardly changed. Adapted from data presented by Scott-Moreton (1991).

From the late 1970s onwards, manufacturing productivity has increased at an exponential rate, as new competition, new technology and – more importantly – new thinking, made themselves felt. In the wake of the decline of the old heavy industries came the rust belts of the US and British manufacturing heartlands; the 'dark satanic mills' that survive only as industrial 'heritage' theme parks by virtue of preservation orders. The figures for the actual work of making things are underestimated by the graph. True manufacturing productivity has increased even more steeply. Seven out of every eight manufacturing jobs as represented on the graph are accounted for by 'indirect' or white collar occupations: consultants, accountants, engineers, designers, researchers, managers, marketers, personnel specialists and so on. Meanwhile, in the non-manufacturing industries, productivity was static between 1975 and 1988; a trend that was never going to be sustainable. As one manager put it to me with refreshing honesty in 1991, "Business Process Re-engineering is simply about extracting more value from white-collar work".

Manufacturing industry absorbed the surplus labour released through agricultural automation, and non-manufacturing industry (and managerial hierarchies) has been, for many, a passport to the securities and comforts of the middle class lifestyle. As the wealth to sustain that lifestyle is created by fewer and fewer people, what happens next? As the Third Wave shake out of the 1990s follows its predecessors, where will the people go? Where, how and on what are they going to live, when the food and goods that nourish and determine their existence can and are being produced by a dwindling few?

The conventional answers of innovation, research and knowledge work may not suffice. The problem is bigger than any one national economy. There already looms a global overcapacity of physicists, geologists, computer programmers, mathematicians, lawyers, accountants, economists, management consultants and advisers. As MIT Economics guru Lester Thurow puts it[6]: "Why should I pay a UK physicist £30,000 a year when I can get a world-class physicist in Russia for $100 per month?"

The manufacturing revolutions of the 1980s, Total Quality, logistics, time based competition, Just-in-Time, zero-defect and the rest had, in mechanical terms, two results above all others. They eliminated the costs, and waste, of inspection and rework, and they eliminated the costs of carrying excessive inventory. The move to emulate such practices in the world of 'management' is having the same effect. Companies no longer want to carry an inventory of professional skills that are used for, in manufacturing terms, inspection and rework. The centrally planned, monolithic corporation is not as competitive as the free market, and firm after firm is being slimmed down, and broken up with part after part 'out-sourced'. Facilities Management, contracting to provide what were previously regarded as essential components of the in-house system, was one of the main growth areas in business in the 1990s.

The downside, in company after company, is that more management attention becomes focused on dividing up a shrinking pie – and for some that implies keeping at least as large a net share for themselves – than on growing the overall pie. "People fight for their place in the golden life-boat", as one director of a large pharmaceutical laboratory put it to us. Is it greed, or is it a sensible human reaction, in a world where the creation of wealth is shrinking?

We are living, in the 1990s, through a period when several 'cycles' of economic or cultural change are apparently coinciding. We have witnessed the severest and longest-lived conventional recession for 60 years. Many would say we are living through the down curve of a 60 year economic long wave, or Kondratieff cycle. Others, for example Peter Drucker, discern us as living through a social and historical change such as occurs perhaps every 100 years. Others still, such as Japanese Historian Taichi Sakaiya[7], author of *The Knowledge Value Revolution,* suggest that the retreat from the apogee of westernised civilisation represents a historical shift experienced no more than once every 500 years or so. Some might even choose to say the silicon revolution represents as profound a switch as the transition from stone age to the use of metal. On the longest scale of all, the geological scale, the cycle may be even more profound. It is only every several hundred million years that one species achieves the chance to poison the planet.

 We will touch again on the interconnectedness of such cycles, and the similarities between the rhythms of biological and economic evolution, in Chapter Four. For now, the explanation does not matter. What does, is the fact that we are either witnessing, or need, a profound shift in and of our patterns. The last Renaissance, the birth of Western, or Westernised civilisation, interrupted a millennium in which, as one historian put it, "religious fatalism paralysed thought". Some say it was a historical accident waiting to happen once certain groups of people started thinking differently. It was certainly a major shift of the prevalent pattern. Similarly, different thinking is being found in the new forms of organisation that are succeeding today. The thinking patterns that have served Western society well, that have evolved with it over 500 years, are having to change. A new Renaissance is needed, and may be happening. Unchanging patterns can only freeze companies and societies in the patterns of the past. Understanding the insidious tendency of all thinking habits to channel thought, to seek maintenance of the status quo, offers the prospect of companies and individuals prospering in, rather than being victims of, a period of profound social, economic technological and business change. It may also enable the societies in which those companies operate to be generative, for societies, too, are a reflection of their patterns.

We have already alluded to the dramatic shifts in the speed with which data, often mislabelled as information, can be moved from place to place. Whether the time taken to really communicate – to share a common understanding of the meaning of the information being transmitted – has fallen is a different question. Indeed it is arguable that, as the rate and volume of information transmission increased, so the rate of true communication and learning has fallen. This is one of the problems. We drown in data. Machiavelli, or for that matter Socrates, might be bewildered by modern technology and might not recognise the specific forms of many organisations. Either could probably recognise immediately the unchanged, or deteriorated, dynamics of human communication and behaviour. The limited evolution of thinking and conversation may be one of the major limits to the evolution of technology, wealth and organisation.

There may also be physical limits. No exponential increase lasts forever and none ever has done since the first positive feedback system in the history of life on earth, the prokaryotic bacteria which enjoyed two billion years of unchecked expansion until they destroyed most of their environmental niches by poisoning their atmosphere with oxygen, two billion years ago[8]. In a finite world, where everything is ultimately connected to everything else, everything is ultimately limited.

As a species we have got where we are by being good at reacting, and specialising on the problem in hand. Contemplating the interconnectedness of the planet was not a useful survival strategy when the problem was to avoid getting eaten by sabre-toothed tigers, or raped by marauding Proto Indo-Europeans. Focusing on the problem in hand, and specialising, was a good strategy when hunting mammoths in 19,950 BC and seems an equally good strategy in the competitive patterns of the late Twentieth Century. But we have outrun our genetic programming. The economic and environmental challenges ahead are those that build slowly, until they turn critical; the kinds of creeping problems that, as Charles Handy[9] reminds through his parable of the boiled frog, are much harder for us to react to. We have filled the planet to the point where there are no 'empty lands' awaiting emigration, and no obvious new resources waiting to be exploited. Our runaway success is in danger of meeting a similar fate to that which befell the prokaryotes, and various other successful species which fatally disrupted their environment.

For some it seems to be human nature when faced with creeping change to cling to what has worked in the past, to try and push harder on today's solutions even if by doing so we merely hasten the onset of the crisis. Or is this just the power of patterns again? Can we recognise and challenge the blind forces programmed into our belief systems as surely as religious fatalism was programmed into medieval Europe? Ultimately, this book is grounded in its authors' optimism. We believe a new Renaissance is not only needed but is possible. We also believe that, without a similarly profound change, humanity risks a new and global dark age. We are not saying we have the answers. We are saying that the answers are to be found in considering the processes by which companies, in the broad sense that we use the word, evolve, proliferate and change. People have the capacity to change their own worlds – but the received strategic wisdom of current management theory and practice may not be adequate to the task of creating organisations that will break the mould of the next millennium as successfully as The East India Company changed the established trading patterns of its time.

The first Renaissance was 'an accident waiting to happen', once certain groups of people started thinking differently. As well as launching an era of unprecedented progress, it launched unprecedented struggles as patterns, languages, religions and the nations they defined, competed for supremacy. The struggles linger on. The challenge is to break the grip such pervading patterns exert on the people who carry them.

Breaking the grip

Where patterns create they also limit. If we want to achieve a greater result, to step beyond the limits of current patterns, then somehow we must extricate ourselves from the familiar; undo old patterns, or at least the grip of old patterns, before creating new. This is key, for if we merely try to add powerful enablers on to powerful disablers, that is, build on what is already limiting, then the result is likely to be more cosmetic than of substance. This helps explain, incidentally, why many executives become frustrated when major initiatives such as Total Quality programmes appear to run out of steam within their organisation.

When we add something that works onto something that limits what we get, at best, is some neutered workability. If we really want to release more potential then we must get a handle on what limits, and some of what limits are the systems, the patterns, in which we ourselves participate and reinforce. We are, whether by default or design, part of the limiting pattern.

What we, the authors, are up to is breaking the grip and breaching the limits of patterns. We are offering an explanation, an approach, rather than discreet recipes as to how that is done; for it is done differently by different people in differing circumstances. This book invites an inquiry of the reader. In the context of your chosen 'company' and the people within it, what serves to limit performance and how might you break through such limits so as to release, and grow, potential? When people step beyond the boundaries of existing patterns, and suspend the comfort of easy answers and quick solutions, they often discover or invent different possibilities, different openings, different ways for breaching performance limits.

Exercise

What serves to limit performance within your company, or some other organisation, and what wider pattern are these limits part of?

....
....
....
....
....
....
....
....
....
....
....

Summary

We have used this chapter to introduce concepts that will be explored in more detail later. Prime among these is a view of companies and organisations as products of their patterns, expressions of a complex and inter-linked set of behavioural codes and conventions, belief systems and language. Such shared patterns are a prerequisite of organisation. They enable planned or spontaneous emergence of order in what would otherwise be chaos. In the process they also limit performance. They coevolve over time in an evolutionary rhythm.

'Pattern cultivation' – understanding and influencing the emergence of order enabled by patterns – is an approach to management which replaces externally imposed control with internal influence on the inner drums of a company's rhythm and march. This suggests that in lieu of managing content we create and manage the context through which inner drums may be engaged.

People and companies have traditionally been good at reacting and focusing on the problem in hand in order to survive. Such reactive capacities need to be expanded to a more creative orientation capable of generating those futures of our choosing. But past successes tend to keep us stuck. Just as the first Renaissance punctuated the historical equilibrium of 'paralysed thought' of the Dark Ages, so a new Renaissance is beginning to emerge in the worlds of business and organisation. New and more fluid forms of organisation are emerging – yet often we witness the stubbornness of established patterns. We need to break the mould and breach the limits of such patterns, patterns in which we knowingly or unwittingly participate and often serve to reinforce.

 ## Primary Sources

The realities of the looming global economic changes are commented on by many. Most influential on our thinking were Drucker (1989), Handy (1989), and Thurow (1994). The ecological challenges we face are likewise much written on. Hawken (1993) draws important connections between them and commercial practice. The Club of Rome (http://www.clubofrome.org) continues to promote discussion on major global trends.

Our historical sources were, for the Renaissance, Roberts (1976) and Harthig (1991) whilst Lawson (1993) traces the origin of the East India Company. Diamond (1992) traces the evolution of PIE and many other aspects of the interconnection of genes and culture in human society. Rothschild (1992) presents many examples of the co-evolution of technology and organisation.

Figure 1.1 is based on a diagram provided many years ago by Scott-Morton (1991). More specific references to the various patterns of scholarship on which we draw are included with later chapters.

2

A walk on the dark side: the realities of companies

"I am struck by the growing list of 'prescriptions' for producing more successful organisations and just how unreliable these gizmos are. MBO, OD, 'Excellence', TQM, BPR ...even 'culture change' and 'empowerment' avoid the nettle of the systemic complexity, power relations and political processes in organisations. So I am likely to be naturally cautious about any new approach heralded as yet another Philosopher's stone."

Prospective client

 ## Joining the 'club'

What have your local golf club and a large multi-national company got in common? What, if anything, do they share with any other form of organisation?

Part of the answer is that they will both possess aspects of "systemic complexity, power relations and political processes"... The prospective client cited above was replying to a suggestion that a company might enquire why its new safety management system, introduced some two years previously, was, after an initial flurry of excitement, not resulting in the reduction of accidents and near misses that they had expected? I had not talked to them about 'patterns', let alone 'mental genes'. All I had said was that it was possible, by under-standing and changing what Peter Scott-Morgan has labelled 'The Unwritten Rules of the Game', to remove some of the barriers which the reality of life in that particular company put in the way of what it was trying to do.

Another part of the answer lies in membership. Anyone joining any organisation has one or more contracts, agreed in the rituals of joining. These can be formal, as with the application, subscription and constitution of the golf club, or the selection process and contract of employment signed with the multi-national company. In addition to the formal there will also exist an unwritten, informal, implicit psychological contract. Such agreements are always being formed and reformed between individuals and any organisation to which they belong. Unlike a legal contract the 'contract of relationship' is dynamic. It is a 'living' agreement; one that is continually being renegotiated, sometimes in very subtle and sometimes in very obvious ways. It produces, or defines, sets of expectations and contributions.

One does not seek, and one is unlikely to be granted, membership of the golf club without at least a passing interest in the game of golf and a level of skill, or connections, commensurate with the expectations of the particular club. With some, that level of skill might be a single figure handicap. With others it suffices to demonstrate to the club professional that you can hit the ball. You receive in return some implied promises concerning the standards of play and social behaviour shown by other members. You may have expectations concerning opportunities for social or commercial networking. You are prepared, in return, to fit in with the codes and conventions of the particular club.

The recruitment process is not that different. Those who do not strike a prospective employer as likely to fit in are unlikely to be employed, nor are companies likely to receive applications from those who have no interest or expectation of fitting in. Research shows that such decisions are typically taken in the first few minutes of a selection interview. In some companies the formal contract may then be no more than a brief and standard letter of agreement. The informal contract mostly reigns supreme. To be, and remain, a member means that we must comply with certain codes, conventions and rules. It defines the standards of membership, of the company as much as the club, and of particular groupings within either. The codes of behaviour for the board are different to those for the shop-floor. Both are an expression of the pattern of the company and are windows through which that pattern can be revealed.

Patterns of survival or success?

Paranoids sometimes have enemies. Hypochondriacs are sometimes ill. Ruthless, calculating corporate politicians are sometimes ruthless, calculating and *rational*. Often, however, the "systemic complexity, power relations and political processes" and the prevailing thinking habits and behaviours, are less the uninhibited choice of individuals in a company and more an expression of their acting consistently within a prevailing pattern, obeying a particular set of unwritten rules and keeping an implicit contract of membership. The pattern preserves the organisation. If everything had to be written explicitly, things would soon cease to function – yet the pattern also acts to stop the organisation changing.

As many have said before, to succeed – even to survive – in today's markets, companies must at least react to, and at best generate, changes in the arenas in which they operate. Doing so requires that they, and their members, learn to continually adapt and change. The need is not lost on most senior managers. New strategies, visions, missions, processes and systems abound; yet, all too often, nothing really changes. 'Plus ça change, plus c'est la même chose'. Powerful forces seek to perpetuate the stability of a particular status quo. This chapter, and the next, seek to reveal some of those forces. This one is dedicated to a simple proposition:

...that the unwritten rules which an individual must follow to succeed or even to survive in many companies foster behaviours which, all too frequently, are not in the company's long- term interest.

Any form of company has rules that people conform to but seldom articulate. They are part of the deep programming of the company and a manifestation of its patterns, understood through the transactions people have with each other; that is, through their direct experience, their tacit learning acquired through working together. People joining a new company soon learn, through processes of socialisation and acculturation, the particular behavioural set fostered by the rules.

This phenomenon extends beyond individual companies. Implicit contracts, rules, exist in any group of people and in wider groupings of companies as well as in entire industries or societies. No less an authority than Michael Porter reminds us that innovators usually come from outside the social elite of a particular industry. Elites often become so steeped in the prevailing thinking that they simply cannot 'see' another way, let alone innovate. All too frequently, membership of an elite carries an implicit obligation not to rock the boat! Either way, the unwritten rule becomes in effect: 'Don't be *too* different'...

In normal times a particular set of unwritten rules may benefit the company or industry. They enable it to function. Working purely to the 'written' rule can be more damaging to the organisation than not working at all. For companies and individuals, however, the rubber hits the road when a change that is good, perhaps even necessary, for the organisation demands that individuals break the unwritten rules. The biggest tensions are created when the unwritten rules, in a sense the unwritten reality, do not match the espoused rules, the spoken and frequently written policy of the company. Those who are naive enough to be unaware of the mismatch, or principled enough not to ignore it, are the ones who suffer. Consider the following vignette.

"I don't mind what you do, provided you don't make me wrong!"

Several years ago, *IP* was managing a Research and Development division, part of a large corporate research laboratory. The senior management of the research organisation had stated policies of focusing more attention on clearly defined targets and objectives, and of judging individual performance by such standards. The company's Chief Executive had announced a much-publicised intention to shift the corporate culture through more empowering and open management. Both campaigns resonated strongly with my own beliefs and I, and those I was managing, duly set out to meet, or exceed our targets for performance, safety, budgets and customer satisfaction in an open and empowering way. We achieved them and, in the process, delivered what we believed to be one of the best performances the division had accomplished in recent years.

I was much surprised and angered when, in turn, I received the worst performance review I had had in my entire career. The best performance in years with the worst performance review. Something did not resonate!

I had, in the course of the year, made public the fact that I was not concerned with the time that highly-trained and well-paid scientists started and finished their day, provided the job got done, colleagues were not inconvenienced, and we achieved results. I was less concerned with time worked than with the results to be achieved. As it happened, with the challenge of a significant result, most people worked longer hours than the official nine-to-five. In any event, forms of official time keeping had withered many years before.

In practice, I had given official sanction to the *de facto* reality of flexitime; something to which the Director of Research had previously stated his vehement opposition. In focusing more on the achievement of clearly defined targets and objectives in a more open manner I broke another more established rule. Regardless of espoused policies on results, and new cultures, what I broke was the overriding unwritten rule that is found in so many companies: *'Don't make the boss wrong'*. My worst performance review was a result of the unintended upset that I had caused my boss, no matter that the substance of actual performance suggested that we had found a new dynamic.

 At the time it was easy to fall into the trap of making my boss wrong. Various vernacular phrases expressed the sentiment! By implication, I made myself right! With the benefit of hindsight it is possible to see the situation in different terms as an example of the inevitable patterns that play out in companies. They reflect 'The Road Most Travelled' of corporate life (see Chapter Three). Consider some other examples, all based on real cases in 'successful' companies:

Rick...

"Please make a difference, but don't cause too many ripples!"
"We don't think you are the right person for the next phase of our strategy."

Rick had been the Managing Director of the company, manufacturers of instruments and sensors, for two years, having been head-hunted from a position as plant manager in a similar business. He had turned the business around. Sales were up 30 per cent. The company was shaping up to be a, still rare, example of the rebirth of successful manufacturing in the UK. A new product, developed faster than previous conventional wisdom considered possible, offered the possibility of redefining their market, from selling components to selling a complete reliability service to major retailers. A new strategic alliance was opening up export markets, particularly to Japan. The staff were coming alive with the new opportunities and the new sense of excitement that was developing in the company; a reflection of the importance Rick attached to "managing downwards" and of his genuine commitment to involving people.

In managing downwards Rick ignored the corporate expectation and politics of managing upwards. He thought his company's performance would speak for itself. It came as something of a shock when the Group Chairman expressed his appreciation for all that he had achieved and then said "We now need someone else to maintain what you have begun."

It was OK to be different up to a point, but in being too different there was a price to pay. Though terminated with a financial package, he was nevertheless fired! Not surprisingly, performance has since deteriorated but at least there are not too many ripples. Mediocrity has once again gained ascendancy.

Mike...

"You are showing the rest of us up: Your success causes us a problem!"

"So you got lucky with a few results, too bad you have such lousy peer relationships."

Mike managed an Engineering Service Unit, one of several in a large workshop supplying complex plant and equipment maintenance. He had committed to achieving a different result, a complete elimination of the unit's service backlog in a company and industry where 80 per cent on-time delivery was considered to be a stretch target. He involved his team in doing things differently, he pushed responsibility down the line, encouraging, praising, and helping with whatever was necessary, in effect discovering a facilitating more than controlling or directive style. Results were very impressive, almost inconceivable. They drew management's attention and Mike's actions were held up as an example of what was possible. But his peers started to complain. This was not the way things were done. He was acting and doing things beneath his station, things which were not commensurate with his role and official title. Rumours started that he had manipulated the system to bias results in his favour.

Mike suffered real misery from his peers for his success. Senior management's support waned, they did not wish to risk the support of his peer group. Mike was criticised for his poor peer relationships and 'promoted' sideways to a 'staff' job. Results returned to normal. So far as we know, the senior management of the department have still not realised what lay at the source of this substantial improvement in performance, how it has since deteriorated, nor, indeed, the overwhelming informal lesson that has been learned by everyone involved. On the one hand the deterioration in performance is probably held by some as vindication of the rumour of cheating the system. On the other, he had genuinely started a higher performance dynamic. The overwhelming lesson learned? Do not take the risk of extraordinary performance, for the risk of success is too great!

What had been broken was an informal peer group rule: don't rock the boat and, in particular, avoid that level of success that may be an embarrassment to others. Interestingly, the senior management group unintentionally conspired with this peer group norm, presumably in the interests of harmony of relations and other, more deeply rooted, conventions. Success does not always go to the successful!

Talk 'teamwork' but stand out yourself

"The visibly successful networker can and will prosper in this organisation. Just make sure you support the idea of teams."

The company was intent on rendering itself more flexible in the future and on building a new management style and competencies which they recognised were needed if greater openness, learning, empowerment and teamwork were the key to future success. But the unwritten rule, for high fliers to fly higher, was that their individual profile was critical, and profile was gained by paying lip-service to the new style rather than by actually managing differently. The company had a large amount of data from attitude surveys and 360° feedback that revealed people's perceptions of a difference between what was espoused and what was actually practised within the enterprise. When confronted with the unwritten rule that personal visibility counted for more in terms of career advancement, no one expressed any surprise. The competency initiative died for lack of support.

Whatever you do, at least look busy!

"We are too busy right now with the efficiency drive to worry about effectiveness."
"Don't bother me with these fancy new ideas, I've got a war to fight."
"Being busy gets rewarded."

"We were caught up in the process of processing – striving for bigger, better, and more complicated in just about everything we did. If something was simple we made it complex. If it was hard, we figured out a way to make it impossible. We operated this way because with all our layers of management we needed to make things difficult so we could keep everybody busy. The more commands and controls we had in the system, the more the system justified its own existence. Unfortunately, in our ever-increasing efforts to micromanage every aspect of operations, we became so focused on ourselves and our processes that we forgot to ask the basic question: What the heck do our customers think about all this[10]?"

This dynamic is common, particularly during periodic waves of re-engineering. So common that we offer the following story.

The treadmill syndrome
(or: how we all get busy without much result)

short story

I was up to my ears as usual. Despite all our efforts to try and minimise fire-fighting we still seemed to be afflicted with cases of spontaneous combustion. It's all very well these management gurus telling you to find the root cause, I just wish they would try it here and find out what it's really like in the front line.

It's odd how stray thoughts prompt a long chain of reasoning. I had been thinking of professional fire-fighters. Now, I admit that I don't actually know any, but my perception is that they are not out there fighting fires all the time. Spare capacity exists to answer other vital calls. When not fire-fighting they get on with training, keeping the equipment in top condition, and even enjoying some well deserved relaxation. Why could we not achieve a similar balance?

At lunch I met up with Geoff, one of my team leaders who I often use as a sounding board. His experience and ability to see the big picture is invaluable. Yet his key quality is his directness. We have had our differences but I have come to respect and value his candour. I talked about my fire-fighting concerns and sought his views.

"It's odd that you should be worried about that," he said. "Only the other day I was thinking very much the same. My analogy was that I would be much better off if I was a piece of machinery rather than a human being. Instead of feeling driven all of the time, I would only be used when and where appropriate, and, in the meantime, I'd be well looked after and maintained."

"And ...?" I prompted, knowing there was more to come.

He continued, "Well, I have this feeling that organisations or systems with a clear sense of purpose only have a few parts or components that are working flat out. Other parts are not always that busy and may, from time to time, appear to be relatively inactive. Human beings, though, are creative creatures, and, in such a system will avoid the risk of appearing to be idle. God forbid that anyone might be accused of having nothing to do! Instead, we make up work to fill the gap. So, when an intelligent person finds him, or herself, with no immediate set task I think there is an element of the Devil finding work for idle minds. What is more I think we naturally encourage this. It is as if being busy gets rewarded!"

"What do you mean, Geoff?", I asked.

"Well, as an example, in most business cultures the number of sub-ordinates is still a measure of a manager's status." I did not disagree, as this was one of the factors taken into consideration when evaluating the relative worth of jobs in our own company. "Also", Geoff continued, "any sign of slack activity levels is interpreted as a sign of overstaffing, which could threaten the numbers employed, and thus their boss's status. Consequently, staff feel obliged to invent work.

"Now, how do they do this? First, they may just look at their own jobs and get busy solving problems and improving processes. Then the light goes on. For they soon realise that this well-intentioned behaviour only makes things worse. As efficiency rises, more slack time is generated.

"In this situation people either have to create enough visibility to move on fast in their career – not so easy in today's flatter organisa-tions – or find an alternative approach. Some of the brighter ones dis-cover something else. They discover that if they 'raise the game' and put forward a larger proposal which affects a cross section of their organisation, all sorts of good things start to happen. First, it makes their boss look good, which is good for them. Second, it makes them look good, not only for being creative, but for taking the wider view.

Third, it generates more interesting work, often more travel, and possibly other perceived benefits.

"Pretty soon there is a powerful signal that this is the way to get on in the company, and everyone is trying to come up with their own initiative. For anyone with ambition this becomes a major driving force, competing with the requirement to concentrate on being an effective specialist in their own work. Workplaces with such ambitious people soon fill up with initiatives.

"Speaking of initiatives, I really must get on. I'll see you later." With this Geoff got up and left!

He had succeeded in making me feel uncomfortable. What he had described came pretty close to how I became noticed in the company, and how I got promoted. Those reorganisation proposals that I had worked so hard on, really were in the best interests of the company. Or were they? Geoff had this uncanny ability to upset my sense of well-being.

I couldn't stop thinking about it. As a manager, I could not deny that I rated any subordinate whose ideas extended beyond his own immediate area. Neither was I averse to helping such subordinates push their ideas forward, as, indeed, some of the credit reflected on me. Was this some form of collusion? I could not believe that we all tacitly conspire to participate in behaviours which in the long run make life more difficult for ourselves.

As a test, I decided to explore whether the consequences of such behaviour really served our business interest.

I started jotting down some thoughts. If slack time gets filled with other activity, activity which appears to be of importance, then what happens? Everyone then has fuller diaries, we become busier, with the possible result that our priorities become less clear. In addition, when the inevitable panic occurs, there is less capacity to cope. To do so requires people to either drop things or work longer hours.

Dropping or postponing things is undesirable. It would impact individual performance and bonuses, so the first reaction is probably to work longer hours.

Then the reward and recognition systems come into play. Those who work the longer hours to counter the panics are seen as the heroes.

Soon everyone is tending to work longer hours in order to be a hero, and this becomes an embedded part of the culture.

Yet far from helping, this just makes matters worse. People who were on the critical path of activities are now buffeted by ever more calls on them and find it increasingly difficult to respond. Overall, the proportion of fringe to core tasks increases and either critical tasks take longer to accomplish or standards have to slide in order to meet deadlines. Either way, the overall performance suffers. Could this be an explanation for our indifferent performance?

I pursued the reasoning a bit further. As people work longer hours they have less time for relaxing and being with their family or friends. They become stressed. Performance and morale are then both at risk.

Was it mere coincidence that we seemed to have three concurrent issues? Performance was, at best, mediocre. Damn near everyone was working longer hours. And morale was low. But what to do? Time for another chat with Geoff. I gave him a call and we arranged to meet for a beer after work.

In the bar I described my reasoning to Geoff. I wanted him to pick holes in it. Geoff, being Geoff, merely took a long sip of his beer and went on to another tack. One I had not considered.

"You know what else might be going on? I think we are seeing survival strategies at work. Everyone knows that performance is under pressure and that a likely response is to reduce expense by cutting jobs. As a company, we have cut jobs before, and, no doubt, we'll do it again. We all know it. As individuals, if we are part of the critical path of a key project or activity, then we may feel fairly secure. If not, it makes good sense to raise visibility, create new activities, and thus get involved on a key project".

I attempted to summarise: "So, if we are right, we would be seeing lots of simultaneous initiatives, people working longer hours, and poor morale. At the same time, there will be lots of fire-fighting and apparent well-intentioned creativity. In short, we'd all be working harder and yet getting no further."

Geoff nodded his agreement and added: "It might even be worse, for, contrary to common-sense, the more effort put into this system the more likely it is that performance will deteriorate. For example, I'd expect in this sort of culture that ideas would be valued more than results, consequently there would be little effort to truly evaluate the implementation of ideas. Initiatives, there being lots of them, would tend to overlap and become blurred. If any changes occurred it would be difficult to establish the impact of any one initiative and probably there would be little incentive to do so."

Geoff's comments were not a million miles from reality. As he was speaking something had clicked. I brought the conversation back to our specific circumstances. "But Geoff, do you think we'd see these sort of behaviours in a manufacturing set-up? Are they peculiar to knowledge and service-based companies?"

Geoff thought for a while. "No, if we were just a manufacturing company I don't think we would have all these problems, at least not to the same extent. There would be some similarities for sure, but I suspect that we may have started to uncover why white collar productivity has been stagnating for such a long time, despite so-called revolutions in IT."

"The trouble is, Geoff, it is becoming much too complicated. We've started to identify a number of issues – capacity, priorities, critical paths, status, initiatives, recognition, stress, and so on – and we have traced some possible connections between them. We've even concluded that despite best intentions, or maybe because of best intentions, things might even get worse! Now, the key question is: Just what can we do?"

My glass was empty. "You know, Geoff, when we start to think about all this logically, it's surprising how we start to build connections and see relationships that serve to limit performance. I've got some ideas I'd like to run by you. But first, let me buy you a drink. Now, what will it be – the same again or something better?"

As Eli Goldratt demonstrated in *The Goal*, the output of a system is determined by a few critical bottlenecks. And the neck of the bottle is often at the top. If everyone is out to make work the top gets busier and busier, often working longer hours and generating a rule that says, in effect, *"Make even more work"*. The same superficial effect can have other causes. The rising complexity of contract negotiations and planning between specialist engineering departments, or between customers and contractors is often exacerbated by the pleasure people take in displaying their professional skills, as well as the incidental increased job security inherent in greater complexity.

Don't tell it like it is: if in doubt, talk it up!

"You really did not want to bring bad news forward to the top of the business."

"People became more interested in impressing (colleagues) than in attracting customers."

"The way to get ahead was to impress your boss, not serve the people."

The company had posted a record loss. It had lost touch with its markets, customers and competitors, through a culture that forced people to focus more on looking good than doing good. And that culture is far from unique. Several companies in the business of investing in major projects and risk ventures have found themselves suffering from 'championship bias', the tendency of those whose job it is to evaluate a particular opportunity to hype it up. Championship bias contributes to the well-known phenomenon of many take-overs and acquisitions not yielding the results expected of them. It has also contributed to the world's oil companies spending countless millions of dollars over-bidding for exploration licences[11]. In case after case people succeed, not for having the right answer, but for selling their particular project or for delivering the answer that is wanted.

Where management development policies also encourage movement every two to three years, and base such movements largely on perceptions, a commonly associated rule concerns moving on before one's judgement is put to the test. Someone else can dig the company out of the hole created by another's legitimate ambition and self interest. And that does not imply that fast movers are wrong; merely that that is how that particular company operates.

Criticism of the team is disloyal!

"Don't make the company wrong; its disloyal."
"You don't like to criticise a colleague – You will need them to get things done some day."

It is not always 'profile' that drives the 'don't bring bad news to the top of the business' syndrome... Another company that suffered a superficially similar problem of getting out of touch with its market did so out of a great premium on teamwork and being 'for' each other. In this case that premium was reflected in the reality. Criticism was regarded as downright disloyal. Unfortunately, nobody wanted to face the reality that their previous success formulae were no longer working. They continued to borrow forward against future contracts until a cyclical downturn in the market nearly destroyed them. The business outcome was similar to the previous example but the pattern behind it was substantially different and the cure that ignores the cause is doomed to failure.

Partnership, what partnership? Evaluating new arrangements with old standards!

"You get on by billing as many man-hours as possible."
"You show how tough you are by screwing your suppliers."
'You get on in the negotiations. Deeds of variation are where it's at."

Two companies, one the owner of a processing facility, the other a leading supplier of Facilities Management services, had announced a new partnership to replace the old style of competitive tendering and adversarial relationships. It was to be the dawn of a new Golden Age. Unfortunately, the purchaser's managers were still stuck with a pattern that judged success in terms of costs saved, and being tough with suppliers. The company did not see itself as a place for wimps. Meanwhile the fact of the contract was that man-hours billed to the project were what made the supplier money. Every unanticipated exigency, every deed of variation was, when it came down to it, an opportunity to make more – to say nothing of also being a satisfying challenge and source of security to the personnel involved. The procurement and legal procedures made lots of satisfying work for all the procurement and legal personnel involved, as well as creating in reality a self-fulfilling prophecy that they were needed, confirming their perceptions of the world. In practice, the contract drove the relationship rather than the other way around.

 We will return to this example in Chapter Nine. In industry after industry, companies seeking 'partnerships' find their rules and other artefacts of the patterns which drive their practices getting in the way. And it is not just between companies that such rules rear their head. Organisations such as technology developers or consultants who require co-operation between teams of different specialists, or the exchange of 'best practice' and innovation between different project groups also find that the unwritten barriers are large when 'man-hours billed for your own project' dominate the implicit reward system

Under-promise and over-perform! Budgets and rules

"Watch the numbers."
"Keep something back."
"Spend it or lose it."

The unwritten rules of budgeting and control processes can be a law unto themselves. Where the company is driven by numbers everyone can so easily fall into a pattern in which more effort is devoted to meeting the plan, the numbers, than to customers or sales. Exceeding targets is dangerous. If you do, 'they' will want more or will want an explanation. Senior managers devote hours of their time to preparing for review meetings, with slides, print-outs and reports to cover every possible question. Reputations and empires are built on the back of being good at coming in on budget. The dangers are that what might be possible is overlooked. New opportunities are ignored.

Dirk...

Dirk ran the national subsidiary of one such company. One year he took a risk (the country he worked in had particularly strong employment protection legislation) and went to the annual budget meeting with only one slide and a powerful request for help in meeting an extraordinary target. After the shock died away there was some different listening. The subsidiary went on to achieve 150 per cent of normal projections in the next quarter.

But such vignettes are the rare exception. All too often the prevailing pattern demands more time and attention focused on the internal systems than on possibilities and opportunities in the outside world. The result may benefit the company whilst the outside world is static, or whilst a particularly dominant and numerically astute man[12] is in charge. The danger is that concentration on the numbers passes from sound managerial practice to an obsession that limits flexibility. The point of looking at unwritten rules, and any patterns, is not usually to say whether they are, in absolute terms, positive or negative. It is whether or not they are currently limiting what a company is, or could be, achieving.

And it is not just commercial companies...

The examples we have used so far all come from commercial companies but the same dilemma of individual interest and the long term benefit for the organisation occurs in every other walk of organisational life.

Elaine...

Elaine ran one of the larger departments in a university for two years
as 'Acting Head'. The teaching and courses improved. Students and
staff recognised the change and the reputation of the department was
starting to grow in the outside world with new courses and distributed
programmes for the local community. Elaine became something of an
indispensable figure, called in by the Vice Chancellor for such key
events as visits from government ministers. Unfortunately she could
not be confirmed in post. She lacked the necessary 'academic qualifications' and, in practice, the track record of publications in refereed
journals on which the department's score depended in periodic
reviews by the Funding Council. As this is written the search for an
outside candidate continues and Elaine's resignation looms. What has
started in the department is unlikely to continue.

Performance 'league tables' generat spurious rules. For example, my
local hospital was praised for meeting government targets for performance in National League tables, among them the percentage of
patients seen within a minimum time of arriving in the casualty clinic.
Two weeks earlier I had been careless enough to need that service
after a minor accident. On arrival in casualty I was politely asked by
the receptionist to wait until they could book me in. After about ninety
minutes she asked me back, and took down the details. Five minutes
later I was seen by the casualty sister, had my wound dressed and
received a referral to the doctor. I noticed others receiving the same
treatment; everyone in fact who came in. There was nothing to complain of, the staff were pressed and under-resourced on a Saturday
night. They could not have been more friendly, diligent or helpful.
The point was, the meeting of the target was achieved by adjusting
formal check-in times to availability of staff, not by any genuine
improvement. The written 'rule' shows a considerable improvement;
one that a government minister can claim as a success. The unwritten
rule was 'business as usual'...

Nor are rules always negative...
Partnership in practice

"We try to put into people as much positive energy as we can."
"If someone asks for help, I treat him as a king."
"We work as a team because we need one another."

Previous examples have all involved unwritten rules that were generating negative side-effects. The choice was deliberate for the intent was to reveal the limiting impact of this aspect of patterns. Negative side-effects of the rules are at their most obvious when they are limiting. Yet rules can also *enable*. To show the difference, consider this last example: a bank whose return on capital employed and growth record place it in first or second place world-wide in its industry.

Among the causes of its success is a culture, and a set of values, that promote mutual support and sharing between the managers of highly decentralised, autonomous, branches and districts. The management of these districts compete, fiercely, to outdo each other on various numerical measures of success, measures viewed both absolutely and as trends over time. Yet they also collaborate to share new ideas and help colleagues whose numbers are not doing so well. Learning is shared with a speed that many companies would envy.

Examine the rules, both written and unwritten, and what does one find? A company with a great sense of membership undoubtedly. Also a company in an industry and a national culture where quantified performance measures are not only accepted but enthusiastically embraced. Senior executives have up to 70 per cent of their take home income in the form of bonuses tied to various levels of performance. And there's the rub, for not all those levels are theirs, or their subordinates', or even their boss's, or the collective performance... People have bonuses specifically tied to the performance of peers over whom they have no direct authority. It is in everyone's interest to collaborate. The formal and informal mirror each other perfectly.

We are not saying this is a miracle recipe. There are many companies and industries where, often fortunately, 'performance-related-pay' does not loom as large in the real world as its advocates would have us believe. Where it does, many companies are discovering the limitations of pay-for-individual-performance in situations where teamwork and flexibility across organisational boundaries are key to success. Leaders in the self-managed team concept have moved to the point, not only of team-based pay, but even of team-determined distribution of performance bonuses. Few have moved to the 'pay-for-other-people's-performance' to the extent of the company on which this example centres.

But the example proves that the dilemma between company and individual interest is not inevitable. It is possible to create systems where the unwritten rules encourage desired behaviour. The first step is to realise how pervasive unwritten rules really are.

The reigning rule

Unwritten rules are as old as organisations themselves. They are 'political reality'. They begin to reveal the systemic patterns of companies. Machiavelli earned his place in history by documenting the pragmatic rules for princes of city states in Renaissance Italy. It was not his fault that they happened to involve poisoning rivals and lesser forms of extreme behaviour that have come to be labelled Machiavellian. Pragmatic but devious unwritten rules still dominate the corridors of power. There is no finer recent exposé than the BBC's *Yes, Minister*[13].

Bob Townsend's 1970 book *Up The Organisation!* was an immensely humorous read, which anticipated many of the messages on empowerment and other, now fashionable, trends in management thinking but did not gain widespread recognition as a manual for doing things differently. 'Eclectic' was one reviewer's description of its challenge to perceived managerial wisdom. Townsend put it rather differently:

"There are already too many organisational orthodoxys (sic) imposed on people, and I don't want to help the walking dead institute another."

...and:

"Most people in organisations have become but mortals conditioned to serve immortal institutions."

Townsend suggested two solutions, and argued for the second if American corporations were not to lose their pre-eminent position over the next twenty years. As he put it:

"Solution One is the cop-out. Decide what is must be inevitable; grab your share of the cash and fringe benefits and comfort yourself with the distractions you call leisure.

"Solution Two is non-violent guerrilla warfare; start dismantling our organisations where we're serving them leaving only the parts where they are serving us."

Unfortunately for corporate America – and the USA is far from alone – Solution One remains the attractive option for most individuals. Unless you have the good fortune to find yourself in a company determined to be different, non-violent guerrilla warfare is a career limiting strategy. It represents an act, either of extreme foolishness or extreme altruism, depending on one's point of view. It breaks the unwritten rules of the average company as much in the late 1990's as it did in 1970. Indeed if anything, at a time of down-sizing and unprecedented insecurity, the pressure to conform, to avoid rocking the boat, to remain a member of the club is stronger. To keep one's spot in the golden life raft is eminently sensible for many.

The twenty-five years since *Up the Organisation!* were to be full of companies going bottom-up: companies in which people adopted what for them was the 'rational' (at least in the short term), Solution One, option. Industries and nations of Solution One companies also had, and continue to have, problems. For example:

❑ Two thirds or more of the companies identified as leaders in Peters and Waterman's 1972 best-seller *In Search of Excellence* were no longer excellent ten years later. Some had ceased trading altogether[14].

❑ Whole industries such as consumer electronics or heavy goods vehicle manufacturing have all but vanished in the UK, and are threatened elsewhere.

❑ Study after study bemoans the declining percentage of school leavers aspiring to careers in technology or manufacturing, but the fact is that there are greater rewards in the financial services industry.

❑ Organised crime is one of the industrial West's, and the 'liberated' Eastern Bloc's, major growth industries.

❑ Jobs are vanishing as executive remuneration rises in privatised utilities; a game that their managers perceive themselves as forced, by the system they are in, to continue playing whether they like it or not.

❑ Industrial decline continues.

Yet the approach we normally take is to persevere with what we already know: specifying and ordering organisations down to the last detail; measuring more, setting standards targets and objectives, developing policies and procedures for every eventuality, improving the efficiency with which the organisation is administered, etc. One might call this the pattern of managing through written rules; removing uncertainty and ambiguity by planning and specifying for every eventuality, by preparing detailed written job descriptions for everybody, and by measuring everything. It forms the substance of those conditions which we describe as 'manual mania' and 'policy proliferation', conditions which assume that to write down nearly everything is the key to salvation!

The alternative one might call 'managing by the unwritten rules', managing the *context* of the company more than its content, ensuring that the behaviours the company informally encourages serve at least its own interests, if not also those of the wider economy. Human beings are, by and large, pragmatic and adaptable creatures. Change the rules, and make the change clear, and new behaviours follow remarkably rapidly. Old patterns are broken. First though we have to see what the rules are for a particular context of company.

'Not here it doesn't!': revealing the rules

Our argument in this book is that by surfacing and revealing corporate patterns one may start to change them. Unwritten rules are only part of the pattern of any company. They may be more a manifestation of a deeper pattern than a pattern in themselves, yet revealing them still offers considerable benefits. One essential is to appreciate that unwritten rules are nobody's 'fault'; they just *are*. They emerge and self-organise over time as a logical combination of, on the one hand, the mental models and motivators of the people in the company, and on the other, its formal structures and systems.

It may be necessary to convince people that unwritten rules will exist in their organisation. At one level this is not difficult. Many people find it easy to accept a mismatch, perhaps a considerable mismatch, between an espoused policy – that which a company says that it wants or stands for – and day to day reality. Take the current enthusiasm for 'visions and missions', a management tool that surveys reveal to be more used than either Total Quality or Process Management[15], and a tool whose adoption is supported by the evidence of high performance in organisations that have formulated a compelling sense of purpose. The problem with many such vision statements is that they are no more than wish lists dreamed up in a management retreat, crafted by HR (or PR), and announced to the corporate world; often supported by a plastic card or a plaque on the wall. As the millennium approaches, the figure '2000' often gets in there somehow. Yet how many of us remember our company's vision, let alone use that vision to guide our behaviour, even if we know how to relate it to our everyday tasks?

Most people we meet, whilst they acknowledge the gap between what is espoused and practised, also regard it as inevitable, and resign themselves to its existence. Seeing the connection between rules, the behaviours they encourage, and business results may be difficult, especially where that connection carries an in-built time lag. When habits and training conspire with the day to day whirl of busy-ness it can be harder to be convinced of longer-term, systemic connections, let alone to be ready to do something about them. Part of the art of revealing the rules, or any pattern, is always to explore the consequences in the context of the company concerned.

Other reactions occur. Some, especially those who are comfortable with, and successful in, an existing pattern; members of a club within a club, may grant the existence of, but vigorously defend, a particular system of rules. Others, especially more senior managers, confronted with the idea, will often react by denying that dramatic conflicts such as those cited above exist in their organisation. "Other companies may have unwritten rules, but not us!" one CEO said.

Three questions then help to convince...

First, consider a situation other than a company; perhaps a social club, or the local traffic regulations or even a marriage or other relationship. Reflect for a minute on the formal, espoused rules of acceptable behaviour (e.g. the prevailing formal speed limit) then reflect on the unwritten rules. Do they match?

Next, consider what your company ideally requires of you, or what you require of your workforce. If you, as a manager, or as managed, could write the Ten Commandments that your company would wish to see used, what would they be? Using the actual format of the commandments can help. If you had to write down the ten, or nine – or eleven, for your company, what would you put?

Thou shalt:	Thou shalt not:
....	....
....	....
....	....
....	....
....	....
....	....
....	....
....	....
....	....
....	....

Now are these the *actual* commandments? Are these the rules that those you see around you are playing by? Are these the rules your staff follow? Really? How do you know? When did you last ask them and would they have told you?

This last question is important, for talking – and more importantly listening – to people is the only way to bring out the unwritten rules. People know what they are, even if they have not made the effort to make all the connections between them. When the unwritten rules get talked about at all it is in the informal conversations of the company, the corridor encounters, the chats over lunch, or the gossip in the pub after work. To reveal the rules, those conversations must be brought out into the open. If you are really serious there is no substitute for a series of interviews in which you sympathetically and empathetically encourage a representative group of individuals to talk about the reality of life in their particular organisation. The amazing fact is how quickly a pattern of consistent answers emerges[16].

Sometimes interviews are essential, particularly if you suspect defensive reactions from participants. Often though, an alternative approach achieves the same end. It is quite possible to invite people to talk to each other about the rules in their company. The trick is to invite them to replicate the sort of conversation they might have in a different setting, say a pub or bar where they happen to meet a stranger genuinely interested in what life is like in that organisation. By creating an imaginary setting (such as strangers meeting in a neutral environment) one can enable people to talk to each other and to draw out, in the space of not much over an hour, the essence of the unwritten rules of their own particular game and also of the forces that drive those rules. We supply them with the following checklist, not as a recipe to be blindly followed but as a series of questions for them to explore in their own way, using their own words. Once they have the answers to these questions a group have the data to understand what the rules are; and, more importantly, the prospect of some insight into why their rules are like that, the behavioural and business consequences that result from such rules, and what they might do to change them.

Exercise: the pub conversation

With a colleague, have a 'pub conversation'. Imagine you are talking about joining their company, or that you are swapping notes on what it is like to work for each other's organisations. Listen, empathise and try to let your colleague do 90 per cent of the talking.

This is not a check list but these are the sort of topics to cover

1 What is it like working for the company?

2 What is the company up to?

3 What is different about the company?

4 What makes it worth working for? – What gets people out of bed in the morning?

5 What is really important?

6 What do you have to do to survive?

7 What do you have to do to succeed?

8 What are the greatest sins to avoid?

9 What are the important events?

10 Who are the important people?

11 What is flavour of the week/month/year What flags have to be saluted?

12 Can you capture the company in a phrase?

Some of these questions bear not on the rules but on the factors that drive them. Before getting to that stage however you must first identify the rules themselves. We find it helps to ask a group who have interviewed each other to then work on identifying their commandments. From the questions, particularly numbers six, seven and eight, you, or they, can readily identify the key do's and don'ts for the company concerned. A real life example is given in the next table. One group's impression of the commandments in their company:

Thou shalt:	**Thou shalt not:**
Hold back good ideas to thyself	Muddy the good name of XYZ Co
Reward inactivity and error	Rock the boat
Always re-invent the wheel	Trust anybody
Pass the buck whenever thou can'st	Communicate more than thou hast to to thy colleagues
	Get over-excited or enthusiastic
	Take risks

When a group has reached this stage they will not need convincing that these are the commandments for their organisation. They may need convincing that those rules matter, in which case it is vital to involve them in exploring the implications for their business. Only then does the exercise cease to be an interesting bit of fun.

The same is true if you have reached the same point of a set of rules after interviewing people. You may need to convince them, or their management. In that case having actual quotations to support your conclusions is invaluable. One CEO we worked with described it as: "The mother of all feedbacks".

But what next?

 # Changing the Rules

A company that can shift its unwritten rules achieves, in very short order, a shift of behaviour. In Chapter Eight there is an explosive (literally) case study.

A similar effect can sometimes be engendered simply by the exercise of revealing the unwritten rules. The very act of talking about them can help people to change them. More usual though is the situation where deliberate action has to be taken to change the rules. To engage those with the power so to do it is necessary to help them see:

First – the side-effects of the rules so as to decide what to change or perhaps reinforce.

Second – what causes those particular rules.

What one is doing is a variant of a theme found in any change to an individual's or a company's pattern, that is revealing the pattern and the effects it generates (see Chapter Six). One is freezing a snapshot of the current reality by demonstrating how the rules and their side-effects form a coherent system that limits an organisation. Any changes to the rules are best facilitated by involving those affected. No-one can remove all the rules. The objective is to identify and change whatever is limiting: the rules which encourage behaviours that run counter to whatever the company judges to be its best interest. It helps if everyone is able to realise that the rules are genuine, logical, and impact upon their business results.

So, having arrived at the rules, or commandments, the next question is to assess their impact. Not all rules are negative and what is negative for one company at one time might be positive for other. If, for example, the company whose commandments are quoted in the last table happened to be in the business of managing, say, nuclear power plants (it wasn't) an unwritten rule that said: "Don't take any risks" would seem to be beneficial. The same rule, however, would slowly kill a company that relied on innovation.

Don't expect to find a neat one-to-one correspondence between particular rules and immediate business consequences. You are asking what, given a set of encouraged behaviours, the cumulative effect is likely to be over time. In practice, the language and discipline of Systems Thinking, and a familiarity with common systems archetypes[17], helps. At some point every common archetype can be found in the dynamics created by a particular set of unwritten rules and almost any situation involving unwritten rules can be described using the language of a systems archetype. Examples are provided elsewhere in the book.

Once you know which rules you wish to change or reinforce, the other need is to establish what drives them. Peter Scott-Morgan's key breakthrough was to discover that the drivers can be understood by answering two questions:

❏   What motivates people in a company?
❏   How is that motivation delivered in practice?

The answers can be found, either in interview notes or in people's answers to other questions in the 'pub conversation'. In any organisation one finds a common set of motivators. They are part of the implicit contract of membership. The joining process filters out those who do not share the motivators, who won't enjoy being part of a particular company and 'culture', who don't want to fit in. Motivators self-select themselves. What they are varies. Money is not always a priority, provided a necessary hygiene level is reached. In the terms of Maslow's classic hierarchy one is asking what grants people – or a subset of people – in a particular company their self-actualisation? It can be belonging and loyalty, it can be a sense of service to others, it can be more money, it can be the challenge and excitement of a particular type of work, it can be professional recognition or career advancement. The point is that, in a given culture, one or two of these will prove surprisingly dominant.

Given a set of motivators some rules follow; as, effectively: 'seek that motivation'; whether it is: 'sell yourself to the highest bidder', or 'enjoy opportunities to display your technical skill'... Other rules stem from the mechanisms that either deliver that motivation or prevent it from being realised. Two further questions help:

❏   Who is important to delivering a particular motivator?
❏   What are the events that can deliver a motivator, and when?

Answering these two provides what is termed, in the jargon of an unwritten rules appraisal, the 'enablers' and 'triggers'. Their effect can be understood from examples. Career progression and greater responsibility are still very common motivators in large organisations where, despite the changing world, managers are seeking moves 'up the organisation'. Career moves remain, for many, the triggers that deliver that motivation. Candidates for career progression are often judged by various superiors, including current boss, would-be boss, and perhaps by the head of a particular specialist function within the company. If reputation with such key people is gained or lost in meetings and presentations, 'Give good slide' becomes a common rule. It can, as we have seen, have the long term side-effect of a business out of touch with the world because it is focused more on style than content.

We also saw an example of a similar outcome generated by very different rules. If the motivators include a sense of loyalty and pride in belonging to a particular company, then peer group opinion can be a very powerful motivator. A group meeting is a trigger, an opportunity to enjoy that sense of belonging and people are then loath to risk the harmony.

Performance appraisals are common triggers. Where the rules are heavily influenced by individual reward systems, common side-effects include compartmentalised thinking and an unwillingness to devote time and energy to cross-functional projects and other occasions for inter-departmental collaboration. Turf-wars and territorial behaviour can often (not always) be traced to performance assessment and reward systems. The simple expedient of making parts of people's rewards dependant upon the performance of others can have a dramatic effect. In other companies the formal, written, performance appraisal system exerts so little impact on the unwritten rules that it is an irrelevance. In those cases tinkering with it is unlikely to shift the pattern one little bit. It can become a great excuse for evading the real issues.

It is rarely as simple as one motivator, enabler or disenabler, one consequent rule, and one business side-effect. Combinations of drivers conspire to generate particular rules and combinations of rules generate particular side-effects. What one is seeking is the dynamic that is at work, the underlying archetype. It helps the process of understanding the rules if the 'consultant' who is interviewing, or the facilitator who is helping a group, has developed a sensitivity to such patterns. She or he can then steer the conversation, exploring for, and helping people to see for themselves, the interconnections between the rules they are verbalising, the dynamics of the pattern. Those interconnections are key. So conditioned are many of us to a pattern of thinking in separate, neat, cause and effect boxes that we frequently fail to see them. Consider an example:

Wytch Farm

The Wytch Farm Oilfield is one of the ten largest in the UK. Unlike all the rest, it lies onshore. The surface facilities of the field, which include well sites, a rail terminal and a gathering station, lie in a designated Area of Outstanding Natural Beauty. In late 1992, when the appraisal described here was conducted, a separate office, stores and workshops were located 12 miles away and a slipway and emergency response base were located on the edge of Poole Harbour approximately 15 miles from the gathering station. Around 150 permanent staff and a significant number of contractors, worked in either the operation and further development of the field.

Prior to this exercise the field had already achieved significant improvements in operating profit by way of a number of projects to involve and empower all staff in the improvement process. Yet the management team shared a hunch that something was missing, that the rate of improvement was slowing, that something more could be done, but what? We were asked: "Are some unwritten rules stopping us achieving the next level of performance?" and given a week on-site to find an answer. Four people, two external and two internal consultants, spent the week interviewing a representative cross section of all 'levels' and functions in the operation. All their comments – interpreted as unwritten rules and edited only to preserve anonymity – were included in a management report. As one interviewee put it: "I could not have been this open to my managers", and, as another said: "It's great that the company sends you here to ask us these questions rather than just giving us attitude surveys!"

The results produced some very positive findings. Employees had recognised and responded to a change in their sense of empowerment. Many negative rules identified elsewhere in the company were not apparent – a benefit of Wytch Farm's geographical isolation. There was a noticeable sense of belonging to what was seen as almost an independent company; one where the rules provided unwritten encouragement of several well-developed networks for making things happen. Nevertheless, the employees shared their management's instinct that more was possible. They told us about performance appraisal and bonus systems being, at best, variable in their influence, about maintenance systems not getting it right first time, about suggesting improvements being something one waited to do until the time was right, and about formal systems not being used to their full potential.

The under-utilisation of systems was the dominant issue. "We are too busy to deal with the paper trail" was a common theme. People, they said, simply did not have time to implement standard systems and processes. In the language of systems archetypes it was a classic 'Shifting the Burden' dynamic (figure 2.1); a case, apparently, of everyone being too busy fixing problems to worry about systems that might have stopped those problems recurring[18].

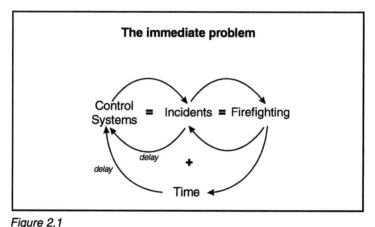

Figure 2.1
The superficial situation at Wytch Farm expressed a 'Shifting the Burden' archetype (Senge et al, 1994). Everyone saw themselves as too busy firefighting to make the more fundamental changes to operating procedures that would avoid there being so many fires to fight. The plea is not unique! (The '+' and '=' symbols reflect systems language notation – see Chapter Six, figure 6.1 for explanation.)

But the unwritten rules kept this informal system perfectly in place. There were three common motivators: a desire for informal recognition (widely perceived as not being provided in the prevailing culture); a sense of pride in working for the Wytch Farm operation, and a desire for challenge and variety in the day to day work. Compared to these, the formal performance appraisal and bonus system had little impact. Activity, being busy solving problems, provided the main motivator, the desired challenge. People motivated by challenge had no incentive to simplify their work by using systems. As one interviewee put it, "My biggest fear is that work will become mundane and boring in a year or two". A shift maintenance hand summed it up: after one and three quarter hours of telling us his problems, especially the fact that, in the pecking order of the site, maintenance hands were regarded as second class citizens compared to the operators, we offered the observation that he might not be getting much fun out of his job. "Away, man" was the reply "Its a great place to work, there's summat different every day"...

Managers enjoyed the challenge of being busy, so had little time to remember to offer informal pats on the back, and spot recognition; so there was only one remaining motivator. Systems were seen as a threat, the formal performance measurement system was an annual exercise soon forgotten, so *challenge* was the only motivator being delivered. The expanded systems diagram is shown in figure 2.2. In essence, everyone was caught in a pattern of 'fighting fires'.

The fact that management was seen to be ready to conduct the appraisal and to receive the direct feedback sent, by itself, a strong and positive signal which shifted certain patterns. The collected quotations from the interviews became one of the most widely read items of managerial communication, sought after even by those not interviewed!

The existing appraisal system was replaced by one based on a team performance. More emphasis was given to rapid, positive encouragement. The major pattern shift, however, was to consider how the use of systems to take care of mundane parts of the operation could increase the technical challenge – through, for example, interdepartmental participation in activities such as safety reviews; a shift of perception that generated a different result. There was an immediate response in terms of incident reporting. Even the visitors from Head Office were credited with providing a fast, pragmatic intervention.

The case illustrates the power of changing the rules so as to enable shifts in patterns of behaviour. The willingness and commitment of

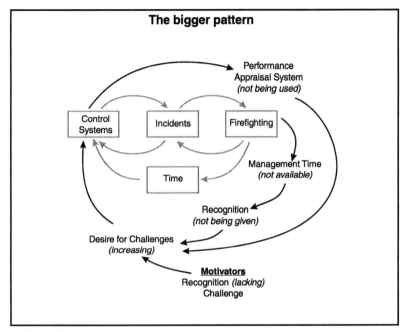

Figure 2.2
A more detailed expansion of the situation shown in figure 2.1. In reality, given the dormant motivators of this group of people, there were perceived disincentives to make life simpler. Until the assumptions behind those perceived disincentives changed, nothing else would change.

those in a position to make the change was, as always, critical to its success. The feedback helped those involved to see the totality of the system generated by the existing patterns.

The example also serves to demonstrate other themes, to be taken up in later chapters. Geographical isolation, physical and – more importantly – perceptual separation from the prevailing patterns of the larger company made the change easier. We will be arguing in Chapters Four and Eight for the power of such separation – peripheral isolation – as an enabler of innovation and change.

The shift also involved a fundamental perceptual move

from seeing systems and procedures as a threat, a dilution of challenge, to seeing them as an opportunity, an enabler. Nothing was different in the physical world; nonetheless, the perceptual pattern changed at the deepest level. This aspect of patterns is so often fundamental. We take it up in the next chapter and continue the theme for the rest of the book.

Finally, there was a shift in the implicit contract between managers and managed – embodied in the commitment to faster, more open, informal feedback; and the demonstration to the managed that subjects previously regarded as taboo could be, and had been, openly aired. In such an example we may begin to see the link between rules and the rest of a company's pattern. When one can change the enablers and triggers, deliver a current motivator in a new way, it is relatively easy to change an associated unwritten rule. Pragmatism works. In the example just described a way was found to deliver 'challenge' differently; though even that shift involved those concerned in seeing 'systems and standards' differently.

The conditioning of contract

 It is much harder to change rules rooted in the motivators of a particular organisation, especially when, behind the motivators, are deep-seated assumptions people have about their business, their company and, indeed, about what any company is or should be. To quote another perceptive director: "This is too close to home. It's like schooling. We all support state education but send our own kids to private schools". Rules are but part of the interconnected pattern introduced in Chapter One.

Revealing the unwritten rules of a company, powerful though it is, may do no more than uncover part of an iceberg. The various sets of expectations and obligations that apply between individuals and their peers, subordinates, superiors, and the company as a whole, often exist simply because they lead to actions that become self-fulfilling drivers of reality. When two or more parties conspire in an informal contract through which each limits their expectations of the other, the result is limited. Rules are often indicative of the informal contract that exists between the players in an enterprise. The nature of that psychological contract is part of the pattern that shapes behaviours. It is informal in so far as it is 'what is understood' as an established and emergent agreement between players.

Such contracts do not have to be limiting but often are. A fundamental surprise in the case of Wytch Farm was the discovery that there were no significant different motivators for managers, professional staff and 'technicians'. All three groups had individual members more concerned about money, career or job security. What everyone shared was the love of a technical challenge. That realisation shifted the mutual perceptions of managers and managed and of different groups within the operation of each other.

We will have more to say on perceptions shortly. For now take the following, hypothetical, conversation:

Management: We have to pay the lowest price compatible with the job.

Managed: So only an idiot would take it?

Management: So we had better make it idiot-proof.

Managed: So it's only a job... Thank God it's Friday!

Management: We need to squeeze harder...

Each side in such a dialogue mirrors its expectations of the other. Managers reinforce their perceived need to be in control, while the managed replicate the mirror image of the managers. "It's not my company, I just work here" provides, or preserves, a limited context for involvement; one which leads to dissociation from the performance of the company. 'Worker' carries a set of mental baggage, a pattern, that says to be managed is to be told what to do, when and how to do it, to convey any problems to management and to seek their answer, and to comply with all reasonable instructions and requests. Being a passive agent, exempt from responsibility, becomes a comfortable pattern in which to exist for the activity called work. Energy can be reserved for the distraction called leisure. Much of schooling and life prepares us well for this role.

If managers attempt to be *different*, to change the set of ideas out of which they work, and the informal contract that applies, then they must deal with the established pattern that exists. Much of that established pattern is deeply rooted in the existing contract and sets of ideas of those being managed. Take, for example, the ideas of 'managing' and 'manager'. What do these words convey to many people? What set of reciprocal expectations are elicited and what form of agreement is implied between parties? Both the managed and the manager have learned the ways of the other in all sorts of environments – the home, school, and work. For one to change without the other is untenable, thus to manage differently means shifting the experience, ideas, and the informal contract of being managed. Either party can limit the movement of the other.

We may be confined within informal contracts – implicit agreements – which form part of the pattern of an under-performing system. To change the pattern requires someone to take the lead. Yet patterns and contracts are often so well-established, so well-mirrored, that the change takes root only in a very small environment – or it withers. We'll see why in the next chapter when we start to examine the deeper structures underpinning rules and contracts.

Summary

We started this chapter with the idea of joining the club and revealed how membership of any one club carries with it certain codes, conventions and contracts. As we proceeded to the end of the chapter we saw that it is not just a matter of membership of one club but a number of 'clubs' – domestic, professional and social – that can keep us locked into a network of rules, expectations and agreements. Within the membership of any one club and certainly between clubs there is "systematic complexity, power relations, and political processes" at work.

These forces manifest themselves as unwritten rules which maintain the status quo. Furthermore, such unwritten rules – which an individual must follow to succeed or even to survive – often foster behaviours which are not in the company's long-term interest. We provided real-life examples. We also pointed out that rules may have a positive effect in different contexts and at different times.

The point is, one first needs to surface these unwritten rules in order to ascertain their contribution in any context; to reveal what rules operate, as it were, in the background. Knowing the rules and 'seeing' their consequences is one thing, changing them is another. It can be achieved. Yet unwritten rules are but part of the informal contract that exists in the membership of any one club and in the multiple memberships of different clubs. Unwitting conspiracies emerge which serve to create underperforming systems.

 Primary Sources

The literature on the culture of companies is extensive. The seed for this chapter was Townsend's (1970) under-appreciated early warning of the dangers inherent in the prevalent pattern of large organisations; germinated by the ideas of Scott-Morgan (1994) and the opportunity IP had to work with him during the later stages of the development of his methodology (see also McGovern, 1995). The power of the unwritten rules of the Game methodology is enhanced when it is combined with systems theory and especially the concept of generic systems or archetypes (Senge 1990, Senge et al, 1994). The Wytch Farm case study is based on one such joint exercise reported more fully elsewhere (Price, 1993) by kind permission of the management involved. The other case studies all relate to real life examples. The classic work on bottlenecks is Goldratt and Cox (1989). Other references to the thinking habits of companies are provided in Chapter Three.

3

The origins within: exposing the patterns of management

"In truth the ideas and images in men's minds are the invisible powers that constantly govern them."

John Locke

The origins within

Chapter Two began to reveal how 'rules, contracts and understandings' shape behaviours, and how many of these are tacit rather than explicit, understood yet seldom articulated, felt, known and experienced, yet not written; how such factors emerge from informal and interpersonal processes of socialisation, negotiation and renegotiation; and how, so often, they remain unchallenged. We attempted to show some of the consequences that can flow from such rules, and some of the influences that serve to support them. They function at an almost invisible operating level: the dark side of the enterprise. They are how the company, the team, the relationship operates beneath the surface. They govern how things really work as distinct from how they are supposed to work. Yet such rules, contracts and agreements are but part of the pattern.

Someone's acquired knowledge of unwritten rules may be described as 'tacit'. It is a knowledge acquired through informal processes of learning rather than through manuals and procedures. It exemplifies how the pattern or system really works. The rules, codes and significant influences of the game in question may be intimately appreciated at a deep level and yet, in a way, not understood. Not 'understood' in that we may be so conditioned to the rules – and even to the game itself – that it is as though we are stuck with them, and in it, as victims. It is as though the game and the rules have us.

Thus it is that outsiders – people who have not been conditioned to particular patterns – tend to change the game and the rules. Whereas insiders are deeply trained in a game and its rules, perhaps stuck with them, the newcomer might just invent a new one. And the newcomer may be a new entrant to a market rather than just a new person in a company. A recent example is the car company Daewoo, changing the rules by its direct sales practices and service arrangements[19].

Common sense reveals the possibility of this conditioning by suggesting that our intimacy with a game and its rules of conduct may make us 'too close to see it'. Distance may help us to see patterns that we would not otherwise be aware of.

Do new rules emerge by design? The Daewoo example shows that they can, just as, as in another example, the laws of the game of Rugby may be changed in order to make it a more open game. Practice, though, does not always meet the design intent. Tacit rules often emerge to counter the intent of an explicit change. In order to counter defensive play in the game of Rugby football, the authorities decided to increase the number of points for a try[20] from three, to (first) four, and then five points. However, despite best intentions, players learnt that it was preferable to give away a penalty for lesser points than to concede a try. In consequence, the number of tries scored in the annual Five Nations tournament stays roughly constant. (In kindness to our American readers, perhaps we should explain that a try is the equivalent of a touchdown.) From the amalgam of explicit changes to the formal rules combined with the desire of participants to win, or at least not to lose, emerged an unintended tacit rule that keeps the game defensive rather than open. Contrary to apparent logic and 'common sense', if the authorities were to decrease the points for a try and increase the points for a penalty, it might be that the informal or tacit rules would be to avoid penalties at all costs and thus play more flowing rugby. Yet we seldom challenge common sense with more uncommon sense!

New rules, then, may emerge by design but often, in turn, encourage new rules of a more tacit, emergent kind. Despite the plethora of formal rules that abound in legislation, in formal codes of conduct, and in legal contracts of one sort or another, the more powerful rules are those that arise tacitly. They are born out of the informal processes of interaction within the prevailing culture, with other persons, and within the context of established or emergent purposes.

 Two further examples demonstrate the emergent nature of informal or tacit rules. First, take a hypothetical domestic relationship of a marriage or close partner and, in this context, see how the rules and practice of 'what is not to be discussed around here' – the 'undiscussables' – might emerge. As a relationship develops, one begins to appreciate that certain topics raise a lot of sensitivity on the part of one's partner. One may observe one's partner becoming upset within a particular subject domain, either by recall of the subject itself, and/or by the nature of one's own assumptions on the subject and one's own dialogue. In short, the two of you argue...

Many people disposed towards the 'quiet life' prefer to avoid arguments and disputes. But what if this particular subject, once the cause of an argument, is important? It is raised again. Let us suppose that a further heated discussion – a row – ensues, this time with even greater intensity than on the first occasion; partly because the first row forms part of the pattern for the second. Both parties end up miserable, even angry, as a consequence of the exchange. The nature of most relationships is that neither party wants to be miserable or angry with the other. With this in mind, important though the subject may be, the parties tacitly agree not to raise it, at least for some time. At least then tempers can cool!

Yet the subject is important, it somehow works in the background to limit the relationship. Both parties tacitly know that past and present sensitivities are blocking its airing. There is a further attempt to raise the matter. Very quickly old upsets are triggered and the past row is renewed, sometimes with increased energy and vigour!

This is a common though not universal dynamic. What may emerge is a rule, a rule that is not made explicit though it is clearly understood and understood through direct experience: it is that this subject is undiscussable. Its undiscussability shouts at you! Furthermore, as Argyris puts it, its *undiscussability* is undiscussable! We have what is technically called a taboo subject, at least taboo within that relationship. Yet the rule may be made known to third parties through eloquent and yet very precise phrases: "Oh, we don't talk about that". The indication and invitation is that this is a taboo subject, an 'invitation' with which most of us duly comply for fear of triggering an upset.

If such a pattern is not within the experience or even the imagination of the reader then perhaps our second example might help. It suggests that experience does not have to be first-hand in order to understand tacit rules. We can come to understand them through the experience of others shared via their descriptions and stories. Imagine that a new boss is due to arrive in the department. What often precedes the physical arrival of the boss is his or her reputation, conveyed through what people say about her or him. *"Oh, he's a great bloke provided you stay on the right side of him"*, or: *"The trouble is she has a fierce temper, so watch what you say."* It is not too difficult to work out the rules here – be cautious in what you say, say things that he might like to hear, and stay on the right side of her. These more specific rules play into a broader cultural rule that reads something like: *"Whatever you do, don't upset the boss".*

What are the consequences? At one, perhaps short-term, level, survival. At another, it is likely that bad news will never be passed up the department to the boss and will instead be concealed; the boss's thinking will not be challenged. There will be few innovative ideas arising from an exchange of different views, because the perspective of the boss dominates, and people will tend to play to the gallery; that is, say only that which they believe he or she wants to hear. A possible long-term consequence of this is the demise of the organisation. Another is the replication of the boss's reputation. But at least no-one was upset in the process of realising such consequences!

 At a deeper level what is it that gives rise to such rules and limiting patterns? How might they be best changed or influenced? This chapter deals with the first of these inquiries, the remainder of the book with the second.

95

The origin of most, if not all, of these tacit rules comes from within: from within the culture, from the mental and social patterns that are shared by participating members. In the domestic example above it is the idea and image, the memory, of a row (which has been directly experienced) that serves to make something undiscussable. In the work example it is even clearer: it is the idea and image of the boss that shapes, in advance, one's experience; experience which, in turn, reinforces one's image and idea. Opportunities can, of course, emerge for one's experience to be different to the idea and image; equally the idea and image can serve to predispose the experience which reinforces the idea and image in a self-fulfilling and self-maintaining pattern.

What was the source or medium of this idea and image of the new boss? The original source may be someone's experience of him or her at some time now lost in antiquity. Alternately, it may be the stereotype of how most bosses are. It matters little how the idea came into the world. What matters is the idea, and the image it conveys, which is passed on through conversation. That conversation may create a future reality as much as reflect a past reality.

If we stay with the example, the interesting phenomenon is not whether the description of the new boss is right or wrong, but what it *produces.* Conversation does not merely describe, it creates. If we play the example further, the story and the reality it generates can lead to the situation where the boss has the monopoly on ideas and, in turn, is frustrated and even angry at the lack of ideas and different thinking on the part of his or her people, resulting in her or him taking on more of that burden, thus reinforcing the condition. From the worker's perspective the pattern can become one where: "It's too bad he won't let us think"; and from the boss's: "It's too bad they can't think". The perspectives mirror and reinforce.

Many of these 'rules' have their origin within: within the experience of the person, the enterprise and the culture in which the rules apply. It is the ideas and images conveyed and created through language – our conversation – that shape or influence the worlds in which we find ourselves. We emphasise the word 'influence', for we must beware of the pattern of linear logic. Systemic and mutually reinforcing relationships emerge between patterns of thinking, patterns of perception, normative or rule-making patterns, patterns of behaviours and patterns of results. But first let us deal with another prevailing pattern – the one that urgently requests an answer.

Getting beyond quick fixes & flavours of the month

Richard Pascale, in *Managing on the Edge*, documented the explosive growth in management recipes since the late 1970s. Others have made the same point. In one graphic metaphor, Jerry Brightman[21] compared the pursuit of the latest management idea with the search for the latest new ice-cream flavour – the one that this time will be tastier and more refreshing than anything we have eaten before, or so we think!

The exponential rise of 'fads' suggests positive feedback at work[22]. Could it be that the fad industry fuels the need for more fads? Each comes with documented case histories of its success, yet none provides the sought-for miracle; the excellent companies do not stay excellent. The outcome is that many companies had, and some still have, veritable floods of initiatives, almost as if the more money thrown at the issue the greater the likelihood of a result. For a while, some, if not most, of these programmes show some result. The effort seems to work, then the benefit levels off. Rates of improvement peter out. The 'new spirit', if ever there was one, slowly dies. Performance fails to register any lasting improvement. Old, more deeply-rooted, patterns re-emerge. Soon it is time to poke the embers again and the cycle repeats itself with a further flood of initiatives taking their course. In 2000 years we seem to have learned little, for this pattern or chain of events was well described even in Roman times:

"We trained hard but it seemed that every time we were beginning to form up into a team, we would be re-organised. I was to learn later in life that we tend to meet a new situation by re-organisation, and a wonderful method it can be for creating the illusion of progress while producing confusion, inefficiency and demoralisation."

Attrib. Gaius Petronius, c. AD66

Whether such initiatives involve 're-organisation' or some other "re"-configuration, it appears that, all-too often, whatever is generated is not sustained. Even the gurus of the currently popular movement for business process re-engineering suggest that up to 70 per cent of all such initiatives fail to deliver the desired results. There is a similar story with many Total Quality initiatives. The spirit and intention behind such programmes does not take hold and grow of its own accord. Why? One reason is that whatever changes in management style the new initiatives require do not blend with the existing unwritten rules. The Chief Executive who not only states "quality is our business", but then demonstrates it by giving priority to quality in management reviews is a rare exception.

Another reason goes deeper. In the thinking behind such programmes, people are frequently 'done unto'. Deep in the minds of many programme designers and implementers, people are considered as a passive resource who need to be taught, trained or programmed to perform new tricks, rather than being given the opportunity of learning – for themselves – to develop and practise new concepts and ideas[23]. Even the idea of The Learning Organisation, which we believe to be a valuable and worthwhile concept – and potentially a great vision – some people seem to hold as some sort of recipe or formula for Nirvana. In the minds of some theorists and practitioners it is reduced to a set of steps or even a banner behind which a Human Resources department justifies the training budget.

What happens in such cases is that recipes, formulas and processes for change fail to interrupt the prevailing thinking habits, mental patterns, or paradigms of a company. Indeed, too much conventional management theory reflects a mental pattern which fails to challenge their assumptions about what a 'company' is. Most of the prevailing recipes, and much of the theory that informs their application, come out of a particular mental pattern and create a pattern of application that is itself limiting. This is not to make the advocates of a particular best way, or the managers of a company that seeks to apply that way, wrong. What is sought and what is offered tacitly combine. There is a powerful temptation to supply a set recipe, formula or process when that is what is expected and sought. In conditions of uncertainty there is equally a great demand for detail and the assurance of something that works, the so-called 'stuff of proof'. It is difficult in these circumstances for either party to help others start down the road of discovering a solution for themselves. Thus we miss the opening for discovery to contribute to action. Goldratt[24] puts it well:

"The minute you supply a person with the answers, by that very action you block them once and for all from the opportunity of inventing these same answers for themselves. If you want to go on an ego trip, to show how smart you are, give the answers. But if what you want is action to be taken then you must refrain from giving the answers."

Why, for so many, is there this penchant for quick fixes, fads, and flavours of the month? We suggest it is reflective of a pattern – a pattern of ideas and images in people's heads – a pattern that is widely shared within our particular culture. The genesis of this search for fixes, fads and flavours lies in the thinking – the mental patterns – which people bring to their company and sometimes to their personal lives. At its simplest, it is that the analysis that there is 'something wrong here' triggers a deeply indoctrinated reflex to search for some remedy that will preferably have a quick result in correcting the situation. We are frequently admonished by other consultants who suggest that all people and companies want is a pill to make them better. If so, why not just give them a pill? A wonderfully symbiotic relationship can then develop in which both parties maintain and extend their dependencies – and at least one makes money. A story concerning one of our own GPs (general medical practitioner) serves to illustrate.

 He is a very thorough and diligent professional whose process is somewhat different from the rapid treatment sometimes given by others. He explains at some length the possible and probable medical cause underlying the symptoms described by the patient, he advises of the medication prescribed, and outlines how it should be taken and to what effect. Through this process of communication and education the patient ends up knowledgeable with regards to the cause of illness, the working of their body, and the treatment. The physician has thus removed any magic and mystery. The communication process is noticeable when compared with the more dispensary practices of others. I asked what lay at the root of this change in pattern. He offered his view that the 'healthy' condition between doctor and patient was when the patient took responsibility for their own health, with occasional assistance from a doctor. If the patient is to exercise this responsibility he or she needs at least some knowledge. The alternative of the doctor being responsible for the patient's health seemed to him to be a limiting start point.

I asked what the consequences were of this approach. The GP replied that each consultation took longer – by virtue of the process of communication. As a result he looked less efficient in terms of time taken. His process did not match the performance criteria of the system in terms of the speed of processing people. Furthermore, some patients suggested they did not have the time to be responsible for their own health. They just wanted to be fixed! In the main, though, people were healthier – Goddammit!

 Whether it is the quick fix of some business consultants, or the rapid treatment of some physicians, why is it that we so often seek superficial cures to deeply seated and deeply rooted malaise? Why do we seek simple cures to components of complex issues? We suggest that this plays into and out of patterns, patterns of urgency, patterns of avoidance, patterns of 'getting fixed'; in short, patterns of belief and practice that are deeply ingrained, so deeply that we think with and through them.

Thinking patterns: the power of paradigms

The performance of a company is inextricably linked with how the people in that company think; that is, with the shared habits of thinking that prevail in the company. There is some connectivity between people, their thinking patterns, and the results they achieve. For what we think of, the ideas and images in people's minds, and what we think with, 'the structures which give rise to these images,' create and limit both what is possible and what is realisable in terms of performance.

These habits of thinking include deeply ingrained structures which influence the ways of being in the company – our perceptions, relationships, and behaviours. Some such patterns are easily recognisable, at least by others, as for example when mechanical engineering companies think in mechanical engineering terms and in mechanical ways as befits their training. Other ways of thinking are more deeply embedded and more widely shared, within for instance an industry, a national culture, or a geographic block. The expression 'Western thinking' conveys something of the shared thinking held by people resident in the West[25] and, by implication, suggests a difference from 'Eastern thinking'. The more widely shared our thinking, the more 'invisible' it seems to be. We are less aware of our particular thinking simply because it is so widely shared, and, in being less aware, we may not challenge or change that thinking. Inherited patterns keep us stuck.

An analogy may make the point. The recognisable patterns in our thinking may be likened to a computer's application programs; thus we can 'see' whether a word processing or a spreadsheet application is running, yet we might not be able to 'see' the operating program underlying the application, let alone the deeper thinking embedded in the system underlying the operating program. Consider also that the analogy conveys something only on the basis of at least some shared background and vocabulary – a common pattern – in the reader's and the authors' experience.

Shared patterns of deep thinking bring one to the concept of paradigms. Thirty-plus years after it was first coined, the word has increasingly entered the vocabulary of management circles; sometimes to the anguished accompaniment of: "Yet more jargon to bemuse and befuddle the poor, practical, practising manager". Is it a 'fad' expression enjoying but a brief bloom of popularity before being condemned to the dustbin of past fashion?

This tendency for periodic populist expressions itself reflects something of an underlying pattern, one usefully termed 'know-about'. It seems to be part of our lot to collect different vocabularies at different times in order to converse with colleagues, or, sometimes, to appear as knowledgeable as our colleagues, who themselves appear to know about such things. In effect we acquire the vocabulary in order to look good, to be on a par with peers who appear to enjoy such 'insight'. Then, when the popularity wanes, we dispense with such terms, having at best only aspired to a superficial understanding, and having therefore little to lose in terms of depth of knowledge or utility. Populists emerge with hugely discounting phrases such as "Paradigms? Oh, don't worry about them. That was last year's language!" Expressions enter and leave our vocabulary like hemlines moving to the whim of fashion. What we once knew about we can discard, because the world has moved on.

 In so doing, we limit ourselves to mere passing knowledge. We miss the chance to explore and, through exploring, to discover something of ourselves and our world. So, rather than know about paradigms, we invite our readers to be more knowing in the matter of their paradigms; that is, to become more knowing in the matter of what they think with: the thinking patterns that shape their thoughts. To do so is to explore those patterns that shape our behaviours, if not our very being; for it may be that: "We are what we think"... What we think conveys an idea or image, and the idea and image that we think we are is played out in the world. As Chapter Four will explore, it may be that we and our companies are quite literally creatures of habit – creations and reflections of our pattern(s).

How, then, can we become more knowing in the matter of paradigms, able to 'see' and shift them, rather than just knowing about them? The process is much more one of discovery than of being taught; and discovery may be much more a reflection of the discoverer, than of the thing being discovered. It is an expression of our relationship to an aspect of our world and our actions aligned to this relationship. Might we discover our 'patterns of thinking' and, if so, what difference can we make with what we discover?

Paradigms have been variously described:

"Example, pattern, especially of noun, verb, etc."
The Concise Oxford Dictionary

"A constellation of concepts, values, perceptions and practices shared by a community which forms a particular vision of reality that is the basis of the way a community organises itself."
Thomas Kuhn's original definition[26]

"A set of rules and regulations that establish boundaries, and tell us what to do to be successful within those boundaries. We view and understand the world through our paradigms."
Joel Barker, 1990

"A framework of thought, a scheme for understanding and explaining certain aspects of reality."
Marilyn Ferguson, 1987

A shared set of assumptions

A paradigm in other words is a pattern or way of thinking with which, and through which, we relate to the world. It is part of a wider 'pattern'. It is what we think with, as well as what we think. It embraces the structure as well as the content of our thinking and our thoughts. Within such patterns there may be many elements: assumptions, concepts, theories, models, expectations, logic, ideas, values, beliefs, rules, connections, boundaries, etc.

Thinking within certain ways, within certain patterns, creates a horizon in which so much is available and no more. Our world is bounded by our thinking. To progress we may need to step beyond the boundary, to move beyond the habit of our current thinking. If this sounds too theoretical, recall the changing nature of work. At one time the real asset of the worker was physical prowess; strength or dexterity. Increasingly, machines have replaced that requirement. We moved into the age of the knowledge worker, where brain replaced brawn as the desired asset. Yet, if 'brain' refers only to the accumulation of explicit knowledge, then perhaps more sophisticated machines – computers – will in turn replace the human worker. What, then, may be required? Perhaps it will be the 'knowing' worker more than the knowledge worker, the worker with the wisdom to change established patterns and thus release different results.

Thomas Kuhn's *The Structure of Scientific Revolutions*, is widely 'known-about' as the birth-place of paradigms[27]. Although first published in 1962, it is worth capturing the spirit of his work for its application to the field of management and its mirror, the field of being managed. Kuhn, in exploring the advance of science, wrestled with how brilliant thinkers of earlier years could get things so wrong when viewed from a modern frame of reference. What he discovered was that, when he looked at their explanations from the prevailing world-view of the time, their explanations made a lot of sense. Kuhn developed the idea that every scientist works within a distinctive paradigm, that, just like the rest of us, they carry out their day-to-day activities within a framework of presuppositions that are, so to speak, taken for granted and yet shape what constitutes a problem, a solution, and a method.

When seen from a distance, and with much hindsight, it may appear as though scientific thought has progressed through successive increments and that current thinking has developed by accumulation. Kuhn sheds profound doubt upon this cumulative interpretation and upon gradual incrementalism. Rather, he argues, the development of science has been one of periodic revolutions, whereby past thinking is upstaged by a radical new outlook. In the early days of a science (and perhaps of a human life) it is as though practitioners are seeing with unprogrammed eyes (an innocence?), and any 'facts' so gathered are gathered without the guidance of established theory. We are then educated, trained and conditioned in ways of seeing and interpreting the world, through which our innocence is lost and our looking is shaped. The body of beliefs we acquire focuses our attention and directs our activities towards permissible selection, evaluation and criticism of available facts. What is lost in terms of restricted field of vision, is gained in terms of depth and detail. The paradigm develops.

As Kuhn states: "Paradigms gain their status because they are more successful than their competitors in solving a few problems that the group of practitioners has come to recognise as acute". More successful does not mean completely successful. The prevailing paradigm gathers momentum, and:

❑ Defines the very problems suitable for scientific inquiry.
❑ Creates standards for the definition of admissible problems and legitimate problem-solutions.
❑ Generates rules of acceptable methodology.
❑ Develops a theoretical framework, including models and concepts, for understanding.
❑ Initiates an educatory process for newcomers.

Along with the development of the paradigm come anomalies, things that the paradigm cannot explain or predict. As the anomalies accumulate, so awareness is raised of the insufficiency of the prevailing paradigm. It breaks down, creating space for a breakthrough as alternative paradigms are created that can better explain and predict what were once classed as anomalies. As Kuhn writes:

"Novelty emerges only for the man who, knowing with precision what he should expect, is able to recognise that something has gone wrong. Anomaly appears only against the background provided by the paradigm. The more precise and far-reaching that paradigm is, the more sensitive an indicator it provides of anomaly and hence of an occasion for paradigm change."

Only where there is a breakdown or crisis of the prevailing paradigm will there be a breakthrough to a newly accepted theory! So long as the tools a paradigm supplies continue to prove capable of solving the problems it defines, science moves fastest and penetrates most deeply through confident employment of those tools. The reason is clear: as in manufacture, so in science – re-tooling is an extravagance to be reserved for the occasion that demands it. The significance of crises is the indication they provide that an occasion for re-tooling has arrived.

The surfacing of significant anomalies; or indeed, fresh challenges that cannot be explained by the prevailing paradigms, provides the essential creative tension for new thinking. At this point 'extraordinary' science emerges to create a new conceptual network, a new system of relations, a new framework through which scientists view the world. Rather than 'progressively incremental', Kuhn describes these changes as 'revolutions' and such revolutions he interprets as fundamental changes of world view:

"... during revolutions people see new and different things when looking with familiar instruments in places they have looked before. It is like being transported to another planet. Paradigm changes do cause scientists to see the world and their research engagement differently. Insofar as their only recourse to the world is through what they see and do, we may want to say that after a revolution, scientists are responding to a different world."

The transformation is less that the world changes and more that the scientist changes, and in changing, changes her or his world.

Paradigms, bound up with other patterns of science, become self-maintaining phenomena intimately interwoven into the structure and unwritten rules of scientific institutions. As Max Plank is reported to have first observed, scientific paradigms do not always change through logic and reason, or by displacement of the old by evidence of the new; rather, they shift when those who carry them die or retire and new centres of influence emerge. People may be motivated to pursue careers in science for a variety of reasons, among them curiosity as to how the world works, a desire for intellectual challenge, or for recognition of their peers. Each science supports a structure of codes of acceptable behaviour, a system for example of peer reviews and precedence, a system that places high premiums on openness; at least, once publication is assured – and a system that generates a very low incidence of deliberate fraud. But scientific institutions, like any organisation have their unwritten rules, rules that aspirants to membership must follow to remain part of the 'company'. The gaining of a PhD, the gaining of reputation through published papers, the gaining of research grants and support whilst building a career are part and parcel of the established rituals. They depend on the tacit, and frequently active, approval of the establishment in particular disciplines and institutions. Overt challenges to the conventional wisdom can be just as career limiting as in other forms of organisation, and the conventional wisdom is judged by those who represent, and perhaps owe their own position to, a given paradigm. The paradigm enables a structure that assists its own preservation.

Kuhn's exposition is a challenge to gradual incrementalism and to the explanation of development as progressive accumulation. This is not to deny the contribution of incrementalism, rather it is to suggest that such processes are periodically interrupted with short bursts of more radical or revolutionary change. This is similar to the modern conception of evolution, with long-term incremental trends being interrupted by short bursts of punctuated equilibrium (see Chapter Four) in which new life forms emerge to be favoured by changes in circumstance. Such 'short bursts' are not simply cumulative, they do not merely add to what already exists, they are themselves profound changes which in turn change patterns around them. For example, the breakthrough to 'total quality' is not gained by simply making the once-common job category of inspectors better at inspecting[28]! New paradigms cannot be grafted onto the store of what is already known. What is known must first be unlearned before the new paradigm can be assimilated. "We can't get there from here!"

What Kuhn points out is that there are other processes at work, radical processes, which are not simply incremental, 'good' though incremental progress may be. What he sees is that patterns are not just added to, but that patterns are shifted and, in their shifting, whole new areas of inquiry, opportunity and performance are opened up. This leads to the idea of 'development' being something other than progressive accumulation, something more disruptive or discontinuous. Best viewed perhaps as a breakthrough to a whole new level of potential where a step-change in performance is made possible. Thus, as Ackoff points out, 'development' can be distinguished from 'growth'[29]. Growth, an increase in certain functional qualities or attainments, may occur without any exercise of choice. Its principal limits are predominantly external, within the environment. Growth is simply more of the same, a volumetric increase. We can properly say that we grow taller, or that companies grow their volume of sales as a result of a growing market. Limits to growth will tend in the one case to be inherited (genetic) and in the other a reflection of the market.

Development does not equal growth. Development suggests some increase in capacity, ability or potential – not simply more of the same. Any constraints usually lie within. One can develop and not grow just as one may grow and not develop. Thus, in a shrinking market, a company may need to develop (its potential) in order to maintain its sales (in a volumetric sense). But our language is confusing; for, in more competitive worlds, where more competitors are chasing fewer customers, we need to develop in order to stand still. That is, to increase and release our internal potential to counter external constraint. What is confusing is that *there is no standing still...* The internal patterns have to change in order to maintain the external result, which would otherwise be decline[30].

The developed company with limited resources may produce more results than the underdeveloped company with unlimited resources. The ever-growing commercial pressure to achieve more with limited resources translates, in these terms, into a challenge to develop our companies; to discover and release new potential from within. Yet there are relatively few companies really up to development. It is not an incremental process. Neither can development be prescribed, given or imposed. There is no 'pill', no magic 'Seven Steps for Development'. It can only be nurtured, encouraged and accessed.

Kuhn describes the process whereby new thinking emerges out of an ever-increasing set of anomalies which together create a 'crisis', out of which a breakthrough to a new paradigm emerges from breakdown in the old. Furthermore, he argues, such 'crises' are essential for creative tension: "The significance of crises is the indication they provide that an occasion for retooling has arrived". We suggest later that paradigm shifts do not have to be solely sourced out of crises, breakthroughs do not have to have their origins in breakdowns. It is possible for a significant challenge of a positive nature to stimulate creative tension, to inspire different thinking, rather than force it.

Paradigms and perception

Kuhn asked whether paradigms were a prerequisite to perception itself? We learn to see, to process and interpret our experience of vision, using the labels and concepts encoded in our shared ways of thinking. Paradigms operate like a shared mindset, 'invisible' yet operating in the background. We may be totally unaware of the way we think until such time that we experience a new culture, perhaps through living and working abroad[31], or until such time as we face a clear deficiency, a crisis, between our thinking and the accumulation of attendant problems or anomalies. Established maps have proven reliability when the territory they represent is stable. When territory itself is changing then maps that once worked may no longer suffice and can even mislead. Widely shared, 'invisible' paradigms, neither known of nor questioned, shape a community's perceptual framework and co-exist with a particular language, a given way of speaking about the world.

We 'learn' to see and interpret the world through our paradigms upon it. It is as though they are a lens through which we translate the images that hit the back of the retina. Our paradigms influence what we notice in the world, our perceptions, and influence the meaning that we give to what we notice, our interpretation of the world. What we 'see' depends to some extent on what there is to see in the world out-there; that is, what exists within our field of vision – but also upon what our previous visual-conceptual experience has taught or prepared us to see. There is a distinction, summarised in figure 3.1, between what is there to be *looked at*, the possibility of perception, and what *is seen*, the practice of perception.

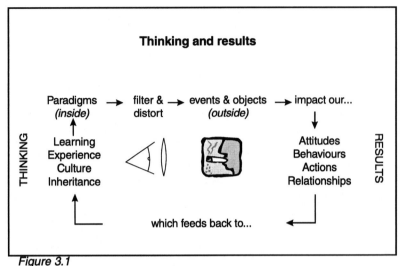

Figure 3.1

Paradigms, or our 'beliefs about a particular context', are the lenses through which we interpret that context. By inducing us to act consistently with our paradigms, those same paradigms are reinforced.

The common paradigm of perception holds what we see as somehow representational of the world 'out there' as though independent of the observer; somehow, through perception, we capture in our mind's eye the recognisable property of some 'thing' in the environment. Reality corresponds to perception. An alternative paradigm suggests that perception is never independent of the observer or the community of observers; that we are trained, or programmed, to 'see'. In effect, the observer participates in what is seen (selection), how it is seen (orientation), and what meaning is given (interpretation). What is seen to be 'there' and how it is 'there' is not independent of the observer[32]. This means that we do not have to be stuck with how we see. We can choose and learn to notice different things and to see things differently. Yet there may be a price to pay for the benefit received!

 The questions asked by a community, the conversation shared by that community, presuppose a world already perceptually and conceptually subdivided in certain ways. Any challenges to that construction of reality can be threatening, in effect a breakdown of current orientation. It can also be very liberating, a breakthrough to a new orientation. For, what we think with, our paradigms, shape what we see and how we interpret the world which, in effect, shapes our relatedness to the world. This explains why two people sharing exactly the same field of vision may see very different things and interpret what they see very differently. What could be a threat to one may be interpreted as a relief and opportunity to another. If this seems strange, recall the example of the symphony in Chapter One. What is heard depends, in part, on the listener.

Within a community, particularly a well-defined community in a relatively stable world, paradigms will be very stable. Acceptance of the paradigm is part of the implicit contract of membership, the unwritten rules, of the community. Alternative ways of thinking may lead to excommunication, a process of withdrawing membership by the host population. Those who choose to see differently might pay a price in terms of their relationships with and within the community. New paradigms tend to start at the edge or with some introduction of a newcomer or newcomers, people who are not so embedded in the established ways. A new paradigm emerges first in the mind of one or a few individuals. Its adoption by the community depends on its utility in solving or resolving the growing crisis or challenge of the moment and upon beating the resistance of those who are deeply embedded in the old way. That resistance manifests itself in at least three ways:

First, it not easy to let go of what has once worked – or at least, what we believe to have worked, and from which we continue to receive some payoff, no matter that something else might work better. Proof often speaks louder than potential.

Second, we get locked-in by being 'right' in what we think. There is an enormous pressure to be right in what we think, say and do, almost as though we believe the only significant contribution we can make is through being right. Being wrong risks relationship, the judgement of others, their scorn and opprobrium. We will not loosen the grip of our patterns without being willing to explore our own as well as other's paradigms. The need to be right in what and how we think limits such exploration.

Last and by no means least, if we were to be different in our thinking, seeing, being and doing we might risk our membership of the group to which we choose to affiliate. There may well be a price to be paid for the gain we might receive.

These patterns of what has worked in the past ('winning formulae'), of being right, and of membership tend to get us to try harder within existing patterns and inhibit a search for different patterns which might release greater performance potential. There is nothing either right or wrong in this, it is just that any pattern limits as well as enables. It makes available a certain horizon and no more. To step beyond the present horizon takes a shift in patterns. This demands much more than just 'thinking about our thinking'. Being mildly curious in the matter of the way we think leads to a certain level of inquiry and no more. Intentionally setting out to change our thinking in order to make more of a difference suggests a freedom from existing patterns that, for many, is already ahead of the game. It takes an act of courage which may or may not be responded to with encouragement.

Henry Ford captured this well:

"If to petrify is success then all one has to do is to humour the lazy side of the mind; but if to grow is success, then one must wake up anew every morning and keep awake all day."

Pascale[33] offers a similar insight:

"The ultimate, and largely ignored, task of management is one of creating and breaking paradigms. The trouble is that 99 per cent of managerial attention today is devoted to the techniques that squeeze more out of the existing paradigm – and it's killing us!"

Perhaps one of the paradigms we might choose to break is the existing paradigm of management?

Exposing the dominant management paradigm

Failure to reach a destination may have nothing whatsoever to do with either the level of our motivation or our competence and skill in reading a map. We may be very highly motivated and great map readers and still not get there if we follow the wrong map! Do we have the 'wrong' map for managing? Does something that once worked either no longer work or not work well enough for the challenges ahead?

The words of M. Konosuke Matshita, Executive Director of the Matsushita Electric Industrial Corporation, have been frequently quoted and less frequently acted upon:

"We are going to win and the industrial West is going to lose. There is nothing much you can do about it, because the reasons for your failure are within yourselves. Your firms are built upon the Taylor Model; even worse, so are your heads. With your bosses doing the thinking while the workers wield the screwdrivers, you're convinced deep down that this is the right way to run a business. For you, the essence of management is getting the ideas out of the heads of the bosses into the hands of labour.

We are beyond the Taylor Model: business, we know, is now so complex and difficult, the survival of firms so hazardous in an environment increasingly unpredictable, competitive and fraught with danger, that their continued existence depends upon the day-to-day mobilisation of every ounce of intelligence. For us, the core of management is precisely the art of mobilising and pulling together the intellectual resources of all employees in the service of the firm. Only by drawing on the combined brain power of all its employees can a firm face up to the turbulence and constraints of today's environment."

We have inherited a way of thinking about management that, whether articulated or not, shapes our behaviours as managers and the behaviours of others being managed. This inheritance is culturally transmitted, part of the reproductive process of culture in replicating the idea (and practices) of managing and of being managed. 'The

Management Paradigm' has been referred to above as though only one paradigm has prevailed. As a generalisation, and with some cultural variation, that assumption has considerable validity for the West. Increasingly, however, the paradigm we have inherited is being challenged to the degree that in some companies one can say that an alternative paradigm prevails and results in different practices of management. One can also say that in some companies there is a shift in vocabulary, in the words used, without a shift in the pattern or way of thinking or in consequential behaviours. For the majority who describe themselves as extremely busy there is no time to think about what they think with when managing!

Our interpretation is that something has started but it is embryonic. Most of us are still caught in the grip of our paradigm. This is as valid for the category of people called managers as it is for the category called 'being managed'. That paradigm, in turn, generates the 'Road Most Travelled'. It is the paradigm variously described as the control paradigm, the command and control paradigm, or the control, prediction, and conformance paradigm. It is the thinking that applies a certain logic to a task; a relatively mechanical, reductionist, and deductive logic.

Put crudely, the pattern goes something like this: there is a big task to be accomplished. I had better break down that task into smaller component parts that are manageable by others (specialisation). As we specialise people will be doing smaller and smaller jobs and we'll need co-ordination (administration). In addition, some of these jobs will be so small that we can employ unskilled and interchangeable labour and concentrate on improving efficiencies at the operator level (operation). To do this, and to offset the possible consequence of low levels of interest in work at this level, we had better make sure they are properly supervised (supervision). All of this will need proper planning, control and co-ordination (the work of management).

A crude simplification of an evolved pattern perhaps. Yet it is a pattern that works and one that has worked for many years. How else are you supposed to organise? The point is that various types of work have been parcelled out, and there is an advantage to this parcelling: one can recruit people suited to the particular parcel. What gets carried with the parcel is a set of expectations, if not assumptions, concerning the people doing that sort of work. Managers do the thinking, the planning, controlling and co-ordinating, while others – operatives – do the doing. It works and works well. And yet it may not suffice for either the change in circumstances that companies face, for the development of our companies, or for the pace of change. Belgard, Fisher, and Rayner describe well the significant dimensions to the control paradigm[34]:

- There is a single best way to perform a job.
- Highly specialised, narrowly defined jobs assure optimal performance.
- Jobs are simplified and easy to perform: training periods are short to assure quick replacement of employees who do not make standard.
- Rewards are based on individual performance against 'scientifically set' standards.
- Technological imperative: technology and process flow are designed for optimal performance and then workers are fitted into jobs.
- Controls are external.
- Job alienation is an accepted phenomenon of industrial life.
- Bureaucratic, function base.
- Isolate employees from one another to minimise distractions.

The perspective of a company is as an instrument to get something done. Management equates to control. People are recruited for their fit with the packages of work that have been designed and described as jobs. People's relationship to 'company', their sense of company, is again instrumental. At all levels it is viewed as a vehicle for making money, a source of income, a matter of earning a wage. Relationships tend to be impersonal, functional, sometimes tribal, and mechanistic. People are related to as objects, at best as 'resources', which need to be maintained (motivated by threat or fear and reward), occasionally upgraded (trained), and sometimes replaced (fired). We design systems for great control and enormous compliance. As a friend says: "It shows on the faces as they come into work in the morning." The interesting phenomena is that, for many, the thinking is so deeply ingrained that we can pose questions and find no answer: if you do not relate to people as human resources, just how do you relate to them?

If the essence of management is to control, then the essence of being managed is being controlled. Being controlled suggests an extremely passive engagement. No wonder it seems so difficult to make such companies come alive. Greater 'life' is often manipulated by greater threat. We forcibly 'change' through the threat of crisis, only to discover that such changes are, all too often, merely structural and superficial. Such instances feed back into the system of control and compliance. The system is further reinforced by the set of rules that build up around it. Peter Block[35] terms them 'The Road Most Travelled' and illustrates, as salient examples :

- ❑   Manipulate situations and at times, people.
- ❑   Manage information and plans carefully and to our own advantage.
- ❑   Invoke the name of the high level people when seeking support for our projects.
- ❑   Become calculating in the way we manage relationships.
- ❑   Pay great attention to what the people above us want from us.
- ❑   Live with the belief that in order to get ahead, we must be cautious in telling the truth.

To which we might add:

- ❑   Speak only when spoken to and be cautious in communication.
- ❑   Tell others only what they want to hear.
- ❑   If you have an idea, feed it to the boss, and let it be their idea.
- ❑   Never, ever, challenge or criticise your company, boss or peers in public (do so only to third parties you can trust).
- ❑   Even when you do not understand, or when you disagree, or see

inconsistencies, it is always wise to salute the flag (at least in public).

❑ Seek the approval of selected others.

❑ Avoid sensitive issues.

❑ Present yourself in a winning way.

❑ Do not let others know the rules of the game, it will give you some advantage.

Before dismissing the above as sycophantic, or merely the rules of survival within an authoritarian regime, consider how many such 'rules' apply in more customary social circumstances? We often avoid saying things for want of avoiding possible upset and often avoid confronting things for want of destroying some illusion and an associated tender network of relationships.

Where some enjoy the power of control over others, others enjoy the comfort of being controlled and having little responsibility. This is not pathological, it is patterned. It also becomes self-reinforcing. For the powerful there are the rewards of individual achievement, status, material well being, and position. For the disempowered there is the comfort of dependency, passivity, of going with the tide. The nature of one's company, relationship with others, indeed, one's nation, innocently reflects the prevailing paradigm on a sustained and self-reinforcing basis. At extremes it may become pathological.

It all comprises a *living system* with substantial workability and repeatability. When we want more result out of the system we put it under greater pressure. We share a language for this: "squeezing until the pips squeak". Great rewards are to be had for great squeezing! We get locked-in and become unable to see beyond the metaphor of the orange and the pips. We fail to invent a different metaphor, and associated set of ideas, that might release yet more performance.

Given an established paradigm it is sometimes difficult to imagine any alternative, any different pattern of managing or of being managed. We become used to the prevailing pattern. After all, is it not true that someone has to be in control, that someone has to have responsibility, that, on occasions, someone has to be willing to carry the can and take the blame? We have been well taught. Yet *what if* we could start to design companies where we enjoyed control and power with others within a community of commitment, where responsibility was less a positional thing and more a matter of choice and alignment with one's commitments? *What if* we created a different sense of responsibility, power and control out of a different orientation to our world?

What if management work became one of cultivating commitment, fostering and coaching performance, where control is in the system through the self-control that comes with aligned intentions? There is a profound shift in relationship to company, to work and to people at work. People become active agents and associates in a real sense of enterprise. Whole sets of ideas shift in an interactive way which, in turn, interact with a shift in one's sense of being when being at work. Belgard, Fisher and Rayner again capture some of this when they refer to the commitment paradigm:

❑ There are many ways to achieve the same level of result.

❑ Jobs are broadly defined and skill sets diverse, so as to assure quick adaptation to change and effective resource utilisation.

❑ Jobs require a variety of skills and areas of knowledge; training and development is considered a life long endeavour.

❑ Work teams control work design and administrative responsibilities.

❑ Rewards are based on contributions made to the effectiveness of the team.

❑ The social and technical systems are designed to assure that the human/machine interface is optimal.

❑ Controls are internal.

❑ Job alienation is considered detrimental to organisation performance.

❑ The organisation is ad hocratic, issue or purpose based.

❑ Groups form to assure continual interaction and problem solving among employees."

Whole sets of ideas and assumptions come together in each paradigm to form a discrete pattern: one that shapes us and the world in its own image. When 'new' ideas are played into an existing paradigm they are so adapted to fit with what is already known and experienced that what was hoped for with the new idea is not realised. Thus, for example, Total Quality; which is interpreted to be a revolution in the mind of someone like Deming[36], turns in practice into yet more refined controls within a controlling paradigm and culture. Disillusion sets in after initial enthusiasm.

It is easier to describe the commitment system than to generate it. Just how do you build an active commitment pattern where there has been a tradition of control and compliance? We return to this from Chapter Seven onwards.

More on the Western tradition

It is easy to read about the dominant management paradigm and be moved to a statement of 'Yes, but'. . .'. "Yes, but it's not like that in my company or department"; "Yes, but we know about all that and about theory Y"; "Yes, but things are changing, we are now empowering our people"; "Yes, but all this is just Taylorism which went out years ago." *It isn't and it didn't!* The prevailing management paradigm is but a reflection of a deeper pattern of Western thinking, one that Winograd and Flores label "The tradition of rationalism and logical empiricism that can be traced back at least to Plato". This tradition has also been the mainspring of Western science and technology, and has demonstrated its effectiveness most clearly in the 'hard sciences', those that explain the operation of deterministic mechanisms whose principles can be captured in formal systems. Briefly, the tradition suggests that, when in search of a solution to a problem or opportunity, one should accurately and comprehensively represent the situation in question, find general rules and theories that apply to such situations, and logically apply such rules to the situation of concern until one arrives at a conclusion about what should be done[37]. At various times different paradigms were dominant within the tradition. But the tradition itself may also be interpreted as a deeper paradigm – one more widely shared – and thus less visible.

Means of describing the tradition vary, yet indicate different perspectives on the same pattern. Where DeBono[38] speaks of critical thinking, the clash system and analysis, others speak of reductionism, of rational and mechanistic thinking. We will use the latter two as examples, not to make any one particular way of thinking wrong and another right; rather, to suggest that different ways of thinking may be suited to different purposes, and different purposes may merit priority at different times. The object is to heighten awareness and appreciation of the way we think and the differences that our ways of thinking make. To be stuck in any habit of thinking will at some time be limiting. We demonstrate with another fable.

In and out of the rut: a short story

I'm Orville D. Hammer the Third, president of Treadmill Inc. and right at this moment I'm listening to a board room presentation, just waiting to press the destruct button. Some of the ideas and proposals we have to listen to you would not believe, they're off the wall. They ignore the realities of commercial life and are presented as if the board were a mere bunch of rubber stampers. Often the proposers seem to think all they have to do is turn up, make their megabuck application and we'll give it to them in a gift wrapped parcel. They present us with a proposal in which it is claimed the options have been thoroughly worked over so that only one choice remains. Any downside is supposed to be catered for so we do not need to worry about risk. Tell me about it. Why is it we hear a very different story when it comes to explaining why projects so often do not live up to their original projections?.

The presentation runs on and I go over my diary for the rest of the day. I've got lunch with the Japanese director of a small diversified business we are hoping to enter into some sort of partnership with. Later I've promised to sort out my schedule for the month with my secretary, and then more inevitable meetings.

The presentation finishes and Don, the speaker, asks for questions. The other board members make a few desultory requests about points of detail. I can tell they are waiting for me to give a lead. I give it. "Don, this is just not our line. You know we have a definite plan to target several Far East areas yet you are proposing something that would put a lot of our eggs into the one basket. What is more, there is no guarantee that any of it will work. You have not shown any detailed analysis to indicate the exposure to exchange rates or the impact of a real market downturn. We don't have the people or the capital to take such a risk." The other board members make approving noises and before long we have agreed to turn the proposal down.

There is a pause, then Don speaks. "In that case O.D., I'm tendering my resignation. This is the eighth major proposal I've put forward to the board and in my opinion one of the best. When I joined this company it had a reputation for bold commercial initiatives ahead of anything else in the industry. Presentations like this used to be exciting sessions about what the proposal might make possible. But now the approach seems to be no surprises, play it safe and by the book. The real listening that we used to have for each other and for the sense of possibility is gone. At one time, O.D., you would have been alive to every opportunity. You would certainly never have consulted your diary in the middle of a presentation, would you?" With that he nodded to the stunned board members. "Good-bye gentlemen and ladies", and left the room.

The eyes swivelled to me. Don's unexpected statement has stunned me but I have to say something. "Pity about that. Don's a good Vice President, but if you are in the kitchen then you must expect some heat. Does anyone feel we made the wrong decision?" I look round the table; there is a noticeable lack of eye contact but no-one says anything.

We get through the rest of the agenda and I head back to my office to think things over for a few minutes before my lunch appointment. I don't like to admit it but Don's comments have struck home, and, damn it, I've got to admit he's got a point. The meetings in the past were much more stimulating and my diary was never out then. So what is changed? Is it that business has become more competitive? Have we all just grown older? Is it *me*? Anyway, something has got to be done about Don. I am beginning to regret my comments in the boardroom and really would not like to see him leave. I give Don a call. He's very stiff but eventually I get him to promise to think things over for a month before making a definite decision.

My luncheon date arrives. He's called Harada and is one of the most entertaining businessmen I have met. He is one of those people with whom one feels immediately at ease and with whom you can engage in deep and personal conversations. He went to college in Japan, then came over to the States to do an MBA before working in Europe and now back here. He has a knack of combining some really different thinking with a very sound commercial approach – an unusual combination. It is partly his originality that attracts me to the idea of some sort of partnership with his firm.

Over lunch we discuss the possibilities and make some pretty tangible progress towards developing our relationship. There is a compelling strategic logic for us to work together so we have a natural commitment to make things work. When it comes to coffee I decide to take Harada into my confidence about Don's presentation and the aftermath, particularly my sense that we no longer approach things in the same exuberant way we once did. Harada stirs his coffee. "Would you accept some advice from me?" he asks. I guess this is a real test of our partnership before it has even begun, but when it comes to it I think I would, so I say: "Yes".

"Well," Harada says, "my brother, as you know, is in business in Japan. He, too, had a similar experience. He appreciated what was happening and went for a fortnight to a well known retreat, to something which, when translated, means 'withdrawing to allow inner debate' and came back entirely refreshed. Although it is essentially for Japanese, they do take foreigners if recommended by someone they know. I could recommend you and I would consider it an honour if you would accept my gift of a fortnight at this retreat."

Well, what could I say? Could I turn the gift down gracefully? Was this something that was important to me? I decided to take the plunge. "Thank you, Harada. I will be delighted to accept your offer. If I go for a fortnight, though, I would like to think you were also experiencing something special while I am away. I know you like sailing so I would insist that in return you make use of a temporary membership of the

Ocean Yacht Club and the use of my boat while I am away." Harada, too, accepted, and we ended our meeting in good spirits.

Back in the office I tried to imagine how I would manage to take two weeks off. I didn't have much time for speculation for, towards the end of the afternoon, there was a special delivery by courier of the most exquisitely drawn invitation to spend two weeks at the School of Wind and Forest starting a week from today. Tickets and directions were included. The place sounded rather strange but most of all I was impressed with Harada's organisation. How had he managed to get all this arranged in such a short time? Well, that settled it, I was going. I called in my secretary and managed to delegate or defer everything so I could go off with a relatively clear conscience. I could imagine the stories that would be circulating when it was discovered that I had attended a place called the School of Wind and Forest. OD was losing his grip they'd be saying – he's taking this Japanese partnership thing far too seriously.

A week later I found myself on a small fishing boat on the last leg of the journey to the retreat. Two other Japanese accompanied me on a boat manned by what looked like monks. Apart from much head nodding, none of the others exchanged any words. I spoke no Japanese and I assumed they could not speak English. We were making for a small island. Already I could see several buildings scattered in pine clad slopes above fields with tended crops and animals. As we got closer I became aware of more figures in the landscape and a small stone jetty where we were no doubt destined to disembark. A far cry from the Treadmill office I thought.

When we arrived at the jetty there were three of the monk- like figures to escort myself and the two Japanese. Instead of staying together we were each taken in separate directions. I found myself heading towards a wooden hut, supported on short carved stilts, with steps leading up to the entrance. My guide gestured for me to enter and I found myself in a small entranceway with what I guessed was a rack for footwear. I took off my shoes and entered a spartan but surprisingly large room, probably comprising half the hut. There were open screens to another room, obviously a bedroom with a bed of simple bamboo construction on which were stacked some rough clothes.

For the first time, my guide spoke. "I have been assigned to you, Hammer san, because I speak English fluently. My first task is to introduce you to the School and what is expected of you over the next two weeks. Know that you have a choice in the matter. If, after having heard the introduction, you decide you do not wish to continue, then the boat will return you to the mainland. However, once you decide to stay, then you must do so until the end of the two weeks." He paused, obviously waiting for me to indicate my understanding of the terms. 'Well here goes', I thought as I nodded. 'I hope you know what you are doing Harada.' The guide continued: "The school requires three things of you: firstly that, like all visitors, you wear the common uniform; secondly, that each task you are given you fulfill without question and thirdly, that you keep a brief diary of your experiences. I must tell you that nothing you are asked to do involves personal danger and no-one who has stayed has regretted it."

Well that didn't sound so bad, what had I got to lose? I accepted. My guide then spoke up again, "Now that you are properly with us, Hammer san, I will give you your first task. After you have changed into our uniform you must put on this blindfold and wear these ear plugs then make your way by smell alone to our eating hall for your evening meal. You will notice that there is a stick which you can use to assist you, but you may not ask any directions or remove the blindfold or earplugs until you are sure you are in the eating hall. You may sense others nearby but they will be there only to ensure that you do not come to any harm."

Looking back now, that fortnight was one of the strangest experiences of my life. I had tried to imagine what it would be like, but nothing had prepared me for the reality. To give you a flavour here are three entries from my diary that I was required to keep. Reading it again brings back every moment of the fortnight just as if I was living it again.

Day 1.

Why do I have to keep this diary? I'm not sure, but I do know I am not keen to record some aspects of the dinner hunt. I have not been blindfolded since I was a child and the sensation was very strange, even odder having ear plugs as well. I felt totally insecure, frightened and foolish starting off down the ladder in my funny uniform with a stick and a black band around my head. 'What a great picture for the company magazine', I thought. When I got to the bottom I felt some gentle fingers coaxing me to turn in a certain direction. That made me feel less nervous about the whole business. I strained for any impression of cooking smells but detected nothing. Oddly, I was more conscious of the light breeze against my hands and the feel of the rough material of the uniform against my skin. With nothing to guide me I resolved to stumble off in the direction I had been pointed. My balance was not as good as usual which I blamed on the ear plugs. That didn't help my confidence which was draining away with each succeeding and diminishing footstep. It was then I noticed that I was on what felt like a gravel path. I explored with my stick and thought I detected plants or shrubs to either side. So far so good. If I stuck with the path then I was probably going in the right direction. I continued my erratic progress for what seemed like hours until I reached a point where the gravel seemed to run out. My legs were exhausted with the effort despite having gone what I am sure was only a short distance. At that point the mysterious arms subtly turned me in a different direction and so I stumbled off again. As I did so I caught my first scent of cooking. 'I'm going to make this', I thought. From there I continued in what I thought was the direction, several times receiving assistance from the helping hands. Sweating and exhausted, I finally detected a buzz of conversation despite the ear plugs. Moving forward again my stick informed me I was in front of an opening, an entrance to the dining hall, I desperately hoped. Cautiously forward once more and I found myself descending a short, spiralling ramp. The conversational buzz seemed stronger and, reaching level ground, again I was grasped and led forward. Ear plugs and blindfold were removed and I found myself looking into the kindly face of an old, white-haired Japanese. All around others, almost all Japanese and, dressed in the same uniform as me, sat on benches pounding the tables in front of them in an obviously good humoured appreciation of my success. Apparently I had coped with the first task but I was too mentally exhausted to really appreciate the fact.

Day 6

I don't understand what is going on. Today everyone had to go down to the beach and find two pebbles with at least fifty differences between them. At first it was rather comical, this gathering of serious-looking individuals scrabbling along the beach after breakfast. Initially I did not worry about the task but tried to find two pebbles which struck me as being very different. However, when I tried to enumerate the differences I was lucky to get to 10. What was really frustrating was that my companions seemed to be having no difficulty finding a suitable pair of stones and most were already heading back to the discussion room. In desperation I decided to make do with the pair I had and made my way back to the room. When I got there I was asked how many differences I had detected. "Perhaps thirteen", I ventured. "That's fine, Hammer san. This is your first attempt, now just observe." At this point the white haired master asked one of the others to bring forth his two pebbles and explain the differences. The selected candidate brought forth two pebbles which to my eyes looked identical. Not to him though! He began to talk in a spirited, flowing, yet almost hypnotic way, presumably outlining the differences he perceived. As he did so my guide came and sat beside me to give a running translation of the descriptions. At first I was just amazed that someone could talk for so long about two pebbles. As the discussion continued I became captivated by the depth of observation the candidate displayed. He talked in minute detail about the finest shades of colour and the patterns present in the stone's surface. An hour later he had only just begun explaining the detail of how the surfaces compared by touch and the different planes and high spots that could be felt. He then went on to talk about taste, warmth and coldness and a 'sense of soul'. I didn't pretend to understand the last category but judging by the total time spent talking we had probably heard about several hundred differences. I found it amazingly impressive and the acuity obviously found favour with the white haired master too. But what is it all about, I ask myself; what does it have to do with me?

Day 10

Are things becoming clearer? I am not sure. Today we had an

exercise in which we had to go off in groups of threes and find a comfortable spot to sit and observe the immediate surroundings. One had to maintain a dialogue of precisely what he was observing at that point. If he noticed either of the other two had lost concentration and was drifting away he could challenge and the description would be continued by the one who had drifted away. The third person acted as a referee if there was any dispute over the challenge. I was paired with two other English speakers and for once thought I was going to do well in the exercise. After all, I am used to listening to long presentations and sitting through extended meetings. I was mistaken. I found myself drifting away and being challenged with alarming frequency. There was then the problem of maintaining a flowing description of a scene in which the change was minimal and slow. Somehow we managed to keep going for most of the day. On reflection, I am beginning to realise how little we do really observe and take in. We have these tremendously powerful senses yet often they are taken for granted and under-used.

Day 14: the boat

I think this will be my last diary entry. Am I glad for Harada's invitation? Yes I am, but it has turned out very different to what I expected. I feel somehow rejuvenated; not by exercise or treatment, but by going back to the fundamentals of how I see the world and reinventing the freshness of doing so for the first time. Even on the boat, which was nothing special when I came, I am now aware of a riot of texture, colour, smell, noises and sensations. It is as if I have returned to my home to find it redecorated as it was when it was new and with that sense of expectation for the life that will evolve in it. I don't know how I will be different back at the office but I know I will.

When my flight arrived back, Harada was there to meet me at the airport. He was wildly enthusiastic about his sailing experiences and eager to hear how I had fared. Strangely, I felt a reluctance to talk about what had happened. I told him this but warmly expressed my appreciation for the experience and thanked him for his part in enabling me to participate. I sensed he knew how I felt and was satisfied with my response.

So, now some months later, what have been the results? Firstly, the venture with Harada is going from strength to strength. Secondly, Don is still with us and heading up a new project similar to the one I turned down. When I got back, I sat down with him and we went through the whole thing again. In reality he had found some good opportunities and we had nearly let them slide. We agreed on what needed more work and I backed him up at the next board meeting. The meeting was one of the liveliest for some time; not least because two of the members chose to depart. Am I different? Everyone seems to think so although I would be hard pressed to say. My secretary is still trying to work out whether there is a hidden message in the Japanese card on my desk which reads, 'To Hammer san, a man alive enough to know the 100 differences between two cherry blossoms.' Underneath there are some lines of script which I can translate as 'Having lived, learnt and understood the lessons from where the Wind meets the Forest.' I have not re-opened the diary for a while, but I will know when to do so, if it is necessary.

The rationalistic tradition

...underlies pure and applied science and enjoys much prestige and success, such that for many it has become the very paradigm of what it means to think and be intelligent. For some, the only conceivable alternative is "some kind of mysticism, religion, or fuzzy thinking that is a throwback to earlier stages of civilisation[39]". In the world of physical sciences the tradition led to the scientific method, and the Laplacian assumption that, given enough data, one could predict the future. The limits to that assumption are now being challenged by the new sciences of Chaos and Complexity, of which more in Chapter Four.

In economics and business theory, tradition generated the assumption of rational economic man, and of managers as being decision makers, processing information to reach solutions. Even though 'objective rationality' has been recognised as an idealisation and replaced in practice by 'bounded rationality', assumptions of complete knowledge, of valuation, and of conscious choice remain. Thinking and action are presumed to be separated. The 'rationalist tradition' still pervades much Western management theory and has been enormously beneficial in the development and application of that theory. Yet even a recent and powerful summary of the need for rational appraisal of business strategy is driven to the conclusion that "the effectiveness of modern advertising is fundamentally an irrational phenomenon[40]", working as it does on the perceptual patterns of the recipient. Just as in the physical sciences rational, deterministic, logic is being challenged as a source of understanding, so we join in the view that argues for the same re-examination in management science.

Ackoff in his book, *Creating the Corporate Future* gives an account of the development of mechanistic thinking through what he describes as the "Machine Age". The age was itself a natural product of the Renaissance, natural insofar as it flowed from this movement perhaps more than it was designed by it. He argues that we are now leaving the machine age and that this change is a change in our minds as well as in our environment. "The most important change taking place, I believe, is in the way we try to understand the world, and in our conception of its nature." He proceeds to label and describe the new age as the 'Systems Age'.

Let us first, though, increase our awareness of where we are coming from with much of our inherited thinking. Ackoff takes us on a quick Cook's Tour of developments since the Renaissance. Liberated from dogma, Renaissance man reawakened his curiosity about the workings of the natural world and attempted to unravel its mysteries analytically, that is, to understand it the better by taking it apart. How, then, did one begin to appreciate and understand the parts? The answer appeared to be by taking the parts apart until one arrived at some essential, indivisible element. Thus the doctrine of reductionism grew: all reality and our experience of it can be reduced to ultimate indivisible elements. "In every domain of inquiry men sought to gain understanding by looking for elements". Having arrived at elements or parts there was then the need to account for the relationship between the parts. Cause-and-effect became the familiar concept linking parts together. In turn, this developed into the doctrine of determinism, that is, that everything had to be taken as the effect of some cause, otherwise it could not be related or understood. Chance or choice played little part.

The form of this thinking is still present both in many of today's institutions and in the manner in which many people think. If the natural world could be analysed into its constituent parts then so, too, could the world of work. Work, interpreted as the application of energy to matter, could be reduced into a set of simple repetitive tasks making it amenable to mechanisation. Machines could start to replace men in many areas of work, 'at a stroke' as it were, removing the drudgery of repetitive labour, whilst promoting untold improvement in efficiencies. Where machines could not economically replace men then at least the task had been simplified, making any particular 'labour' easily replaceable and therefore expendable, admittedly whilst dehumanising the work and alienating the worker.

In a grossly oversimplified scenario, the analytical way of thinking permitted one to 'see' work in terms of simple constituent elements. Many of these elements could be, and were, progressively mechanised, and what remained could be undertaken by easily replaceable labour. This created a certain type of workplace which had many economic benefits. These benefits, for some at least, reinforced the thinking and its further development and application. Yet this pattern has for many reached the limits of its potential. Different types or patterns of workplace are necessary for a different level of result. In turn, these require different patterns of thinking.

The 'Human Remains Department' – How old habits die hard

Let us first acknowledge a client organisation for this 'play' on the term and on the function of the HR department. The error of expression was, for the company concerned, deliberate and served two purposes. One was to shape the relationship between the 'line' – where 'real' work was undertaken – and the function. In context, the term served as an expression of denigration. The other purpose, at a deeper level, was as a token recognition of current reality, that is, not as an expression of the department but as an expression of the way of being for many people in this enterprise. This was a company that had come to depend on passive conformance to its systems and procedures, one where people left a lot of their individuality at home in the morning. Only their 'human remains' or what was left over after they had discarded their spirit body was expected to be present at the workplace; an expectation that could be observed and witnessed in the language used and in the practices of 'people' when at work.

This condition is no-one's fault. It reflects a set of ideas and images in men's minds; a confluence, a pattern that was reinforcing. The prevailing thinking, the prevailing metaphor of the company was *mechanical*. It was, after all, a very significant mechanical engineering company. It used mechanical and financial resources in the course of its business. In a similar manner of thinking it used human 'resources'. In being used as a human resource, one had a 'job' and became a 'job holder'. A job in this company was seen as a highly-prized possession. It gave certain 'rights' in the scheme of things. The level of involvement in any purpose was limited to possessing a valued job. Motivation was supplied by management threat to valued jobs, only somewhat weakened by the protective power of trade unionism. Some readers may be familiar with the pattern.

The role of a manager was to use human resources. So the 'being' of human beings in this company was as a resource, one that could choose to have a job or not. Incidentally, what is often conveyed by such companies is the impression of human beings as expendable resources. It provided for a well-ordered world, significant controls, and not much in terms of capacity (development) to 'see' or attain totally new performance horizons. In this company, as with many others, one was easily dissuaded from even considering significant step-changes in performance by the high value placed on being realistic. "That's not possible here!" echoes in the corridors. Attempts to actually make a difference resulted in the system fighting back. All sorts of stuff could not be done here! The role of such a function as the Human Resource department at the one level was to resource human resources, that is, to recruit people who would fit requirements, people who were willing to be a 'resource', and a lesser number of people willing to be users of such resources (managers).

The Human Resource department in this company had, like nearly all others, succumbed in the past five years to the metamorphosis of 'personnel' into HR, a change often intended to signal a belief that "people are our greatest resource", and to acknowledge the need for new styles and practices of management; a need, let it be said, that the personnel profession has been in the forefront of recognising. Yet, in making the change, the company, like so many others, had not in fact shifted the pattern of thinking that was met by the old personnel department. Old habits prevailed behind a new name.

The assumptions underpinning the expression 'human remains' and the arrangement of the company were widely shared and mirrored. This is why changing habits is so hard. For it is not just a matter of an isolated change, as with the change of name, but of a change to a pattern of habits, each of which supports and triggers others. There were many habits within this company; habits of practices, thinking, relating, being and seeing that were deeply entrenched and reinforcing. Habits are known and proven, they work, or at least have worked. To change them is to risk the unknown and to challenge current workability. Such companies when they see the need to change continue with their habits. They tend to engage in initiatives with armies of rational consultants engaged to identify the components that need changing and to re-design them. Little attention is given to the process of discovery and development from within. And 'changes' tend, as a result, to be short-lived. Old habits die hard.

When the relationship to work is seen as purely economic, the boundary to possible development is severely restricted. The being associated with being a member of the company may be very focused – an advantage – but it is tremendously confined. The background of this relationship can occur at many levels in a company, from the shop floor to the boardroom. It was recently powerfully captured in an overheard conversation when a presumably upwardly mobile professional person was speaking with his colleague: "I know I am good at my work", he said. "What I do is I sell myself to the highest bidder.

If they are not prepared to pay what I think I am worth then I go elsewhere." There was a certain 'dominant logic' in his thinking and speaking, and a certain level of confidence in how he said what he said. Whatever his field one can presume that companies were mirroring the same logic.

The exchange at one level is crystal clear: he will provide that service commensurate with his remuneration, with a complete detachment from his work, i.e., not much of the person in the work. There is much of the economic relationship present in the context of many companies; which is not to say that it is a bad thing, but that when it is the dominant thing it may be limiting to a higher sense of purpose and possible commitment. The relationship will limit the result.

Greater development and greater result is possible when we shift our relatedness to company. Instead of human resource, imagine the difference when people are source and agent in the matter of their enterprise. For example: Servicemaster, a company who have achieved their position in the contract cleaning market through the motivation they grant to a workforce traditionally regarded as part of the casual fringe, have chosen to have a People Services function rather than a Human Resource department.

Images of reality: the invisible hand of metaphor

The switch of label from 'Personnel' to 'Human Resources', or to 'People Services' may seem cosmetic – yet it provides some clue to the ideas and images in the company. A window on how people think – on their patterns – is provided by the language people use to describe their business and, in particular, within their language, through the metaphors they use in order to tell the story of their business, its past, present and future: the etymology of business.

A metaphor is a figure of speech in which a name or quality is attributed to something to which it is not literally applicable. So, in using a metaphor when speaking of companies, we attribute certain qualities or 'states' to our companies. It is an 'as-if' or 'as-though' way of speaking. And people often speak of their companies as though they were a machine. The machine is a commonly used metaphor revealed when people use such phrases as 'running like clockwork', 'ticking over' or 'in the driving seat'.

Metaphors can do more than reveal patterns of thinking. They can also shape a perceptual framework. We 'see' through a lens that the metaphor has coloured. This 'seeing' in turn influences our relationship with the object being looked at, in this case the company. The metaphor shapes our interpretation of 'company'. Thus, in using the machine metaphor, we interpret aspects of company in mechanistic ways, we are propelled to reductionist thinking, to thinking of component parts assembled into a functioning whole. Dependent upon inclination there can be a certain beauty in thinking this way, captured in expressions such as 'working like a well-oiled machine'.

This is not to say that the use of a machine as a metaphor for a company is wrong. There are certain advantages to it. What may limit is to confuse a particular metaphor with reality; to hold it as the 'only' or the 'correct' interpretation of reality. In doing so, we may make ourselves blind to the limits of the metaphor. For example, the strength of the machine metaphor is also its weakness, for the component parts of a machine tend to be inflexible and passive. When seen as parts, people tend to think only within the limited horizon of their 'part' of the total 'machine'. The great advantage in thinking this way is that it is very easy to replace component parts, after all we may be but 'small cogs' in some giant machine, itself in turn part of a mechanistic, Laplacian universe.

The invisible hand of metaphor in our language and thinking subtly but powerfully influences perception, action, and performance in the world of business[41]. Our choice or inheritance of metaphor colours our modes of perception and thinking. It becomes part of how we think and of what we think with. The huge advantage of metaphor is that it serves to reduce the enormous complexities of the interaction of human, material, technical and knowledge elements of business – this tangled mass of interactions – into something understandable. In reducing complexity, it organises our thinking. It also channels it into a particular groove.

Our next chapter will challenge a very dominant metaphor.

 ## Summary

We have seen how rules often emerge over time through tacit learning, with both intended and unintended consequences. These operate in the background, for the most part unchallenged, shaping both experience and results. Such rules are but part of bigger patterns. Most, if not all, rules come from within; from the cultural, mental and social patterns shared by participating members. They influence and are influenced by the 'ideas and images in men's minds', ideas and images that already exist within established patterns of thinking and ideas and images that are transplanted via conversation. We saw how conversation has a creative as well as a descriptive function.

We explored the penchant for the quick fix; the management fad, a pattern that seems to have been in existence since at least Roman times. There is a tendency to seek superficial cures to deep-seated, highly complex and dynamic issues. We saw how paradigms shape unwritten rules, and hence behaviours, within a community. Rules reflect deeply ingrained webs of beliefs, values, myths, etc. – in short, webs of thoughts and of ways of thinking. Paradigms define accepted domains of inquiry. 'Re-tooling' of our paradigms – new ways of thinking and new thoughts – is necessary to provide a new bloom of progress. Revealing and making visible our paradigms provides the opportunity for paradigm shifts, for a new set of mental tools and patterns to be shared within a community.

We exposed the dominant management paradigm of control. This 'Road Most Travelled' has a set of rules with which, for the most part, we are very familiar. The manager and the managed mirror each other in their thinking and rules, unwittingly serving to maintain the pattern in place. An alternative 'commitment' paradigm has been described; yet to describe is easy, the key challenge is how to generate commitment, particularly when control prevails.

We saw how this dominant management paradigm was but reflective of deeper traditions of Western thinking, particularly traditions of reductionism and rationalism. We saw how old habits die hard when 'new' ideas are interpreted within old, established frameworks. The metaphors people use are indicators of the operant paradigms, they provide a window upon the ways in which people interpret organisations. Yet often, we do not challenge the assumptions of the metaphor, the assumptions on which we base our interpretation of what a company *is*...

 Primary Sources

The distinction of tacit and explicit knowledge is drawn by Nonaka (1991). Nonaka and Takeuchi (1995) extend it and compare the 'Western' and 'Eastern' traditions of thinking with the particular dominance, in the former, of the Platonic and Cartesian separation of mind and object. They describe the different philosophical traditions of Japanese management and their consequence; management as the mobilisation of knowledge resources. Winograd and Flores (1987) specifically define 'traditions'; shared heritages of thinking analogous to the operating programs of computers. Argyris (e.g. 1982, 1991) has documented the extent to which theories in use, tacit mental models, manifest themselves in organisational defensive routines. For many practising managers Senge (1990) or Senge et al (1994) provided the accessible insight into the power of mental models to govern corporate thinking and behaviour. Their paradigm of the Learning Organisation is very different from the recipe approach suggested by, for example, Thurbin (1994) or the equating of the Learning Organisation with Training and Development (e.g. Mumford 1993). The translation of a different philosophy on organisation (e.g. Deming 1986) into the quality manual is a similar absorption of a new idea by a prevailing paradigm.

It is to Pascale (1991) that we owe the insight into management as the art of making and breaking paradigms. Pascale is also one of many authors who have commented on the failure of numerous managerial fads (see also for example Shapiro 1995; Schaffer and Thompson 1992; Price and Evans 1993; Brightman 1994; Scott-Morgan 1994).

Kuhn's work on paradigms and the development of science has been extended to an assessment of the origin and preservation of science's unwritten rules and institutions by Hull (1988). Gersick (1991) and Price and Evans (1993) discuss punctuated equilibrium as a model for organisational change (see also Chapter Four). Ackoff (1981, 1994), Barker (1990) and Covey (1989) are among those who have drawn on Kuhnian paradigm shifts as a metaphor for development, and for personal and organisational breakthrough. Walton (1985) and Block (1991) discuss the limits of the prevailing Western managerial paradigm. Ackoff (op. cit.) and DeBono (e.g. 1990) are others who have challenged the limits of the rationalistic tradition. Morgan (1986) covers metaphor in organisational theory as well as offering a fine review of older work on organisational theory. Clancy (1989) introduces a separate distinction of metaphors into two prime classes: metaphors that interpret the company as a description of processes (as in journey, game, and war), and those that interpret the company as a description of systems (as in machine, organism, or society). For a more recent and wider treatment of metaphor see Grant and Oswick (1996). Lloyd (1990) explicitly goes beyond metaphor in suggesting a company is a living organism.

4

The pattern's eye view: companies as self-maintaining systems

"So when deciding what a company should do, it is first essential to determine what it is. Corporate phenomenology has precedence of corporate strategy."

Tom Lloyd

"Darwin derived natural selection more by wondering how he might transfer the laissez-faire principle of Adam Smith's economics into nature than by observing the tortoises on the Galapagos Islands."

Stephen J. Gould

 We may witness the actions of people in companies and the results they obtain; all the more easily visible manifestations – the stuff of human and corporate behaviour and of periodic business reports. But what lies behind? When we inquire deeper we begin to see how the mental models we think, speak and listen with and through shape our actions and results; but what assumptions do we carry about what a company is? What is the phenomenon called a company? This chapter explores an unconventional answer to that question, one that carries a significant benefit in terms of understanding and action.

In brief: we suggest a company, or any organisation, becomes a system dedicated to the maintenance and reproduction, the replication, of its own corporate 'genes', its patterns, its mentalic code. Seeing a company from the pattern's perspective and asking how that prevalent pattern seeks to replicate itself within its host[42], much as the gene seeks to replicate itself within biological hosts, helps to explain much that we put down to resistance to change and preservation of the status quo. In seeking to preserve itself, the pattern uses the organisation, as least as much as the organisation uses the pattern. Without a pattern no organisation, no form of company, could exist. Imagine a nation without a shared language, a corporation without some shared perception of its business, a science without an accepted set of principles, a society without a shared code of ethics. Yet in each case the organisation also preserves the pattern. To paraphrase John F. Kennedy, "Think not of what the pattern does for the organisation, but rather what the organisation does for the pattern."

This perspective owes much to the work of Richard Dawkins whose book *The Selfish Gene* invited readers to consider evolution and natural selection from the perspective not of organisms but of their genes; replicators whose 'purpose in life', is, without conscious forethought, to distribute copies of themselves. As well as writing a brilliant manifesto for a gene's-eye view of biology Dawkins created the concept of the meme (pronounced to rhyme with cream) as a basic element of cultural replication; in effect, the equivalent of a mental gene, protein or virus. In a similar way, consider this chapter as being concerned with the *selfish meme*... The term used is less important than the image of an abstract entity seeking its own replication by preserving the status quo – an invisible antibody to change.

We will also draw on other insights into the workings of evolving biological systems, and on what has come to be called Complexity – the science of complex adaptive systems – to suggest a view of companies as self-organising, and self-maintaining, entities. 'Self-organisation' refers to an ability, seen in many natural systems, to spontaneously develop some ordered dynamic out of random interactions. Turbulent cells in heated water, or weather systems, are two commonly cited examples. Both create dynamic order from the random interaction of dispersed molecules.

The comparisons we draw between the biological and organisational worlds involve summarising a considerable amount of biological and geological theory in as little space as possible. It is worth being clear at the outset why. We are neither using biology as a metaphor, nor saying organisations are biologically 'alive'. We are saying organisms and organisations are both entities maintained by their replicators. Insights from the biological process of evolution, played out over geological time, provide the platform from which to begin constructing a comparable perspective on organisations. As organisms form ecosystems, so companies interact to form economic and social systems. As gene complexes define organisms, so meme complexes define companies. As genes are carried and transmitted through biological reproduction, so memes are transmitted and mutated through the conversation they create within and between human minds. The result is a self-organising hierarchy of co-evolving memetic systems with at least four levels: personal, inter-personal, organisational and inter-organisational. We will examine these in the rest of the book – after first setting out a theoretical foundation.

But first a statement of intent. As we developed the ideas recorded here we have frequently encountered the argument that we are trying to deny human choice and free will. On the contrary, we seek to liberate it... A person, or even a 'company' can be more than a passively adaptive agent in a self-maintaining system. He, she, or it, can be self-generative in a way that an organism cannot. As Dawkins puts it in concluding *The Selfish Gene:*

"We, and we alone, can, if we choose, free ourselves from *the tyranny of the selfish replicators."* (emphasis added).

In other words, human beings are unique because they can choose to shift their patterns. Stepping into a pattern's perspective, recognising the power or grip of patterns, their inherent 'self-interest' in reproducing themselves, and the consequent inertia built into the self-maintaining systems they specify, helps reveal how, in practice, that choice is not often exercised.

Organisation and organism: a tale of two systems

Organisations, and organisms are both complex adaptive systems. They share attributes of relationships, complex order, evolution, natural hierarchy and strategy. Consider each in turn:

Relationships

Individual organisms and complete species live in ecological niches defined by their relationship to other members of a particular ecological system. Within that set of relationships, individual players – and whole species – 'compete' for differential survival. Exactly what 'compete' means in this context will require clarification. As will become clear, we are not implying the simple nostrum of 'survival of the fittest'. A company is likewise an entity that lives in a web of relationships, in this case economic transactions with other players. There is again a 'competition' for their differential survival. Economy and ecology are both defined by the repeated interactions of their component agents.

Complex order

One of the best definitions of 'life' is again owed to Richard Dawkins, this time in his third book, *The Blind Watchmaker*.

> (Life is) "...a property of improbable complexity possessed by an entity that works to keep itself out of equilibrium with its environment."

To use Dawkins' most graphic example, a dead pigeon thrown into the air obeys the laws of physics, describes a perfect parabola and falls back to earth. A live one disappears over the county boundary; its component parts working together to maintain their collective entity against the force of gravity.

In a similar way the component parts of living companies and networks of companies work collectively to maintain their order against the natural forces of decomposition and atrophy.

Evolution

Organic species evolve and adapt through natural selection, in their system of repeated interactions. Such selection, played out over time, produces all the infinite variety of organic designs[43]. The mechanisms and rhythm we will come to; for now, the key point is that evolution is blind. It creates intricacy and order with no designer, no watchmaker. Small errors in nature's genetic copying process create small differences in the instruction set from which new bodies are built. The essence of evolution is the differential survival of different designs, because of their greater success at reproducing. Out of differential survival stem all the organic designs that have populated the planet, from the first strands of DNA to float in the primordial soup, to dinosaurs and humans. At a rate orders of magnitude faster, but through a fundamentally similar process, companies and organisations evolve in the broth of human culture and economics. Old organisational certainties, and the designs which embodied them, disappear. New organisations form. One image of today is of many individuals, abandoned by, or voluntarily disassociated from, their old companies, floating like free strands of protoplasm through the soup of the modern economy. A bewildering mix of technologies, products, services, ideas, organisations and relationships is continually shifting and forming.

There is no overall economic designer any more than there is an overall biological designer. As we sought to show in Chapter One, civilisations, nations, companies and organisations coalesce around patterns of language, belief and technology. The broad similarity with evolution has been commented on many times. Organisations that do not adapt become extinct.

Hierarchy

There are several distinct levels to the agents in the biological system. Individual genes combine to define various specialised cells, and a given arrangement of cells defines an individual organism. Individuals who share a common design are recognisable as a distinct species, a population whose members can reproduce copies of themselves. A remarkable fact of nature is that, whereas there may be a wide and continuous variation between members of one species (just think of our own) there is no such gradation from one species into another. Each is an entity with its own pattern. Biologically, evolution produces entities – not endless and continuous variation.

Related species can in turn be classified into genera – groups that have large elements of their design in common; that, in business language, share a high overlap of core capabilities. Genera in turn can be grouped into larger biological units, conventionally Families, Classes, Phyla, Kingdoms and Super Kingdoms. Each level has its particular set of shared capabilities. For example, all domestic dogs belong to one species, *Canis familiaris*, their place in the larger scheme of things given by:

Super Kingdom ....Eukaryotes..........Cells with nuclei

Kingdom ....Animals ....Ability to move

Phylum.....................Vertebrates ....Animals with backbones

Class ....Mammals ....Vertebrates that have
hair and produce milk

Family ....Carnivores ....Mammals that eat meat

Genus ....Canidae ....Dogs: wild and domestic

Species ....familiaris.............Domestic dogs

Each step in the table represents a step change in a fundamental organic design, or natural technology. Many mammals exploit the same basic design archetype to compete in different environments. Bats, birds, and insects compete for airborne 'markets' using different basic design competencies[44].

 Similar albeit more fluid hierarchies exist among social and economic agents. Thus, people group themselves into organisational units, units into companies and companies into networks of specialist relationships.

Languages split from common roots, as illustrated in Chapter One, and ultimately divide themselves into dialects. Analogous hierarchies exist in religions or scholarly disciplines – though none are as clear- cut, rigid or fixed as is an organic species; a point to which we return shortly.

Strategies which anticipate the future

At first glance it may seem strange to consider an organism having a strategy, an anticipation of the future, but in one sense a gene can be considered exactly that. It is an explicit set of instructions which says, "build a body to this set of parameters, anticipating an environment in which that body will successfully occupy an ecological niche". The instructions are of course based on a projection of the past; an implicit assumption that the rules of the game for the next generation will be the same as they are for the present one. A gene can do no more than pass on the recipe of a past success.

An organisation anticipates the future through the strategy it follows, explicitly or implicitly. Strategy, as we come back to in Chapter Nine, concerns the design, the unique capabilities, the relationships by which the company accesses resources, and perpetuates itself at a node within its own web of relationships. A company has, in theory, a freedom to define the future that no genetic agent can ever possess. In practice, however, many strategies boil down to no more than an anticipation that past formulae will continue to succeed in the future. Even in organisations whose management have embraced change as a permanent need, unwritten rules, paradigms, industry recipes, common mental models and traditions – all the stuff of patterns – all too frequently conspire in presuming that the future will be much the same as the past[45].

But there are differences!

The comparison of biological and cultural evolution, especially when presented in such a potted form, can appear seductively simple. As several writers have observed, it is easy to overlook key differences. Another eminent natural historian with a gift for writing for the lay audience, Harvard's Stephen J Gould[46], expressed them as: speed, interbreeding, and the transmittal of acquired characteristics.

Organic species are, with minor exceptions, incapable of interbreeding. Once formed, a species (or a gene) is a distinct entity, in principle forever. Organisational entities can, in theory, merge and blend at will. In practice, significant barriers stop individuals or groups cross-pollinating, learning from one another. Witness the familiar 'not-invented-here' response to exchange of ideas along even one corridor of a firm, the difficulties that speakers of any two languages have in appreciating each other or the schisms and disciplines of both science and religion.

An organism cannot pass on acquired characteristics. Interactions with the environment do not affect the genes. That fundamental tenet – part of the central dogma of modern biology – distinguishes 'Darwinian' from 'Lamarckian' evolutionary theory. To cover, briefly, the difference: Lamarck's theory (which pre-dated Darwin's) advocated that organisms could pass on characteristics acquired during their lifetime. Lamarckian evolution would have a giraffe exercising its neck by feeding and then producing longer necked offspring. Darwinian evolution argues that longer necked giraffes got a preferential share of leaves from tall Acacia trees. ('Post-modernist' evolution argues that giraffes and Acacia trees actually co-evolved in an evolutionary arms-race, but that is getting ahead of the argument[47]).

Cultural and technological evolution is essentially Lamarkian. The patterns an organisation acquires, as well as the patterns embodied in culture and language, are passed on through cultural programming: education (training!) and socialisation. But the distinction is blurred by the fact that we are not the only species with the capacity to transmit acquired knowledge. Blue tits living near humans have learnt, and have taught their young, to drink from milk bottles. Foxes have discovered the possibilities of urban and suburban environments, learning to forage from garbage bins. As even the response of wild species to recent technological and economic developments shows, the evolution of behaviours which do not require genes as agents of transmittal can be orders of magnitudes faster.

Blue-tits or foxes illustrate the sound, Darwinian, explanation for the evolution of brains. A capacity to learn, to respond to a changing world, to exploit the new opportunities of milk bottles on doorsteps (a uniquely English ecological niche now disappearing again) or suburban refuse bins, and to teach your offspring the same trick, increases immeasurably the probability that your offspring will survive to reproduce in their turn. Patterns of learnt behaviour, and an ability to change them, grant the agents which carry them an ability to adapt which genes, by themselves, cannot aspire to emulate. A set of genes which say 'build a brain' creates a more efficient survival machine than one which tries to code for every eventuality. Brains are to nature what empowering individuals to use their judgement is to management.

There remains a fundamental difference between evolution in human and non-human systems. Nature is 'red in tooth and claw'. Species eat and parasitise each other in ways that strike most people as decidedly unpleasant if judged by most current human ethical and moral standards. One has to accept that nature cannot have any such ethical capacity nor can we judge it by our own standards. The converse is that we have no reason to judge human behaviour by nature's standards. Organisations and the individuals in them can, uniquely, make an ethical choice[48]; though many choose to compete as ferociously as any natural predator and common ethics may be 'bred out' of the willing participants, in return for whatever material 'rewards' the company has to offer.

The edge of chaos: order for free!

Complex adaptive systems are one example of the phenomenon variously referred to as 'Chaos', self-organisation, bounded instability or non-linear dynamics; recognition of which has been contributing over at least the last twenty years to a fundamentally new scientific paradigm. The shift is now impacting thinking in other fields, including for example, weather forecasting, the management of oil production, economics and organisational theory. It is part of the growing recognition of the limits of the deterministic or reductionist tradition[49]. As Ralph Stacey[50], one of the pioneers in applying this new science to management theory, expresses: "It is the conceptual content rather than the mathematical precision (of the new paradigm) which is key to management or organisational theorising". We aim in this section to provide an unfamiliar reader with a brief summary of that conceptual content.

Even very simple systems can generate unpredictable behaviour. Consider two ice-cream sellers on a beach, with nothing to differentiate their product save the distance their customers must walk to purchase an ice-cream. Imagine the beach is 400 metres long. Customers are equally spread out along its entire length.

❑ What is the ideal position for the ice-cream sellers and the customers?

❑ Where will the ice-cream sellers end up?

Everyone's convenience is served if each ice-cream stall ends up 100m from either end of the beach. That way the distance customers must walk is minimised and both sellers access an equal market. Great for everybody if they agree to do that and stick to it. But if both sales people behave as rational economic theory says they should (we are not saying that they will, you could equally say "if they are victims of a particular economic pattern"), then there is an incentive for one to try and increase market share by moving towards the middle of the beach. The other must respond, and so on, until the only 'logical' equilibrium is that they are both next to each other in the middle of the beach, again with an equal 'share' of the market, but now causing maximum discomfort to prospective customers. The situation is shown in figure 4.1.

Ignore for a minute the fact that pragmatic small businessmen are not necessarily going to be as irrational as rational economic theory suggests they should be. Leave out the possibility of creative thinking, and the system is, in theory, fully determined. It has one predictable outcome. On a map of the beach there is only one possible stable position for both ice-cream sellers: a single point in the middle of the map. Physicists call such a map of all possible outcomes 'phase space', and refer to points a system can reach as 'attractors'. The fully determined system has a single point attractor. Newtonian science held nature was ultimately the same. If we knew enough we could predict any outcome.

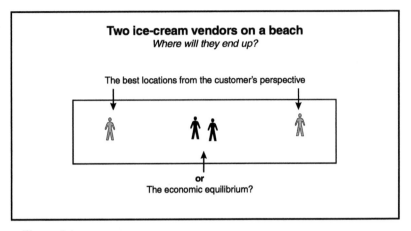

Figure 4.1

A predictable situation – in economic theory, at least. By presuming 'rational economic action' one can predict where two ice cream sellers will position themselves on a beach in such a way that neither can, by moving, gain any competitive advantage over the other. As even this simple example will also demonstrate, presumptions of rationality may not equate with reality.

Most economic theory operates on the same basis, (a bad case of 'physics envy' as one leading economist put it).

Now add a third ice-cream seller. There is no longer a logical stable position because our third entrant can force a response from one of the other two by positioning herself a little way to one side or the other. Trace out maps of their possible behaviour and they will wander up and down the beach in a constantly shifting pattern. There is no attractor in this truly random, or completely undetermined, unstable system.

Classical physics concerned only these two states, fully determined or random. A fully determined system, obeying fixed and simple laws, will reach a given equilibrium and only that equilibrium. Its attractor is a single point in possibility space: the two ice-cream sellers in the middle of the beach. The random system has no attractor whatsoever. Its possible states, its phase map, looks like the beach with three, or more, ice-cream sellers wandering anywhere on the surface.

With the advent of computers and graphics mathematicians were able to explore a third domain, wherein simple, deterministic equations (such as the one which provides our 'underpinning theory' icon) would describe behaviour that did not settle to any equilibrium. The attractors of such systems came to be called 'strange'; they had a recognisable order but never actually repeated themselves. So sensitive are such systems to their initial values, that small differences in starting point make phenomenal differences to the outcome after only a few iterations. One of the most famous strange attractors is reproduced in figure 4.2. It represents a simulation of a system of three variables, each of which is a simple function of the others. Such an outcome could arise if each of three ice-cream vendors decided to keep moving, simultaneously, to a position given by some constant rule which dictated the next move as a function of where they and the other two stood this time round. For some rules their footsteps would trace a pattern in the sand not unlike the butterfly in figure 4.2.

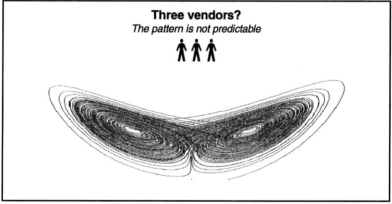

Three vendors?
The pattern is not predictable

Figure 4.2
With only one more ice-cream seller the equilibrium is not predictable, even within the simplifying assumptions of standard economic theory. Many natural systems, even those which can be described by quite simple formulae, show this outcome. The 'Lorenz attractor' illustrated here is one of the classic examples. If the behaviour of three feedback equations is simulated over time the result is a graph which never repeats itself, or settles to a final equilibrium, but which is nevertheless bounded within limits and displays an obvious form or pattern – in this case, the butterfly shape.

Such systems have the property of producing unpredictable order, instability within limits, because of their internal feedback, because the current values of any variable determine its future behaviour. Their study is coming to be called the science of Complexity – while the systems themselves, as they display characteristics intermediate between the ordered and the chaotic domains, are coming to be thought of as operating on the edge-of-chaos, or under conditions of bounded instability[51]. Many examples, both natural and commercial, are now recognised, weather being the classic case. You cannot predict it accurately but you can say with reasonable confidence what range of weather conditions is likely at a given time (or at least you can if you ignore the probable gathering pace of global warming). Stock markets show a similar pattern of bounded fluctuation, and many millions of dollars have been spent in fruitless efforts to use the science of complex systems to forecast their behaviour more accurately[52].

Complexity science is now most notably associated with New Mexico's Santa Fe Institute, whose founders deliberately sought cross-pollination of ideas from physics, biology, and economics in an environment physically separated from the main bastions of normal research in any of the contributing disciplines. (We shall see later that such paradigmatic isolation is, in and of itself, not a bad recipe for organisational innovation.) The phenomenon of spontaneous, yet unpredictable, order is coming to be called self-organisation. Systems on the 'edge of chaos' are described as possessing self-organising criticality. When in this state they are highly sensitive to even small disturbances. To vary the beach theme, consider a pile of sand. Adding more sand grains may do nothing, it may trigger a small sandslide, or perhaps a massive avalanche. The variation, and the unpredictability, is a property of the interconnectedness of stresses, the feedback, between all the grains in the pile. Anyone catching each sandslide and measuring its volume would observe what is called a 'power-law' relationship. The average frequency of a given size of slide is inversely proportional to some power of that size. Avalanches, storms, earthquakes, stock markets, or the size and market share of firms in a new industry all display similar power-law patterns. The distribution is the natural product of self-organised criticality in complex systems, the sign of a system on the edge of chaos.

Recall the three ice-cream sellers. If their movements were falling into a state of self-organised criticality, if the pattern they traced on the sand resembled figure 4.2, then the individual moves would display a power-law pattern; lots of small steps and fewer giant leaps. In practice of course the three-seller system is unlikely to remain in such a spontaneous state. All three players would have a common interest in forming a cartel to define some mutually accepted pattern of operation, say one in which each had a territory and they collectively made sure that no other player intruded on their joint patch. If they did not reach agreement a higher authority, the local council, a franchise operator or even the boss of a local protection racket would be likely to reach it for them. By force or implicit agreement, by written or unwritten rule, a particular order would emerge and move the system from chaos towards a more ordered, predictable state. Because of human thinking and communication some form of stability is likely, even without imposition from a higher authority. Leave it a few seasons and one could imagine the ice-cream sellers doing it "because we've always done it this way", vulnerable to a new entrant who shifts the rules. Compare the example of the car market and Daewoo in Chapter Three.

Evolution and revolution

Mature, stable markets do not show the power-law pattern characteristic of stock-market fluctuations or emergent markets. They may end up with a few players sharing a pie between them, like, say, Coca-Cola and Pepsi or any two national carriers on a regulated airline service between two European capitals. They may end up with a single dominant player, or with a tacit cartel where no-one wants to start a price war. They may end up, like most biological systems, with every species (company) in a unique and differentiated niche. Either way the system, without overt design, seeks more order. It becomes set in its ways until some new innovation, or new entrant to the market disrupts it.

Over geological time life shows the same pattern. The history of evolution is not of species continually coming and going, of change at a steady, gradual rate. It is one of large periods of time during which there was relatively little change to a dominant biological system, interspersed with 'events' during which large numbers of species perished and new ones arose to occupy equivalent ecological niches. At least one such event was truly that, when, some 65 million years ago, an asteroid impact on the coast of southern Mexico (seemingly) ended the dominance of the dinosaurs, along with 95 percent of life forms on Earth. Most mass extinctions are less dramatic; what a geologist calls an 'event' might represent tens of thousands of years. The 'event' only merits the label when seen against the millions of years in between. If life on earth was a purely self-organising system, one might expect extinctions events to show a power-law distribution with occasional large disturbances and numerous smaller ones. They don't, or at least not a perfect one. They show a distribution biased towards order. The periods of stability are longer than would be predicted in a totally critical system and the bursts of change are less frequent. Nature maintains her own cartels, empires and monopolies.

To the extent that evolution has penetrated management thinking it is as a metaphor for gradual and even managed change. "Evolution not revolution" is the plea, not least of those seeking to limit the pace and impact of change in their particular company. Yet the evidence of geological history is that evolution does not work like this: its tempo, relative to the time available, is stasis or near stasis interspersed with crisis. Evolution is either revolution or it is nothing.

The human species may have come of age in 1859 when Charles Darwin[53] first worked out the reason for its existence, but he still couched his theory within the cultural and scientific patterns of his day; patterns of thinking that were only just coming to terms with the age of the earth and the fact that it had not been created in the state that Victorian gentlemen scientists then newly observed. The new geological paradigm of the day, supported by the power structure of science, was the theory of uniformitarianism which held that physical processes observed in the present could – given time and a constant rate – explain all geophysical history[54]. The world was conceived, if not as a created constant, at least as changing slowly and almost imperceptibly. Darwin cast evolution in the same terms – as a continuous gradual process – even though he was fully aware of a possible conflict with the fossil record, where the naturalists of the day had found little or no record of the gradual transition of one species to another demanded by the uniformitarian paradigm[55]. His only answer was to point out how incomplete the record is, how it is but "fragments of pages from the last Chapter of the Book of Life". Once people got over the pattern interrupt of being descended from apes and accepted the fact of evolution, it became the paradigm to seek examples of gradual change, sequences of fossils displaying a pattern of continuous, incremental adaptation. Most of the science of palaeontology was to spend the next hundred years doing just that. Even so, by the 1960s precious few examples had turned up. The best there was, (as certain undergraduate geologists in Australia were required to memorise!) concerned a particular 200 million year old oyster evolving in southern England[56]!

Twenty-five years later the evidence, whilst still recognised as fragmentary, is at least accepted at face value. Continuous records provided by oil exploration helped. From palaeontology and other branches of geology has come the recognition that the rhythm of evolution has undoubtedly been episodic. Long periods of little change in global biological diversity or in the dominant species in a particular system alternate with bursts of sudden extinction and rapid evolution. (Few extinctions compare with the present day...) The greatest booms follow the appearance of new biological technologies: the ability to colonise new habitats say; or to metabolise oxygen, or to fly, or develop skeletons, or brains.

Economic and historical 'cycles' show the same dynamic on a different scale. Civilisations are separated by 'events'; shorter periods of fundamental rearrangement, such as the Renaissance, or the PIE invasions of Europe. On a shorter scale, Andrew Tylecote has shown how many economic cycles, especially the so-called long-wave or Kondratieff Cycle of sixty to seventy years' duration are driven by what he terms fundamental shifts of technological style. Water-power enabled the first industrial revolution. Subsequent dramatic shifts in the entire economic pattern occurred after :

153

- The explosion of steam powered transport from the late 1820's.

- The co-evolution of steel making and the electricity industry from the late 1870s.

- Fordism: mass manufacturing methods and the motor industry from c. 1915.

- Microelectronics and biotechnology from the late 1970s.

 Such 'pattern shifts' periodically engender a 'revolution' in the whole dynamic of an economy; not as an instantaneous event, but as a short interval compared to the total time available. Many would say, as alluded to in Chapter One, that we are now living through such a shift. On any scale, from the geological to the life of the individual firm, the same dynamic is seen: long periods of stability or incremental change and shorter bursts of radical rearrangement which usually involve crises for the established order. (Recall the pattern of scientific paradigms described in Chapter Three.) Organic species, entire ecosystems, cultural and social systems, firms, scientific or political paradigms, economies and markets are not merely self-organising, adaptive systems; they maintain themselves and possess an in- built tendency to seek stability. *Why?*

Our concern is with the tendency of companies to seek such stability and the need to interrupt that trend, if a company is not to find itself failing to change the world around it, or at least change as the world around it changes. Patterns, we argue, cause in the economic adaptive system the same rhythm as genes in the biological system. To understand the case it is easier to first digress, again, into the workings of the genetic replicator.

The gene's eye view

Deoxyribonucleic Acid (DNA), the stuff of which genes are made, is a chemical molecule with a property not shared by any other yet invented or discovered. It can copy itself. The capability is inherent in DNA's structure, the famous double-helix first described by James Watson and Francis Crick in 1953. One way of imagining this structure is to think of a long ladder twisted into a corkscrew. The uprights of the ladder are chains of sugars and phosphates. Rungs are formed by only four compounds, adenine (A), thyamine (T), guanine (G) and cytosine (C) arranged in pairs. A and T and G and C molecules lock into each other like molecular plug-and-socket joints. The ladder has two halves which slot uniquely together. Either is a blueprint for reproducing the whole. Provide a DNA molecule the right supply of chemical feedstock and sufficient energy and its two strands will separate and assemble new twins: the basis of all growth and reproduction and the source of Dawkins' metaphor of the immortal coils.

DNA is also a natural bar-code, one that stores digitised information on a scale of miniaturisation far beyond that of even the most advanced manmade media for information handling. The code is written in an alphabet of four letters, A, T, C and G and is a set of instructions for copying itself. It does so each time, the molecule unzips and then assembles two new copies, one from the each strand of the zip. The same code serves a second function. It is a set of instructions for building proteins and hence for assembling parts of a body. DNA in the nucleus of an organic cell can copy part of itself as a similar, shorter molecule of RNA (ribonucleic acid). RNA is converted in the rest of the cell into proteins and hence, organic tissue. The process can be thought of as a miniaturised chemical production plant whose operating systems are written in the DNA code. Each segment of DNA, each gene, is a coded instruction for both reproducing itself and contributing to a manufacturing process. Several thousand genes constitute, between them, the blueprint for a particular organic design. The total set could be conceived as the procedure manual for a particular organism. If we think, as urged by Steve Jones, of the bases of DNA as the alphabet of a genetic language, then the alphabet has four letters, but the manual contains many thousands of words and phrases, three thousand million characters. What it is, is a set of instructions on how to build a body, and which can reproduce one or many more copies of the manual.

Organisms are, from the gene's perspective, no more than survival machines, photocopiers that a gene must construct in order to reproduce. Reproduction does however provide an opportunity for spelling mistakes to creep into the genetic language, for genetic words and codes to assume new meanings, for changes to the design parameters for the next generation. Were it not so, the primordial soup would still be the primordial soup. Out of variation, and the preferential survival of particular designs of copier, emerged, with time, all the complex order of the living world.

There is however one critical flaw in the metaphor of a genetic barcode or instruction manual. It tends to convey a picture of a neat, linear, structured set of instructions: build skull to specification XYZ, add hair red, eyes blue, nose Roman etc., etc. It is not that simple. The full genetic code, the 'genotype' of an individual or the genome of a species, is an interacting complex of many genes. The context of the manual affects the meaning of the phrase and the interaction is a network, not a linear script. One strand of DNA might, to take an hypothetical example, contribute in a given context to both redness of hair and an abundant supply of adrenaline. Any body is the result of a complex interplay or fudge between many different strands. It depends on cross-connections and feedback. The selfish gene is shorthand for a complex of interacting genes in:

a co-operative venture of such intricacy that it is almost impossible to disentangle the contribution of one gene from that of another.[57]

 That very inter-connectedness may grant DNA its functionality. Computer simulations of other complex systems are revealing that the property of emergent order depends on a critical density of interactions. Too few (two ice cream vendors) and the system stays stable, too many and it is completely random. Stuart Kauffman, one of the founders of Complexity, suggests that it is the degree of interconnection in genetic networks that gives biological systems the ability to generate order. Genes are, in aggregate, actually closer to 'patterns', interconnecting signals from several components of a symphony orchestra (in the metaphor of Chapter One), than they are to instruction manuals. As with any other rich conversation, the meaning of words and phrases in the language of the genes depends on the context and order in which they are placed and on the other words and phrases with which they interact.

Nonetheless, genetic replication generates and maintains order. Genes which code for a more successful copier, a body that can access the resources to copy them, get passed on. Others don't. Such, in a nutshell, is the modern restatement of Darwin's theory of evolution through natural selection. From the gene's perspective, stability is a good thing. If you are yesterday's recipe, and want to ensure your own replication, it helps if tomorrow will be the same as yesterday. If your survival depends on your place in an intricate genome you want the genome, and the system in which it thrives, maintained.

Do organisations have an equivalent replicator?

Of Memes and Men

 The essential parallel between natural selection and differential survival in economics and biology has, as Geoffrey Hodgson's Economics and Evolution makes clear, a long history. 'Survival of the fittest' is a much used metaphor for commercial and social competition. Fewer authors have sought to extend the parallel by seeking a replicator, an economic or cultural gene. Consider what any candidate for the role must perform:

❑ It must specify the behaviour of whatever host carries it, in a way that enhances its chances of self replication.

❑ It must have a means of being transmitted and copied.

❑ It must be involved in a selective competition.

157

Various cases have been advanced[58]. The most developed was made by Friedrich Hayek, who argued for the economy as a selective competition between 'rules of behaviour', "irrespective of whether the rule is 'known' to the individuals who carry it in any other sense than that they normally act in accordance with it". Cast in the language of Chapter Two, this amounts to a suggestion that rules, written or unwritten, are the 'genes' that drive firms and are selected as those firms compete. As Hayek put it, they specify 'institutions and practices' that compete with each other for resources. A not-dissimilar case has been made by Nelson and Winter for the role of 'habits and routines' in organisations. In neither instance is it clear how the rules or 'habits' are propagated. Tom Lloyd, in The Nice Company, recognised that difficulty. He argues rather more pragmatically for strategy as a replicator. Successful strategies are imitated, unsuccessful ones fall victims to the market, hence his suggestion of the 'streme', or strategic meme.

Whereas most economists who sought inspiration in evolution were concerned strictly with commercial companies, trading entities, other writers have considered the selection process in different cultural spheres. Biologist and scientific philosopher David Hull's *Science as a Process* uses the history of biology, its paradigmatic schisms, schools and institutions, biases in particular journals and other emergent behaviours to make a compelling case for science itself evolving through a process of selection between competing paradigms, each replicated by their success in convincing a body of adherents[59]. And the biological competition was not restricted to purely scientific paradigms but was also influenced by cultural context and the lessons particular authors either tried to draw, or were perceived to have tried to draw, for cultural evolution and the morality and inevitability or otherwise of particular social systems.

 Winograd and Flores, whose work we cited in Chapter Three, drew on one of the less prominent concepts of modern biology, the theory of self-referring or self-producing systems, to argue for 'traditions' and language as self-maintaining. In essence, and without going into a further scientific detour, they grant language and tradition the role of replicator.

In the two previous chapters, we have argued the case for each of these alternatives. Rules of behaviour, paradigms, strategic perceptions, traditions and language all contribute to the pattern of an organisation; but equally, each is a snapshot, a perspective on, and a part of, some more intangible whole. It is the whole that replicates in organisations and institutions, interwoven with the ideas and images in people's minds. In biological terms the pattern is the genome of the organisation (see below).What is it built from? Is there a gene for the organisational genome, a unit of transmission of ideas and images, rules and culture? Dawkins' suggestion of the meme serves the purpose.

Many critics have sought to dismiss *The Selfish Gene* as overly 'atomistic' or reductionist; a criticism that Dawkins answers by pointing out that the title is more likely to engage a reader, and convey a message than is:

"The ill-defined bit of a chromosome that one could argue is selfish because of the way it interacts with a lot of other poorly defined bits of a complex chromosome system."

...which is what he really meant! We have to remember in other words that despite the increasing facility with which the term gene is used a gene is, in fact, an ill-defined entity. There is no hard and fast rule for saying where in a genetic paragraph one gene stops and another starts. The word meme was coined to convey a similarly imprecise unit of cultural transmission: say, a tune, idea, catch-phrase, fashion, recipe or design. The title *The Selfish Gene* is itself a good example of a meme; an entity or element of cultural transmission that propagates from mind to mind conveying a meaning in the process; a meaning that may mutate each time it is transmitted but one that is captured and remembered. Any other cultural artefact can serve the same purpose. As Dawkins puts it:

"When you plant a fertile meme in my mind you literally parasitise my brain, turning it into a vehicle for the meme's propagation in just the way that a virus may parasitise the genetic mechanism of a host cell."

The comparison with a virus is apt, for viruses are essentially free strands of DNA or RNA that replicate, not by building their own copying machines, but by inducing the machines of others to make the copies; freeloading on other genes' photocopiers. Such freedom enables viruses to evolve many times faster than genes which are tied into larger genomes. Just think of the annual varieties on the theme of the 'flu virus! They also promote actions in their hosts which will facilitate their own, not their host's (or host's genes') replication. Sneezing is a classic example. Slightly more sinister is the supposed increase in libido in the early stages of syphilis.

The word 'meme' is a meme in its own right. The meme is a unit as a gene is a unit, and the boundaries of both are somewhat vague. A gene is a particular subset of the letters on a strip of DNA; a phrase in DNA's language, the smallest unit capable of seeking its own replication. A similar distinction is intended by 'meme': it is an entity that will be recognised as such but may be repeated or combined with others to form some larger unit of replication. If you want your wider ideas – your memotype – to propagate, giving them an infectious title helps[60].

If we think of patterns as built of memes in the way genomes are built of genes, we reach the following comparison:

An organism is coded via chemical strands of DNA, sections of which form genes, the smallest units capable of being copied. An *organisation* is coded via 'ideas and images of the mind', abstract strands of thinking, perception and language, the smallest units of which can be thought of as memes which may be interpreted as: *the smallest element capable of being exchanged, with an associated sense of meaning and interpretation, to another brain.*

Genes, in aggregate, form chromosomes: recognisable, discreet units of a genetic code. Memes, in aggregate, constitute mental models, paradigms, languages, traditions, habits and rules; interrelated units of a cultural or economic code; widely shared patterns of perception, communication, understanding, appreciation and tradition. (Advertising works intensively with memes, if its practitioners only knew it. So does poetry.) Only scale and scholastic origins differentiate a meme, an industrial recipe, a mental model, a paradigm or a language as building blocks of a composite pattern. In an important sense, and in the context of other memes and patterns, memes enable organisations as genes enable organisms in an environment created by other genes.

Several chromosomes constitute a genotype: the total genetic code of a particular organism or genome, the code of a complete species. Without the code neither organism nor species would exist, but they can only become what the code permits. The genotype defines the phenotype, the bodily structure and capabilities, the 'strategy', and behaviour of an organism in its environment and its interactions with other organisms. In aggregate, 'ideas and images of the mind' form a pattern, the memotype of an individual and the memome or 'cultural code' that enables, shapes and influences any organisation and underpins its internal behavioural rules and external stance to strategic relationships.

A pattern requires memes, language, artefacts and symbols to communicate from mind to mind. The converse does not hold. Memes can survive, and adapt themselves to many patterns. The knowledge of how to brew beer is an example. Variants on a 'brewing meme' have survived as a component of thousands of years' worth of cultural evolution. The meme 'alcohol' has an even longer pedigree. It can be traced to a root in the oldest recorded written language, Sumerian, and has, ever since, both enabled, but on occasion limited, the hosts which carried it!

Tom Lloyd[61] suggested considering companies as "alien entities, the first our species has encountered". It may be more helpful to consider memes or patterns in this way, replicators that, once created, seek to take on a life of their own – whether or not that life necessarily benefits the hosts through which they replicate. In doing so, we can consider them as 'selfish', that is *successful* if they encourage behaviour that ensures their own preservation.

The Selfish Meme

 Given the context, the environment, both genes and memes work by ensuring their own propagation rather than necessarily the best interests of the vehicles they create. A prevailing mental infection will blindly seek its own, short term, replication even if by so doing it actually acts against the longer-term interests of its host. Think of doomed corporations clinging to a mental model of a market, or religious fanaticism condemning its adherents to self-destruction. The collective mindset of an organisation is a memetic pattern that resists invasion by competing 'ideas'. It generates its own mental antibodies. The 'not-invented-here syndrome', the 'it cannot be, it isn't possible' response to a new paradigm, or the defensive routines recognised by students of individual learning (see Chapter Five) can all be considered examples.

If the meme is an alien replicator then, from its perspective, success equates with copies made, minds or brains infected. Some viruses confer benefits on their hosts in return for a free ride. Others don't. A parasitic virus that kills its host succeeds if it is copied first. It need not matter to a meme that, several memetic generations from now, it will destroy its host. A gene has no foresight. It carries blindly on until it can replicate no more, when the host body either evolves or dies. One can consider memes as equally blind. They compete only with other memes for success in infecting, and increasing if they can, the available set of infectable hosts, the patterns in the individual and collective minds of organisations. Through competing hosts, natural selection weeds out memes that have no niche in the collective meme pool – just as the same process weeds out genes.

Patterns, memes, may spread, like strategies, through imitation; but they do not rely on it. They propagate, and mutate through societal conditioning, education and linguistic programming, and especially through language: conversation and communication. A meme is transmitted, like a good joke, when it 'infects' another mind. A paradigm is transmitted the more adherents it has. The act of replication is less conscious copying and more unconscious conversion. We learn when we discover something for ourselves – when, in essence, our minds are infected. In biological terms, a brain is a component of a survival machine; one that, by virtue of its being programmable, frees the gene from having to specify everything in advance. By evolving brains, especially human brains, selection has also created the living space of a new, and totally non-genetic, class of replicators. They do not automatically have to act in each other's interests. What is good for the meme, from its perspective, may or may not be good for the genes of the memetic host.

Two examples, the first trivial, may serve to make the point of the meme's perspective. Each is easier to express by attributing to a meme a level of foresight that we are not actually saying it possesses. Bearing that in mind, imagine for a moment that you represent a very simple meme, the phrase 'The Earth is Flat'. The more people who believe this the more successful you are. What is your strategy and market? Two answers spring to (our) mind. There was a time when this meme was able to employ a 'mass-market' strategy. By co-existing with other memes in the religious paralysis of pre-Renaissance Europe it achieved a measure of success in delaying acceptance of the contrary view. In today's world it is restricted to a niche in mildly eccentric flat earth societies.

The flat-earth thought experiment serves to demonstrate another point. For most of history, it simply did not matter to most people whether or not the earth was flat; they were never likely to travel far enough to approach the edge. In that context, the flat earth meme is not granted an environment where its existence matters. The same holds for any new idea. To catch on, to infect minds, it must find or create a context, some niche in the pre-existing pattern, at least to begin with.

Our second example seeks to demonstrate, and to translate the meme's perspective to a more current business issue. Imagine yourself now to be a set of memes for a particular business recipe or fad, say Business Process Re-engineering[62]. You have just arisen through the flux of variation and mental mutation that is the soup of business theory and practice. What determines whether you get copied?

An unfit meme, an experiment that does not generate a result or an idea that is out of step with its time, has less chance of replication. Note by the way that this 'fitness' is relative. It depends on the wider context of other memes in the environment. A recipe that would work perfectly well for one company may not work for another. The unfit may be simply be unlucky enough to evolve in the wrong place; an issue of contingency in evolution that we have yet to examine. But let's assume that you are a fit meme for the particular environment in which you first arise. You work, that is you confer some advantage on your first host organisation.

This may not be enough if you are unfortunate enough to miss out on the confluence of a catchy title, and a skilful advocate. Many companies in the late 1980s and early 1990s evolved or invented something similar, for example Business Process Improvement, Business Process Review, Business Process Transformation, Business Process Management or Business Process Simplification. The dissimilar names described similar recipes for achieving a common business aim, one we examined in Chapter One. Some early inventors of a very similar concept simply gave Business Process Re-engineering a different name. For various reasons, none of the alternative memes caught on. Perhaps they were not catchy enough, perhaps they lacked such an articulate host as Michael Hammer, perhaps 're-engineering' played to the existing memes of the dominant managerial paradigm (c.f. Chapter Three, company as mechanism), or perhaps the alternatives were just unlucky. We may never know. Back to the meme's perspective...

Having survived these first few hurdles you become an established and infectious meme. Positive reinforcement can then take over. Consultants seeking to impress clients, managers seeking to impress shareholders, and business journalists seeking to fill column inches, are all susceptible to catching your particular virus. If you are really successful, institutes and journals devoted to you will create niches for themselves. Somewhere in this process a fundamental switch occurs. Once the bandwagon is rolling, then – from the immediate point of view of the replicative success of a given meme – what counts is less the results to which it originally contributed, in the context in which it first evolved; and more, how infectious it is in a wider world.

Once a meme succeeds in becoming a new fad, gets copied as a recipe or grasped as a new panacea, then it no longer matters that it generates no lasting results, provided only that it keeps spreading. This is the moment when, from the meme's perspective, the momentum it has rather than the difference it makes becomes the determinant of successful replication, at least in the short term. And no replicator can be expected to look beyond its immediate replication. The selfish meme cares not that getting infected may kill the patient. The syphilis virus (again no judgement of BPR is intended!) succeeds, providing it provokes its hosts into transmitting it before it kills them. There is at least an argument that BPR, by evolving to focus exclusively on reducing costs rather than increasing value, has had a not-dissimilar effect, inducing what has been labelled 'corporate anorexia'[63].

The comparison is apt – for anorexia, in its medical form rather than as a metaphor for a business, is a totally memetic disease; one that infects by some estimates one in five of the population of teenage girls in affluent parts of suburban England. It thrives because of the growing prevalence of a pattern of fashion and life-style that is transmitted purely by mental infection. It co-exists with the commercial patterns of numerous companies in the fashion industry, advertising and the media.

And the advertising industry, as we have suggested, also demonstrates the commercial potential of memes. They can add value. People who purchase a particular brand of cigarette, or clothing, or scotch whisky, or vintage cognac in a designer bottle at a duty free shop, are paying for nothing more than the memes associated with the product, the pattern it creates in their minds[64]. Advertising is an industry that taps the practical power of memes, without worrying for a moment about the theory. It is an almost universal component of the industry pattern that any TV commercial ends with a catch phrase: a single meme whose sole purpose is to infect the decision process of the recipient. Consider for example, from the motor industry, "the ultimate driving machine"; "safety in style"; "better by design"; "where quality comes first"; "cars with flair"; "vorsprung durch technik", or: "above all, its a Rover". Those same memes also offer windows into the patterns of the particular companies that use them.

Strategic intents, engaging missions that motivate and release energy in a company, are likewise successful memes. "Put a man on the moon by 1970" or "Maru C", Komatsu's assault on Caterpillar, were infectious visions that became part of a successful pattern in the companies which they enabled. They released purpose and intention. They have been imitated by empty slogans, memes successful at replicating without needing to make a difference. And bland, anodyne wish lists gathering dust on the plaque by reception, lists that even the management who crafted them in a visionary leadership workshop or similar event have forgotten, demonstrate that 'vision and mission', like Business Process Re-engineering, is itself a meme which has spread beyond the need to grant utility to its hosts.

No replicator can exist for long in splendid isolation. Each is subject for its existence to the wider context created by those around it, the other genes in a genotype or the other memes in a pattern. Just as the elements must co-exist, co-evolve, so too must the other levels of the hierarchy; a fact that brings us to the next step in the argument.

Dances with wolves: co-evolving levels of selection

A large part of the selection process in biological research concerns the argument over which unit of the biological hierarchy selection acts on. Is it the individual gene? The complex of co-adapted genes? The individual body built by that complex? The species to which that body belongs? Or is it an altogether higher unit of the taxonomic classification? Careers and institutions have been built on the debate, a debate which nonetheless misses a point in presupposing a unique answer and focusing attention on any one entity.

No organism lives or evolves in isolation. It co-exists and co-evolves with others in its system of relationships. Consider grass, buffaloes and wolves. Conventional linear logic argues on the following lines: the high plains of North America were geologically and climatically suitable for grass. Grass therefore evolved to colonise that niche. Buffaloes then evolved as the fittest organisms for eating the grass. Wolves evolved to eat buffaloes. In reality the three species depend on each other. Grass genes thrive on being grazed, because being grazed encourages their propagation through spreading root systems. By supporting a large population of grazing buffaloes they also defend their territory against competitors such as flowering plants or trees which might otherwise win the competition for sun, soil and sex (genetic replication). Grass and buffaloes are mutually symbiotic. Wolves keep the buffalo population in check and provide an inbuilt constraint against over-grazing. This is not, by the way, an argument for genetic altruism, for the evolution of behaviour that deliberately helps other genes. Each gene, individual and species acts in its own best interests. The result is still a biological oligopoly which set, until less than 250 years ago, the overall rules for most of the other players in the grass-buffalo-wolf ecosystem. From the perspective of each set of genes the other species are 'partners' as well as competitors. Each, in furthering its own replication, contributes to a biological cartel that maintains entry barriers against competition.

 The system need not be entirely stable. The American plains had their own geological learning curve or arms race; encouraging, for example, the evolution of buffaloes with teeth better adapted to grazing, and grasses with stronger stems and more vigorous root systems, but it was locked into an overall pattern, one that did not change until its equilibrium was broken by the arrival of a new biological agent, in this case a wave of human predators. The horse, which enabled not only that invasion but also the linguistic spread of Proto-Indo European (see Chapter One), also evolved on North America's great plains but failed to survive the extinction of large mammals which coincided with the arrival of the first wave of human settlers some 11,000 years ago. Horse genes only survived in Asia (to which they had migrated) and it was from there that they subsequently helped to enable what became, in time, the spread of the Western pattern. Horses were then re-introduced to North America by Europeans in the sixteenth century. They had barely 200 years to become part of the pattern immortalised in countless 'westerns'. Co-evolution moves in mysterious ways, its wonders to self-organise!

Co-evolution is not restricted to the genetic realm. Patterns or memes for fashion, advertising and a media industry co-evolved, as we have seen, into a mutually supporting system. Patterns for motor cars, roads, oil companies, motels, drive-in movie cinemas and out-of-town shopping malls have likewise co-evolved for the last seventy years or so. The personal computer industry shows the same trend, with the apparent lock-in of the PC standard.

So, in both the genetic and the memetic domains, co-evolving entities create stable systems. How? How does a genetic or memetic pattern get locked-in in a world of selfish replicators? How does the self-organising system that is evolution bias itself towards self-maintenance, the ordered domain, the dynamic of stasis interspersed with revolution?

The dynamics of selection

The BPR illustration and similar memetic recipes demonstrate many of the dynamics of natural evolution: an origin in isolation, a struggle among many entrants for an new niche, and a progressive stability. The outcome can owe as much to contingency as to absolute 'fitness'. Why?

We have already alluded to long periods during which a species, or a population of different species, does not change substantially. Five to ten million years is typical and several hundred million possible. Stability is interspersed with mass extinctions and evolutionary radiations. Arguably the most cataclysmic pattern shift on record occurred 65 million years ago when a 10 km diameter asteroid crashed into the sea off southern Mexico[65]. For the preceding 130 million years, dinosaurs and mammals had co-existed but dinosaur genes had established the dominant position. Our ancestors survived in the marginal niches of the Mesozoic economy. For some reason, perhaps a propensity to hibernate, they survived when dinosaurs did not, and were free to radiate into all the newly-vacated ecological niches. Plants also seized the moment. With the demise of the great grazers they took the opportunity to cover as much land as possible in forests.

Few extinctions have such a dramatic cause. Few have such a magnitude. Some are global. Many are confined to particular parts of the earth's surface and are enabled by geological contingency. Some two million years ago, for example, the appearance of the Isthmus of Panama exposed the indigenous South American population to competition that destroyed most of it. Others relate to changes in the world's climates or sea levels, and sometimes to the introduction of new biological competitors, breakthroughs in biological technology.

Whatever the cause, what follows such events shows a similar dynamic. The initial expansion frequently shows a burst of biological experimentation followed by a progressive locking-in to a few species that, between them, dominate a system of ecological relationships. Long before the appearance of human predators, horse evolution on the great plains experimented with different lineages until a single survivor emerged. Any co-adapted set of genomes which can define and dominate a mature system so as to exclude competitors have, in their own selfish interest, a good recipe for survival and replication if they can prevent the entry of competitors. It is not only genes that behave that way. So, too, does any prevailing pattern and the economic or social elite who benefit from it. If the whole population believes in – is 'infected' by – a meme called the 'divine right of kings', then that suits kings. In this instance, the memetic pattern is a natural ally of the king's genes which have an unrivalled opportunity to replicate themselves[66]! Biologists call such an established pattern an Evolutionary Stable Strategy, or ESS. A cartel of genes that achieves an ESS has it made. They set the rules and keep the system stable, which suits their own replication just fine. Mutation is bred-out, swamped in the larger gene pool.

Where, then, do new species come from – particularly if they do not happen to have the assistance of a convenient extinction? The answer seems to be small, reproductively isolated populations; 'peripheral isolates', in the jargon of biology. In a small population, a biological innovation has more chance of surviving, less risk of being swamped by prevailing genetic norms. In 1972 Nils Eldredge and Stephen Gould described geological examples and coined the term 'punctuated equilibrium' to suggest the evolution of new species in short discreet bursts, rather than through a process of continual, gradual, change. Contrary to interpretations by some subsequent guardians of the gradualist paradigm they were not, in so doing, suggesting that evolution worked by any process but natural, Darwinian, selection. They merely pointed out that its rate varied; that it was, geologically, fast relative to the time available. A new species may, if it is a sufficient breakthrough, disturb the wider equilibrium itself. Our own is as good an example as any. A species that does not have such an immediate opportunity may simply bide its time in its niche, like our distant mammalian ancestors, until some other factor grants it the opportunity of spreading and diversifying. Paradoxically, punctuated equilibrium is a natural consequence of systems in which one or more replicators seek to preserve an established order in their own best interests.

A punctuated dynamic has been observed in computer simulations of evolving adaptive systems. It also characterises memetic systems, as does the evolution of new thinking in 'peripheral isolates'. We have already alluded in Chapter Three to the observation that paradigm change mirrors punctuated evolution. It tends to start in populations isolated from the paradigmatic main-stream. The punctuated equilibrium theory itself serves as a handy example, having been born in the minds of two palaeontologists, rather than in the biological community that regarded itself as the custodians of the science of evolution. One eminent British biologist responded that, right or wrong, it was good to see palaeontologists 'returning to the high table'; a metaphor which speaks volumes for the hidden power of patterns! Recall also the example of the science of Complexity evolving in the paradigmatic isolation of Santa Fe.

It is not only paradigms that change first when small populations are isolated from a memetic norm. Corporate change and innovation shows a similar dynamic. Daewoo is Korean, testimony to Michael Porter's observation that innovators typically come from outside the elite of a particular industry. Witness also the relative success of large, centralised change programmes and local initiatives; projects chasing a particular result. Successful companies are finding that product breakthroughs are made by teams taken out of the normal structure and hierarchy of the organisation and deliberately permitted and encouraged to think differently. The technology for personal photocopying, with which Canon nearly destroyed Xerox when they rewrote the rules of the industry, was invented in Xerox's own laboratory but rejected as having no proper commercial application. It depended on a perception of the market as one that competed with photographs to make single copies, not one that competed with printing for bulk, low cost reprographics. It was also driven by Canon's American sales office rather than their own central research structure. One very successful British medical products firm now applies a similar formula to their development projects. As their research director expresses it: "Research is just too important to us to be left to our own laboratory."

In every case the same theme can be seen. It is not the mandated programme, the centralised thinking habits, or the behaviour within normal rules, that produces change and innovation. Mandated programmes of change usually preserve existing patterns, as when people are 'done unto' by new recipes. It is memetically isolated populations that find it easiest to break old codes and change old rules. Interruptions of the established equilibrium, new patterns, threaten old ones as surely as new genes threaten the old, and old patterns resist change as much as old genes. A new species cannot be reinvaded by old genes. An isolated population can be reconverted to old rules and beliefs. Memes benefit from the relative fuzziness of cultural evolution. There is another difference. A gene has no choice but to replicate whilst it may, and neither perhaps does a meme, but we do not have to be victims of passively evolving and adapting replicators. People can choose to break the grip of a prevailing pattern. Punctuating organisational equilibria intentionally, shifting patterns rather than waiting for history to shift them for you, is the key to the self-generative system. Contrary to some very prevalent patterns, leaving it to natural selection does not guarantee a best outcome.

It can be luck

A frequent metaphor for an ecology of evolving species is the fitness 'landscape'. If the landscape is a series of hills, each species represents a particular summit. Once genetically locked-in, a pattern can only grow its own peak. Yet climbing may be a recipe for only limited success. Imagine starting a walk and deciding which direction to go by always going up. You will reach a summit but it may not be the one you want. To reach a different place, a trip downwards is needed. Natural selection is frequently misunderstood, not least by those who regard it as a justification of unconstrained economic competition, as a mechanism that will, inevitably, produce some 'best' result, some survival of the 'fittest'. There is a powerful argument to the contrary. Selection may only magnify initial differences, grow particular peaks. Which peaks get locked-in is a matter of chance as much as any absolute fitness.

The greatest evolutionary flowering in history followed the emergence of multi-celled life. That 'event', the so-called Cambrian explosion 570 million years ago, actually lasted 30 million years during which organisms 'experimented' with the new 'technologies' of multi-celling and skeletons. The first multi-celled designs to evolve found a world of unparalleled opportunity with a sea full of bacteria to eat. One of the bacteria's side-effects was to regulate the oxygen in the atmosphere. As the new predators grazed their way through the ocean the oxygen balance was disturbed, favouring further evolution of the new arrivals on the organic scene. All the high level organic designs for the next 600 million years, today's phyla, were locked-in in the process. Everything since has been a variant on one or other of those basic themes; peaks coming and going on the main ranges of the fitness landscape. What's more, several other phyla attempted to enter the Cambrian 'market'. As Stephen Gould has argued in *Wonderful Life* and many essays, luck, contingency and blind chance played just as large a part in determining the eventual survivors as did selection through absolute 'fitness'.

Wonderful Life narrates the story of a geological freak known as The Burgess Shale: a rock formation found only in one cliff 8,000 feet up a Canadian mountain. It preserves a chance accident 550 odd million years old, when a mud slide buried the population of a particular lagoon. This chance event happened to kill and bury, indiscriminately, everything living in the lagoon at the time, including animals that, because they had no hard shells, would not normally leave behind traces of their existence. In the early 1970s, the professor of Geology at Cambridge University, Harry Whittington, and two research students re-examined the fossils from the Burgess Shale; the first such re-examination since their discovery sixty years earlier by the then *eminence gris* of American palaeontology, Burgess, who had managed to convince himself and others that each of these strange creatures was a recognisable precursor of a better known group of animals: that they all belonged to known phyla and were thus entirely consistent with an orderly, linear paradigm of evolution.

Truth proved stranger. When re-examined, the fossils turned out to represent, not slightly unusual members of known phyla, but instead fundamentally different organic designs. More unique phyla were found in that one rock formation than in the entire record of life on earth everywhere – and every when – else combined[67]. When the biological competency for multi-celled life was just getting into its stride as an organic technology, it experimented with a vengeance. And the smallest, puniest, and least abundant design of all was the ancestor of all chordates, including ourselves: an insignificant worm. It is easy after the event to justify why the chordate design was inherently superior, but then, post-hoc historical rationalisation is the perquisite of the victor. Perceptions apart, there is no *a priori* reason why some designs survived and others did not.

The manuscript of this book is being prepared on a computer equipped with a QWERTY keyboard. It happens that the keyboard layout is not the critical constraint, the bottleneck, that governs the speed of production. Two fingers are quite enough for my thinking speed. For a skilled typist, however, the QWERTY keyboard is, most assuredly, a bottleneck. Such a person underutilises the processing speed of any computer to which the keyboard is attached. Yet the QWERTY meme survived the evolution of the microchip because it dominated an established pattern; one that evolved for a different world. It was originally designed to slow typists down; a solution to the endemic problem of typewriters continually jamming – not typewriters of the 'modern', that is the immediately pre-electronic, design but typewriters of a much older, nineteenth century design[68]. The slow keyboard happened to be adopted by Remington for its conventional typewriters. The Remington design then happened to be chosen as a standard for shorthand and typing courses. There was no obvious technological superiority in QWERTY, even in the 1880s when alternative designs of keyboard were last seriously competing with each other. It happened to attract more users, and the more it had, the less chance a competitor had of penetrating the market. Later, far more ergonomic designs of computer 'interfaces' employing massive ingenuity, have sunk without trace. To them that hath an edge, evolution giveth more!

Orthodox economic and business theory is beginning to recognise and acknowledge the same phenomenon, dubbing it 'The Law of Increasing Returns'. The story of the gradual acknowledgement by economic orthodoxy of this challenge to the conventional paradigm of equilibrium economics is told in Mitchell Waldrop's *Complexity*. The coining of new ideas in the relative isolation of an institute in Vienna by Brian Arthur, now Professor of Population Studies and Economics at Stanford University, provides another case of the punctuated equilibrium model of academic innovation and a new idea resisted by the defensive routines of established patterns (in this case the economic establishment wedded to a paradigm of equilibrium economics).

A now classic example of increasing returns in action is the evolution of domestic videotape formats. Three designs were brought to the market when the technology first appeared. Phillips' Video-2000 format perished quickly, leaving the field to the competition between VHS and Beta. Much rational judgement still says that the latter was the superior technology; however chance variation, (or perhaps JVC's different dispersal strategy for the technology) gave VHS an early lead in market share[69]. The result was a growing incentive, in terms of choice of pre-recorded tapes and of lower costs, for subsequent buyers of video recorders to choose the VHS format, increasing its relative share and competitive advantage, and so on. It is a graphic example of what Systems Thinking would call a successful dynamic. Market selection acts, not necessarily to choose the 'best' solution, but to reinforce and magnify an initial difference, to grow a fitness peak out of a small hummock. Which particular hummock grows may be as much blind chance as superiority of initial design. The emergence of Business Process Re-engineering from the competing memes of process management is another case, as are the development of many new technologies and new markets.

Closing the circle

Both the genetic and the memetic domain show similar cycles of punctuation, adaptive radiation, lock-in and stability then punctuation again. In the language of complexity theory it is the radiative phase, the new market, that is closest to the edge-of-chaos, that state of self-organising criticality or bounded instability pilots know as 'fly-by-wire'. This is when new genetic or memetic entities, new patterns, emerge; self-organising out of the interconnection of either genetic codes or a critical density of ideas and language. Through selection and contingent chance in the early dynamics of the system, certain entities survive and replicate more successfully than others. As they do so they are increasingly able to impose and maintain stability. The selfish pattern is served if it can move the system away from the generative to the more stable and predictable; imposing its own order on natural 'chaos'.

Ultimately, the tension between emergent order, new evolution, and preservation of the existing pattern becomes too great. Either through pure chance (asteroid impacts), the system reaching its inherent limits to growth (environmental feedback) or the evolution of new, equilibrium shifting competitors (new organic or cultural capabilities) the equilibrium is punctuated. The system is pulled back towards the edge of chaos, as when crisis forces change upon a company. Evolution forces revolution.

Companies, and other forms of organisation, seek the ordered domain where the dominant patterns can prevail. But consider either the former Soviet Union or the command economy of a large corporation. Unfortunately for either, in a complex and co-evolving world, the price of too much order, the cost of being too far from the edge of chaos, is the loss of adaptive capacity and the risk that the crash, when it comes, throws the organisation straight into total chaos, completely fragments it. We consider what this means for companies in Chapter Eight.

One can see the phases at work in one of the simplest models of the formation of teams, individuals coming together to achieve a collective end that they cannot achieve separately; a microcosm of the emergence of a company. At its simplest, the process has been modelled as:

- *Forming*   The coming together of the team members.

- *Storming*   The tension, dialogue, discussion[70], and uncertainty of the early stages of a team, or indeed a new business.

- *Norming*   The development of a tacit set of rules, a shared context out of which the team can operate, one that implicitly determines membership of the team.

- *Performing*   Getting on with whatever task is needed – and in the world of the control paradigm, whatever task is assigned.

One could view this as a journey from chaos, through emergent order, to stability. The storming phase equates with the 'edge-of-chaos' of complexity theory, the domain of emergent order. New ideas emerge and compete for mental space. Norming, and what is conventionally held to be performing, represents the lock-in of a particular order. Unfortunately, as many who have participated in teams, or in advising teams will know, the storming process is one that people are usually anxious to have done with as soon as possible. The subsequent norming may leave unresolved tensions and uneasy compromise but a certain pattern of thinking prevails. Performing is then both enabled and limited, for the fixed domain is not one of spontaneous creativity. Neither is a stable ecosystem or a company in the grip of a dominant pattern, a set of rules, and thinking that is keeping it stuck. Achieving different levels of performance frequently requires a return to storming before re-forming and performing differently. And such a departure is not easy to achieve; the very name we give it – 'storming' – carries connotations of disruption. Yet getting to different norms and a different level of performance requires an interruption of prevailing patterns, a departure from too much order. The interruption is frequently avoided until forced by some crisis.

There are two routes to the transformation in the memetic system. One is to wait until the crisis forces a response; to have your equilibria punctuated for you. The other is to intentionally shift the limiting pattern. To do so is to venture towards chaos. One cannot get from a peak, from one point on a co-evolved fitness landscape to another, without returning to the valley. You can't get there from here... The departure is easier if one can acknowledge patterns as just that; replicators, bent on their own preservation; and question them, not as 'right or wrong', but as 'limiting or not'.

 ## Summary

We have set out an unconventional perspective on companies, arguing that they are best interpreted as vehicles, or hosts, for a meme's – or pattern's – replication. This perspective explains the similar rhythms, at vastly different timescales, of organic and organisational evolution.

Companies, by virtue of 'the selfish meme' and the pattern's desire to self-replicate, demonstrate strong stability-seeking tendencies that provide significant order and stability. Too much order, however, and the system is unable to adapt to changes around it, or to create changes which may be more favoured by the environment around it.

When looked at in a context of a co-evolving pattern with other companies – competitors, suppliers, customers etc., whole industries may
similarly become apparently locked-in to an established pattern of
order, and sometimes, despite the rhetoric of apparent good intention,
appear unable to break out.

Evolution points to punctuated equilibria and complexity theory to
new emergent order from the edge of chaos, yet the established patterns seem very persistent. The breakdown of established order for a
new order has always involved a price to be paid. It doesn't come for
free. There's the price of disorder, the letting-go of what is known and
comfortable for something unknown. This cost, this price, is clearly
less to the new entrant for they have less invested in the established
order, they have less to lose and much more to win. Thus it is, in
human terms, that new patterns are likely to be found at the edge, in
isolated populations from the mainstream.

Does that then mean that established mainstream organisations
cannot evolve at a pace that is needed to adapt to changing circumstances, if at all? One reaction is defensive, it is to protect established
patterns and to fight off any new entrant. This often serves merely to
delay the day of reckoning when patterns need to shift, whilst serving
at the same time to lock people in to the prevailing pattern. The key
question is less how are patterns shifted, and more how we ourselves
can shift patterns, particularly when they are well-established.

Primary Sources

(Hodgson 1993) reviews the intertwining epistemolo-
gies of economics and biology since the eighteenth century and makes the case for renewed efforts towards a
synthesis. Morgan (1986) summarises the equivalent tradition in
organisational theory. Modern thinking in biology and palaeontology
concerning the evolutionary process and history is made accessible
through a number of works, notably Dawkins (1976 & 1989, 1982,
1986) and Gould (e.g. 1987, 1989, 1991, 1993). Other useful intro-
ductions are Wills (1989), Maynard-Smith (1989), Diamond (1993)

and Jones (1993). The theory of punctuated equilibrium in evolution (Eldredge and Gould 1972) is finding its way slowly into debates concerning the social sciences (Somit and Petersen, 1992), even whilst it and many other debates in biology compete for paradigmatic space (Hull 1988). Gersick (1991) explicitly used punctuated equilibrium as a model for organisational change, as did Price and Evans (1993) who coupled it with the idea of paradigmatic isolation (Price 1994, 1995). Price and Shaw (1995) discuss the evolution of business fads as memes. They and Beer et al (1992) provide case examples of change programmes not producing change, whilst Nonaka and Takeuchi (1995) explore the Japanese process of new product development and knowledge creation as analogous to punctuated equilibria. Pascale (1991) also alludes to the analogy. Rothschild (1992) draws an explicit parallel between DNA and technological information, his candidate as a corporate replicator. He provides interesting case histories of the punctuated model of technological evolution, especially the case of the displacement of the Newcomen steam engine by James Watt's improved design. Lloyd (1990) prefers strategy as the replicator, whilst Nelson and Winter (1982) make the case for habits and routines. A wide literature referred to in other chapters discusses the power of organisational and individual defensive routines. The comparison of memetic infection with learning can be contrasted with the theory of Neuro Linguistic Programming, one of whose pioneers, Bateson (1973, 1979), was explicit about evolution as learning.

The departure from a uniformitarian paradigm in geology is marked, among others by Ager (1973) who coined the 'Life of a Soldier' metaphor. Offshore oil technology gave us the science of sequence stratigraphy. The pattern of extinctions in geological history owes much to David Raup (1993) whose original work is also cited by Eldredge's (1991) discussion of the causes of mass extinctions. Kauffman (1993) uses the same data to posit a departure from pure self-organised criticality in the biological record. His contribution, and that of other pioneers to the more general theory of complexity and Holland's theory of complex adaptive systems is summarised by Waldrop (1992), whilst Cohen and Stewart (1994) provide a different perspective and a review of Chaos theory. They, and Kay (1993) use the example of the ice-cream sellers on the beach which we have modified. Gell-Mann (1995) discusses the theory of self-organising systems from the perspective of a theoretical physicist and suggests the generic term 'schemata' for all patterns or replicators. Dennett (1995) has written a detailed examination of the philosophy of selection in both genetic and memetic domains. The concepts of self-organising systems in social and economic contexts is receiving increasing attention (e.g. Stacey 1993a, 1993b; Allen 1994; Parker and Stacey 1994). Winograd and Flores (1987) and Mingers (1995) draw on another approach to biological systems, the concept of autopoiesis or self-referral (e.g. Maturana 1970, 1975; Maturana and Varela, 1980). Tylecote (1993) presents an evolutionary account of economic long waves. Our comments were also informed by Forrester (1961). References to work on business strategy and business process re-engineering are covered in Chapters Eight and Nine. Brodie (1995) and Lynch (1996) have recently published popular books on the subject of memetics. The comparisons of organisations and organisms have been advanced by Hurst (1995) and De Geus (1997).

While this book was in press we have seen MacCarthy et al's (1997) demonstration that an evolutionary tree – a cladogram in biological terminology – of manufacturing technologies can be constructed. Their work provides striking, and independent support for the scientific ideas advanced in this chapter.

5

Patterns that prison: an exploration of personal and interpersonal dynamics

"On the basis of avoided tests, people conclude that constraints exist in the environment and that limits exist in their repertoire of responses. Inaction is justified by the implantation, in fantasy, of constraints and barriers that make action 'impossible'. These constraints, barriers, (and) prohibitions then become prominent 'things' in the environment. They also become self-imposed restrictions on the options that managers consider and exercise when confronted with problems. Finally, these presumed constraints, when breached by someone who is more doubting, naive, or uninformed, often generate sizeable advantages for the breacher."

Karl Weick[71]

Having argued that organisations are the creations of their memetic patterns we now turn to look at the reality and effect of such patterns at the individual and interpersonal level.

 A capacity for 'memetic transposition' enables companies and people to change. That capacity implies interrupting the patterns encoded in individual minds and the 'conversation' by which patterns of memes are replicated from mind to mind. This chapter seeks the theoretical foundation for such interventions. A view of minds as the creations of memetic patterns, transmitted by, in the broadest sense, language, explains many observations from the sciences of cognition and behaviour and shows how 'patterns' become established. Indeed, they exist in the 'alreadiness' of the patterns we encounter. We participate in their self-maintenance. For an individual or group the phenomenon of lock-in to a particular, self-maintaining, memetic configuration can be described as 'stuckness': a more abrupt word, yet perhaps one that is easier to relate to on a personal and interpersonal basis. In essence this chapter seeks to explain why people tend to get stuck in interpersonal and personal patterns; patterns that limit what could be. What 'is' – that is, what is perceived to be from the perspective of a given pattern, – limits what is possible.

Most of the time we cannot 'see' that we are stuck and when challenged in the matter of our stuckness tend to deny it. Somehow stuckness is viewed in negative terms, as a challenge to our independence and freedom, our intelligence, or whatever. Yet without such stuckness, in the sense of constraints and limits, social living would hardly be possible. The patterns that exist provide order where there might otherwise be anarchy and chaos.

Too much order though, and we can be frozen in time, unable to evolve for the rigidity of the patterns that we are in. Just as variability, genetic diversity, is a key requirement for biological evolution so, too, is memetic diversity a key for company and societal evolution. Yet there is a tendency to seek the efficiencies of the routine and to avoid the edges of chaos. The routine offers the comfort of the known. It is tempting to say that, by comparison, the unknown offers only discomfort. A peculiar state of affairs when, earlier in our lives, the unknown offered the promise of daring adventure. What has changed? It is perhaps only our orientation to the unknown. Perhaps our pattern has shifted as we have matured, we have become less adventurous, more knowledgeable, more stuck!

But we are not equating knowledge with stuckness. Although it may be said that some are stuck with their knowledge whilst others are liberated by their innocence, this may be mere trickery of words, or perhaps says something of the relatedness of the person to their knowledge. He or she who is able to say, with humility, that the more they know the more they 'see' what they don't know, is perhaps less stuck in a pattern. But then there's a wider pattern, an unwritten rule, that suggests that humility does not pay, at least in commercial and academic worlds!

We are all stuck in patterns and this condition is neither to be celebrated nor castigated; it merely is. What provides an opportunity for someone to make a difference is enough freedom from an established pattern to create a new pattern. This is not without risk. To accept what is, and to play to what is, offers a less risky strategy – yet less opportunity to make a difference. In what follows, we attempt to unfold, to reveal, some of what exists in terms of the patterns at the personal and interpersonal levels. We will be inquiring into how these operate and asking what happens when such patterns are put under increased tension? In doing so, we begin to dance with some of that which is uniquely human, and to suggest that people are sufficiently gifted to generate new patterns that can influence their future. We invite readers to join with us in exploring this whole 'mess'[72] – this complexity – of patterns that operate at the personal and interpersonal level. Yet we might also be grateful for the mess, for without its inherent variability, without the chaos of the human condition, our stuckness would be severe indeed.

The brain and meme to mind

We have so far discussed patterns without considering their physical existence. But we argue that, in fact, they have existence, in human brains and in the languages and cultural artefacts that are used to transmit ideas and images between brains. The brain, a biological endowment whose capacity and composition results from genetic inheritance, is the living space for a host of mental and perceptual patterns, the living space for a plethora of memes. Philosopher Daniel Dennett[73] puts it well:

"A human mind is an artefact constructed when memes restructure a human brain in order to make it a better habitat for memes."

 We introduced the meme in Chapter Four. It is any unit of cultural transmission propagated from mind to mind. As Dawkins invited readers to consider with the idea of 'God', some memes can be traced back through many centuries, if not millennia. They demonstrate enduring survival value and even, as with 'God', evolve independently, with different arrangements of particular memes in different and separate communities[74]. Over time the 'God' meme has attracted physical cultural artefacts such as temples and churches and powerful symbolic behaviours such as sacrifices, excommunication or baptism. As Dawkins put it, the meme of God, in a process similar to the survival of genes, survived in the context of "a large complex of mutually assisting religious memes", where ideas such as heaven, hell, faith, and Satan combined to forge powerful memetic patterns. How have they endured? He suggests that the God meme's survival value in the meme pool results from its "great psychological appeal". It provides at least a superficially plausible answer to deep and profound questions and some hope of a difference in the next world if not in this.

Lest this seem an overly cynical rationale for the meme's survival we would add the social appeal, and even benefit, of the pattern. Faith makes a profound difference, conveys a benefit, to many individuals. In a wider context it provides order, albeit religious order, and a source of values and beliefs. Without some such shared and pervasive pattern the foundation for joint social undertakings is severely weakened. But the same society that is enabled and bonded by shared faith is limited and weakened, when blind faith obstructs change or encourages actions to assure a meme's propagation at the expense of its host's, or other, lives. (The doctrine of celibacy is an interesting use of a meme to demonstrate the power of spiritual belief over the genetic imperative.)

The capability of our brains to contain and transmit shared patterns is the foundation for consistency and organisation in our personal and social worlds. The latent potential of the brain provides for the concept and the reality of the 'mind'. But note that the nature of reality has shifted from a referent to a physical reality of grey matter located in the skull of Homo Sapiens, to a human concept and the somewhat more abstract construction of the 'mind'. The biological capacity of the brain, with the progressive development of the species, has permitted the evolution of the idea or meme of the mind. There is a pattern to any mind, a pattern that is in part-permitted – enabled and limited – by the structure of the brain and the information encoded in

DNA; and, in part, by the information encoded in our memetic inheritance. In short, the information encoded in genes gives rise to brains and that in memes gives rise to mind. Thus, similar biological endowments in terms of brains, exposed to different memetic inheritances, produce very dissimilar minds!

The distinction between brain and mind can be captured in the dance between the two. The physiological capacity of the brain, particularly in humans the higher cortex, provided the capacity, over time and through a pattern of ideas, to make available and increase our awareness of the brain. Thus the brain's capacity, with learning over time, provides the mind through which we can study the brain. We have the brain to mind, and the mind to study the brain. The mind is more than the brain; it is the brain-in-use, programmed with the memetic inheritance of the culture and the unique experience of the individual. Thus we may speak of mindsets at the individual level and of shared mindsets or paradigms between groups of people.

 The brain is an evolutionary endowment to the human species that, by providing a context for memetic evolution and the advent of various human technologies, now grants us the capacity to potentially destroy our world, to go in search of other physical worlds, and/or to create environments of our choosing. The human brain, its capacity and potential has been so useful to the species largely because it has been so relatively little prescribed or programmed, at least in its origins. It is minimally specified; a trick many companies are now trying to emulate (Chapter Eight). Though committed areas of the brain perform certain mental functioning, capacity, plasticity, and redundancy are built in to the system. Some parts can perform the function of others. We are born with spare, or unused capacity. This pinkish grey blob of living tissue that is our brain has been estimated to be made up of 10,000 million neurones in the cerebral cortex alone, some of these with an estimated total of ten thousand synaptic links. Patterns are, in some way, stored in this neural network. We may imagine that the interconnectedness of this complex system is profound, with the brain in aggregate being responsible for all of our mental functions, the control centre for movement, the centre of human emotion, and the central receiver and interpreter of a host of sensors from around the body. No wonder that it is but a small margin of our brain activity that enters consciousness!

Our brains and other aspects of our anatomical apparatus also endow us with the capacity for speech and communication. That capacity, or more accurately that potential (for it is a latent capacity) is released through our cultural inheritance. We are provided with the physical and mental apparatus; yet the level of speech and the degree of communication is, at least in part, a reflection of cultural transmission. Whereas our brain is a level of construct – a linguistic term – that refers to a physical reality, our mind is a level of construct that is more abstract, a stage removed from physical reality. As our brain has evolved over time so too has our mind: each through the processes of variation, natural selection, and replication. The difference is that whereas we cannot change what we have inherited as a brain, we can change our mind. What gives us this potential is our capacity to learn; though learning itself is more than a mental phenomenon, it takes place within a society and within a history of others.

How we learn to 'see' is a good example of an innate capacity developed within such a society of others.

How perception works

A geological metaphor provides an image of the physiology and psychology of perception[75]. Imagine a landscape, eroded over time to provide streams, rivulets, and rivers interspersed between higher plateaux. It provides a simple example of a self-organising, locked-in, system. If one can imagine the virgin landscape as being relatively flat, perhaps gently undulating, then as rain falls so it tends to find the paths of least resistance: the soft rocks and minor depressions of the undulating territory. Over time, accumulations of rainfall carve out stream and river beds and settle into pools and lakes. Any new rainfall will no longer find its own way but will rather take, and reinforce, the already sculpted way. Though the falling rain may be evenly distributed across the landscape, in its collection and flow across the land, it will tend towards a predetermined route, one taken by previous rainfalls.

Just as the rainfall follows established routes, so perception follows established ways of 'seeing'. Technically, even if the light sources which perturb the back of the retina are identical, what will be noticed from all that can be seen will depend on the perceptual lens through which we view the world. The optimist's half-full glass is the pessimist's half-empty one. What is 'there' is not wholly independent of the viewer, as experts in quantum physics will acknowledge. What is there is what we have been 'trained' (or conditioned or have learnt) to see. (So what is 'really' there?) Our training in terms of our maps and our lenses means that we will not see certain other things which do not fit with the map or lens we carry. We may discard, indeed we can be blind to, anomalies that do not fit. The self-organised pattern which we call our thinking grants a particular perceptual blindness and rigidity to our perceptions of the world – the very foundation of such things as stereotypes and prejudices – common to all human experience and found, for example, in the way one department in a company may view another.

What holds for light waves perturbing the retina, holds equally for acoustic perturbances of the eardrum. Exploring the analogy further we could say that an idea, a single thought, an utterance, a meme in fact, is like the single raindrop. It falls with others upon a pre-formed perceptual landscape. Isolated thoughts gather together in a string – a pattern of co-existing memes – which we might compare to a few drops congregating together in a splash of water. With sufficient mass the splash of water starts to flow into streams and rivers which are, if we like, the connectors between the raindrops and the pools and lakes, if not the oceans, of our thoughts. The pools and lakes we may view as concept pools and theory lakes. Thus a self-organising system is inherited and developed in which the flow of perception takes a certain course, it follows a certain pattern, a largely given paradigm.

Patterns in the brain influence 'seeing' (or more accurately perceiving). Patterns, and seeing, influence behaviour – so that behaviour follows certain patterns. It may be argued that we see the world less as it is and more as we are, and that we act perfectly consistently with how we see the world. There is a certain alignment with our thinking, our perceptions and our actions-in-the-world. Thinking, seeing, and behaving tend to follow pre-existing patterns[76].

Well-established patterns become social and cultural norms and preserve and replicate themselves through their influence on people's ongoing perception of the world. The cultural tradition is passed on by the language and perceptual habits acquired by succeeding generations and by that which we inherit through the cultural artefacts of previous generations, for example their temples, books, theories, myths and legends, as well as through our own processes of informal and formal education. These may take the form of individual units of cultural transmission – 'memes' – or the broader patterns of thinking which Kuhn dubbed paradigms.

What this amounts to is the assertion that our perceptions of the world provide for our very relatedness to the world before us – both in terms of what is seen or noticed, and the meaning or interpretation we grant to what is noticed. Perception grants what may be termed our Being-in-the-world (an expression first coined by Heidegger[77] in the term 'Dasein'). If we can interrupt the pattern of thinking, eschew our memetic and paradigmatic inheritance so as to think, and see, newly, then new behaviours may naturally follow. To achieve such a difference in thinking and seeing we may need to create a different language.

The constraints and liberation of language

By language we mean any description of a perceived reality, any form of symbolic representation or expression of some selected aspect of reality, imagination, or exploration, whether such relates to internal or external domains. The nature of the symbolism can vary and will include among others the spoken word, the written word, mathematics, various sign languages, and art as language. Communication we take as the conveyance of meaning, whether or not the meaning actually conveyed was intended. Conversation for us is the process of communication. It embraces more than speaking and listening and includes conversation that is communicated in physical forms through art and architecture, texts, and other media as well as meaning conveyed by actions and reactions. Human action carries with it communication and is itself a conversation. Small acts can convey much meaning. Defined thus, 'conversation' is the act of memetic transmission[78], the medium of memetic exchange, the 'currency of companies' by which shared meanings, understandings and patterns are created and expressed as unwritten codes and conventions. (Thus we arrive at an explanation for phenomena discussed in Chapters One to Three).

We 'see' and interpret the world largely through language. Language grants the ability, not only to describe and explain, but to pass on such descriptions and explanations through the myths, stories and theories of successive generations. It falls on, and moulds or reinforces, the existing perceptual landscape, yet also grants the potential, through different thinking and through invention or configuration of a different language, to create new theories, descriptions and even realities. The narrative of language permits not only description of what is – perceived current reality – but also description of what could be there, what is desirable, etc. In describing some future state and delineating some ways of getting there, it is possible for that reality – that future state of affairs – to be not only invented but also realised.

The great gift of language is not only that it enables us to think, for there are ways of thinking that do not require language, but that it enables us to communicate to one another and across generations. This transmission through the generations is the stuff of myths and legends (verbally transmitted culture), enormously abetted in more recent centuries by the technologies of the written word and, more recently, by those of electronic transmission and computerisation. (Recall PIE from Chapter One as an evolving linguistic tradition.)

The languages we inherit, how we represent and express things, package the world in a certain way. Just as with cartoons of political figures, the distinctions encoded in language call forth a certain noticing; they call attention to some things and not others in the environment within and around one. Our languages differ not only on a national and regional scale but also on a technical, company or social group scale, providing a different, culturally attuned, noticing. What the geologist 'sees' with his vocabulary and where he goes to look is different from what the psychologist sees! Our different languages provide different frames of reference for interpreting the world. At one level these are encoded in the grammar (the structure) of the language, at another in the distinctions (the content) of the language itself. Such interpretations have not only a utility or expressive value; more simply, they are the way that the world is understood. Our languages are simultaneously the maps of our perceptual landscape and the agents that modify that landscape.

Bruce Gregory in his book *Inventing Reality: Physics as Language*[79] explores the relationship between language and the world. Even with the relatively precise language of physics, he asks: "How much of what we find in the world is the result of the way we talk about it?". He goes on to suggest that:

"Language tells us what the world is made of, not because language somehow accurately captures a world independent of language, but because it is the heart of our way of dealing with the world. When we create a new way of talking about the world, we virtually create a new world."

Language constantly frames the way we see and understand the world. This interpretation does not deny a physical world independent of, and in interaction with, human beings. That world did without us for 4.5 billion years until memes and minds evolved which could describe or theorise about that world. They do so in terms of categories and relations encoded in language. Our ways of talking about the world are not 'the world' as though independent of us and our concepts, just as talking about or describing our experiences is not the same as the actual experience at a unique moment in time. Gregory first quotes, and then expands upon, Einstein:

"This universe of ideas is just as little independent of our experience as clothes are from the human body. What we say about the world, our theories, are like garments – they fit the world to a lesser or greater degree, but none fit perfectly, and none are right for every occasion. There seems to be no already-made world, waiting to be discovered. The fabric of nature, like all fabrics, is woven by human beings for human purposes."

 The correspondence theory of language on which much of the rationalistic tradition is based can be questioned. Language is, rather, a self-organised system of symbolic utterances by which we make our way in the world by virtue of a 'community of shared assumptions, conventions, and understandings'. In the terms of Chapter Two, there is a rich body of unwritten rules in which we participate in the game of language.

The *potential* of language is enabled by our biological endowment of brain capacity, larynx, hearing, etc. The *practice* of language, its patterns, our ways of speaking and listening, has evolved over time and is more a matter of our cultural inheritance and individual learning. It continues to evolve as an aspect of living human systems. Witness, for example, the emergent language of our computer age: completely baffling to the uninitiated, yet offering useful(?) distinctions to the experts.

Words take on meaning in the context of their use. Without a shared referential background there is no shared communication. If two people literally do not speak each other's language they are likely to take no meaning from each other's utterances[80]. If they do there is a greater risk of each taking different meanings from the same linguistic meme. The shared background both enables and limits. It enables communication to the extent that the parties share broadly similar interpretations. The lock-in of a particular vocabulary grants the 'benefit' of a shared sense of reality, confirmed membership of a world of similar dwellers – 'insiders' – and a measure of apparent certainty. It limits in so far as the members may be stuck in those interpretations.

Outsiders can offer the potential of a different language. As such they may offer the freshness of new insights and interpretations. But recall the view-point of the selfish meme, pursuing its own replication. The new language, the different meme species, threatens the territory (the mind) of the current meme. At the memetic level, rejection of the new serves the interests of the old. Such a thing as, say, the idea of commitment, when viewed from the controller's world, occurs as a constraint or threat. In this process of memetic defence one can see an explanation for much that has been observed about human learning and cognitive patterns.

Cognitive patterns

Cognition is a term that largely refers to the processes of knowing, learning and thinking. Without undertaking a detailed psychological review of these phenomena we do wish to see how such processes combine into a cognitive system or pattern that is, in the absence of any variation, self-maintaining. The relationships between these processes and the communities and contexts in which they take place may be complex yet they are sufficiently reinforcing to form stable patterns. If cognition is the mental processing that is to do with knowing, then what is it that goes on inside (and between) the heads of people that influences *action*? Its importance to organisations is summed up in Karl Weick's[81] provocative suggestion:

"Insufficient attention has been paid to the possibility that, for want of a thought, the organisation was lost."

Weick describes an organisation as "a body of thought thought by thinking thinkers" and suggests that the term 'organisation' is but a snapshot of ongoing processes in which there are thoughts, thinking practices, and thinkers. This brings us close to the paradigms of Chapter Three which were described as not only the content of thinking – our thoughts – but also the process or pattern of thinking applied to such thoughts: what we think with. Combining conversation with thinking Weick says:

"Managerial work can be viewed as managing myths, images, symbols and labels. The much-touted 'bottom line' of the organisation is a symbol, if not a myth. The manager who controls labels that are meaningful to organisational members can segment and point to portions of their experience and label it in consequential ways so that employees take that segment more seriously and deal with it in a more organisationally appropriate manner. Because managers traffic so often in images, the appropriate role for the manager may be evangelist rather than accountant."

From the perspective of the controlling manager talk of evangelism may not strike a chord. Yet the literal evangelist seeks to convert others to a particular set of religious beliefs and associated memes. In just the same way, does not the new manager seek to convert others to some set of shared purposes, meanings and actions?

 Organisations and environments are not just objective entities in the world out-there. They are also constructed and interpreted through the eyes and minds of an organisation's members. How we choose to talk and think about our organisations and environments in part creates them. Organisation and environment are interpreted, in the language of Chapter Three, through the tradition of which we are part and it is that interpreted or constructed context which we perceive as unwritten rules and respond to through our organisational acts.

Chapter Three introduced the idea of paradigms as our mental maps upon the world, and reminded that the map is not the territory. Our representations of the world are just that, representations. Yet the map *is* the territory if people treat it as such. Things are real if we treat them as real. Weick refers to the work of Axelrod, Bartlett, Neisser and others to introduce the notion of schema as:

"...an abridged, generalised, corrigible organisation of experience that serves as an initial frame of reference for action and perception."

A schema is a shorthand pattern which, like a map, represents a much more complicated reality. Take walking, a complex dynamic movement of a bipedal mammal. To programme this mammal for every eventuality in the matter of walking would necessitate a complex and conditional specification. Nature's solution was to merely programme the capacity to walk alongside the capacity to learn to respond to different surfaces and conditions; a simple schema of relatively minimal specification which can guide us, yet be adapted to meet changing circumstances. Like the schema for the driving of a motor vehicle, it can become a habit.

The sophistication of the twentieth century belies our acquired capacity to perform the feat of driving. The technology of the car is largely taken for granted. In the West, at least, cars are a common reality. They occur as 'normal'. Familiarity tends to breed acceptance. We do not 'see' the complex array of different technologies and the history of memes that constitute such a thing as 'car'. Our language denotes a tool, sometimes a love affair, which we learn to drive. With experience our driving mostly becomes routine, we can do it without thinking about it, at least until some significant change in circumstance, for example the 'peripherique' around Paris at rush hour, shifts our awareness. Driving when you have to constantly maintain awareness and concentration can be exhausting; driving with familiarity and ease leaves spare capacity for other things[82].

Weick refers to Neisser's perceptual cycle to demonstrate how schemata constrain seeing. This can be paralleled to the view of perception as a self-organising system described above.

Weick reports Neisser as noting that schemata are:

"...analogous to things like formats in computer programming language, plans for finding out about objects and events, and genotypes (emphasis added) that offer possibilities for development along certain lines. Neisser posits a perceptual cycle to illustrate how schemata operate and this graphic provides a useful medium to describe how organisations affect their own cognition."

Where Neisser suggests that the schema directs perceptual exploration, we are suggesting that it operates through memetic patterns held in the mind which direct or frame what we notice in the world around us. We are adding the suggestion that memes create a mind of their own. Perceptual exploration samples the available perceptual horizon providing information on the basis of which the original schema may be confirmed or modified. In other terms, the noticing granted by the memetic pattern operates in such a way as to get us to select, or sample, from the array of all possible information available in the environment, that information which abets the pattern's primary concern: its own replication.

Two or more people given the same perceptual horizon or environment may notice very different things, because they are each looking through different memetic patterns. They may even 'see' what is not there, either because they expect or imagine it to be there. We can and do create illusions that are reality for us.

Weick uses the idea of the schema to describe the condition of groupthink:

"The phenomena of groupthink is important because it demonstrates some of the dysfunctional consequences when people are dominated by a single schema and this domination becomes self-reinforcing. Having become true believers of a specific schema, group members direct their attention toward an environment and sample it in such a way that the true belief becomes self-validating and the group becomes ever more fervent in its attachment to the schema. What is seriously underestimated is the degree to which the direction and sampling are becoming increasingly narrow under the influence of growing consensus and enthusiasm for the restricted set of beliefs. . . . this spiral frequently is associated with serious misjudgements of situations."

Where we speak of memetic patterns influencing or channelling behaviours Weick describes "directed exploration of objects". We endorse his conclusion: "This directed exploration samples features that typically affirm and strengthen schemata, which means they become even more binding as recipes that organisational members apply" In other words, a self-organising and self-maintaining system is set in motion.

We are born into or, in the case of companies, recruited into, communities of conversation in which the shared narratives, stories and myths influence collective and individual belief systems. In effect, the linguistic practices of particular social groups are internalised in memetic patterns in the brain and in the ways of thinking (paradigms) within the community. Such belief systems can be viewed as patterns of thoughts or knowledge which provide the basis for interpretative or appreciative systems of the world around us. Understanding is grounded in such systems and reflected back to our sense of reality, a socially-constructed reality of how the world is and what we can do within it. By guiding and constraining our actions this view of reality or context, this set of memes, replicates; endorsing the narrative, story or myth with which it started. What is revealed is the interaction between context and people (see figure 5.1). Contexts create us as we create contexts.

 They are not mere givens, independent, as it were, of participants' actions and sense-making constructions. For example, recall the creation of reality out of conversation concerning a new boss described in Chapter Three. The figure below serves to illustrate the overall pattern.

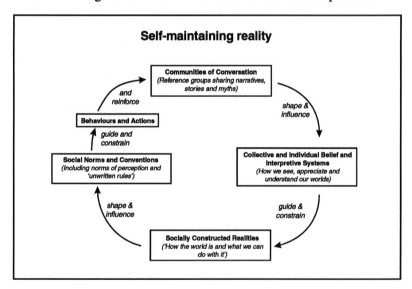

Figure 5.1

The workings of socially constructed systems. Memes, expressed in shared stories, language and belief systems, induce actions on the world, which serve to reinforce the meme's hold on one, or more, minds.

Relatedness and Relationship

What we are seeing here is a shared memetic pattern, a common hold on the minds of a group of individuals within a certain context. Just as members of a particular religious group are united by their shared memes (in certain contexts they may otherwise lead separate lives), so members of an organisation, or of a group within it, are drawn into a common cognitive system in the sense of a mutual pattern of appreciation, knowledge and understanding through which they relate to the context in question. The context cannot be independent of human interpretation. The language people use to describe it, and their relatedness, signals to others just who they are in the matter of the context in question. Such signalling forms the basis of our relationships and the informal political structures in which we participate. Our patterns of interpersonal relationships provide a living space for, and are shaped by, shared memes. Similar thoughts and similar thinking practices provide the background for the various tribes of human endeavour. In turn, such relationships reinforce the memetic pattern which helped the relationship to be forged in the first place. By such processes we can become trapped by our relationships, victims of groupthink. Human tribes become memetic species.

Stable systems of belief about the world can provide a comforting background of relationship and a relatedness of relative certainty to what is deemed by shared convention to be real. They also provide an ability to distinguish between tribes, between 'us' and 'them' in self-maintaining competitive and sometimes conflicting patterns. To risk relationship for a different reality is often seen as a risk too far, particularly when any new reality is uncertain: better the devil you know than the devil you don't! Even to raise such 'stuckness' can be sufficiently provocative to one's peers as to invite denial and be a threat to established relationship.

An example is afforded by what we term 'the busyness pattern'; one very prevalent in the language, rules and practice of many managers in companies. We illustrated it in Chapter Two as the treadmill syndrome. Whilst any isolated case might seem to be justified by the unique circumstances of a particular company and market, the pattern is rife in management circles and is not restricted to management groups or commercial companies. Many voluntary sector organisations show exactly the same behaviour. We describe this pattern not to further stress the already exceedingly busy executive; rather, as a demonstration of how a pattern can take hold, quite independent of that pattern's effectiveness in terms of either business results or quality of life. The pattern – as a pattern – merely seeks to reproduce itself. It can prevail even where, at an individual level, there is unanimous agreement that the group could produce more result by being less busy.

The pattern is complex, supported in any one case by particular sets of beliefs, constructed contexts, rules and reinforcement. Interestingly, whether an organisation is lean or fat the pattern of busy-ness still appears. It is quite independent of the relative number of managers! Part of the pattern is that time in attendance reflects one's commitment. 'Good' managers work long hours; they arrive early and leave late. With that belief, and with the desire to be thought of as a 'good' manager people will spend time in meetings, generating work to keep themselves busy. Long hours come to equal commitment (people even feel guilty if they leave 'early', i.e., on time). And so the pattern gets embellished and shared. People relate to each other out of their respective busy-ness and some almost seem to compete with each other on just how busy they can appear to be, with the one with the heaviest schedule and working the longest hours clearly being the most committed. That relatedness in turn shapes relationship both inside and outside the place of work. It might be said that this is all the result of ineffective time management – or of the leaner organisation placing more burden on the remaining managers. But, whilst these may indeed contribute, provided the belief exists that working long hours – being busy and being seen to be busy – is what makes a 'good' manager, then long hours will be worked, no matter what!

This pattern, in Anglo-Saxon cultures, predates the business process revolution. In 1980, when first working in Norway, one of us encountered the contrast between the Norwegian pattern of working from 8:00am to 3:30pm, with, at most, a short break for lunch, and the expatriate pattern of feeling guilty leaving the office before 5:30. Both patterns were deeply ingrained in the cultures of those who carried them. Both were mutually incomprehensible to carriers of the other. Koestler[83] suggests that what he terms perceptual habits are:

> "... as stubborn as our motor habits. It is as difficult to alter our way of seeing the world as it is to alter our signature or accent of speech; each habit is governed by its own canon of rules."

So 'where habits enable they also limit'. A habit is a pattern, often a complex pattern governed by a canon of rules that control lower - order hierarchies of response. What triggers the motor or organisational habit can itself be a habit, a habit of perception or interpretation. For now, be it sufficient to see the pattern of habit to which we can get triggered, hooked or thrown at personal, interpersonal, organisational and even cultural levels.

Whatever is in the head of the perceiver when perceiving, or of the listener when listening, or of the speaker when speaking, points to the routines of mental patterns; and even to established knowledge and perceptual frameworks. Koestler speaks of the need for "escapes from the bondage of mental habits" – yet new or different thinkers often meet with considerable resistance: the 'Galileo' syndrome.

To undo a mental habit sanctified by dogma or tradition one has to overcome immensely powerful intellectual and emotional obstacles. It is not only the inertial forces in society; the primary locus of resistance against heretical novelty is inside the skull of the individual who conceives of it.

Defensive routines

The mutual incomprehension of those inculcated in different cultural traditions provides a small example of what Chris Argyris[84] has termed defensive routines in the field of management and organisations. Defensive routines serve, as the language suggests, as a protective habit but can also be grossly limiting to result. Defensive routines also tend to be a complex habit of perceptual selection, interpretation and conversation that are difficult to surface and often denied. We tend not to like being caught in our defensive and limiting patterns. The surfacing of defensive routines invokes defensive routines!

Argyris defines a defensive routine as:

"Thoughts and actions designed to protect individuals', groups', and organisations' usual ways of dealing with reality. (They) come between the individual or organisation and any threats in the environment and can be both productive and counter-productive. They are counter-productive when they inhibit learning and productive when they protect the present level of competence without inhibiting learning."

In brief, Argyris discovered patterns of 'governing values' which influenced 'action strategies', which in turn had 'consequences' which created a bigger pattern which he described as "modes of reasoning". He discovered these patterns in the course of asking three questions:

❑ How is it that organisations seldom appear to achieve their potential?

❑ How is it that when everyone is agreed that a new strategy, new values and important organisational changes need to be made these strategies and changes never seem to achieve their potential? The old values about performance still blunt the new ones.

❑ How come, when we all agree on what's needed, we still seem to deal with each other in such a way that mediocrity, if not failure, is assured?

He suggests that part of the difficulty is the conditioning that individuals bring with them into organisations:

"Individuals create organisational environments consistent with their defensive routines. For example, we tend to act in ways that lead us to avoid threatening issues by making them undiscussable and by making the undiscussability of the subjects also undiscussable."

He describes defensive reasoning[85] as having the following governing values:

❑ control of the purpose of the meeting or encounter
❑ maximise winning and minimise losing
❑ minimise negative feelings
❑ maximise rationality

These in turn lead to action strategies in which people:

❑ advocate their position in order to be in control and win
❑ unilaterally save face – their own and others

The consequences of the behaviours that flow from the action strategies include:

❑ miscommunication   ❑ mistrust
❑ protectiveness   ❑ self-fulfilling prophecies
❑ self-sealing processes ❑ and escalating error

Threatening or difficult issues which we are prone to avoid become undiscussable subjects, the undiscussability of which in time becomes undiscussable. The subjects become taboo. This can lead to the discouragement of risk-taking; self-fulfilling, self-sealing processes and error escalation; competitive win-lose dynamics; groupthink; polarisation; games of deception, cover-up, and protectionism.

In brief, we could call at least some of that 'stuckness'. If it all sounds too dramatic, then is it sufficient to ask oneself: what, in what is not spoken about, could make a significant difference to performance and results? Many of us unwittingly, and sometimes knowingly, conspire in the pattern. The meme parasitises the individual and collective mind to ensure its own survival.

The nature of human systems

I am indebted to a client and colleague for starkly confronting me with the training many people have when entering and staying within organisations. He put it this way:

"Look Ray, you have to appreciate the deep training that many of these people have. You are asking them to think. I applaud you for that. Yet please understand that many of them have been deeply ingrained within school and onwards *not* to think. Rather, they have waited on being told what to do and then maybe, just maybe, depending on the carrots and sticks, the rewards and threats, they've gone and done it. We've treated them just the same way within our own organisation for years. They've grown used to being passive agents picking up some pay now and then. After all, it's pretty comfortable having no responsibilities. Now you're asking them to think and make a difference. Well, it might take some time!"

So that the reader does not become too alarmed, it is surprising how quickly one can undo past training. It is our experience that most people, when given the opportunity, want to make a difference at work. But the context in which they are enabled so to do has first to be created. The equilibrium has to be punctuated. Otherwise, as we have sought to demonstrate, there are many personal and interpersonal dynamics that serve to keep us locked-in to a relatively stable, self-maintaining system. There are patterns that serve as prisons, constraining and limiting us within certain horizons.

This sense of imprisonment and release is well captured by a European client:

"Looking back to the period before and after I would say that the best comparison I can think of is releasing someone from prison. You are your own prison. Your thoughts cripple you, you are not able to 'see' in spite of your eyes being wide open. We could have gone back to our own prison. We chose for the future and the risky path. A few were more comfortable in their own paradigm and declined the journey we chose."

People bring with them to their organisations their prior conditioning, their values, interests, expertise, habits of thinking and ways of seeing. Much of this conditioning has been learnt from and, in turn taught by, the primary groups of which the individual has had membership. Powerful and often subtle processes of socialisation have served to effect a memetic transfer through which we have been taught to 'see' and interpret the world. We see what we have learned to see. This 'seeing', and its associated memetic foundations, is further reinforced by process of selection and advancement into and within organisations. People are recruited and promoted for their fit with, and fitness in, tacitly approved memetic patterns – hence the unwritten rules of Chapter Two.

All this is conducive to the efficiency, smooth running and incremental development of the established way. We become locked-in or imprisoned by interconnected patterns – the patterns of shared perceptual frames, language, thinking, expectations, values, and lifestyles. Patterns that are reinforcing and self-maintaining, patterns that simultaneously enable and limit. Whist they provide the benefit of collective frameworks and shared focus they also carry the seeds of rigidity and perceptual blindness or myopia. Isolated memetic pools carry risk as well as benefit.

The same condition applies to isolated genetic pools. The domestic pond may provide a safe haven for frogs to propagate, but without the invasion of some foreign frog's spawn, the population risks the consequential effects of in-breeding or insufficient variety. It is interesting to note the public request of informed biologists to "Please introduce some foreign frog spawn into your pond". Until a similar request is applied to the memetic world, we may simply be restricted to greater and greater refinement of already established ideas – for example, greater refinement in inspecting poor quality out rather than the more 'foreign' idea of building good quality in.

Likening patterns to prisons may seem to take the idea too far[86]. Is it being too deterministic concerning memes or patterns and their consequences? It could be, if that was all we were saying. But it is not as simple as that. What we have said is that patterns release as well as confine and, further, that we do not have to be stuck or imprisoned by our patterns. We can break out.

So, what is it in the nature of human systems that can propel us beyond the limits of existing self-maintaining systems? How is it that we are not inevitably stuck, forever victims of such systems?

Translated into the language of this book, being 'released' may be interpreted as being freed from a mental infection, or of discovering a different one. To use the words of Dawkins:

> "Just as genes propagate themselves in the gene pool by leaping from body to body via sperm and eggs, so memes propagate themselves in the meme pool by leaping from brain to brain via a process which, in the broad sense, can be called imitation. When you plant a fertile meme in my mind you literally parasitise my brain, turning it into a vehicle for the meme's propagation in just the same way that a virus may parasitise the genetic mechanism of a host cell. And this isn't just a way of talking – the meme for, say, 'belief in life after death' is actually realised physically, millions of times over, as a structure in the nervous system of individual men the world over."

Not only is this meme realised physically in an electro-chemical trace in the brain, it is also preserved in the literature and physical artefacts of cultures.

Meme propagation, and an idea is but one form of meme, is then a process by which the informal system (such as a conversation between two people) can generate and stimulate tiny changes from which there may be major outcomes. Yet all too frequently such 'tiny changes' are nipped in the bud; we – or our existing memes – appear skilled in taking an idea early in its life and killing it. The same sets of formal, and more importantly informal, habits, rules, schema, structures, conventions, relationships that enable organisation to emerge from the complex, chaotic, non-linear feedback that is a human system can, if allowed to prevail unchecked, impose a stability that serves their interests. We believe it helps to consider patterns as alien entities bent on their own survival, We also believe that many of the established methods for helping individuals and groups to change amount to memetic re-engineering, through either crisis or intention.

We turn, for the rest of the book, to an examination of those processes of change at various scales.

Summary

Individual and collective mindsets, framed and trans-mitted through language, have been shown in numerous studies to shape behaviour and action. We frame these observations within the concept of the memetic pattern, seeking its own survival. The literature of organisational science is replete with observations of individual and collective mindsets: observations which may be more readily grasped if we see them as the effect of memes literally 'parasitising' the brains which host them. The process enables. Without it there would not be culture. It also limits, entrapping individuals in patterns of seeing, hearing, speaking, thinking and acting that are self-reinforcing and self-fulfilling. Realities are declared into existence. It may help to grasp this process, not as an act of human intentionality, but as one of blind memetic replication. *You are your memes* – unless you choose to examine whether you have them rather than they have you!

Primary Sources

DeBono (1990), through his many works, has long been an advocate of theories as to how the brain and percep-tion work. Popper and Eccles (1977) put forward an argument for an interactionist perspective between the self, its brain and the world. Wilson (1990) explores inner worlds, whilst Koestler (1990) has long argued for much greater consideration of 'the ghost in the machine'. Bruce Gregory (1990) acknowledges the contribution of Werner Erhard to his connection between language and reality as, perhaps more indirectly, do we. Weick (e.g. 1969, 1995) has written many articles dealing with cognition and sense-making to the differ-ence management could and does make to organisational results.

Hosking and Morley (1991) take aspects of this work further in developing and pursuing a relational perspective to understanding the 'organising' process. Relatedness and relationship is developed further by Batchelor and Shaw (1996). The arch- proponent of both personal and organisational defensive routines is Argyris (1990). Ackoff (1981, 1994), Senge (1990), Mitroff and Linstone (1996) and Checkland (1981, 1990) are but a few among an increasing number of people who give emphasis to the need for much greater systems thinking so that we may understand how elements interact within more complex wholes.

6

Stop the world: I want to get on!

"At any moment we are prisoners caught in the framework of our theories; our expectations; our past experiences; our language. But we are only prisoners in a Pickwickian sense: if we try we can break out of our framework at any time. Admittedly, we shall find ourselves again in a framework; but it will be a better and roomier one, and we can at any moment break out of it again."

Arthur Koestler[87]

"Language is the net that keeps thoughts and thinking trapped within the bounds of culture."

Anon

If minds and organisations are specified and maintained by shared patterns, how can such patterns be shifted so that different outcomes can be created? We turn now to explore that question, seeking over the next two chapters a generic explanation to this process of change

New patterns grow in the minds of individuals. The process of transformation therefore starts with one, or a few people, first 'seeing' differently, and then thinking, and acting out of, a different pattern or patterns. Transformation starts in the mind of an individual. This chapter concerns the possibility and practice of seeing our patterns. The next concerns acting differently.

 An oft-quoted change formula[88] states that in order for change to occur, it is necessary to first 'unfreeze' old patterns, change, and then 'refreeze'. This can be interpreted as moving from established order, through disorder, to a new established order. The emphasis on rationality often leads to 'cases for change' being drawn up, designed to increase the so-called 'readiness-to-change', after which various initiatives are undertaken to create the new order of things in a fairly logical, progressive manner. The whole plan and scheme of things is designed to get you 'there' from 'here'. Yet the more fundamental change is discontinuous, you simply cannot get 'there' from 'here'. You must first undo, unlearn, step back, before leaping forward. All too often, logical progressivism misses this point. Great plans for change are laid to waste, seldom delivering their full potential. Short-comings are attributed to resistance to change. Yet perhaps it is the case that people less resist change than they resist being changed, that is, having change done unto them. Such resistance one can con-ceive as the meme 'defending' its 'territory'.

We suggest that when you help people to discover – to see – their patterns and how those patterns grant and limit performance, then they may choose to change such patterns, and, in the process, effec-tively become authors of their own pattern shifts. To catch our pat-terns, and to create new ones, we first have to 'see' them, in a sense to slow them down or 'freeze' them, just like a slow-action replay of a fast-action sequence on a video tape. When we do, and if we begin to see that we cannot get 'there' from a current pattern, then we may start to think and see from a different place. Many tools and technologies of facilitation, creative thinking and learning work because, inten-tionally or not, they serve to help the freezing, the discovery of the current pattern and its limits.

Only through exploring our own patterns, and in the process dis-covering something of ourselves and our world, do we change. Oth-erwise, our memetic pattern traps our thinking and behaviour within the bonds and bounds of personal and collective, cultural and corpo-rate, existence. In short: to change a company, the minds of its mem-bers must change. We must eschew our memetic inheritance and break the grip of established patterns. Not perhaps easy when to do so risks membership.

Why 'stop the world'?

The inspiration for the title derives from Casteneda's book, *Journey to*

Ixtlan. Casteneda's story concerns an American youth coming into contact with, and learning the wisdom of, a Yaqui Indian named don Juan. The book represents the essence of that wisdom delivered in a narrative form. Among his learning was the notion of 'stopping the world', acknowledging and freezing a current perceptual reality, as the first step to 'seeing' – rather than merely 'looking' at the world. We all look at the world out of a largely self-maintaining system of perceptions. How do we interrupt such 'looking' and 'see' our world differently, particularly when perceptual habits are so deeply ingrained? How, then, do we help others to interrupt their patterns?

The young American took many notes of his conversations with don Juan and remained faithful to the interpretation of his mentor by referring to his set of beliefs as 'sorcery' and to don Juan himself as a 'sorcerer', "because these were categories he himself used." Some readers might prefer the term magic.

> I must first explain the basic premise of sorcery as don Juan presented it to me. He said that for a sorcerer, the world of everyday life is not real, or out there, as we believe it is. For a sorcerer, reality, or the world we all know, is only a description.
>
> For the sake of validating this premise don Juan concentrated the best of his efforts into leading me to a genuine conviction that what I held in mind as the world at hand was merely a description of the world; *a description that had been pounded into me from the moment I was born* (emphasis added).
>
> He pointed out that everyone who comes into contact with a child is a teacher who incessantly describes the world to him, until the moment when the child is capable of perceiving the world as it is described. According to don Juan, we have no memory of that portentous moment, simply because none of us could possibly have had any point of reference to compare it to anything else. From that moment on, however, the child is a member. He knows the description of the world; and his membership becomes full-fledged, I suppose, when he is capable of making all the proper perceptual interpretations which, by conforming to that description, validate it.

For don Juan, then, the reality of our day-to-day life consists of an endless flow of perceptual interpretations which we, the individuals who share a specific membership, have learned to make in common.

> The idea that the perceptual interpretations that make up the world have a flow is congruous with the fact that they run uninterruptedly and are rarely, if ever, open to question. In fact, the reality of the world we know is so taken for granted that the basic premise of sorcery, that *our reality is merely one of many descriptions*, could hardly be taken as a serious proposition. (Emphasis added)

The young American could hardly grasp the point, his understanding was stretched, he became incredulous, his mind so opposed to what he was hearing. He continued:

> My difficulty in grasping his concepts and methods stemmed from the fact that the units of his description were alien and incompatible with those of my own.
>
> His contention was that he was teaching me how to 'see' as opposed to merely 'looking', and that 'stopping the world' was the first step to 'seeing'.

'Stopping the world'. What did he mean? What difference does stopping the world make to 'seeing'? Is this anything more than mystical, New Age-speak: anything more than some cryptic metaphor between indulgent and consenting adults?

Don Juan stated that in order to arrive at 'seeing', one first had to 'stop the world'. 'Stopping the world' was indeed an appropriate rendition of certain states of awareness in which the reality of everyday life is altered because the flow of interpretation, which ordinarily runs uninterruptedly, has been stopped by a set of circumstances alien to that flow. In the young American's case, the set of circumstances alien to his normal flow of interpretation was the sorcery description of the world. Don Juan's precondition for 'stopping the world' was that one had to be convinced; in other words, one had to learn the new description in a total sense, for the purpose of pitting it against the old one, and in that way break the dogmatic certainty, which we all share, that the validity of our perceptions, or our reality of the world, is not to be questioned.

After 'stopping the world' the next step was 'seeing'. By that don Juan meant what I would like to categorise as 'responding to the perceptual solicitations of a world outside the description we have learned to call reality'.

Don Juan has it, then, that we are taught to 'see'. The last chapter argued that, we are all conditioned to see and interpret the world in a certain way, reflecting what we think with – our paradigms and memes – when looking at the world. Who we are, our way of being, what we stand for and how we interpret the world around us reflects that which we interpret it through, and that which we interpret it through acts as if it were trying to preserve its hold on us and gain a hold on others. Our thinking-seeing-being grants a certain operability or workability within the world that surrounds us. Having learned – having been taught within a community – we 'see' according to the concepts and labels granted by that community, our learning forms part of a self-maintaining system – one in which there are many self-fulfilling prophecies in operation.

Many have learned a certain formula for success, or at least survival, in this world. More accurately, it is a formula for success/survival in a world that we have experienced, one that is now past. Like genetic formulas, such memetic formulas may continue to be useful provided there is a continuation of that past world into the future. Yet, unlike the genetic world, that assumption may be challenged. Otherwise, by default, any future may be no more than a reasonable extension of the past, framed and limited, as it were, by our experience.

From a background of 'teachers', teachers who stand before the world with a shared 'culture', a shared sense of reality, we acquire a description of the world. That description influences our perceptual interpretation of, and relatedness to, the world; and grants us membership of a group carrying that description. Thus a 'taken-for-granted world' is established, an 'uninterrupted flow of perceptual interpretation', out of which we relate to the world, and in turn teach others. An unchallenged reality, a 'dogmatic certainty', is perpetuated. We participate in a self-maintaining system, where to be less than dogmatic, to be uncertain, is to court opprobrium.

Don Juan's fundamental proposition was that our reality was just one of many possible descriptions. With this as a proposition he could issue a challenge: to 'see', as opposed to merely 'looking'. We will return to the distinction shortly but first let us slow, if not stop the world, at his proposition: "Any individual's reality is merely one of many descriptions. Any reality that we share with others is but a shared description of reality. There may always be another reality to 'our' reality."

 At this point let me illustrate with a brief story from my very early career. At an early age, I had been appointed to a senior position in a young offender correctional establishment. Note that young in the expression 'young offender' was not too far from my own age at the time! The establishment ran fairly intensive group counselling sessions designed to explore, and raise awareness of, the influences on the individual's criminal or anti-social behaviours. Conducting these inquiries in the context of a peer group rendered them all the more intensive. The same development process was mirrored within staff groups, though here the emphasis was on our correctional and working behaviours. The staff team which I joined, to all intents and purposes as head of the team, was keen to point out what a good team it was, how honest and open they were in communication with each other, and generally how supportive they were to the team, the unit's purpose, and the wider institution beyond. In different ways these same themes were repeated for all of the first meeting, for all of the second meeting, and for much of the third. It seemed to be their shared story or description of reality. And yet... to the newcomer, reality appeared to be different. Though there was a lot of 'talk', nothing much seemed to be said, issues were skated over, and any sensitivities were massively avoided. It was almost as if there could not be any issues or sensitivities in such a great team!

You may imagine what happened when I described an alternative reality: one which intruded into, made fiction of, the reality they thought they had arrived at. The intrusion, which confronted an established and very comforting way of thinking, was not welcomed to say the least. I guess I should have been better trained! Such an abrupt interruption to the established pattern led to significant and immediate denial and to the rejection of both the interrupt and the interrupter. There was a price to pay for shattering the reality, that price was a period of excommunication: being 'sent to Coventry'. Yet it was a price worth paying for the new reality we could now invent.

 The story helps to illustrate a process. Our description of reality is not just an individual phenomenon but also a group or social phenomenon. In choosing to describe reality differently we risk membership, even the wrath of, or the belittling of ourselves by significant others. So we continue to describe reality a certain way until we begin to merge the description of reality with reality. We become acculturated, infected if you will, by the interpretative stance, the memes, of the dominant group. When successful, this process gives us that "uninterrupted flow of perceptual interpretation" and the memes an uninterrupted flow of perceptual replication.

 A reader concerned at this point that what is being read concerns solely the obscure past of one of the authors or, perhaps, just mere fiction, might care to contemplate their own management team, their own peer group. What is the group's description of reality? What is yours? How does describing reality that way affect their, or your, actions and relationship to that peer group? What difference might be made by describing the reality of your business differently, by, for example, redescribing *what your business is?*

At this sort of time, the question "what is reality?" rears its head. It is fairly easy to get our description of reality. It is what we say. Public reality is that which we say in public, private reality is that which we say in private. You may have noted that the two are not always the same! Yet what is reality? And is there a reality separate from our description of it? The answer to this latter question is Yes, but we know not what it is! It is like the difference between experience and the description of experience: one's description is never the experience. No two witnesses agree.

Now this is great news, for we can choose never to be stuck before the 'dogmatic certainty' of our particular description of reality. Yet, when the social process is one for such dogmatic certainty, it takes real courage, some might say foolishness, to go against the flow. If we speak of the world being round in a committed group of flat-earth dwellers we run the risk of getting locked up, of being cast aside, for that sort of crazy talk! Why risk one's career, or more, for a different description of reality? H. G Wells' short story, *In the Country of the Blind* captures the point well. It concerns a climber stumbling into a remote valley whose inhabitants suffer an endemic blindness. He dreams of being king but is forced to discover that the society does not value what he claims to see. Out of sympathy for his 'illness', out of desire to grant him full membership of their community, they lay hold of him to put out his eyes, from which they have concluded his affliction derives!

Don Juan issued a challenge: to 'see' as opposed to 'looking'. What might be meant by this? I am not too sure about the "opposed to", for my primary education had much to say about look and see! Yet Casteneda reminds us of a difference, a difference captured in a phrase such as "look, can you see?" To look is to direct our attention, to make an effort to see. To 'see' is to grasp something, to perceive, to form an image or mental picture of something, to understand. They are not the same, yet they are related. For our 'seeings' perhaps follow our 'lookings', though we may not always 'see', having 'looked'. To 'see' is to appreciate how we are looking.

In the context of Casteneda's exposition, looking, directing attention towards, is framed by what is taken-for-granted, the given aspects of our cultural inheritance to which we are directed by virtue of what we have been taught. Seeing may be an interruption to that way, so that, perhaps for the first time, we 'see' more than we have been shown; in effect, we see beyond our customary way of seeing: that taken-for granted 'world' to which we relate. To 'see', he cites the sorcerer's steps:

❑ Stopping the World
(Interrupting the uninterrupted flow of perceptual interpretations)

❑ Awareness

❑ 'Seeing'
(Responding to the perceptual solicitations of a world outside the descriptions we have learned to call reality)

When we 'see' we usually get that 'Oh, gosh' or 'Oh, s...' feeling, but even the latter is not bad news!

'Yes, but!'

Consider that harmless and ubiquitous little conjunction: 'but'. Used constructively, it can fulfil a powerful role as an adjunct to a conversation of inquiry and possibility. "*But* if we assume that, doesn't it mean that we cannot do such and such?" or: "That is one valid interpretation, *but* on the other hand what becomes possible if we assume ...?" More frequently in conversation, 'Yes, but', signals a meaning closer to "I have not really listened to what you are saying however my assertion concerning my perception of the issue at hand (or even my agenda forced to fit the issue at hand) is ....".

'But', becomes, intentionally or unintentionally, a hugely discounting put-down, provoking either antagonism or withdrawal from the other party. The space of what can be created in a conversation is immediately limited. The payoff for those using 'But' in this way is that it is a very controlling mechanism in conversation.

One small tip, but a giant leap for pattern shifting...

Catch yourself, catch others, or catch it – as a group practice: that 'Yes, but' whether spoken or thought, is a *limit* about to happen... 'Yes, but' is a dead giveaway for one set of

215

memes, those which currently have your head arranged their way, defending their patch. What examples of 'yes, but' are most commonly used by yourself and others within your organisation?

....
....
....
....
....
....
....
....
....
....
....

Seeing the wood and the trees...

While we are stuck in the defensive routines of 'yes, but', there is little chance of an opening in our minds for a different reality; little chance of a glade appearing in the woods, where the green shoots of a different outcome may germinate.

Casteneda suggests that a precondition for stopping the world is being 'convinced', and that being convinced means that "one had to learn the new description in a total sense, for the purpose of pitting it against the old one, and in that way break the dogmatic certainty, which we all share, that the validity of our perceptions, or our reality of the world, is not to be questioned."

Being 'convinced' and 'pitting a new description against the old one' may, though, frame the case too strongly, and throw one to an interpretation of struggle and conflict. If we can interrupt our inherited attachment to being right for something that may be more practical, like being useful, then we can liberate ourselves from the rightness of one perspective – this 'dogmatic certainty' which suggests that the 'validity of our perceptions, or our reality of the world, is not to be questioned'. We may see the perceived reality as being but one package or set of interpretations to which we are accustomed, or with which we are infected. 'Dogmatic certainty' becomes a 'bounded certainty'; that is, it becomes just a way of viewing the world that carries with it a certain usefulness. With this greater detachment from certainty we may be the more willing to engage with other ways of seeing and interpreting the world – with other languages – for the usefulness they offer. In so doing we may discover the basis of a new power; a power to produce results out of uncertainty as distinct from being right and certain in the matter.

Casteneda does, though, touch on an important aspect. We are so well schooled in 'seeing' the world a certain way, that different ways of seeing the world may be mouthed and yet not operant; that is, we can have the words, the language, without seeing through or with them. It is the equivalent of what Argyris[89] calls "the theory espoused and the theory in action".

We can, for example, speak of empowerment; the term may even be in wide circulation within a company, and yet we may operate in ways that serve to disempower. The language is merely espoused and there is something deeper-in-action that produces the opposite of what is said. The control meme may generate a deeper underlying conditioning that keeps the expression 'empowerment' at a superficial level: rationing out 'power' on behalf of managers, or generating 'Yes, but' rejection in the minds of those who perceive themselves as 'managed' and are as deeply infected by the same meme. Interestingly, the word 'empowerment', which is born out of the mechanical metaphor, is most likely to inspire in organisations which have moved beyond the mechanical paradigm.

So do we need to be 'convinced', and, if so, of what? There is a danger of replacing one set of rightness with another. "Yes, you're right. I am convinced" appears to collude in the game of righteousness – this game which DeBono[90] calls "I am right. You are wrong." There may be something more fundamental that can serve to help us to interrupt the normal uninterrupted flow of our perceptual interpretations. That something is to distinguish between truth and validity. It is to interrupt the whole notion of dogmatic certainty. We can accept as valid our perceptions of the world which grant a certain reality, perhaps a widely shared reality, without confusing them with truth. When we do, 'truth' may be questioned. If we are less stuck with the 'truth' meme it becomes easier to hold and operate from two, or more, equally valid perceptions of the world: perceptions that grant different realities. It is then easier to create the results we want – rather than be stuck with the world we endure.

The theme of this book illustrates the distinction: "Are memes real, or an invention of language?" Asked thus, the question immediately frames opinions in the matter of the answer, and potentially limits the utility of any discussion. "Are memes valid?" can enable a different answer, one that permits a description of a world where behaviour, culture and organisation can be perceived in terms of self-replicating patterns, and the structures they create. Seeing the process as an operant manifestation of the natural world is valid if it helps one step outside the context of individual judgement and reaction. It provides the space to examine what patterns might be at work in any particular situation; to, so to speak, stop the world.

"Yes, but why stop the world?" may still be the automatic response. Hopefully so, for in seeking to pursue the inquiry, much more than answer the question, we may start to reveal so much more that can be discovered or rediscovered. Two things spring to mind as we slow the world by repeating – perhaps in greater depth – the inquiry with which we started.

First, for many of us there is a pace and urgency, a busy-ness in our world which may disincline us towards slowing it down or stopping it. Thus "I haven't got time!". We may be so caught up in the rush that we fear being left behind should we slow it down. What is it that common sense tells us? "The world waits for no man..." What difference might some uncommon sense make?

Second, we may start to 'see' the thinking that we bring to the situation. The thinking that exists is that we need a reason to stop the world, the more so as we are so busy. So, we live in a very reasoned world, one where nothing much happens without a reason – we say! The rational world of business calls for many reasons. Thus "there is no reason to stop, or even slow down, the world". We witness these reasons, for example, in the presentations people make. Wonderful presentations with great reasons, yet they somehow do not create the result!

So what reasons might we 'see' for interrupting the uninterrupted flow of perceptual interpretation? If we apply the utility criteria it might be that alternative perceptual interpretations give others some competitive advantage in the results they achieve, whether of quality or quantity. It might also be the case that it provides a less painful means of changing. If we do not challenge our own patterns we can become so stuck in actions which we know are not producing the results we want, so habituated to our customary ways of thinking, that nothing changes until some external crisis serves to rudely interrupt the established pattern. Whether in business or marriage, the danger with crisis is that the business or marriage may not recover, never mind be renewed. Yet some people have this strange thinking that if you want things to really change then a crisis is essential. Do patterns have to break down before there can be a breakthrough?

In the domain of genes it seems they do. An ecosystem locked in to a prevailing system of interacting genetic codes finds it hard to change until interrupted by crisis, as we have discussed in Chapter Four. The arrival of new competitors, of climatic shifts, or of asteroids creates the space for new creativity. Pragmatically, there is a strong case that most organisations do not change until confronted by crisis, one well made by David Hurst[91] in *Crisis and Renewal*. He draws on the metaphor of the forest fire as an episode which opens space for colonisation by new species, even as it destroys[92]. Yet fire is also an evolved defensive routine by which dominant species – genes – keep competitors out of their territory. The same trees re-establish themselves.

When we adopt crisis thinking we may, in effect, reassert the dominance of existing memes. Managers who thrive on crises can become dependent on them, not so much to interrupt prevailing patterns as to reinforce the authority of a deeper paradigm. Even after the 'crisis' things may continue much as they are. We may or may not respond well through our adaptive capacity. We can, of course, expand our adaptive capacity by anticipating what could occur as a crisis and planning in advance of it. This is the stuff of contingency planning and the more powerful scenario planning of Arie de Geus[93] and Peter Schwartz. It can present significant competitive advantage.

Are there ways of powerfully interrupting patterns without crises? Can we create space in our mental forests without having to burn or destroy the existing trees? In lieu of our patterns being interrupted, can we ourselves be authors of the interrupting? We are unable to do so when we are too right in the matter of the patterns that we hold. Yet if we can suspend righteousness, and access a different language, one which grants a different thinking and a different seeing, we may find ourselves inventing and choosing a pattern that is not the one we have inherited.

What sort of language might this be? Well, in one sense it would need to be a 'foreign' language, though not in the normal sense of using that term. It would need to be a foreign language in so far as it would need to be different so as to open up different perceptions upon the world. A different body of distinctions, used differently, can open up a new world and possibly, new worlds. With this it might be that we could develop much more of creative orientations to whichever worlds are our concern.

Stopping the world is the equivalent of making the paradigm visible, of unconcealing or revealing the underlying patterns that shape performance, of opening space in our minds for equally valid perspectives. Stopping the world is the process. The mechanisms for doing it, for interrupting the uninterrupted pattern of perceptual interpretations, are many. They differ in the space they create for making a difference. They range, among others, from being convinced, to reacting to crises, to anticipating crises. They include building scenarios of different futures, exposing unwritten rules, using systems thinking and dialogue, changing the physical space in which conversations are enacted, using visual tools, meditation, reframing, and relanguaging. They are much easier to benefit from if those using them have an appreciation of what they are doing; namely surfacing the patterns from which they choose to see and act in a particular context.

Modelling change and learning

The deeper sense of pattern which we attempt to reveal throughout this book suggests a different model of the process of change from the traditional Lewinian and rationalistic approaches. To effect change it may not be sufficient to simply add to the store of what already exists. We may need to first unlearn, create space in the mind, before learning anew. Rational approaches to unfreezing via acts of persuasion, convincing, etc. are often ineffective. We remain in the language of what we should do and yet do the same as we have always done. Unfreezing the invisible suggests first making it visible.

Lewin's formula and the associated force-field analysis techniques have offered, and continue to offer, a powerful process and methodology for furthering change. The process is simple. It is to unfreeze, change, and then refreeze behaviours. But consider the underlying assumption, inherent in the language, in which the procedure is expressed: the frozen condition is the ideal state!

Unfreezing established patterns – changing those patterns – and reinforcing any changes. It sounds logical. Yet established patterns are so often so damn well established! Convincing people of the need to change does not always sufficiently unfreeze! As outlined, the process appears to call for an unfreezing of a current ordered state to a more fluid state in which things can be changed, after which order – a different order – 'will be resumed as soon as possible'. Change occurs during a brief departure from order. In terms of complexity and self-organisation, order – the solid, frozen, state – is taken as the natural and even desired condition. Disorder is a necessary phase to be endured in achieving a change.

But *what if* change is the normal and natural condition? What if our mind-brain systems are 'designed' (i.e., evolved as biological survival tools) to embrace a constant flux of new ideas. What if it is memes, not us, which benefit from stability? What if the natural state is less order and more movement; spontaneous, self-organising criticality closer to the edge of chaos? What if, what seeks order is simply a pattern bent on its own replication? Then perhaps we need to be careful not to confuse a solid base with a static base. In a dynamic world a static base is no longer a solid base. The solid base is no longer one of certainty, it is no longer one of past formulas for success extending uninterruptedly into the future. It is much more one of development and learning, of being much more fluid in a fluid world, of being crystal clear in an uncertain world.

So what then is the secret of learning? How do we best learn or how do we best learn how to learn? Again, by asking a limiting question, we may limit what is possible from the answer. A process of change may begin with freezing; that is, capturing what it is that governs our response of the moment. When we catch it as an expression of a pattern, we immediately interrupt our mental replicator, and create space in the memetic landscape of our minds. If we consider that the pattern has been 'learnt', that is programmed by prior infection, parasitised in our brains by previously acquired memes, then freezing, acknowledging the pattern as no more than a particular 'cultural' infection, can start the process of unlearning. If we ask ourselves "How do we learn to unlearn?" that, in itself, can create the space for learning, not in the sense of adding to the store of what already exists but in the sense of creating something that did not previously exist in the pattern from which we viewed the world. If that new pattern permits a different result then we advance by stepping back, for we unfetter and release ourselves from prior knowledge that perhaps limits the future. And thus we may enjoy the paradox of slowing things down to make them go faster!

The dilemma is that undoing, or unlearning, means we have to stop, or slow, the world and we may feel we haven't got time. So we continue to add to the store of what we already know. We tend to extend a particular peak on our memetic fitness landscape and are less willing to enter the valleys – the unknown – between peaks. We tend to retain only that which is compatible with what we already know. Yet only when we interrupt what we already know in a profound way do we achieve deep learning. It is impossible to learn deeply when one is committed to being right in what one already knows.

Deep learning equates with what Argyris[94] calls 'double-loop' learning. He draws a simple analogy to compare single- and double-loop learning:

"A thermostat that automatically turns on the heat whenever the temperature in a room drops below 68 degrees is a good example of single-loop learning. A thermostat that could ask, "Why am I set at 68 degrees?" and then explore whether or not some other temperature might more economically achieve the goal of heating the room would be engaging in double loop learning. Double-loop learning is not simply a function of how people feel. It is a reflection of how they think – that is, the cognitive rules or reasoning they use to design and implement their actions. Think of these rules as a kind of 'master program' stored in the brain, governing all behaviour."

Think one step further. Think of the master program as acting as if its agenda was its own survival. Like any virus, the virus of the mind is not there for the host's benefit. If its replication and your performance coincide then fine. If not, then the choice may be one between the host and the infection.

The best 'learners', those who are most successful under an existing pattern, are also the worst. This apparent paradox was revealed by Argyris' research in which he observed that those who had been most successful under current rules had least inclination to question any underlying 'why'. He put it this way:

"Highly skilled professionals are frequently very good at single-loop learning. After all, they have spent much of their lives acquiring academic credentials, mastering one or a number of intellectual disciplines, and applying those disciplines to real-world problems. But ironically, this very fact helps explain why professionals are often so bad at double-loop learning.

Put simply, because many professionals are almost always successful at what they do, they rarely experience failure. And because they have rarely failed, they have never learned how to learn from failure. So whenever their single-loop learning strategies go wrong, they become defensive, screen out criticism, and put the 'blame' on anyone and everyone but themselves. In short, their ability to learn shuts down precisely at the moment they need it most."

(Reprinted by kind permission of Harvard Business Review)

The 'prat' barrier...

Deep learning only occurs if the 'master program' itself, the 'cognitive rules and reasoning that govern all behaviours', is changed. It is more demanding and in some ways more threatening, less comfortable. If we are to achieve a step difference in what we do it is nonetheless necessary.

Another model of learning, beloved of trainers, is that of acquiring a new skill. It states that one moves from unconscious incompetence through conscious incompetence, to conscious competence, and finally unconscious competence. By becoming aware of what limits us we may, so the model holds, be ready to practise a new skill until, with time, it becomes second nature. The step from conscious incompetence to conscious competence, the period of exposure when we risk self-image or peer image, when we fear failure, is colloquially known as the 'prat barrier'.

In deep learning, the process starts the other way round. We have already an unconscious competence in something that is invisible to us, but that we have learned implicitly or explicitly. Being unconscious, we do not even know that we are competent at it; we just do it, like walking. On slowing our world, we may become more aware of what we do, more conscious of our skill and practices in a certain area. We may find that what we are competent in is limiting the results we achieve. Such awareness can be discomforting, for we may come to 'see' the ways in which we contribute as being an obstacle to our own success, the ways in which we sabotage ourselves. It can equally be liberating if we accept the freedom from a limiting way of being in the world. There is often a period of confusion whilst we still have the habit of the past and yet experiment with the new. It can be eased by recalling the distinction of truth and validity. We can become simultaneously conscious of our incompetence in the new and more aware of the grip of habit.

Unlearning has then started. It is not easy. Old habits die hard. Old memes do not yield easily their hard-won space in a given mind. It requires conscious intention to apply the new. Yet, as unlearning of the old progresses and the new becomes more widely practised, it emerges in turn as new unconscious competence. Where the unlearning falters, however, there is a re-emergence of the old with potential reinforcement and, in particular, increased cynicism concerning the new. Argyris coined the term 'skilled incompetence' to reflect that in which we are skilled, but where the 'skill' serves to limit results. We are so accustomed and familiar with such skills that it is as though we are unaware of them; we are, so to speak, unconscious in our skilled incompetence. If we perceive learning as including the possible rearrangement of what is 'known', i.e., the ingrained memetic pattern, then it can include 'unlearning' as well as merely acquiring what is new. We can then reformulate the model. Little writing on change and change management refers in any great degree to this matter of unlearning. And yet, can we make significant strides without letting go of that which limits and that which has already been so well learned? Machiavelli[95] again anticipated Argyris by 500 years or so:

"There is nothing more difficult to carry out than to initiate a new order of things. For the reformer has enemies in all those who profit by the old order, and only lukewarm defenders in all those who would profit by the new."

The enemies of change are those caught in the grip of patterns, sometimes patterns in which there is no or only a limited profit. Why, for example, do some people limit rather than assert themselves? Is there some limited payoff from avoiding responsibility and the possibility of any upset? Even 'defenders' of the new may be acting more out of 'what they believe they know', the patterns that have infected their minds, rather than enlightened calculation. We have not developed a language for addressing our minds and our paradigms in the way we discuss, say, our bodies. We may even be stuck with the limits of a biological inheritance in which brains and language have largely evolved for the purposes of dealing with reaction to immediate threats. Or is this just part of a mechanistic, Western, cultural inheritance? Cause-and-effect thinking which says 'run!' when approached by a lion, or: 'solve a problem by the use of deductive logic', grants a great deal of utility and validity, even survival! Yet linear logic and linear language makes it the more difficult to perceive and share conversations concerning the systemic interconnections in the world around us, and between us and our world.

Talking pictures – systems thinking to systems language

We have already alluded to the widely expressed concern at the limits of 'reductionist' or 'Cartesian' or 'mechanistic' thinking. Indeed, in cultivating this book we have drawn inspiration from the growing movement for a more holistic interpretation of the world, including the world of organisations. Now among many advocates of that holistic or systemic perspective one finds 'reductionism' or 'determinism' used as terms of scholastic abuse. Among some carriers of the holistic memome, to label something 'reductionist' is sufficient reason to invalidate it from further consideration. Groups of, say, post-modernist sociologists, who can perhaps agree on little else, can be enabled by a shared language of anti-reductionism.[96]

One barrier to exploration of the role of genes or memes in complex adaptive systems is that they have attracted the reductionist tag. It is time to invite the switch that we referred to above. What if reductionism/holism, or determinism/emergence, or linear thinking/systems thinking are not right or wrong, but equally valid perspectives which – held in tandem – can grant a much greater access to that which limits people in companies?

We have at times chosen to write of memes as if they were simple, atomistic entities. In that simplification there is considerable insight into the all-pervading power of 'ideas and images in men's minds' created and transmitted through linguistic intercourse. The simplicity of the idea avoids, circumvents, an awful lot of complexity. On the other hand, we have tried to stress the interconnectedness of patterns. Thinking, seeing, perceiving, being, speaking, listening and acting are themselves linked and grounded in bafflingly complex and interconnected systems of language, beliefs, faiths, values, mental models, concepts and paradigms.

One language or way of thinking that helps one to see the interconnection between things, or at least how we perceive those interconnections, is Systems Thinking[97], a management discipline which has received a considerable boost since the publication of Peter Senge's *The Fifth Discipline* and the subsequent *Fifth Discipline Field-*

book[98]. Where Senge considers mental models, we are perhaps trying to suggest an even deeper pattern, one grounded in the natural process of evolution and replicators, one which emerges through language and one that transmits itself in the codes, practices and artefacts of organisations. Indeed we prefer to consider Systems Thinking as a language; a language which, once learnt, helps those who speak it to explore and communicate in the matter of moving and dynamic, rather than static, relationships. Systems Language provides a relational perspective upon the world. Rather than reducing things to their elements one looks at the pattern of things in combination. There is a profound shift when one holds both the reductionist habit and the relational.

Dynamic phenomena are an everyday part of existence in an interconnected world; yet our everyday language, and our commercial and business language, makes them hard to discuss. Our whole memetic conditioning programs us towards reductionism; thinking of problems in isolation, and breaking larger ones down into smaller, solvable, chunks. It is more than just education. The very structure of our language makes it hard to express the idea of a system co-evolving with time. The basic grammar of 'subject – verb – object' makes the expression of feedback difficult[99]. 'Interconnected', 'influences as part of a system', or 'contributes to and is in turn contributed to' are expressions that people find it difficult to get their minds around. 'A causes B', or 'from X to Y' are easier concepts to grasp than are expressions conveying complex inter-relationships. We lack a shared language for seeing components as part of a whole. 'Linear' memes are not about to cede their territory.

Systems Thinking or Systems Language will not cure a business locked-in to a particular limiting pattern. It does however provide, if widely enough shared, a language for describing the effects, with time, of a pattern. As with any new language its power as a vehicle for sharing ways of thinking is under-utilised until it is not only employed in acts of speech but also as a way to think, one that displaces simple linearity. We 'see' the world differently, as a dynamic set of relationships, when we see it from a systemic rather than a linear lens. To achieve that 'seeing' we may have to learn a new, and at first an essentially pictorial, language.

That language and habit is slowly evolving. 'Systems Theory' as a meme in its own right is enjoying an evolutionary radiation[100] which shows all the hallmarks of emergent self-organisation. Often, however, it remains grafted on to deeper conditioning concerning a predictable, deterministic world. Only when this barrier is overcome, when Systems Language becomes a vehicle for communicating a different perspective, is its real benefit discovered.

One of the great simplifications made clear by the approach of Peter Senge and co-workers was the degree to which complex systems could be reduced to only two types of feedback, positive (or reinforcing) and negative (or balancing)[101]. One causes a variable to get larger, or smaller, at an ever-increasing rate. The other seeks a return to the status quo or stability.

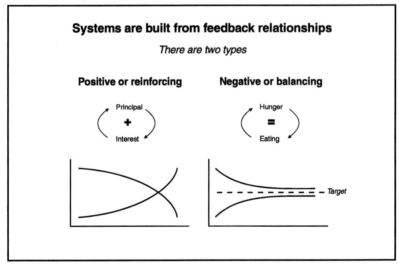

Systems are built from feedback relationships

There are two types

Positive or reinforcing   **Negative or balancing**

Principal   Hunger

+   =

Interest   Eating

— Target

Figure 6.1

The essence of a Systems Language is to appreciate the dynamics of two forms of feedback. Positive of reinforcing feedback acts to produce faster and faster change, over time, in any variable involved. The direction of the change may seem 'negative' in the sense of 'undesirable'. However, negative feedback, in systems language, does not denote any value judgement. It simply refers to the style of feedback that tends to return a system to an explicitly or implicitly defined equilibrium.

The basic action of a pattern in seeking its replication is to exert negative or balancing feedback. Any change – new behaviours, new thinking, new actions – produces a gap between the new state and the desired equilibrium of the existing pattern. Like a governor on a steam engine, or a thermostat on a boiler, pressure for corrective action is exerted. We rarely examine the pattern to see whence comes the pressure for corrective action. We let our memes declare denials into existence, the "It cannot exist" and "It's not possible" reaction so common of scientists when presented with challenges to existing paradigms; of managers when corporate orthodoxy is challenged, and of individuals when deeply-held convictions are called into question. When we only conceive of Systems Thinking as a tool that we can deploy to analyse the world we risk becoming victims of such unconscious defensive routines. When we use it as a language of inquiry we can begin slowing the world down.

What is a tool? Something we pick up, use to make a task easier and then put down, right? Language is more than a tool, it is the capability that allows memetic interaction, that enables the webs of relationship from which mentalic order emerges. If language is more than a tool then what is it? It is a window. Interestingly, both window and language are cultural artefacts of living existence. A systemic language grants a new window on the world, a window that is hard to access through the linear grammar of most Western dialects. By 'talking in pictures' we can circumvent the bottlenecks through which we are otherwise conditioned to think and speak[102].

Expanding our interpretative capacity

From the language we inherit and use to describe our world, from the patterns transmitted in our memetic environment, flows our perceptual interpretation of the world and the stance we take in the world. From that stance flows our action and the actions of others with whom we interact. One can summarise it visually as a systemic relationship between perception and action.

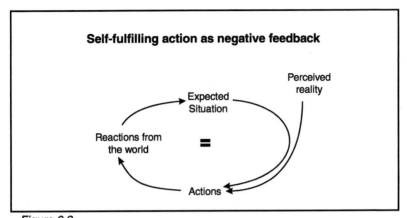

Figure 6.2

The operation of memetic patterns, at any level, can be seen as setting the norms and standards which negative feedback maintains. While these norms enable, the effect is desirable. when the pattern is limiting it is necessary to 'see' or appreciate the negative feedback in order to arrive at an intentional shift.

Many other established methodologies exist in the theory and practice of organisational change for accessing a perceptual framework; once, that is, we have established in our own minds how prevalent and important perceptions can be. Ultimately, these methodologies depend on inquiry. What assumptions of the world are operating here? Are they valid? Why? It becomes difficult, often impossible, to distinguish reality from perception. What we see, or hear, in the world around us is not what a tape recorder, or a video camera, would record. Rigorous logic and analysis, application of the much-espoused but rarely practised scientific method of 'hypothesis, prediction and experiment', may help, as may a variety of visual methods designed to create and test shared pictures of influences upon an issue at hand.

An individual committed to facilitating a shared inquiry (not necessarily the same thing as a facilitator) can help a group if she or he is able to create a shared visual space in which they may process their ideas and images. At its simplest this is the art of using a flip chart.

Through use of flip-charts, white-boards, wall space, or even computer 'groupware', the facilitator can create what amounts to a shared space for a group to process ideas. If each observation can be rendered movable, by representing it on, say, a Post-it note, magnetic shape, or piece of coloured plastic film, then influence diagrams and maps of shared perceptual frameworks may be created.

At one level there is a skill and proficiency in using any of these techniques to assist a group with say:

- ☐ Developing as a team
- ☐ Solving a problem
- ☐ Agreeing priorities
- ☐ Reducing and clustering ideas into a systems influence diagram
- ☐ Analysing a process
- ☐ Understanding dilemmas
- ☐ Thinking creatively

The danger, is that, in working with the methodology the facilitator and the group become tacit partners in a shared view of the world, members of a club, with a common, even if temporary, perceptual framework. The facilitator, even if he or she is not an independent consultant with a mortgage to pay, is under strong pressure to conform to the client's pattern. In so doing, there is the danger that they cease to question whatever pattern they are operating from. Any desire to establish 'the' answer, as though only one exists, should be resisted. Instead, 'answers' are better seen in context of perceptual frameworks. Different 'languages', through which we share and explore perceptual frameworks, grant both a different thinking or interpretation and hence a different seeing. We may then, and only then, invent and choose a different pattern from the one we have inherited.

Such colluding feedback is one way of bringing a shared reality into the world. Actions that are consistent with a particular perceptual interpretations of the world tend to be reinforcing. Acting in a manner consistent with our perception tends to strengthen our opinion that the perception is correct. In the process, we are trapped in an archetype of positive feedback. Thus my perception of another as 'difficult', leads to actions consistent with dealing with him or her as a negative or difficult individual, and to an interpretation of their response that is consistent with my initial perception. Equally, if I perceive someone else to be acting towards me in a certain way that will influence my actions. The 'accidental adversaries' dynamic (figure 6.3) is common:

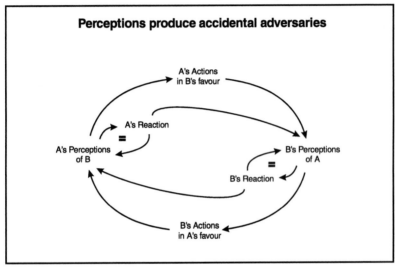

Figure 6.3
The 'accidental adversaries archetype' (Senge et al, 1994) arises, at various levels, when two parties, acting consistently with their perceptions of the world, mutually reinforce each other's misconceptions. Any larger result that they might achieve through joint action or partnership is not realised. But the perceptions get replicated.

Accidental adversarial patterns emerge from nothing more than two perceptual interpretations. Whether it concerns two individuals in an escalating quarrel or deteriorating relationship, a business partnership turning sour, or a price war, the same basic dynamic plays itself out. The danger is that, with time, the rigidity of both party's perception of the situation as one of 'If you win, I, or we, lose' is increased. The penalties for thinking, and acting, differently become larger.

As with any positive feedback, the dynamic may be reversed. Choosing a stand for co-operation, becoming committed to another party's success – as well as, rather than instead of, one's own – may, in turn, engender a response that enables not only their success but one's own. A partnership may grow and strengthen. A seemingly impossible synergy, or future, may be brought into being; one that might not have been conceived as possible by either agent at the start of a given relationship. The same dynamic occurs between units within a 'company' and between companies, as we address in Chapters Eight and Nine.

Self-fulfilling speaking

A significant part of our training, our prior conditioning, is to see ourselves in a certain way. Our perceptual habit becomes our horizon. The way that we see ourselves creates a certain horizon or space for us to work and be in, and no more. This is no more than a recognition that statements such as "I can't do that" actually creates a future as well as perhaps reflecting something of the past.

'Cannot do's' offer some protection in the world. I am willing to accept general and not personal experience that I cannot fly. I do not need personal experience to inform me that jumping off cliffs is a less than sensible course of action. Yet, without the limiting aspect of that 'cannot do' being questioned or challenged in some way, I may become stuck. So, for example, if I replace the language 'Man cannot fly', with the question: 'Why can't I fly?' or 'I cannot fly unaided', the possibility of powered flight, or hang-gliding may be created. And 'flying' is a very concrete example. 'I cannot write a report, or give a presentation, or see how life could be different in this organisation' usually gets granted the same certainty of meaning. Thus are realities declared into existence.

The language of some companies and some cultures abounds with 'what cannot be done' or at least with 'what cannot be done *here*'. One also tends to hear of people being 'right' about what cannot be done here. They provide masses of well-reasoned evidence dug from the stories, legends and myths of their company, as to why something 'cannot be done'. People talk themselves into very limited and limiting horizons. "That project is impossible." "This market is mature and cutting costs is our only option." A similar dynamic often emerges in other social and personal arrangements, such as marriage and interpersonal or team relationships. Furthermore, it is perceived as difficult and sometimes dangerous to attempt to be different from what is known and understood; for, in doing so, one risks membership and past relationship. The can-do attitude of some individuals is described, by others, as their 'gung-ho' approach.

To shift the limits of such interpretational stances takes a different language – a different way of speaking – from that which limits. We can then expand our stance and, in a sense, free ourselves from the language that limits. But we may need to speak and listen differently from how we have been taught and from the prevailing conversation around us. To 'get out there and start having a new kind of conversation . . .' requires not only different speaking but, firstly, a different 'hearing', for hearing is to listening as seeing is to looking. As we may look so as to see, so we may listen so as to hear. It is sad that patterns, memes, interfere as if with their own agenda!

It is easily said perhaps, yet a new kind of conversation sets us apart, and many have neither the courage nor commitment to set themselves apart. Note at this juncture, how easy it is to slip into limiting language. "Many have neither the courage nor commitment to set themselves apart" is an enormously limiting stance to take to a vague notion of other people expressed as 'many'. It is also enormously righteous. Compare the opening created by an expression such as: "everyone is willing to set themselves apart when they find something worthwhile to set themselves apart for". We expand our interpretative capacity less when we learn the 'right way' to interpret, and more when we unlearn the limiting ways in which we use, and are used and abused by, our language. For many of us this translates to interrupting habit – the habits of our speaking, listening, thinking, reading and writing. The difficulty is that much of this habit is widely shared and, at times, very pervasive. Remember, the selfish meme *wants* it that way!

Creating space

Slowing the world could be equated to making space in our minds for different possibilities. Creating different physical space can help enormously, as can moving to a different place in search of a different conversation. Again, however, so much of our memetic conditioning is in controlling and limiting space through prescriptions, rules, physical layout, etc.

Space pervades patterns in many senses of the word. People exist in an existential relationship with the buildings they construct, and those buildings, as some of the most enduring of cultural artefacts, can be both a powerful bastion of the existing patterns or a powerful source of leverage for resetting the patterns. Consider, for example, religious architecture as defending the faith that generated it. Consider also the resplendent new office block that is erected as a monument to the permanence of its creator. Such a block can be the last act of an old guard, seeking to perpetuate an organisation in their own image[103].

One can observe it in the way that organisations used to a hierarchical tradition, in which a manager's 'space' is a sign of his standing in the hierarchy, seek to preserve that tradition on moving into a new building, In this situation, buildings designed for creative possibilities become filled with rectilinear workstations in which everyone seeks their defining space...

 I recall many years ago discussing with the HR manager, who was also in charge of administration for a new office, the fact that geologists needed offices large enough to display maps in. Failure to examine such maps (this predated workstations) risked millions spent drilling exploration wells in the wrong place. He could not see the point for a long time, but he then ruled that this requirement obviously created the standard for all other staff as well!

At a more immediate level, physical layout and surroundings are one of the simplest tools available to set the culture and thinking patterns of a group. Walls onto which it is easy to pin diagrams, or better still, magnetic walls create an environment in which a shared space for mental processing is easily established – yet most offices, and even conference rooms are still designed in a manner that limits the style of conversation which may occur, to frame the job description rather than the job. By design or habit, a formal conference table with limited room for shared visual space, an interview across the power space of an executive desk or a warren of work stations that limits individual interaction, frames the thinking habits of an organisation. Interconnection to a sufficient density, a critical mass of feedback, is, as we have seen in Chapter Four, a prerequisite of self-organisation. So far as the best simulation can testify, this facet of complex adaptive systems applies as much in the natural world as it does in the world of social and psychological interaction. *The emergence of new patterns is facilitated by creating space which makes it possible!* In stopping the world, freezing and questioning a given pattern, one is, at least in metaphor and perhaps in neuro-physiological fact, creating space for new possibilities to emerge. Yet so often we limit our possibility space to the single point attractor of our current meme-set. From that point in mental space it may be impossible to get to a different place.

We can get 'there' but not from 'here'!

Every nation has its stereotype of whom jokes of the more stupid variety are told. English and Irish reciprocate, as do Cork men and Kerry, Swedes and Norwegians, or Cantonese and Hakka. All of them, to my knowledge, have the joke about the native asked for directions who replied that, were he going to destination 'x', he wouldn't start from here.

In the genetic world this may be a statement of fact. *Natura non facit saltum*: nature does not make jumps, may be true[104]. Evolution must work with what it has, with peaks on an existing fitness landscape. We hold, however, that it need not be true of patterns. For this to be the case, human choice and intention must prevail over the blind tyranny of memetic replication. Consider a train journey. There is comfort in moving, being part of something going to a certain destination. But if the destination of the train is fixed, and you are committed to reaching a different destination, you must make a switch, either re-routing the train or boarding another which offers the destination you seek. It is easily said, but minds accustomed to their own ways can be almost as firmly welded to a particular direction as is a rail line. Re-routing is not necessarily easy, and getting off to board an alternative train of thought is a challenge to one's own sense of comfort. An even more difficult situation occurs when there is no train, no pre-established route, to the new destination. In those cases the really committed people make a way. In either instance we must risk leaving the comfort of what is known for something unknown in terms of our own experience. Chaos and confusion often looms when the comfort of what is known and well-practised is left behind What might encourage us to undertake such a risk, to venture on a new journey to a different place?

Catching the assumptions out of which one is managing, and challenging them, can put at risk the 'reality' called managing. To take up a new design and practice one has to move from the old habit, the old pattern. Only then can one start to design and practise a new way of managing that leads to different results. Through this process the act of managing may no longer mean what it once meant. This is an example of slowing or stopping the world. We are too often caught up in the doing of management to think about it. In undertaking the inquiry into what it is to manage and to be managed and the consequences that flow therefrom, one may see limits and proceed to initiate a new design and practice of managing that leads to different consequences.

For example, through process of inquiry one may start to see some connections and differences between, say, managing to secure compliance and 'managing' so as to foster commitment. In doing so, one may begin to appreciate that you cannot get to commitment from control, there is no extension from control to commitment. One has to give up some form of control, and go back to zero, to get to real and not manipulated commitment. This is the equivalent of going back to zero when a paradigm shifts. To the controllers, and their control memes, it is threatening, for they give up their way of being: thinking, rules and practices that have been hard learned. To let go of one set of competencies and to learn anew is difficult. To simultaneously make room for an alternative set of beliefs and believe anew is very difficult. To switch worlds, to change the train, is harder still, for controllers live in, and perpetuate, controlling worlds: worlds full of institutionalised controls. The control and the commitment worlds are not opposite, they are different. To be effective in these different worlds takes different approaches.

Given an established paradigm it is sometimes difficult to imagine any alternative. After all, is it not true that someone has to be in control? and if so, then it might as well be me... that someone has to have responsibility and if so, then it might as well be me... that, someone has to carry the rewards of all this control and responsibility as well as the risk if things go wrong, and if so then... (you know how this ends). We have been well taught. Yet *what if* we could start to design companies where we enjoyed control and power with others, within a community of commitment, where responsibility was less a positional thing and more a matter of choice and alignment with one's commitments? What if we created a different sense of responsibility, power and control out of a different orientation to our world?

What if the contribution of being a manager is to engage and inspire the commitment of others, that through one's sense of being and of being alive to a purpose, through one's presence, and way of being, one helps to inspire others and ignite action? In so being, one may be more of a creative rather than a controlling force:

We are but candles in the wind,
Sometimes burning brightly,
Sometimes dimmed.

What is it turns the ember of an extinguished soul,
To flicker and flame,
To be emboldened in their purpose?

Are we so well trained
In damping the flame,

In controlling ourselves
And influencing others,
To be content with existence,
When there is so much more
To 'Being Alive!'?

A service, then, to let our flame shine brightly?
When some are so disposed to extinguish
And manipulate the many to their will.
Serving to constrain and contain.
People but passively imprisoned to their purpose.

For the many,
Controlling ways breed compliance,
Seemingly secure in the comfort of complicity,
With not much space to make much difference.

A difference, then, in being different?

Another difficulty is that the thinking is exactly mirrored on the 'other side'. Perceiving oneself as controlled can bring a great sense of relief. Others, 'bosses', have to have the answers, so that we can then be exempt from responsibility; mere agents for another. Compliance carries little risk. The managed also serve as hosts for the replication of the prevailing meme. Thus, as 'worker', one carries a set of mental baggage that says to be managed is to be told what to do, when and how. Convey any problems to management and seek their answer. Comply with all reasonable instructions and requests. 'Take the money'... Much of schooling and life prepares us well for this role. If management attempt to be different, to change the ideas out of which they work, then they request workers to, in turn, change the ideas out of which they work. Both have learned the ways of the other in all sorts of environments: home, school, and work. For one to change without the other is untenable, thus to manage differently means shifting the experience and ideas of being managed. Either party can limit the movement of the other. Whether they, or any two individuals, do so reflects the patterns of perception organised and maintained at the personal and inter-personal level.

Lest this be interpreted as a problem on the shop-floor, let it be said that it can also prevail in professional service firms, middle management teams (particularly in public sector bodies) and universities. Many innovative private sector organisations, and some in the public sector, have discovered the virtues of reducing traditional managerial hierarchies. Each 'layer' typically adds true costs that are many times more than the apparent costs of salaries and offices because of the additional work and complication they generate; complication which reduces overall throughput. Meanwhile, faced by cost pressures, many UK public sector organisations have sought to *add* management layers, so as to *control* costs. And the managed become even more passive, demanding change from the managers, yet resisting it when it happens.

There is an alternative. Recent research by colleagues[105] has shown some instances of portering operations in NHS hospitals where, as manager-to-porter ratios fall, i.e., there is less control, not only do managerial costs fall but porters' motivation rises, absenteeism reduces, and customers' perceptions of the service they receive improve.

If we begin to understand, not that we can't get to commitment from compliance; but that, when we do, the commitment that we end up with is something less than commitment, then we will start to see that we cannot get there from here. We will need to take a few steps back to leap forward. Commitment is not progressive from compliance. We need to stop the world, to undo before we do. What we are undoing is our interpretative stance. In order to *be* different we first need to 'unbe'. At one level it is obvious: the person who is arrogant cannot get to being humble by continuing to be arrogant!

Translated into the context of our story, the person who wants to generate commitment had better first let go of the compliance that he or she normally works with. Easily said. Yet it is not so easy to let go of something that once worked so well, and that continues to have at least some effect, for something we are not experienced in and have not been trained to. Presented with the evidence of the studies into portering performance cited above, other managers' typical reaction has been along the lines of "It wouldn't work with my lads. They'd be skiving off as soon as my back was turned". And if that is their expectation they are probably right! It is not easy to let go of what seems like certainty, confidence and comfort for something that at first may appear like chaos and confusion. Yet is this not true of all renewal and of development, of reaching new boundaries where whole new horizons of potential and performance open up? Did we not let go of crawling in order to walk?

This change of being, this change in our interpretative stance, can happen by design or accident. Why not by design more than accident? Why rely on some external traumatic event to shift our way of being, when we could choose to do so by design?

 As I write this I reflect upon a colleague who enjoyed a job which placed him in front of the 'public' – a company and customer public – where he made business, product and educational presentations. He was good. He was certainly competent. He had an air of confidence that bordered on the arrogant. And then, quite unexpectedly, a major coronary left him with significant paralysis and slurred speech. After many months of absence he returned to work. One could observe progressive and significant improvement up to today, when there is but some slight remaining paralysis. But, for the more observant, there is tremendous humility, a transcendent humility that enables him to communicate in a different, more powerful way. It is easy to say that this humility was forced. It was, I believe, rather discovered; and he speaks the more powerfully for it. He speaks in such a way that "It's pointed out to you". Through the trauma and recuperation, he found that he "reassessed things unwittingly"; he began to 'see', relate to, and to live out of his circumstance in a way which read as "aren't I lucky" – a time when "different things become important"; a process of rediscovery in which he was "not sure you even know..."

My colleague has been able to take a catastrophe and turn it into a developmental experience, crossing new thresholds in the process. Unfortunately, whether it be a company or personal experience, all too often it takes a major crisis to interrupt our comfortable and routine patterns, and so get us to think and see differently. Yet if and when we can or could see and think differently by design, then our worlds could and will be moved on by something other than crises.

 ## Summary

What we have sought in this chapter is to show how in slowing things down – stopping the world – we may speed them up. This is particularly the case when we cannot get 'there' from 'here', that is, when the destination we want cannot be reached by continuing in the direction in which we are already headed. The established pattern must be interrupted and breached, the memetic inheritance challenged, so that we may get to 'there' from a different place. We must first 'see' the prison – the "framework of our theories, our expectations, our past experience, our language" – in order to break out.

We have indicated an altogether deeper sense of change, one that is not merely additive but discontinuous, one where there is some undoing before doing. It does not proceed in logically incremental steps but is something more radical, something which challenges and confronts participants within their existing patterns. The change is from within. As our settings change, that is, the patterns through we see and relate to the world change, then we enact a different world. The power of logic, being convinced or persuaded, offers one route to shifting patterns. A more powerful route, we suggest, is that of choice and commitment. It requires some freedom from the grip of existing patterns, a freedom gained by stopping or slowing the world.

To do so we may have to be more aware of our language, as an expression of our perceptions. A more dynamic or systemic language can help us to paint pictures – talking pictures – with others, in which we first reveal and then draw or outline how we see the relationships between things. Attempting to uncover the unfolding whole is vastly different to the reductionist approach in which we are largely skilled and which has served us so well. The pattern or system is more than the sum of its parts!

Seeing the pattern alone though is not enough to move beyond it. That takes some risk. For, in challenging the assumption, one challenges the world in which "we cannot do that here". By way of example, we considered managing and asked how one may not so much manage better as better manage... The first takes the fundamental assumptions of managing and of being managed for granted, the latter creates the space for something more of a fundamental redesign. As an example, we explored how one cannot simply get to commitment from compliance, one first has to undo some of the patterns of compliance.

Primary Sources

We have drawn considerable inspiration, as will be apparent, from Casteneda (1986) for a different window on the social construction of reality. That process has received much more attention through the school of social constructionism (Berger and Luckman 1966). Lodge (1988) gives an entertaining introduction, en passant, to the field of professional linguistics. Lissack (http://www.lissack.com) offers several more scholastic summaries of the bridge between linguistics and organisational science. Winograd and Flores (1987) is a brief but major work that explores human cognition as it applies to organisational and managerial conduct. For the difference language makes see Eccles et al (1992).

The theory of management learning, and individual learning, has its own considerable body of research. We, like many others, have been influenced by the work of Chris Argyris (e.g. 1978, 1990) and his influence on Senge (1990) and Senge et al (1994). Schwarz (1994) and De Geus (1988, 1997) illustrate scenario planning as a method for interrupting the mental maps of organisations. There is a vast literature on change, thinking, learning, and facilitation: some of our sources include Waterman (1987), Tushman et al (1986), Pfeffer (1996), Mittroff (1987), Hayes et al (1988). Hurst (1995) presents an excellent view of the role of crisis, and the need for ethical crisis, if organisations are to change However, we seek to make the case that crisis is not always needed.

This chapter also owes much to discussions on two Internet lists, Rick Karash's *Learning-Org* and Mike Lissack's *Complexity-Management*. Contributions by numerous friends on both lists are gratefully acknowledged.

7

Beyond the 'I' that beholds: from 'seeing' to 'shifting' patterns

"To observations which ourselves we make,
We grow more partial for th'observer's sake."
Alexander Pope

"It's no use raising a shout.
No, Honey, you can cut that right out.
I don't want any more hugs;
Make me some fresh tea, fetch me some rugs.
Here I am, here are you:
But what does it mean? What are we going to do?"
W. H. Auden

We can then, with some effort and practice, 'see' the patterns which provide structure and shape to our behaviours within a given context. They may be simple or complex; they may involve only a few others and a stable context, or a multitude of others in a dynamic, shifting context. Whatever the pattern we are part of and that we are able to 'see', we may in 'seeing,' only arrive at Auden's refrain: "But what does it mean? What are we going to do?".

This chapter concerns doing and helping others do. What can we do to create a pattern of our choosing rather than suffer the one that has us – or others – in its grip? How can we break out of our memetic inheritance? How can we help others break out of theirs? In short, how do we move beyond seeing?

Beyond 'seeing'

"Here I am, here you are: But what does it mean? What are we going to do?" We inherit structures, they become part of our traditions. We find ourselves together in some institution, some company. But what does it mean? What are we going to do? In so many social, or economic, institutions what we are going to do is already well-structured: often, indeed, so well-structured that we do it routinely, without conscious awareness. We follow the rules, think the paradigms and abide by the routines and habits of our daily busy-ness.

Those structures – they are part of our tradition – shape not just our behaviours but who and how we are in any given context. We have routine and habitual ways of being – ways that grant the benefit of order, prediction and control by limiting what could be. One such structure or pattern (one into which we are so easily cast and therefore one in which we are all well-taught) is that of the 'observer and commentator' upon events in the world.

In part, the observer's role is enabled by our sense-making capacity. We seek to explain circumstances and events which impact not just us but also the lives of others. We create our 'story', our map or model of what happened (or is happening!). We share such stories and often seek confirmation in them. When confirmed, which is often a condition of membership of a particular group, we are locked-in to what has emerged as a shared story. The same memes infect many brains!

This role – 'observer upon the scene' – is easy to slip into and is much present and demonstrated in the media which surround us. We can divorce ourselves from influence and action and yet cloak ourselves in the mantle of appearing very knowledgeable, even righteous, in the matter in question. Observers can often be witnessed after the event; whether it be a football game, an inner city riot, or a poor business result. They also operate more subtly, as when two or more individuals agree that a certain result is not possible, or that the environment is stopping or curtailing their accomplishment. The professional 'committee person', he or she of the carefully crafted reaction becomes, perhaps, the more skilled observer upon the scene. Observers demonstrate their knowledge, expertise, and strong opinions and yet neither call upon themselves, nor allow themselves to be called upon, to act. Any call to action is framed in terms of what others should do. There can be great, and self-reinforcing, comfort in such commentaries. In observing, we "grow more partial to our observations".

Like any pattern, that of observing, reporting and commenting upon, both enables and limits. It enables the advance of knowledge, a free and inquiring press, and the would-be impartial (??) researcher. Yet it facilitates a growing tradition of being-in-the-world only as commentator or reporter. It promotes a passive, disengaged (even if 'interested') way of being. In being passive, even with interest, we limit the difference we may make to others, or ourselves, at least in a particular context. Our learning so easily slips into this everyday habit. We become adept at reporting what is going on, at complaining, which is often the nature of a report about what should be going on and isn't, and at observing upon others in a way which detaches us from any responsibility. There is a huge payoff. We look and feel good when reporting and exempt ourselves from any action.

 I think I noticed this most at dinner one evening in Brussels with some work colleagues. We spent all of our time describing exactly what we thought was wrong with our company and saying what was needed to put it right. The involvement in the conversation was significant, everybody had something they wanted to say and said it. Yet the whole evening was no more than a report or commentary. We danced in the virtual world of our shared story of the company. Not one of us challenged the others as to who or what they were up to in the matter: the difference that we could and would actually make...

Many organisations foster unwitting passivity in that their unwritten rules favour what we might call 'great collectors'. Great collectors are those people who have built a capacity to be up with all of the latest phrases. They are eloquent in the use of all of the in-vogue buzzwords and magic potions that will serve to give themselves and their companies a better future. They excel in their command of the expressions. They give 'good slide'. They are up to looking good and, at least superficially, to many they do. People buy the advert. Yet the substance is missing.

We paint pictures. We paint pictures of our companies, in terms of how they are or how they could be, and yet somehow fail to put ourselves into the picture. It is much easier to talk about making a difference than to actually be committed to making one. It is easier still to justify how one would make a difference, if only someone else would make the first move! At a fairly profound level the shift of pattern only comes when we do make that difference that so often we think we cannot make, when we bust a self-imposed boundary, when we breach the self-organising system. Once we begin to see that a different reality may be equally valid, once we accept the distinction of truth and validity (see Chapter Six) then we can begin to say, "I am committed to such and such": where such and such can be another's, or a group's, 'success' as much as our own. By declaring into existence, and acting consistently with, a different reality you begin to make that reality possible. You switch from observer to performer, from audience to actor, from passive to active engagement. It helps enormously if you can engage and enrol others in making the same switch. Then perhaps they, too, access a different sense of purpose. George Bernard Shaw captured it eloquently:

"The reasonable man adapts himself to the world. The unreasonable man persists in adapting the world unto himself. Therefore all progress depends upon the unreasonable man."

Putting meaning into company

One way to interrupt passivity is for an active minority to cajole, motivate, threaten, persuade and manipulate the passive majority. This is what is meant by 'upping the ante'. It is an often-used formula, shifting a prevalent pattern for people stuck in systemic structures.

Much attention is given to increasing the force by which the ante is upped, to designing better and better mechanisms for, at its simplest, increasing the pressure. A recent case serves to illustrate:

 The company is highly-driven and cost focused. Much attention over the years has been given to continuously reducing costs, improving value to the customer through lower real prices and/ or value to the shareholder by maintaining real prices. The company's mythology is that managers had better meet the monthly targets that are expected of them, or else! "Meet your expecteds" is Rule One!

It is not surprising that managers budget very cautiously. Most want to keep their jobs, if not get promoted. When keeping your job means meeting your 'expecteds' you will tend towards caution in declaring your expected result. Safer still is to declare a result that you know you will achieve. So there is a built-in tendency to talk things down, to use the language of how difficult things are. Being adventurous is just too risky.

Over the years senior managers have grown more exasperated with the conservative budgeting of their operations. The company issued an instruction, a head office edict, that they wanted managers to be more adventurous in their approach. Nothing much changed. They repeated the instruction with greater force. Still nothing much changed. They are now threatening their managers that if they do not become more adventurous, they had better start looking elsewhere for employment (this might be called 'motivation'!).

Imagine your predicament if you were an operating manager of this fictitious composite company. You face a dilemma. Damned if you do and damned if you don't. What would you do?

The solution of many managers is to be adventurous to a minimalist degree, yet to make it sound as if as if they are being significantly adventurous. One way is to place even greater emphasis on just how bad things are, so any improvement in results, no matter how small, looks really adventurous. Survival becomes a matter of meeting a carefully camouflaged adventurous 'expected'!

The personal objective of continued employment can probably be met, provided everyone plays by the same rules. God forbid if a single member of the peer group, one's managerial colleagues, was really adventurous, placed themselves at risk, *and delivered*! That's unhealthy! The peer group must then ensure that such a successful person does not stay around for long. You can imagine how.

Within this company it is as if a silent conspiracy is at work, a conspiracy which has emerged without conscious intention by anyone. The game and the rules are an emergent property of the adaptive system that is this company. They are known and understood yet seldom articulated – as such. They are conveyed by the myths and legends of the company and particularly by the conversation of the managerial group.

Once upon a time, the issue was publicly addressed. The president himself raised the cautious budgeting practices of the company at a large gathering of senior world-wide executives. Both he and the vice-president went to some length to convey to the assembled company how they wanted more innovative performance, with people willing both to invest time and take some risk in pursuing high potential business initiatives. They pointed out that during their period of tenure not one manager had been dismissed for being willing to take considered risk for the benefit of improved results. They then emphasised the risk assessment procedures and practices that the company had established and invited managers to push out the frontiers for their businesses and positively pursue innovative ideas within their divisions.

I recall one or two polite questions and a few statements of support for the "direction we were taking" by some with an eye for their own career. Yet one could sense that the invitation fell on stony ground for the vast majority. There was simply no listening for what was being said. Even worse, the coffee and corridor conversation revealed that most people thought that what the president said was not what he meant. Granted, most people in the room wanted to see more innovative performance, but they heard 'considered' and 'established procedures', and saw the risk of not delivering against a more challenging 'expected' as just too great. They were able to cite many cases of managers who had 'parted company' for failing to deliver against a target. The names and images of departed managers came to mind, managers who had once achieved significant performance, risen rapidly, and then fallen from grace. What was not said, but was hinted at by many, was that they would not even wish to be like the so-called 'high flyers' who, they presumed, were the risk takers to whom the president alluded. There were two reasons. One was what they thought of these people, and the second, that they expected their fall.

In the room, again, there was a completely spontaneous conspiracy of silence. No-one raised their concerns with the president. No-one dared to challenge. For there was another rule at play. That rule was simple: in the best interest of self-preservation and one's career, never upset the president! Better not to say anything than to say something which might challenge his interpretation of the world, particularly when that challenge might in some way be as bearer of bad news. We chose, or were thrown, then, to conspire.

What influences the state of being of managers in this company? We may not know with any great precision. Such accurate knowing may not even be necessary. What we can see, yet again, is people influenced by certain patterns, patterns which serve to limit individual and collective potential, patterns in which the unwritten rules of the game emerge from a blend of tradition, paradigm and individual self-interest. To shift the pattern it is essential to shift the perceptual and relational processes at work in the background, the unsaid and undeclared stuff that impacts behaviours in such profound ways. How? How can we shift the patterns of being, doing, and performing? Is more and more pressure, greater and greater threat or, indeed greater and greater reward, sufficient to shift the passive condition that so many find themselves in? While the push of the bully or the seduction of the temptation may invoke plenty of activity, the source of action fundamentally remains external to the actor, they are reacting to the threat or promise of others. Remove the threat or promise and things return to their prior condition. How can meaning be put into the idea of 'company' such that people are enrolled and act of their own accord, in which action is more a matter of self-expression than either push or pull? How can we best interrupt limiting patterns and create contexts that serve to inspire and engage?

One way to help people to play a great game is to create a game worth playing. This might mean interrupting the more routine and orderly nature of what's already known and experienced with a context of creative tension[106] and challenging purpose. When we help people access a target or challenge worthy of their personal effort and commitment we put a different meaning into company. Might we then shift some of the patterns of being, doing and performing? Might we help to convert "contractual employees of an economic entity" into "committed members of a purposeful organisation"[107]?

It becomes a lot easier when we can help people see their own patterns and empower their own choice. So doing requires a shared language in which to talk about them; one that, once acquired, enables a group to discuss a pattern and ask how it is affecting them. The pattern which enables and disables is to blame, not the people who may be trapped by it. At some deep, memetic level, the pattern is an alien entity acting blindly to ensure its own survival. Would that it could become that easy to shift! One has to consider how and when to plant the seeds of new patterns in individual and collective minds. We have talked of the leader's role – and the leader does not have to be the he or she of formal power – as a pattern cultivator. Sowing seeds is an apt metaphor, for what one is doing is seeking to have new patterns begin germinating in the minds of others. It may take more time than trying to transplant a full-grown tree into another's mental garden, but it offers greater prospect of taking root!

Jumping the s-curve: when to interrupt patterns

We have said that patterns enable but also limit. A commonsense extrapolation might then suggest the time to shift a pattern is either when it is no longer producing the desired results (implying that either something has shifted in environmental patterns beyond our control or that desired results have been elevated), or when we can see that the pattern is approaching the limits of its workability.

Commonsense might say that, yet all too often it doesn't! The commonsense that frequently prevails serves to keep us locked into that which has begun to limit. "Let's simply try harder!" encourages perhaps greater effort to little, if any, greater effect. We may need to engage in some uncommon sense that, once seen, seems obvious. Consider the ubiquitous S-curve:

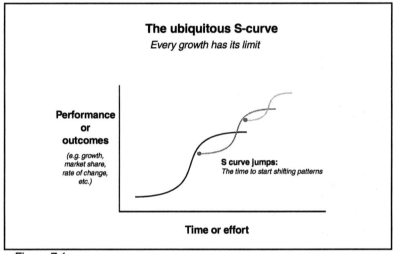

The ubiquitous S-curve
Every growth has its limit

**Performance
or
outcomes**

*(e.g. growth,
market share,
rate of change,
etc.)*

S curve jumps:
The time to start shifting patterns

Time or effort

Figure 7.1

The ubiquitous S-curve, found in returns on projects, in product life-cycles, in new market opportunities, in the growth of new business sectors... indeed, in almost any area of organisational or individual development. It is nearly always a sign of a 'limits to growth' archetype, where initial positive feedback generates rapid growth, then encounters more negative feedbacks. The curve starts slowly, then rises increasingly rapidly. When success under the existing pattern seems most pronounced it is time to start thinking about a shift to a different curve.

The S-curve generalises a positive feedback between incremental effort and performance: one that gradually encounters its limits to growth. Take the example of skill acquisition: say, learning to type. It takes a lot of effort at the beginning to realise even a limited performance.

So much time is spent in learning keyboard layout and key strokes (which fingers for which keys) that speed and accuracy are both relatively poor. Much effort produces only limited performance. Yet as we go up the learning curve relatively little extra effort yields substantial improvements. We may become competent in ten-fingered typing, at 80 words per minute, with 100 per cent accuracy. Then, beyond a certain point, diminishing returns set in and extra effort makes less and less difference. We become limited, victims of a meme that resides not, for once, in our minds but in the cultural artefact that is the QWERTY keyboard (c.f. Chapter Four).

The S-curve generalises to new products in new markets, to successful initiatives to change working practices, to business cycles – to, in fact, virtually any dynamic of business performance over time. Early perseverance within the pattern brings a subsequent return in terms of performance; the danger is one of giving up before positive feedback steepens the slope of the curve. Late in the curve putting more and more resources into yesterday's recipe actually *accelerates* diminishing returns; a lesson hard learnt by whole industries which have, in recent years, found their fundamental operating paradigms challenged by new competitors. Some, particularly fast moving technology and consumer goods companies, now speak of 'S-curve jumping': a phrase born out of the recognition that the time to launch the next product is when the existing one is achieving its peak sales. More often – and the booming Facilities Services market in the UK is a classic current example – companies succumb to S-curve jump-in, spending enormous sums to try and capture a share of projected market growth just before the downturn begins. The ideal time to question a pattern is probably the very time when it is apparently enjoying unprecedented success.

Yet how often does common sense point in this direction of 'less of what has worked well so far', just at the time when the incremental rewards seem greatest? All too often we are driven by 'commonsense' to the Rule of Repeated Action: "When in doubt, do what you did yesterday. If it isn't working, do it twice as hard, twice as fast and twice as carefully". We apply this, even if we know Rita Mae Brown's oft-quoted definition of insanity: "Doing the same thing over and over and expecting a different result!" It is easy to say: "shift the patterns when they are reaching their limits or when they are no longer producing the results they once produced". In practice, we all tend to be stuck in patterns, habits and winning formulas. What has worked in the past will, we hope and, with a little more effort, work in the future. And that of course is just how the pattern wants it. "Don't fix what isn't broken" can be a great defensive routine. What then happens is that any shift of pattern is left until the moment of crisis; the hardest time to actually accomplish a change.

 What also happens is that there is little time, sometimes too little, to grow a new pattern; to cultivate the fragile emergent shoots of a different way of working. Watch any discussion on leadership and it is almost guaranteed that someone will refer to the need for a 'crisis manager': someone who takes command when the going gets tough. Thus is a deeper underlying meme of the modern management tradition (Chapter Three) perpetuated. The pattern cultivator always has to work with emergence.

 I still recall the incredulity when groups of managers from the North Sea oil business first discovered this principle. They were from an offshore engineering environment that had a long tradition of tough minded project management. Here they were a year or two into the beginnings of a transformation process that was to shift the pattern and the profitability of their business in a profound way and was to extend gradually to the entire industry (see Chapter Nine). What had they learnt? I asked one group. "Biorhythms", was the response! "Organisations have a life of their own and sometimes we have to sit back and let what we've planted take hold". It was 'slowing down to speed up' in a big way!

From lock-in to breakout: the discontinuity of pattern interrupts

Let us take a little time to trace the connections between some of the key ideas of this book: memes are intent upon replicating themselves. They do so in the host communities of the human brain, and in the shared patterns of thinking (paradigms) and cultural artefacts of human communities. People are born into – or, if not born into, soon settle into – stable patterns. Most natural systems, including people, if left to themselves, self-organise to avoid chaotic behaviour. Such patterns create a certain horizon of performance; they make a certain level of performance available and no more, they simultaneously release and limit. If you want a different result from that 'allowed' by the pattern, a result that is not released from within the pattern, then the pattern must shift. Simply trying harder and harder within a limiting pattern is only likely to heighten frustration!

 If this idea is valid, then the lock-in presumably happens in the neurological connections of the human brain. We are, some argue, neuro-linguistically programmed. Negative feedback operates through perceptions, language and action to maintain an established order in the mind, a memetically encoded pattern of perception. If we consider this in terms of the domains of complex systems discussed in Chapter Four, we might imagine the mind frozen into, or at least veering towards, the ordered domain. If we seek to help others to interrupt their patterns – especially those whose existing pattern may discount either the notion of patterns, or of stuckness – then how may we go about it? How may we move beyond being an 'I' who simply beholds.

Crisis can form one such interruption, be it a commercial crisis in a company, or the personal crisis of an individual. The danger is that if we leave it to crisis it is often too late. The alternative is to bring some other source of disorder into the prevailing order. As Ralph Stacey puts it, one needs to introduce some 'disorderly dynamics' into the prevailing stability. Such disorderly dynamics are the equivalent of punctuated equilibria[108] which enable new patterns to emerge. Why introduce them? If not because of a reaction to crisis, then perhaps because:

❏ You anticipate changes in the environment to which the current patterns will not be suited.

❏ You, or someone else, wants a greater result than is possible from the established order.

❏ You envision that a new generation or pattern of order will release more potential and create new horizons for performance.

But why 'disorderly' dynamics? Stacey[109] argues that the formal organisation is meant to resist change and sustain the status quo in the interests of efficiency and will therefore be orderly and stable, while the informal system provides opportunity for disorder through the chaos latent or expressed in informal networks. The informal system therefore holds the key to transformational change.

One difficulty in the way of moving from an established order to a new order of things is the premium we place on order and the vested interests in the established order. Order is very highly valued, to the extent that disorder is often held as something to be avoided. When we think of change we tend to do so in orderly ways which follow the logical incrementalism of much of our training. To entertain disorder in a much valued orderly world seems close to heresy, so patterned are we in the esteem in which we hold order. At personal levels the uncertainties and confusion surrounding disorder may be avoided for the security and certainty of what is known and experienced.

We will return to this later. First, how might we entertain disorderly dynamics without triggering the fear, if not the practice, of anarchy? One way, so obvious that we may be blind to it, is to use the dynamic of *humour*. Others that we will deal with are inquiry; challenge and contradiction, confrontation, creative tension, dialogue, reframing, relanguaging and the possibility system.

Humour

Humour, more often than not, is a wonderful pattern interrupt. Recall how often humour, when well-placed, interrupts the dour pattern of a meeting and fosters a different dynamic out of which the meeting seems to make greater progress. When misplaced it tends to be heard as 'bad-taste'. So, we see again that interpretation depends not just upon content but also upon context.

DeBono suggests that humour is by far the most significant phenomenon in the human mind. Largely ignored by philosophers, psychologists, logicians and information theorists, humour only happens within:

> "...the asymmetric patterns created in a self-organising patterning system. So humour is significant because it tells us a great deal about the information system acting in the brain. Even in behavioural terms humour tells us to beware of absolute dogmatism because suddenly something can be looked at in a new way."

Ignored by the classical rational and reasoning theorists because they have been dealing with what are called 'passive' information systems (essentially table-top symbol manipulation according to rules), humour occurs in "active information systems" (self-organising).

It is worth exploring further what DeBono is saying so that we may better understand not only how humour works, but how other interruptions to established patterns may work. First, humour arises only in asymmetry within self-organising systems. Asymmetry is lack of symmetry, lack of the 'quality of possessing exactly corresponding parts on either side of an axis'; dissimilarity or un-alikeness. It provides non-linearity in the network of feedback systems through which people interact.

A locked-in mind gives priority to a main track of thought. At one level this attention is key to survival and progress. Yet what is key to an asymmetric system is that not all points may lead to the same result. Side-tracks may yield either better destinations or more efficient routes than previous experience. If we could somehow jump from the main to the side-track we might 'see' such a better route or destination. Humour works in just this way. For we are led to a certain pattern in the story that runs up to the punch line, only to find that the punch line throws us to an entirely different pattern. The 'surprise' results in spontaneous bodily and verbal motions such as laughter. For the pattern to get established and interrupted does not take long. For example, consider the following:

> "Men who don't drink live longer."
> "Serves 'em right!"

The pattern and image of the world that has been established in the first sentence – where we anticipate some exhortation to drink less – is shattered by the extreme sentiment and imagery of the second: the punishment of a longer life without the solace of drink! The second takes us down a path totally unexpected from the first.

Humour often helps reposition, and shift, the relationship between things in our mind's eye. When we get bogged down in heavy, serious and significant debate, thrown to the pattern of being right in all that we argue, then an intervention of humour can help us to see that perhaps our perspective is but one among many and that, when seriousness is lightened, a different result is possible. The interventionist, as with any intervention, takes a risk that his or her intervention may not be accepted. Thus attempts at humour may be met by the scorn of the group or of the powerful elite. Intervening in the established patterns, whatever the technique or techniques used, is never without risk.

Inquiry

The term 'inquiry' tends to speak into a listening pattern of serious, selective, and significant investigation. The pattern has been established by the use of the term to refer to investigations when things have gone wrong and there is a search for something, or someone, to blame. It is often aligned with an investigation into fault, or even to inquisition. In using 'inquiry' we mean not that limited sense of the word, but rather some process of exploration, where we 'seek by asking' and proceed to ask some questions that would not otherwise be asked. By virtue of this process what is, or has been, is challenged. One has chosen to interrupt a pattern of unconscious acceptance or resignation concerning some context, and instead to ask some questions.

Inquiry has been claimed to be the 'engine of vitality and renewal'[110]; yet inquiry, or at least profound inquiry, is not that common. For, inquiry often leads to uncertainty insofar as, through questions, one challenges what appears as the certainty of what 'is', this thing we call our current reality. Imagine challenging a long-established practice – how things are done here – by asking *why* they are done this way! Imagine challenging long established thoughts – how we think – by asking why we think this way.

The flip side of inquiry is *advocacy*; asserting a particular view or opinion. Often, advocacy is preceded by phrases such as "the fact is…" or "but, in reality…". More often, perhaps, it is concealed. We declare realities into existence by stating them to be true, unaware of our assertion in the matter. People in general, and executives in particular, are well-trained in advocating their position, in presenting and arguing strongly for their views. It fits well with the climate of competitive exchange, debate and argument in which many of us are inculcated, namely, "I am right and you are wrong". The dynamic that advocacy tends to engender, the pattern in which it is often prevalent, is one of win/lose. The advocacy meme thrives in such an environment!

Advocacy can of course enable. Things happen. The danger with competitive advocacy is that the exchange tends to be confined to what is presented and its counter from the opposition. It creates more a conversation of point and counter-point than mutual exploration of any advocated or alternative possibility. Winning can take precedence over optimising.

Inquiry is itself an interruption to the pattern of advocacy for some people. For many, the strength of their case is grounded upon their sense of righteousness, of being right in what they say, such righteousness being untested by processes of inquiry. More powerful advocacy is based upon wisdom, not righteousness. Wisdom is often gained through process of inquiry, having already challenged at least some of one's most cherished assumptions. Combining advocacy with inquiry suggests that one lays out the pattern of one's thinking, purpose and intention so that the assumptions and connections within them may be challenged. The process of inquiry might well make one's opening stand and thinking vulnerable, in the sense that one's untested assumptions and connections get revealed. Yet the vulnerability permits contribution. The power comes from the ability to hold both styles of conversation and recognise which is which.

There are various formal processes for helping individuals and groups to articulate the thinking they may share within any context, in effect, these may be viewed as rigorous processes of inquiry. The scientific method, systems thinking or language as referred to in the previous Chapter, and the Goldratt Institute's 'Thinking Process' come to mind, as, less formally, does the technique of asking 'Why?' *five times*... The problem is usually less one of method and more one of discipline.

Challenge and contradiction

To interrupt and shift the pull of a prevailing pattern often involves a significant challenge, one that can sometimes be provided by provocation or even contradiction. We are generally not well-schooled in effectively challenging either ourselves or others. Pre-dispositions to "be nice" and possible perceived threats to, and of, relationship limit our capacity to challenge, provoke and contradict. We tend not to have contracts or understandings, agreements in our way of relating to each other, that foster challenging. Our habitual relationships are so often based in the past. To challenge, provoke, or contradict someone is too much of a risk, whether that someone is a boss, fellow worker, or subordinate, though appreciation of hierarchy may make it easier in one direction than another!

Clearly challenges, provocations and contradictions can be clumsy and may not be perceived as, or even meant as, well-intentioned. When challenged, provoked or contradicted by another in the absence of any relationship, shared purpose, or coaching agreement, our memes throw us easily to perceiving an infringement upon our own space in the world. Needling, wind-ups, and bullying can be, or can be perceived as, highly manipulative tactics. The reactions of anger or unease that they can engender serve to keep recipients as victims of their own patterns. Yet when we share a sense that to challenge is 'to call forth and test', to provoke is 'to excite'; and to contradict is 'to deny the truth of, to assert the contrary to, or to be inconsistent with' then we can see how each of these, given relationship, can help to interrupt and shift patterns. Contradiction, for example, provides the opportunity to offer an alternative interpretation to challenge the truth or utility of interpretation that the person may be locked into; although the contradictor better have a good story! An example comes to mind.

 It concerns a lady who had time off work due to stress. She was a highly committed individual who held a senior post as director of sales and marketing. Prior to and on return to work, she was convinced that her managing director, together with another member of the management team, were intent upon replacing her. All this despite good results in recent years. She began to dread management meetings, imagined all sorts of plotting and manoeuvres, and worked hard on writing and presenting detailed reports that, in effect, defended her position and department. All this was rather different to her earlier, more creative approach and fresh ideas when first appointed.

Through conversation, she was able to 'see' the pattern that had evolved. She also understood that that pattern carried the danger of playing into any intention that the managing director may have had. That is, she was able to see that she was now spending more time on the defensive than on creating and making a difference in results, which was something she wanted and preferred to do. 'Seeing' was key but not enough, for her behavioural pattern was perfectly aligned with how she saw or interpreted the world; that is, defensiveness followed what she perceived to be the attacks, latent and expressed, of others.

Was there any other opening – another window – through which one could help her shift her perceptual framework? At a crude level, some of what she was working out of was an interpretation which read something like: 'The MD wants rid of me!' She related to this as if it were true, and, not surprisingly, it influenced or shaped her behaviours. One could conjecture, in turn, that her defensive behaviours could become self-fulfilling. What alternatives were there to the lock-in of this pattern? What difference might it make if she invented an alternative interpretation, such as: 'The MD is doing the best job he knows how, he has troubles enough of his own, and we're all being tested by the commercial pressures upon the business'? Through inventing an alternative interpretation, space was created in which the background pattern of relatednesss and relationship could shift. Our sales director, in turn, became much less defensive and started to enrol the team – her colleagues – in the challenges facing the business as well as restoring a performance climate within her own function. Some said that it was almost as though she got back to her old self. Restoration was released by rendering less powerful the distraction of a crippling story.

Many 'commentators upon' might question whether she had been right in her initial interpretation. Adopting an alternative might be naive, even gullible. Indeed, sharing this story recently a listener became deeply quiet and reflective. I asked him what he was thinking. With some reluctance he said: "But what if she was right. Have you not now sent her to her slaughter because she will be totally unguarded?" It was a good, concerned question. I replied that I had not engaged in any alternatives out of being right but rather in terms of utility.

She might well have been right that her boss wanted rid of her. If so, why collude with his intentions by becoming so defensive? Some might also say it would have been better had she confronted her boss and asked him outright whether his intentions were to be rid of her or not. Such acts of confrontation assume a straight reply. Had there been one, and had this been to confirm suspicions, then what then? What difference would confirmation make? It might be said that getting it straight extended her option to either leave or slug it out. The pattern, though, would still have been locked-in. She would still have been stuck with a limited number of options. Inventing something else as an interpretation created the space for a different set of behaviours. It didn't really matter that the interpretation was either wrong or right; the different interpretation expanded choice. We will now never know what the MD's intention was. It matters little, for the world has moved on. As Heraclitus first put it, "We never stand in the same river twice!"

The story illustrates yet again the limitations we place ourselves in when we can only operate out of being right, as though that were the real gift that we have to share with others. Righteous people enjoy calling others Philistines and thus place themselves above all others that are 'wrong'. Hardly a noble act of separation, yet it serves to maintain divisions and replicate memes.

 One more, this time more personal, story will stress the utility of contradiction and challenge. It concerns a close relative who had joined a convent order as a nun after completing a degree course at university:

Her work in the order involved overseas missions as well as periods in her home country. After 25 years, for reasons that matter not, she decided to leave the convent. This, as you might imagine, was no insignificant change. In effect, she had no civilian clothes, very little money, no accommodation, and no job. She chose to teach religious education at a co-educational secondary school and was appointed as a probationer for one year under the mentorship of a fully qualified teacher.

It may come as no surprise to learn that some pupils hardly wanted to be in school, let alone in a religious education class; and, on top of that, with a probationary teacher who had previously been a nun and lived, according to them, a very sheltered life with little knowledge or understanding of modern pressures. To be brief, the pupils helped her to experience some pressures very early in her exposure to teaching!

The result was that towards the end of that first term the dominant thought pattern in our new teacher's mind became: 'Oh no! I don't think I can cope.' She meant it. It was another point of crisis. Almost in despair, she shared this thought with her mentor. Her mentor hesitated for a brief moment and said in reply: "Oh, that surprises me. You impress me as a pretty tough lady. Not many could have been what you've been through and do what you've done." This contradiction, this perfectly inconsistent message to: 'I don't think I can cope', opened up a new window, a new pattern in the mind of this mature, yet fledgling, teacher. It served to challenge her prevailing view of herself in the world, not out of righteousness, but out of something altogether richer.

From a different, more clinical, perspective in the chaos of the new experiences of this teacher a new order was in the process of emerging – one well-summarised in the phrase: "I don't think I can cope". I am certain that it was not an isolated statement of order but played in concert with similar thoughts in different contexts. A powerful expression easily becomes a self-fulfilling prophecy as doubt gnaws away at ability. This order, this pattern, was, thankfully, not colluded with, but was rather interrupted, contradicted and challenged. "A pretty tough lady" and "I don't think I can cope" do not sit easily together, they conflict. In the mind, I suspect there was some disorder, some confusion, some vying and wrestling, before a new level of order emerged from the chaos, a level of order in which a different and more enabling meme infected her mind.

Confrontation

To help someone to catch themselves in their stuckness is a rare gift, for, all too often, we collude with others in their stuckness and, in the process, keep ourselves stuck. There are payoffs. We do not risk relationship, we can be seen to be right, we assume little responsibility, we off-load onto others. In effect, we reinforce the pattern that locks us in, we further endorse our stuckness. It may be less risky, even 'nice', for us to collude with another, so that we neither challenge, confront nor risk conflict. In colluding we can render a disservice, despite the best of intention. Yet what are we trained in?

To confront someone with the pattern that they appear to be stuck in can help them to 'see' that pattern, provided it is not denied. To further confront and challenge by offering some provocation that might take the form of "So when are you going to get off it?" or a nudge of "Just so, and . . ." creates some conflict and space between what is and what could be. It can serve to expand choice and create openings for helping the person move beyond being a victim of their circumstance. A brief and dramatic example makes the point:

 A friend's husband had left her for another woman. At around the same time her daughter, one of two children, was taken seriously ill with a debilitating, incurable disease. The husband appeared to shut himself off from the seriousness of the disease and seemed intent on creating for himself a new life outside his family. Amid all this, the family home was up for sale and there were practical issues of securing new accommodation with little capital and little prospect of work, let alone careers, for either mother or daughter. There was much pain, physical and emotional, in the household.

Our friend, the wife and mother, spoke at length about how much she felt the victim of circumstance: of an uncaring husband, of her daughter's illness. She elicited, and deserved, massive sympathy as she related her story and experiences: an innocent party in a vicious world where things are so black that there was hardly any light in her life.

There's a pattern and there's a pay-off to the pattern. She was right and he was wrong. But how to intrude in such a way as to help her to make a difference? Sometimes it is necessary to confront, and in confronting one risks relationship and chances conflict. How could I, and should I, interrupt the pattern of her being victim in the matter?.

I chanced saying something that perhaps many would not risk: "When will you give up being so right about being so wronged?"

The effect was to help her to see her pattern and to move beyond. A new chapter opened in her story.

This dramatic example helps to reveal what often occurs. It is sometimes necessary to be sensitively abrupt to help people to 'see' their pattern. On its own, though, it is not enough. For, in seeing the pattern, there is, in a way, a prop removed. It is easy for people to substitute one prop for another when what you want to do is to help people live out of a different story – a different interpretation of events – that enables them to expand their choice in life. Ultimately, the possible risk of upset may be more beneficial than sympathising and colluding in a pattern that keeps someone locked-into a pattern. It proved possible to help my friend discover a new level of order from out of the chaos, confusion, and current disorder of one story, by challenging its fundamental assumptions of 'right' and 'wronged'.

Such a domestic tale invites the question of what possible relevance it has to business. Equally for the macho male, two recent tales concerning women may invite the question of what possible relevance this is to men. If so, then we may start to see some patterns at work! Within the pattern of such questions we may see how we box ourselves in, tie ourselves down to discrete categories that says of one that it is and of another that it isn't... If you prefer, they are examples of what other schools of management writing have come to call 'creative tension'.

Creative tension

Necessity, as the old phrase has it, is the mother of invention. And necessity can be a gap between ambition and current resources. Provided that ambition is firmly enough held, treated, in our words, as a commitment, it can be a source of the energy which is needed for self-organisation. Patterns, when not under tension, tend to be stable. When they are put under tension a new order of things may arise. The tension may be one of crisis leading to a respondent or adaptive position, or one of vision leading to a generative position. The tension seems necessary to shift the pattern. Yet, as we said earlier, tension can also lead to memetic rigidity. So what is it about tension, what is the nature of that tension that stimulates creativity, memetic diversity, and effort?

At a practical level a gap is just a gap. It may inspire and engage, it may disillusion and negate. A conventional pattern of managerial writing would tell at this point a story of how shared visions and values, or a 'strategic intent[111],' have inspired extraordinary performance. There are many such well-authenticated tales. So, for something completely different, I recall from my earlier career a different but equally illustrative example.

 It concerns a newly appointed VP for Europe of a recently formed international company. Performance had not been good, so he set very challenging sales and profit targets. Results remained poor. The following year he set even more challenging sales and profit targets, with threats of dire consequences if the results were not met. The results were poor. The next year he really meant business... Europe had earned for itself a really bad reputation in world-wide performance terms, people were beginning to ask what was wrong with European management, his job was on the line. He set really high targets with distinct promises if results were met, and distinct threats if they were not. Results were still poor. All the tension was there, but somehow there was no creativity.

I suspect that the undeclared, and yet widely shared, commitment of most of the Europeans was to see that manager fall!

A gap is just a gap. People grant meaning to a gap through their relatedness and relationship to each other, and to the gap. Whether the tension of a gap is 'creative', that is whether it stimulates a search for a different result, depends on the pattern of relationship and relatedness, to the gap in question and to one's colleagues in the context of that gap.

Dialogue

Dialogue may be best understood as an exchange of speaking and listening which is directed not at proving one right and another wrong, as for example with debate, but more at a process of exploration or joint inquiry. Through dialogue hidden assumptions are articulated, new, deeper, appreciations gained, and unseen possibilities surfaced. Through being witness to, and participant in, a shared conversation, people can 'see' different perspectives and connections and achieve insights that are just not possible on their own. Genuine dialogue has something of an emergent nature where what emerges is less pre-planned (with pre-knowledge of an intended conclusion) and more spontaneous, emerging as it were from the apparent chaos and confusion of the exchange.

It is said that groups when in dialogue learn how to think together and this process of shared conception and involvement is highly beneficial to implementation. As Bohm has indicated, when the roots of thoughts are observed thought itself seems to change for the better. As covered in Chapter Six, seeing how we think can be the spur to new thinking.

True dialogue is a disorderly dynamic. One does not know in advance where it may lead (yet with hindsight conclusions may look obvious). Dialogue also upsets and intrudes upon the prior understanding with which people start. It challenges established order leading, where successful, to a new higher level of order. Isaacs[112] captures this well when he refers to David Bohm's contribution to the development of the theory and practice of dialogue:

"This new form of conversation should focus on bringing to the surface, and altering (our emphasis), the *tacit infrastructure' of thought.* As Bohm conceives it, dialogue would kindle a new mode of paying attention, to perceive – as they arose in conversation – the assumptions taken for granted, the polarisation of opinions, the rules for acceptable and unacceptable conversation, and the methods for managing differences. Since these are collective, individual reflection would not be enough to bring these matters to the surface. Instead, the group would have to learn to watch or experience its own tacit processes in action. Dialogue's purpose, as we now understand it, would be to create a setting where conscious collective mindfulness could be maintained."

What is a memetic pattern if not a 'tacit infrastructure of thought'. Isaacs' summary of the stuckness which dialogue helps to shift is brilliant:

> "The theory of dialogue suggests that breakdowns in the effectiveness of teams and organisations are reflective of a broader crisis in the nature of how human beings perceive the world. As a natural mechanism to develop meaning, people learn to divide the world into categories and distinctions in our thoughts. We then tend to become hypnotised by these distinctions, forgetting that we created them. 'The economy is falling apart' or 'The people are corrupt', becomes our reality, with a seemingly independent power over us."

More significantly, we create and enter these 'hypnotic states' collectively (groups fragment their understanding, with a group seeing the same phenomena in very similar ways and different groups seeing perhaps different phenomena or the same thing in very different ways). Fragmentation of thought is like a virus that has infected every field of human endeavour. Specialists in most fields cannot talk across specialities. Instead of reasoning together, people defend their 'part', seeking to defeat others. If fragmentation is a condition of our times, then dialogue is one tentative proven strategy for stepping back from the way of thinking which fragmentation produces.

 People come to dialogue with their own categories, distinctions, frames of reference, unwritten rules, and, yes, sometimes agendas; in short, all of the tacit or informal stuff that was the subject of Chapters Two and Three. The normal mode of discourse is to be locked-in to what we bring with us: to advocate our case and seek support. Dialogue offers the opportunity for a different exchange, an opportunity to suspend and examine our views and thinking in a context of exploration, discovery, and an 'unconcealing' with others. The certainty of one's prior held views gives way to the chaos of different views and the uncertainty of alternative perspectives; something Isaacs describes as the 'crisis of suspension', when there is the temptation to either withdraw or fight for the rightness of one's view. Yet, when people hold onto to the spirit of dialogue and continue to listen, search and inquire, then a new level is reached, one of shared awareness, sometimes pain, in which insights are gained and new possibilities and openings emerge.

Dialogue serves to shift the pattern by helping people to see their view in a sea of other views of equal validity. The dawning awareness of different ways of seeing encourages self-inquiry into the assumptions underpinning one's view, a reflective inquiry in which one appreciates that one's view is not the only way in which reality may be interpreted. This realisation and appreciation serves to unlock one – and all – from the rigidity and defence of established views, to share concern, and to think anew, thereby creating and generating new perspectives and different openings for possible action. Easily said; yet the experience of effective dialogue is at one at the same time an enormously revealing and releasing process.

Reframing

Our perceptual habits are some of the most stubborn. We come to see things from a certain perspective and seem stuck before that perspective, too close and/or too right in the matter to 'see' it any differently. Reframing helps to shift perspective. It is an old and well-established technique often included within the fables and fairy tales passed down in folklore as well as in humour, where the shock or suddenness of the reframe contained in the punch line induces laughter. It refers to a process whereby the perceptual frame in which a person sees and interprets something or someone is changed in order to create a different meaning or interpretation. A different meaning or interpretation is sought on the basis that with a change in meaning flows a change in a person's responses and behaviours.

"Too bad that Mary does such a bad job" might be a statement made by Mary's boss. It could conceal any number of perceptions: that the boss thinks Mary's attitude is awful, that she is incompetent, that she won't 'play ball', or whatever. A reframe might be something in the order of: "What if Mary were the best person you could possibly get for this job?" First, it interrupts the pattern (though, of course, the interruption can be rejected as not fitting with experience). Let's suppose one persevered. "But what if Mary were *really* the best person for the job?" One has established some incongruence or conflict; for, if the reframe can be entertained, 'Mary being the best person for the job' and a 'bad job being performed', somehow have to be reconciled. This may lead to a search for other plausible explanations for bad performance outwith of the character or potential of Mary.

Reframes which help to shift perspectives over time are also useful for changing meaning. "What would you like to see written on your epitaph?" has always seemed to me a useful question for the reframing of things within some wider purpose, and, in so doing, potentially changing the perspective in which current activities and behaviours are seen. Other facilitators have other tricks. 'Future pacing', a technique in which one takes oneself to a future accomplishment and looks back, or recalls what one has done, serves as a sophisticated reframe that can loosen rigidities, particularly when the challenge looks too great from a current perspective. Similarly, scenario planning provides alternative and at the time unlikely frames – scenarios – in which managers can plan contingency action should the actual business context turn out to be similar to the scenario.

Relanguaging[113]

If language frames how we see the world, if it packages the world a certain way, then relanguaging our world provides the opportunity for release from those frames and packages. In being released the space is provided for new concepts, ideas, distinctions, memes; in short, for new frames and packages to emerge. With such new or rediscovered language we may see and interpret the world differently, thus providing the opportunity for a difference in our being and action in the world, no longer constrained as 'prisoners in the framework of our language[114]'.

 Where language provides the 'house of being[115]', relanguaging provides the prospect of a new 'house' so that we may both be different and, potentially, differently be. Language and thus relanguaging occurs within what we refer to as 'conversation' and conversation we have referred to as the currency of companies (see Chapter One). Yet conversation is not just the currency of companies, it is the currency of human being. To be human is to live, to dwell, to be embedded within conversation. Change the conversation in a profound way and all sorts of new emergent patterns unfold. But to change the conversation is not to parrot[116] some new conversation; rather, it is to live within that conversation. Many of the techniques illustrated provide some means for shifting the conversation and, where the 'new house' fits first into the mind and the conversation of the person, it will later manifest itself in the world.

A simple personal example serves to illustrate. I was once a heavy smoker, a heavy smoker who had tried many times to stop but couldn't (this conversation may resonate with some readers!). With this conversation in the background my infrequent attempts at stopping smoking were short-lived. To increase tension and perhaps motivation I had even challenged a close friend that if she would cross an 'impossible' boundary (one that happened to be a significant personal phobia) then I, too, would cross the 'impossible' boundary of stopping smoking. I thought I was on a winner until she did and I didn't! She later, and not too politely, confronted and challenged me. Yet I had not the will-power to stop. Could I somehow invent another conversation that might enable the same or similar result? If I couldn't 'stop', could I instead 'become'... *could I become a non-smoker?* This new 'house of being' seeded in my mind and, with some surprise at its ease, soon became manifest in the world – I *was* a non-smoker! People who dwell in the conversation that goes something like: "I can't speak in public or give a presentation" offer a similar example when, with great aplomb, they finally speak in public.

These are but relatively trite examples of what's possible when one entertains the possibility of another conversation. Yet such examples are often not believed. This disbelief is perhaps a reflection of the power of conversation and of the house that many people dwell in. We sometimes occupy such fixed dwelling places that we cannot, almost dare not, shed light on what's possible when possibility is entertained. It is as though some of us will not let possibility enter our lives (see next section).

Whilst we may seek to relanguage our companies it is often key to relanguage ourselves, for in relanguaging our 'selves' there can be a new emergence from the I-that-simply-beholds to the I that sees themselves as in the picture, committed to making a difference and being in action. We can, of course, relanguage ourselves to a new sense of self and a new presence and being-in-the-world.

Relanguaging, then, is the art of creating a new conversation for the house of being of either an individual or a company. As Chia[117] has argued, a new metaphor can serve to relax the "boundaries of thought", the "deeply entrenched and therefore taken-for-granted modes of ordering, concepts, categories and priorities, all of which collectively work to circumscribe the outer limits of contemporary management discourse". Whether metaphor or other form of conversation, we sometimes need to change houses; we could, of course, choose to speak of 'contemporary human discourse' as much as management discourse.

Possibility and the 'possibility system'

Possibility provides for patterns of memetic variation where, otherwise, we might be fixed and almost transfixed – stuck – before what 'is'. Thus there can be another route out of lock-in. We are relatively unfamiliar with possibility because we are already substantially locked-in to the tradition of which we are a part, the tradition of our particular way of being. For many, locked-in to a pattern that disposes us towards thinking only within the boundaries of that pattern, all else is deemed to be 'impossible'. We think of something in bounded ways; it is difficult to jump outside a cognitive boundary.

Another way in which this might be expressed is to suggest that we have enormously expanded our capacity to process thought in a logical way, given certain perceptual frameworks and rules. Such processing capacity is granted by the discipline and rigour of logical thought which is embodied in our own training as well as in the programmes of computers. What largely remains unchallenged is the perceptual framework and the rules with which we start. Complexity theory teaches us that significant consequences can arise from small beginnings. Possibility permits us to begin differently.

Instead of starting with what 'is', we start with what 'could be', and what could be, when skilled in possibility, is not limited by what 'is'. Possibility is somewhat chaotic for it interrupts the certainty of what 'is'. Possibility permits exploration, discovery, and design beyond the boundaries of established, perceptually rooted and stable processing of thought. It is not prompted by a search for truth in the matter of what 'is', but rather a search for potential and opening in the matter of what could be.

DeBono in recent work makes reference to the 'possibility system' in a way which captures some of the limits of traditional thinking:

> "Most people believe that Western progress, in those areas where it has occurred, is due to our traditional thinking system with its search for absolute truth; with its classifications and category judgements; with its arguments and refutations. I do not believe this to be so. The main driving force of Western progress has been the 'possibility' system. This is immensely powerful and also essential. It is essential because of the way that the brain works. As a patterning system, the brain can only 'see' what it is prepared to see. The analysis of information will not produce new ideas – merely a selection from existing standard ideas. It is the possibility system that creates a hypothesis. We can organise our information, experience and perceptions according to that hypothesis. A hypothesis does not prove anything at all: it is merely an organising framework."

Other aspects to the possibility system that he refers to are 'vision', resulting from the use of imagination; and 'experimentation', in so far as the system opens up levels of creativity in which you can try out various ideas to see where they might lead without having to be right at each step.

We want to look at possibility and possibility systems from a different perspective, that of patterns and their tendency to perpetuate themselves via the replication of dominant memes. Before doing so it is useful to point out that DeBono has introduced a meme into the world, the meme of lateral thinking. It might well be a meme that in some parts of the world would raise enormous curiosity in the sense that the distinction between 'lateral' and 'vertical' thinking might be seen to be highly arbitrary. Nevertheless, for the 'vertical thinker' to be made aware of, and practised in, some different thinking can be very useful.

Yet possibility which can come from thinking laterally, from imagination, from specific techniques, from dialogue, and from sheer accident is a catalyst to freeing up stuckness. It intrudes upon the established pattern to open new windows to different horizons. Possibility stands as the epitome of all the glorious disorder that is our potential in the dynamic of human communication. For it is in the differences between people that the human community has both prospered and suffered. If all minds think alike the prospect of memetic diversity is severely and dramatically curtailed. The possibility system provides space for the random, mutant meme to infect the mind, to think the 'impossible', which in turn can impact action. Hence, possibility may be realised.

Is 'break-out' accomplished?

We have detailed a number of disorderly dynamics or pattern interrupts, some more intrusive than others, that can serve to intrude upon the stuckness of an established pattern. The trick is that none of these techniques work in isolation. It is easy for any interrupt to simply interrupt for but a brief moment after which normal service is resumed. Patterns, you will notice, tend to persist!

Such interrupts work better in combination, and when interconnected in a broader pattern. Let us first deal with the latter and take one of the more intrusive techniques, that of confrontation. On its own, confrontation simply confronts and, when confronted, many of us resort to either counter-confrontation and conflict, or rejection and withdrawal. For confrontation to work constructively, a shared background of relatedness and relationship is required. If confrontation is seen by the receiver as an attempt to make them wrong then it doesn't work, it simply evokes defensive routines. When it is seen by them in a different context, as an attempt to help release from a limiting pattern, then it is considered differently. The receiver interprets not just what's said but the way its said, the intention, the background, even the way of being of the sayer, all in nano-seconds, out of some deeper, interconnected pattern.

Whatever is said is always said in the context of a background, a background or pattern of appreciation that may lead to acceptance or rejection of any interrupt. The interrupt itself is doing no more than sowing the seeds of another possible pattern, a different horizon or framework, with which the person might see themselves and the matter in hand. It's creating no more than another space out of which the pattern might shift. If the interrupt does serve as an interruption, then any alternative may need to be nurtured and expanded upon. Thus confrontation may lead to inquiry or dialogue in a more powerful combination of techniques.

Let us not forget that in interrupting, one is interrupting either a personal or a shared sense of reality, of order. The interruption itself is immediate disorder to that sense of reality. It may occur as weird, certainly as different to the established order. Thus dialogue, inquiry. possibility, exploration may all be required to help the new order establish itself in the mind of the listener. Unless it is first established in that mind, no new order will manifest itself in the listener's world. A pattern has only shifted when the person becomes an advocate of the new order and committed in their way of being-in-the-world, their action, as well as in their word.

This nurturing is akin to Argyris' concept of 'productive reasoning', reasoning driven by different governing values. Valid information, free and informed choice and internal commitment to the choice, lead to action strategies of advocacy combined with inquiry and public testing, and the minimisation of unilateral face-saving. The result can be more effective problem solving and the reduction of self-fulfilling errors and escalation. Such productive reasoning can, of course, be extended to more productive action and more productive modes of being.

Beyond the I that does: the inner game

To recap and move on. The 'I' that beholds the observing, in the sense that he or she who can 'see' their observing, can move beyond the 'I' that beholds. To do so perhaps involves some risk. Not to do so involves a higher risk of being stuck within a pattern and not developing. Beyond the 'I' that beholds, is the 'I' that does. Beyond the 'I' that does is the 'I' that is. For when being and action are in unity there is a spirit, force and presence in the action that generates a different result.

And there we may discover a still more powerful inquiry. When we find ourselves in structures, when we find ourselves cast together in some arrangement or pattern, we may choose to ask: "Here I am, here you are, but what does it mean? Who are we going to be?" There are, as ever, assumptions present in this inquiry. First that there is some relationship between being, doing, and the results we may achieve. Second, that we can exercise some choice in being. And third, that our choice in being may reflect meaning; the horizon of meaning associated with the pattern, and the horizon of meaning we bring, or convey, to that pattern through our own interpretative stance.

If, through language, we can sow the seed that infects the mind that influences the way of being out of which we act, then there will be movement from within and a new alignment of being, action and potential result. This could be called changing the internal or inner game.

The inner world of the individual influences his or her relations with others. In this sense, who I am as a self-organising system affects my interrelationships. I train the world unto me as the world trains me unto it. The set of interrelationships influences how we are as a company. How we are as a company influences the business we seek and secure, that is, influences our relationships with others external to our company. This patterning forms a complex web with reinforcing and balancing loops.

For things to change, we tend to view it that things *have* to change. And these 'things' are either other people, or processes or events external to ourselves. We tend, as a result, to be less the author but more the victim, or at least passive recipient, of any change. Change is construed as being from the outside-in. If we can 'see' this 'is' as no more than an "is construed as", we may see the construction. We can then choose to change the construction of our thinking and inquire into what it would mean to change from the inside-out. In so doing we start to access the inner game, a game that perhaps has the potential to initiate and empower change from a different basis.

This notion of the inner game is well known to sports players. Golf, for example, is an inner game, as anyone who is on, or off, 'song' will agree. W. Timothy Gallwey deals with it in his book *The Inner Game of Tennis* (subsequent books have dealt with other inner games). He argues that every game is composed of two parts, an outer game and an inner game. In the field of sport the outer game is played against an external opponent to overcome external obstacles and to reach an external goal. Many books provide recipes, suggestions and advice for this game. Many are easier to remember than to execute.

What Gallwey discovered through his own coaching was that instructing someone to play a shot differently, or to hold the racket differently, had limited effect. Mastery in sport could not be gained without giving some attention to the relatively neglected skills of the inner game: "This is the game that takes place in the mind of the player, and it is played against such obstacles as lapses in concentration, nervousness, self-doubt and self-condemnation. In short, it is played to overcome all habits of mind which inhibit excellence in performance."

Gallwey began to see a different, more natural, learning process. Traditional learning tended to operate on the basis of a judgement that something was wrong, or at least not right, with one's game or skills. Learning was fundamentally based upon taking corrective action and trying hard to do it right. The exercise of critical evaluation was essential throughout the process. Instead, he proposed letting go of the old process of correcting faults. When we let go of judgement we grant ourselves the space to 'see' what is happening. In different language, we slow the world sufficiently to raise awareness of what 'is' in a non-judgmental manner. In Gallwey's terms we then ask ourselves to change, we programme ourselves for change with images and feelings, and then proceed not so much to make it as to let it happen. All this until a new habit is learned. The process of unlearning for Gallwey is a process of letting go.

Unfortunately, we are conditioned as observers to observe *with an assessment*, frequently an assessment as to whether something, or someone, is right, wrong, as it should or ought to be, or whatever. The observation is grounded within an pre-existing tradition of how things should be. The 'I' beholds through a critical frame of reference. When we suspend that 'I' for another that is free from judgement and assessment we start to 'see' differently. Having seen, as it were, newly, we can start to 'see' the relationship between what we do and the result that we get. Should we wish to get a different result we can then ask ourselves to change and proceed toward letting it happen.

What has been key is a subtle yet significant shift in perceptual framework and a choice in the matter of change. We have not 'had to change' out of some judgmental stand, but have rather chosen to change out of 'seeing' differently what we do and what we are up to.

How might this translate more generally to the world of business? Can we speak of an inner game of business? Business tends to be more complicated than the world of individual sport. Yet when we engage in some aspects of business we may start to see a direct translation. For example, when we take the world of the individual salesperson much of their success reflects their inner game. When lacking in concentration, confidence, and belief, when full of self-doubt and self-condemnation of either themselves, their company, and/or their products and services, they do not achieve the result to which they aspire (unless of course they do not aspire to much).

Are we not all in some way salespeople for our companies? In whatever capacity we might work, when we are full of doubt and condemnation, not necessarily of ourselves, but of others within the company, does this not serve to limit potential performance? When management is full of woes with regard to its workforce, and the workforce treats its management with contempt, then have we not got mutually reinforcing limits? Limits that will last the longer the more we are up to being right concerning our judgements?

What will more strongly interrupt this pattern is not so much positive thinking as 'seeing it differently'. Perhaps seeing it in such a way that we can start to put a new meaning to our company. The tough bit is that it starts from the inside-out. Gallwey again:

> "It takes years to change behaviour if that's what you're looking for. But behaviour comes out of how a player sees things. If he sees a tennis ball as a threat, he swings out as if he's defending himself and he does 33 wrong things. Help him see the tennis ball as a tennis ball, not as a threat, and he'll stop doing those 33 wrong things. In this way, you can make radical changes in performance with only a few sentences on perception. See what he sees, before you start coaching. In business, if someone turns in a lousy report, first find out what his objectives were."

So how might one be able to help someone, some group, some company to see things differently? The first step is to help both oneself and others to see things as they are, the pattern, free from any judgement. This, in turn, takes a different listening and sharing from that to which we are culturally prone. Next, having seen what is, one may choose to explore the beneficial and limiting consequences that arise from what is, again free from assessment, other than that implicit in drawing connections between what is present and the consequences that result. Having modelled this map of the world, one can then experiment to see if either what is present, the connections, or indeed what is missing, can be altered to generate a different outcome. This takes a form of joint inquiry, a process to which many are not well-accustomed. It is also extremely easy to speak in abstract terms, as though an observer upon the scene; as though with some detachment. In a different sense, then, we need to get beyond the 'I' that beholds, and ask ourselves what difference we can make to this complex web of relationships. Herein is a difficulty compared with the individual sports analogy for our tradition often has it that we cannot make much of a difference. That tradition has a certain payoff, for we do not have to do anything, or be different. Instead of asking ourselves to change, we engage in wishfulness concerning others – "If only he or she, if only they, will change!" In so doing we continue to divorce ourselves from the picture. We fail to ask ourselves to change.

The inner game as Gallwey describes it "is played to overcome all habits of mind which inhibit excellence in performance". A company does not have a mind. What has a mind are all of the people who work for and are associated with a company, that is, all of its stakeholders. A company is an interconnected web of people. And, as we have seen, starting in Chapter Two, people are prone to a corporate 'inner game', one which often inhibits excellence in performance.

Where one can help to reveal that inner game one may help the company overcome the habits of mind and ways of being that are reflected in their conversation. Given that recognition people may then be free to change their inner game, and the rules by which it is played. That change can, in turn, make a difference to the outer game, the one played in a competitive and collaborative context with external obstacles and toward an external goal.

We spoke earlier of various disorderly dynamics that might help to shift patterns. Such dynamics applied solely as techniques are likely to have limited impact. When such techniques are applied out of a background of relatedness and relationship that is shaped by a concerned way of being, then patterns are more likely to be interrupted in something more than an abstract or superficial way. Through such shift in patterns one helps to get beyond the 'I' that beholds – observers – to pattern shifters, people who are up to being-in-action to make a difference to the patterns that exist. Additionally, such pattern interrupts, when undertaken on a widespread basis, avoid placing pattern-shifting in the hands of a few and offer the opening for the inclusion of the many as pattern shifters.

The fallacy of independent 'I's

Some cultures strongly promote individuation and the atomic view. Events and people are viewed in isolation, as though independent of each other. The individual, and individualism, are applauded, with economic systems reflecting the notion that everything is grounded on rational, if not 'selfish', self-interest. Any debate between self-interest and altruism seems to have been firmly settled in recent times. This perspective of self-interest – this way of being – is a reflection of memetic transfer, of cultural transmission. Work may be viewed as the pursuance of self-interest, it may be viewed as something grander, something called 'enlightened self-interest', it could also be viewed in a different way, as the pursuance of self-expression. We can develop a freedom to interpret 'work' in any way we choose. We can invent a conversation that can interrupt the flow of memetic evolution, that begins to shift thinking patterns, in ways that such shifts in thinking and being enable greater potential and result to be released.

For many this possible interpretation of work will smack of naiveté. They might choose to point to recent developments in the UK, where the heads of only-recently privatised public service monopolies appear to have richly rewarded themselves with huge salary increases and share option benefits, or cashed-in by acquiescing readily in hostile takeovers, profiting from the original under-valuation of assets; thereby vastly extending the differential between themselves and other workers in their enterprise. The particular merits, in terms of reward structures, may be argued by some. Part of the unintended consequence is the message conveyed: at its simplest, that people are in business only for what they can get out. It fits the interpretative stance that self-interest is the order of the day. The action taken may not be very important. Whether or not a senior executive doubles his or her salary may make little difference to the overall salary bill. What does make the difference is the meaning given to his or her action. What conversation, what thinking and values, what memes or ideas did they wish to convey?

It may be that their companies will pay a high price in the number of service complaints, the disaffection of customers, and the learning of other employee groups. It is clear that events do not occur in isolation, they fit into a scheme or pattern of things, they fit into the interpretative stance of observers and other actors. This is where the systemic view of the world (Chapter Six) has some advantage in revealing the connections and dynamic relationships between what might otherwise be viewed as independent events.

Our 'I's are hardly independent. We are, at least in part, the result of our genetic and cultural inheritance; and, of all the species on the planet, the contribution of our cultural inheritance is the greatest. As infants we are highly vulnerable, with great dependence on our parents for security, protection and care. This state of dependence is not conducive to growth and development and so we seek independence. We seek to expand our capacity to stand on our own, free from the protection of elders. For some this stage appears as though the zenith of human development; man or woman as independent entities, their own castle, among other independent entities. Others perceive a level beyond this, a level of interdependence where, together, independent mature adults see the results that can be achieved through interdependent relationships; namely, we can see that so much is possible on our own, and so much more is possible with others.

Constructive interdependence takes a lot of maturity, a maturity that is gained only through the struggle for independence. This language of interdependence is relatively new language. It points to a connection between things which sometimes can only be guessed at; it leads to the connections inherent in Chaos theory. It is a language that is helping us start to see the possibilities of, and for, interdependence between nations on the globe, the possible constructive interdependence between companies, the possible constructive interdependence between individuals. We may also be learning that we often lack the maturity – the independence – for such interdependence.

The concept of partnering between companies serves to illustrate. Partnering (covered in more detail in Chapter Nine) suggests a powerful opening for new performance horizons through leveraging off individual and collective interdependence. For many, though, the practice does not appear to live up to the potential. There are many sources for this. Two stand out: first that many partnerships start or rapidly deteriorate toward an unequal partnership with one party fostering dependency on the part of another. Second, that much of our memetic inheritance, our thinking, being, seeing, is not aligned with partnering. To really partner, at any level, takes some learning which, in turn, takes some unlearning. Indeed, the very starting place for some partnerships seems to be very limited and limiting at the outset. "I wish to partner with you out of my own self-interest and profit" seems to extend a limited invitation. "I wish to partner with you for our profit, that is, to our mutual benefit" extends quite another.

One of the great benefits of interdependence is the contribution it permits with others. Through disorderly processes different worlds open up. Language serves as a window to worlds that cannot be seen from our own limited perspectives, in turn releasing potential that is neither possible nor sustainable given our own commencing frameworks. And there are companies and organisations starting to see those forms of design. It may even be that they offer optimistic scenarios for the future world of work. We turn next to the design and action of companies, once we see them as creatures of their patterns, but also as possible creations of people's choice.

 ## Summary

We have tried to place many observations on change at the personal level within the overall construct of a view of minds, individual actions, and collective performance as a product of memetic patterns seeking their own survival. We suggested a benefit. It is easier, perhaps, when one works from that standpoint to accept individual responsibility for one's interpretative stance, and all that flows from it. We only change ourselves when we act, intentionally or otherwise, from a different pattern, a shift of interpretative stance. To do so requires letting go of, or acting with much greater freedom in, what are often deeply held opinions or assertions concerning the world; patterns that have parasitised our mind over long periods of time.

None of this practice is easy, for it requires the unlocking of deeply ingrained mental connections, the introduction of punctuated equilibria or disorderly dynamics at times, and in situations, where we might crave some certainty. On the other hand the potential, and the possibility so released, is enormous. The potential of communities of pattern shifters may be even greater, especially if we can design organisations which are better able to release it.

 ## Primary Sources

Erich Fromm (1994, 1996) provides insight into different modes of existence and the art of being; existentialism also provides useful insights on the unique nature of human being and commitment (Cooper, 1990). Stacey (1993b) covers disorderly dynamics, whilst Gersick (1991) and Price and Evans (1993) expand upon the idea of punctuated equilibrium. For further exploration of techniques and approaches refer to DeBono (1990) and his other writings for humour and provocation; Senge et al (1994) for inquiry; Pascale (1991) for conflict, challenge and contradiction; Hamel and Prahalad (1989) for creative tension; Isaacs (1994) and Schein (1993) for dialogue and culture. For NLP and reframing applied to management and business refer to Fairhurst and Sarr (1996), and Knight (1996), and for background on NLP try Bandler (1981). DeBono (1990) refers to the contribution of the possibility system. There are various inner game books written by Gallwey (1985) and others. Winograd and Flores (1987) deal well with the subject of human commitment whilst Kofman and Senge (1993) expand upon communities of commitment.

8

The fifth attribute: from adaptive to generative systems

"My objective now is to create the conditions where those involved in the manufacturing operation change it. It is not a matter of me changing it, I could do that in a couple of months. I have to grow the capability of the organisation to change itself."

Chief Exec., Anon. [118]

An individual does not then have to be entirely a slave to his or her memes. We can, if we so choose, decide to operate from a different interpretation of a world, or hold an interpretation as just one among several possibilities. In so doing we may progress towards the realisation of a different future. We may innovate, or learn. It can be difficult, not least because in challenging a given meme we risk losing membership of whatever organisation we value in which that meme flourishes. Yet for so many organisations today, large and small, commercial or otherwise, the overriding challenge is to find ways of either changing as the world around them changes or changing that world before some other organisation does so. Can we design organisations so that they find it easier to make such changes? That is the question to which we now turn, looking here at the properties of the organisation and, in Chapter Nine, at the interaction of the organisation with other 'meme carriers' in its ecology. As may be suggested by the number of signposts, we begin to draw together many of the threads started earlier in the book into a conversation for the design of organisations.

Design for a difference?

Recall the example of the East India Company in Chapter One. Whilst adaptive and generative it created an organisation far removed from, and vastly richer than, its original objectives. It imposed its patterns of management on a sub-continent only to fall victim to a revolution when those same patterns, and those of a wider society, denied it the possibility of further evolution. A company is a creation of its memes. It is influenced by wider social patterns; but the corporate pattern, the organisational memome, influences and usually dominates the thinking and behaviour of the organisation's members. Can we design organisations that are not doomed to fall victim to their own learning difficulties, to the hidden presumption that the future is a continuation of the present; or where adaptation simply means a response to, or at best an anticipation of, some environmental change?

It amounts to the question of evolvability of organisations. If some organic designs have proven themselves more evolvable than others, if genetic selection can evolve evolvability, what might grant a memetically specified company similar properties?

Luck may have more to do with it than many managers, or many leaders and writers on management, would care to admit. History is, after all, written by survivors who may not want to admit – or who may have no historical perspective on – how lucky they were. Can an organisation do more to stack the odds in its favour? Can it change from within, in the absence of the helpful threat of crisis? Much case history, interpreted from the pattern of conventional wisdom, suggests the opposite; that the role of management is to maintain the existing order, to collude with the prevailing pattern. "Companies do not really change unless you change their managers", as one MD expressed it, meaning 'change' in the sense of 'replace'. Pressure of circumstances, crisis, is held to be a pre-requisite of change. Yet some innovative companies are able not just to respond to external change, but even to be the source of change, in themselves and in the market.

We have already observed in Chapter Four that teams, companies, markets and ecosystems display a similar dynamic. Stable relationships between a given set of organisations are periodically punctuated by the evolution of, in the one case new species, in the other new technologies, new organisational forms and new structures of relative power. New organisations then emerge[119]. The search for order and stability is always elusive, and ultimately futile. Every overly-ordered system that has existed on this planet has, sooner or later, endured a catastrophic collapse. When it does, there is a rapid shift from extreme order into chaos.

The company facing such a shift in its strategic equilibrium has choices along a spectrum from what might be characterised as passive, through adaptive or reactive, to proactive or even generative. The passive company may 'keep its head down', cling to stability for as long as possible. The reactive company may seek to respond to changing conditions in the world around it and adapt, manoeuvring for fragmented advantage when thrown towards chaos. The proactive company may anticipate such changes and react early, gaining some advantage in so doing. The generative company may decide to cause such changes. It may require them in order to live with the turbulence of an existence closer to the edge-of-chaos, closer to a state of self-organising criticality.

The passive state suits the prevalent pattern. It is the state to which, left to themselves, self-maintaining systems naturally gravitate; survival of the current replicator in a stable niche. If that niche happens to be relatively free of competitive pressure, so much the better. Really lucky companies can become the memetic equivalent of Australian rabbits; adept at eating, sleeping and reproducing without a predator to keep them in check. Organisations that dominate their ecosystems risk becoming similarly passive; growing members, carriers of the same memes who survive and perhaps thrive in a state of passive conformity. Such companies have a greater tendency to pick up passengers, luxuries that are nice to have, given that one can afford it; more minds to share the same memes until interrupted by crisis, real or induced.

Crisis, or the threat of it, then forces an adaptive response. The danger of crisis is that the response may come too late. Just as the crisis of a heart attack may force the overweight middle-aged male to slim so the response to competitive pressures is to become what some describe as 'lean and mean'. The focus becomes cutting costs, at all costs.

So can real change occur any other way? Can a self-organising system develop, and maintain, a greater capability to change? Can it renew from within? Four lines of evidence argue that it can, that change may be accomplished by a change in, rather than a change of, managers.

One is the biological analogy. Some organic designs, genetic archetypes, possess a greater capacity to evolve than others – an inherent genetic flexibility. In other words, some complex adaptive systems are more equal than others. Intuition suggests that if one class of adaptive systems can possess these inherent differences so, too, can another.

Second is the proven adaptability of people in organisations. Given the trigger, even if it is a new CEO determined to show that the game has changed, some organisations have done more than simply cut costs. Crisis, or the threat of crisis may have been the trigger but the response, the reaction to the future, was more than denominator management[120].

Third is the existence of companies with far longer life spans than the average 35 to 45 years. The now much-cited studies done by the corporate planning group of Shell Oil proved the point. In the words of the leader of those studies[121], *"An organisation's capacity to learn is its only sustainable source of competitive advantage"*.

Fourth, and most powerful, is direct experience of companies changing without a crisis. The MD quoted at the head of the chapter was asked by his head office to cut costs because their projections showed a mature product within a mature market, a 'no growth but let's have more profits' scenario. He declined and chose, instead a different journey, posting 20 per cent growth with 50 per cent growth in profitability within two years. The head office interpretation? He just got lucky!

 Reduced to its essentials, our argument is that each such case involves interrupting the mental equilibrium of the company concerned. Continuous change and innovation implies designing companies which can continually interrupt some part of their mental equilibrium. There is not, and can never be, one recipe for doing it. We do not puncture the patterns in our own heads (see Chapter Seven) by following recipes, but – by crisis or intention – the pattern must be shifted. Nurturing an environment that encourages and fosters different thinking and thinking differently facilitates that shift.

Organisations, we argue, maintain themselves by hierarchies of memes; memes that replicate in the language of the organisation, in its belief systems and values, in the types of buildings and physical space it chooses for itself, in its values and its 'rules', written or not. For any organisation to march to a different drum these need to shift at multiple levels. Any particular paradigm, any one meme, only survives in the context of a certain overall pattern of thinking. There is so much interconnectedness in these patterns that it is as if they conspire to limit progress and provide stability. Managers are confronted, not with separate problems but with situations that consist of complex systems of strongly interacting problems, what Ackoff[122] calls 'messes'. He argues that the behaviour of a system, and in his terms a 'mess' *is* a system, depends more on how its parts interact, than on how they act independently of each other:

"Therefore the effectiveness with which a mess is treated depends on how the treatments of the problems that make it up interact, not on how they act independently of each other. However, students are taught to reduce messes to aggregations of problems, prioritise them, and treat them separately. They are not taught, and do not learn, how to deal effectively with messes as a whole."

The work of managers may be interpreted as managing a whole set of dynamics toward a result. Put another way, what managers manage is complexity and they mostly attempt to manage this in an orderly way toward an orderly result.

A difficulty with the term 'mess' is that some, if not many, may interpret the expression in a negative way, even though this is clearly not Ackoff's intention. It is perhaps not easy to own up to managing messes or a mess! The term 'pattern' conveys the same interactive complexity with less risk of any disparagement. The interactions that apply are both temporal and concern major subsystems such as the personal, interpersonal, company and inter-company patterns that comprise a company within its network of relationships (figure 8.1). Experience informs the astute practitioner that these are not separate. He or she is at least informed by his or her intuition if not by any previously accessed theory.

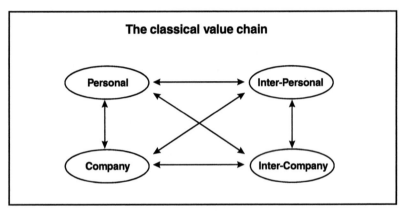

Figure 8.1

In reality, memetic patterns are much more complex and interconnected at many levels. Each may induce resistance to change at another level.

 For example, the Group Procurement Director of a leading airport operator has encouraged considerable initiative in forging different relationships, contracts, operating principles and practices of work with key strategic suppliers, all, so far, with considerable benefits in terms of results. In the configuration we have described above, this may be termed a shift of patterns at the inter-company initiative level.

However, what he now sees is that current progress may hit the wall when such initiatives come into more pervasive contact with the established culture of his own organisation, let alone the inter-personal rules and the mental models and training of individual employees. His intuition informs him that inter-company initiatives will not realise their full potential in isolation, other patterns need to shift as well.

As the layers of the onion unpeel, the emphasis often shifts; for example, from a concern that starts with how we can forge enhanced performance and value with suppliers, we may find ourselves moving to how we ourselves behave as customers... We may need to change to make most difference with these new relationships. This same dynamic of an initiative in one subsystem being constrained or limited by what exists in other subsystems repeats itself time and time again. One result is that, all too frequently, significant initial results run out of steam and often grind to a halt. What then happens is that people move onto another initiative, another popular prescription of the time, without looking deeper into the interconnection of patterns. Some companies appear to drown in initiatives while few, if any, are seen through to a conclusion: a likely indicator that another pattern is at work!

So what properties might characterise evolvability; make it easier to handle the 'mess'? Here we encounter, again, the need to describe, in a linear order, a set of properties which are, inevitably, interconnected. The intention – as throughout the book – is not to reduce management to yet another instant recipe. Rather, it is to inquire into the properties, the attributes, of evolvability in the organic domain and ask what are the equivalents in a memetic system. That inquiry yields four attributes, numbered 1 to 4 in figure 8.2. They are not independent, and none works without the others. However, organisations are not restricted to these four. They have a fifth attribute, an attribute denied their genetic brethren, an attribute born out of the choice and intentionality that people, at least potentially, possess. That fifth attribute is *pattern shifting leadership* which may be displayed at all scales, or levels of an organisation. It is primarily, through such leadership that the other four attributes may connect, as suggested in the following figure 8.2.

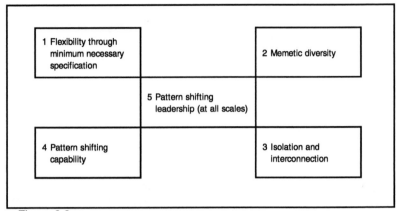

Figure 8.2
The five attributes of a pattern-shifting organisation.

Recognising their inter-connectedness we now look at each in turn:

Flexibility through minimal specification

The prevalent response of managers to the uncertainties of organisational life remains planning and control. If we can just plan sufficiently carefully, implement the right measures and performance management systems, and put in place the necessary controls, then (so goes the argument) we will succeed in business where those around us fail. The pattern has spread in recent years to organisations such as universities, the health service or even charities. Indeed many 'not-for-profit' organisations are experiencing a growing hierarchy of management, a growing overhead of complicated control systems, and a growing cost burden, as the pursuit of 'efficiency' drives them to replicate what the leaders of the commercial world have, arguably, already learnt does not work. One perspective on the public sector side of the UK economy is that the 'pattern' that has already destroyed most of the country's manufacturing industry is now happily exploiting whatever pastures are left to it while it can.

We have seen already how organisations live by sets of unwritten rules that are sourced in the prevailing pattern. The antidote is not to try to put in place ever-more complex written rules specifying what will happen in every contingency. Firstly, it is impossible. Secondly, the rule book is a perfect opportunity for the existing memes to tighten their grip on the organisation, subverting even more strongly its purposes to their own.

The basic rule of survival for a recruit into the British Army used to be stated as: "If it moves, salute it (and, if not, paint it...)". Many American hotels, pursuing standards of customer service, have replaced 'salute' by "tell it to 'have a nice day'". Said with meaning, perhaps even variety, the phrase conveys something that makes a difference to the recipient. Said as part of the fixed routine of a well drilled and specified 'standard' of customer service it conveys at best nothing and at worst exactly the opposite of what the company intends. One self-service petrol station we know took a different approach, encouraging the staff to think for themselves what was essential, and what would differentiate the transaction in the customers' eyes, loosening the rules The result was a list of 76 different ways of differentiating the provision of an opportunity for motorists to serve themselves, and a 10 per cent increase in throughput.

Over-specification?, complicated rules for every contingency, denies the individuals concerned the opportunity to be anything more than automata going through the motions. Compare the biological world's use of 'schemata' discussed in Chapters Four and Five. Replicators, schemata, in any self-organising system, generate rules of behaviour for the agents which carry them. A genotype must build a body capable of coping with the vagaries of seasons, climate, interactions with other genes' host bodies, bad hotel food and all the other complexity of a natural environment. Simple organisms cope with the problem by encoding every conceivable contingency into their genetic instructions. Start growing when the temperature reaches 10°C, stop hen it falls, grow (or move) towards light and moisture. Without such genetic rules the primordial soup would still be the primordial soup. But a code that must program instructions to cope with every foreseeable contingency cannot grant its copier a chance of survival outside a narrow band of foreseen conditions. There is simply not enough space in the manual to write all the requisite instructions. Over time, evolution 'discovered' the benefits of building organisms capable of reacting to, and learning from, circumstance. It takes less genetic code to build a large-brained mammal than to build a frog. Genes, and the organisms they build, gain replicative efficiency from the resultant flexibility. That, as covered in Chapter Five, is the explanation for the evolution of brains. They empower the organism to vary the means by which it fulfils its genetic mission. A learning organism has a better chance of staying alive in a complicated and changing world.

The organisational equivalent, the learning organisation, is one where people are enabled to exercise judgement and initiative, permitted and indeed encouraged to be themselves in delivering a benefit to the collective organisation. The danger, or rather the perceived threat to many an established pattern, is that by so doing we lose control. 'How to control the empowered?' is a question frequently heard in management retreats. A seemingly ordered world is far more predictable. It provides a false comfort of greater certainty. By having control we can delude ourselves that we are in control. Not controlling is interpreted as chaos, and chaos is to be avoided. Despite the manifold evidence of the benefits of empowerment many organisations still act in practice rather like the British Army in World War I. Out of a belief in the need to maintain control of operations, its generals issued detailed instructions for troops to advance in serried ranks regardless of the location of opposing machine guns. It failed. The German Army broke the pattern in 1917 by entrusting its troops to move forward in flexible units[123]. Loss of central control generated a better overall result. Those trusted, educated and supported in using their own judgement will deliver a greater result, faster, than those obliged to do things by the book.

And when the requirement is to do things by the book, the book strikes back. Every time there is an incident or a malfunction, every time the system is seen to have risked departing from control, the reaction is to introduce a procedure to ensure that it doesn't happen again, or if it does, that at least senior management cannot be blamed. Do it by the book and the book gets bigger. Adaptability, let alone generativity, soon becomes frozen. A bank wanted to empower its staff to improve the service to customers. It was committed to such service and invested heavily in providing training and support to its counter staff. It also wanted the security of control and fired tellers the second time their tills did not balance at the end of a day. Its managers were genuinely puzzled as to why queues kept building up!

Twice already in this section we have used the word 'empowerment', which is the current vogue term for the process we are describing. We must again slow the world and inquire what pattern lurks therein, for the term empowerment is often used out of a sense of "I have power and am giving you some (perhaps)"; the old 'responsibility without authority' conundrum. Equally, delegation of power is often perceived as a trap. Then the companies which attempt it, while they are operating under the control pattern, wonder why it does not seem to happen? There is, however, no easily understood alternative term so we will continue to use it, meaning perhaps something closer to 'true empowerment'. True empowerment grants to the 'empowered' a self-authorisation; a responsibility for the outcome.

Empowerment is not just delegation, "Here's what I want you to do"; let alone, "and here's how you do it" – for delegation rendered thus grants the empowered no control over their destiny, no freedom to use their flexibility. It may even leave them feeling alone and under-supported, a vulnerable state – particularly if the control-by-punishment pattern lurks in the not-too distant background. *So what is empowerment?* The brain, as the device of the cunning replicator, may serve as a metaphor. Genes grant a brain considerable freedom, staking their future on its decisions. Its success or failure in competition with other brains determines the survival, not only of brain genes, but also of other genes in a particular genome. Their success is bound up with that of their 'fellow genes.' They 'empower' by staking their own success on the success of the empowered. Yet how many managers, even when they depend for their success on those they manage, wish the relationship to be reciprocated?

The truly empowered are not controlled, limited to certain ways of behaviour, but rather trusted as members of a group enabled by a shared pattern; an accepted way of thinking and behaving. What is shared and lived by, whether formally specified or not, are standards and values, of, say, financial integrity, or safety, or behaviour towards, and management of, others – shared patterns rather than systems. Control by specification is replaced by the creation of an 'identity'[124]; an 'idea and image' of the company with which its members, as well as other stakeholders, identify; a pattern or meme that enables the organisation in such a way that the need for traditional control diminishes. A strong, shared memome is created.

Identities cannot be 'engineered', machined into existence in a one-off project or operation. They need to be cultivated, grown over time; hence again, pattern cultivation rather than engineering. A friend in advertising was once briefed by a prospective client: "I want my product to have an image like BMW's." My friend replied, "Okay, so do you have thirty years and three hundred million pounds to spend?" He didn't get the account! It may seem slower, particularly when compared with the apparent ease of adding yet more specifications. The difference is, we still see companies full of excessive specifications being slowly strangled by them.

The alternative is to allow shared processes, systems, standards and procedures to become the equivalent of minimally specified organic schemata, routines that take care of the routine, so that the brain is more able to concentrate on enhancing a product or service delivered and on creating, with other brains, a collective outcome. The purpose of the routine is then to enable, rather than to restrict: a profound shift from the usual pattern. The comparison extends to software, where conventional computer programmes, sets of rules that specified every step a computer would take to reach a programmer's desired goal, are being displaced in complex applications by 'genetic algorithms', codes that mimic natural selection by converging on a solution[125]. The programmer's desired outcome is met, not by specifying every step, but by specifying what is rewarded, the bits of code that are replicated in the next iteration, and the boundary rules; then letting the solution emerge through a process of selective self-organisation.

Why then are so many companies still full of detailed specifications? Why are some still trying to impose additional specifications[126]? Part of the answer is that we may see it as memetic infection; infection by a strain of the prevailing managerial pattern. Part is that minimal specification is not, by itself, sufficient. There must also be a sufficient source of ideas for the minimally specified to work with. Generative companies need generative people, more than compliance with ISO 9000.

Memetic diversity

The global environmental debate, and in particular the growing concern at the loss of natural habitats, has focused attention on the longer-term threats of the loss of genetic diversity – the ultimate source of variation and creativity in nature. The same danger lurks, less well appreciated, in an organisation. Diversity, requisite variety, is not only essential at the level of an entire ecosystem, it is a prerequisite of evolvability in any complex system. Adaptive designs carry an excess genetic capacity. Only a small percentage of their genes are used in the normal process of building body tissues. Few organisations encourage, or have a listening for, the equivalent mentalic variety.

Evolutionary survival may be partly a matter of luck, having the right capability at the right time. It is also a matter of riding the booms, and stimulating positive feedback, increasing returns. But this by no means explains everything; for, to evolve new biological structures, organisms require sufficient surplus capability, a minimum requisite variety. Animals first 'tackled the land market' 400 million years ago, when some fish, trapped in an environment where the lakes in which they lived were prone to dry out, developed the ability to breathe air. Whilst they were evolving lungs the fish still needed to go on breathing. Their solution was to evolve lungs, not from gills, the existing breathing technology, but from their buoyancy structures, their internal 'airbags.' Birds probably evolved wings as a new use for

299

cooling fins. You need the ability to live in the present world whilst you develop the capability to prosper in whatever is coming in the next.

The genomes of most multi-celled organisms contain far more genetic material than is absolutely necessary to reconstruct a particular organic design. This is what enables organic innovation. The optimally efficient, perfectly honed, lean-mean genome[127], which carries only the information needed to carry out its 'mission', is trapped when the world around it changes. It cannot simultaneously mutate and carry on sufficient business as usual to survive. Species with the smallest surplus of genetic capability are also those with few close biologic relatives, condemned to a future as niche players by their lack of a strategic capability for evolving.

Contrast what the efficiency pattern often seeks to force on a company. In honing the functions of the company (the body that the pattern builds) to be perfectly adapted to its competitive niche, to be efficient and specialised, it all too frequently eliminates variety. Pursuit of efficiency can lead to corporate anorexia[128], a reduced capacity to compete in the future. Another symptom is reduced diversity. Talk to the survivors (the word is often theirs) of most programmes of cost-reduction and you will often find that those who were most different – including sometimes the more able – were the first to go. The survivors are those who toe most closely the company line, who conform most precisely to the unwritten rules, who carry most completely the prevailing pattern. The result can become the downward spiral of failure shown in figure 8.3.

The cycle plays itself out over eighteen months to two years. As the lay-offs bite, the old paradigms of the business become more and more firmly established. People are even more afraid to stick their heads above the parapet. Fear and insecurity increase. Being different risks membership. Adaptation, let alone generativity, is even harder in what is already a focused organisation and the competitive position declines further. Somebody renews the drive to focus and, guess what, another round of lay-offs is announced. Peter Scott-Morgan[129] dubbed it the "Honey, I shrank the Business" syndrome.

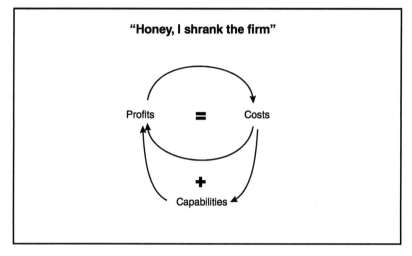

Figure 8.3

The stark dynamics of the slide towards corporate anorexia when cutting costs reduces, over time, the ability of an organisation to generate revenue. Unwritten rules, and patterns of thinking, are nearly always there behind the scenes. The overall dynamic is a vicious circle. (See Chapter 6 for an explanation of the (+) and (=) systems language notation.) The dynamics of individual anorexia are identical.

The lesson is not that downsizing and focusing is wrong. This is not an argument for preserving excess physical capacity 'in case it is needed', or even for over-staffing. But organisations that have never lost their focus find it a lot easier to learn. The lesson is that, in improving the focus and efficiency of the corporate body, it is vital not to destroy the surplus capacity of the corporate mind. The evolvable organism carries its surplus capacity in the most efficient way possible, as genes. The alternative of carrying surplus in the corporate body offers far too much opportunity to competitors.

For organisations the equivalent translates, in practice, into carrying a surplus and diversity of *ideas* or mental models. It implies a culture that not only tolerates, but even encourages, ideas and thinking that do not fit prevailing norms. The generative company must be willing to include people who are different, people who can catalyse different thinking. Thanks to the Lamarckian rather than the Darwinian model of memetic evolution, such companies have an advantage over a genetic species. Unlike species they do not necessarily have to carry the full surplus all the time. Provision of requisite mental variety is a, perhaps the, natural role for the external advisor, the executive coach, the non-executive director or the creatively deployed consultant. Companies have the option to use such people as 'meme adjusters': an option denied to their genetic precursors. The dilemma is that someone who is too different is usually the last person to be employed, even as a part-time source of requisite variety. They threaten the pattern, so ably defended by the gatekeepers in HR.

The generation of variety may be even more simple. It can come simply from encouraging and enabling different conversations in the company. Consider for example two simple questions:

☐ What's wrong here and how do we fix it?
☐ What's possible here and how do we achieve it?

The first implicitly presumes a problem, a departure from a desired state of order, a threat. The second presumes an opportunity – if we can slow the world down enough to imagine one. Prevailing patterns of control, specification and efficiency throw their victims easily to the first question, to a restoration, if possible, of a former state of affairs or a further refining of an existing way of operating. Possibility is the essence of a generative system – yet the efficiency pattern steeps us in diagnostics. We may be thrown, without thinking, to respond to the second question with, "No, that's impossible here and here's why...". Thus is the pattern preserved. Possibility is more easily created in smaller groups isolated from that wider pattern, but how then is it *shared*? This brings us to attribute three.

One company or many? Isolation and interconnection

 We observed in Chapter Four how isolated populations facilitate speciation, organic innovation, and how a comparable phenomenon enables organisational change and innovation. Smaller populations find it easier to punctuate an existing equilibrium, break the mould of an existing organisational pattern. In sector after sector of the economy, whether privately or publicly run, the dispersal of decisions and accountability to local units has proved an essential stimulus to faster adaptation and change. Decentralisation works; but not, or not only, for the oft-stated reason that it exposes organisations to greater competition from market forces. It works *because it permits memetic variation.* Planned economies, national or corporate, are doomed, not because they are planned per se, but because they are the natural breeding grounds of complacency; of a dominant meme bent only on its own survival. They have an inherent tendency to drift into stasis.

The different explanation exposes the dilemma that, for the whole to be more than the sum of its competing parts, isolation, which aids innovation, has to be complimented by interconnection. The component units must somehow share knowledge and resources. A recent televised debate on the subject of schools opting out of the control of local education authorities encapsulated the dilemma. On the one hand, argued a representative of a successful opted-out school, the freedom from bureaucratic control by local authority committee enabled a more flexible, proactive approach to improved teaching. The apparently opposite case, argued for the greater level of service and diversity that was possible from a group of schools connected with a collaborative framework under a single authority.

 The dilemma, yet again, has its genetic equivalent, for genetic instructions work through the cross connections in a genetic network. Genes do not act in isolation. Simulations of complex systems show that critical densities of interconnection are essential to the emergence of order[130]. Without interaction there are limits to the order that may be created. Simultaneous collaboration and competition are, we argue in Chapter Nine, the secret of any organic design more complicated than a bacterium. Co-operation in your own best interests is too good a trick for a selfish gene to ignore. Organisations pursuing a paradigm of apparent efficiency, with everyone in their appointed place and slot, all too often, actively or covertly, discourage interconnection. So, often, do individual reward systems and Strategic Business Units. Both frequently produce situations where individuals, or individual business units, are more concerned to extract as much from the whole as they can. They compete with each other, more than with the outside world[131]. A company of discrete, unconnected units may create the space for greater innovation but lose the multiplier effect of interconnection – unless there is simultaneously an implicit inducement to collaboration and cross-fertilisation. One phrase which expresses the sentiment, and derives from the MD of a company that has transformed itself along these lines, is the 'Federation of Assets'[132].

Simple genomes can only generate simple species. Complex order depends on a complex cross-connection of different genetic phrases. The phenomenon is more general. In any complex system, self-organisation; spontaneous and emergent order, depends on the density of agents in a network. Ideas and new patterns are born out of conversation between people, and economic systems are born out of interaction between companies. Trade and exchange are the basis of growth. Recall the story of Aniko in Chapter One. The difference was not so much the different drum, as the connections that it enabled.

The dilemma of the virtues and dangers of isolation is well illustrated by the recent changes in the UK's National Health Service. Independent trusts, created out of what was previously a dominant bureaucracy, have been able to evolve different and flexible responses to more effective, and efficient, customer care. At the same time they have been forced, through the formal and informal reward systems imposed on senior managers, to see each other as competition. There are now considerable barriers to sharing ideas and information between trusts. (The December 1997 White Paper, 'The New NHS', published while this book was in press, seeks to address the problem.) Many large corporations divided into either business units or national operating companies report a similar disincentive to collaboration as one of the side-effects of structures designed to encourage greater efficiency. Meanwhile, others have succeeded in creating workable 'federal' structures; organisations that combine the virtues of local innovation with the synergy of collaboration and shared learning.

Achieving such a change demands a shift from the paradigm of a reward structure in which individuals are rewarded for individual performance, and managers for the performance of their individual departments. There has to be an incentive for collaboration, one which many companies are recognising under the name of 'gain sharing', or team-based pay. A few go further and link individual managerial reward not to a higher collective performance but to the specific performance of peers over whom individuals have no direct, or formal, influence. Chapter Two gave an example.

An interconnected organisation also demands a profound shift in paradigm for any functions at its centre. The classic role of such departments, whether they are specialised technologists, finance, audit or personnel (see Chapter Three) has been to see themselves, and be seen, as the enforcers of law and order, bastions of control whose role is to define, and ensure compliance with, prevailing standards. The classic dichotomy of staff and line is another case of self-fulfilling paradigms. Both parties in company after company act consistently with their view of the world. (See Chapters Three and Seven.) In essence the function becomes, in the name of preservation of order, the guardians of a prevailing paradigm, the high priests of a pattern. Their stance in the world is then dedicated not to innovation but to preservation and refinement of an existing way of doing things. Rather than encouraging innovation by moving new ideas around, supporting the shifting of patterns, they more often become dedicated to suppressing it, enforcing conformity by reducing diversity.

A profound shift in the pattern of performance measurement may be essential. The measurement meme is having a field day in today's organisation, spreading from bookkeeping to private and public sector management, replicating through all kinds of variants. Indeed, by co-existing with the word 'performance' as in 'performance measures' or 'performance measurement system', the measurement meme dangles a seductive hook to catch the mind of many a modern management and supports its own replication. The hook runs along the lines of "Just really refine the performance measures and you will finally succeed." Hah!!!

 Perhaps controversially, consider the hypothetical example of a police force, established to contribute to a safer society. What are the appropriate measures to apply to compare different forces and how strongly should they be linked to the reward structure of senior officers? (It is a safe presumption that the senior officers will translate their own reward structure into the reward structure for other ranks). One much touted measure is the number of arrests made, or the number of convictions gained. Unfortunately such a measure, like any other, can easily be biased. In this instance apparent success can be gained by large numbers of arrests/convictions for relatively trivial crimes. Such a reward system does not actually encourage the prevention of crime, indeed it could happily co-exist with high levels of crime, a proportion of which was detectable. Increased crime levels permit increased detection rates. Criminal organisations are as emergent in a given context as any other form of company and the police force can, if reward systems are distorted, become a symbiotic memetic partner.

Many similar instances arise in both financial and non-financial performance measurement systems. Schools focused by exam league tables on marginal candidates who can be squeezed into a qualifying band, or production line managers producing stock for inventory are equally distorted by an imbalance in reward systems; an unintended consequence evolved over time. All systems evolve in the direction of satisfying the perceived reward criteria. And numbers used to judge people, whatever those numbers are, become as unreliable as numbers with which to judge what is happening in the outside world. Overemphasis on periodic accounting statements contributes, not only to cost systems that are irrelevant for many other management decisions, but to performance geared solely to manipulating quarterly accounts.

The control pattern carries the presumption that order is established from the top down, imposed on what would otherwise be chaos. Complex systems show the opposite. Order emerges equally from the bottom up. Interacting networks of genes build genomes, and individuals. Those individuals are entities that function as systems of mutually adapted organs. A body is a system, not – as the control paradigm would have us believe – just an entity ruled by a commanding brain. Interacting individuals create species and interacting species create ecological systems. Memes coalesce into paradigms, ideas and language. Shared language and intention creates companies and interacting companies form complex economies. Again, we will cover the theory in the next chapter; but basically, symbiosis, interdependence between 'selfish' replicators, pays.

Spontaneous collaboration is favoured by, and favours, a positive-sum game. Companies that are growing, whether it is by virtue of a fortuitous strategic position or by well-established competitive capabilities, find it easier to establish a fundamentally collaborative internal architecture, a sense of partnership around some common enterprise and values, than do companies which find themselves in a static or shrinking market. Equally, companies where everyone shares a fundamentally collaborative stance find it easier to grow.

The controlling pattern, by making things happen, enforcing common standards and setting the drum to which an organisation marches, can generate great competitive success. It enables large organisations to emerge from entrepreneurial innovation and near-chaos. It easily evolves to a point where it becomes parasitic, where, by supporting a small elite and a subservient majority, it commands the maximum number of minds it can. Parasitic behaviour shows up whenever a small 'elite' organisation, a company within a company, gains control of an enterprise. Boards enriching their status and power beyond what is good for other stakeholders in the enterprise, government bureaucracies and quangos, or the 'nomenklatura' of the former Soviet Union are, or were, all parasitic 'companies' founded on the meme of control; like their biological counterparts, they suck the lifeblood of the larger companies they infect. As Michael Rothschild puts it in *Bionomics*[133], a book that is, by the way, intended as a vigorous defence of capitalism:

> "Without question, our standard of living would rise significantly if the corpocracies were purged from corporate America. In all likelihood however the required reforms will not be implemented. Like enormous tapeworms, these persistent, unobtrusive parasites will be sapping our economic strength for some time to come."

When too much lifeblood is sapped, the generation of new wealth slows or ceases. The competition for advantage within the company becomes more intense and the vicious circle starts. When people are fighting for their place in the golden life-boat, especially when the life-boat is shrinking, the cycle of denominator management, diversity reduction and enforced adaptation is easily started. Severe cases of the corporate parasite might be compared not merely to a tapeworm sapping lifeblood but to a more refined parasite such as the barnacle *Sacculina*, which has developed a strategy, extremely effective from its point of view, of programmed consumption of the crabs on which it feeds. It first attacks their testicles or ovaries, effectively castrating the host which then, bullock-like, devotes all resources into growing food for the reproduction of the parasite's genes.

The parasitised crab is forced into an extremely passive orientation on the world and the inevitable consequence of parasitic management is a passive stance in the company – not in the sense of a lack of action, for people may be very busy and passive, but in the sense of their fundamental orientation. It is easy to stimulate activity but in the absence of the stimulant the action ceases: the fundamental orientation remains passive. The overseer on a slave galley can stimulate the slaves to row; but remove whip and overseer and the overseen will row less, if at all. Throw some slaves to the sharks and one might stimulate activity again. This does not mean that slaves – people – are passive by nature. It merely means that they do not feel part of the enterprise, the undertaking, of the ship. Offer an alternative enterprise, perhaps escape to freedom, and their orientation might become very active.

How, then, to shift an underlying passive orientation? The slave ship holds the clue. A few – the masters – are clear about their intention. The rest are only required to row. To do something they do not wish to do they are threatened with punishments and promised rewards, all extrinsic to their sense of purpose or choice in the matter of what they are doing. What is missing for the slaves is any sense of shared purpose, any context in which they may willingly act. Their work is a function of the most limited of motivators, simple survival. The example is extreme. It is used for dramatic purpose and to highlight some stark realities. Today, we are not enslaved, at least not so obviously. We may not be imprisoned within physical boundaries but we can still be imprisoned within mental, perceptual, and relational boundaries.

It is gradually dawning on political ideology and economic orthodoxy, even in the bastions of Anglo-Saxon free enterprise, that the relative success of Japanese or German commercial organisations may derive, in part, from their greater equality in sharing out the available pie; their much smaller differential in the share of the rewards received at the top and bottom of a company[134]. A similar observation is being made in study after study of individual firms that are succeeding in exceeding the performance norms of their industries. *Cultures of common commitment outperform cultures of manipulative control.*

Communities of commitment both thrive on the process of wealth generation and support it by enabling new and different wealth creating strategies. Communities of control thrive in a world of fixed or shrinking pots, yet also perpetuate such worlds by sapping the wealth creating process. In contributing to economic decline they also encourage the conditions for their own survival. Truly, there is no route from control to commitment. You cannot get there from here. To break out of the mental prisons that sap an organisation one must indeed think and converse differently. The point is that it is within everyone's power and potential so to do. The genetic organism cannot re-engineer beyond the facilitative capacity of its genes. The organisation can be 're-cultivated' but the process is memetic, and the organisation needs the seedcorn, the different ideas and images to work with. But that diversity of ideas and images can only thrive in an environment where the capability to re-cultivate exists, which brings us to the fourth attribute:

Pattern shifting capability

One way to change an organism's, or an organisation's, behaviour is random natural selection. Patterns that are unfortunate enough to code for a particular structure may lose out through no fault of their own when the environment changes or when a superior genetic technology appears. A second is conditioning and selective breeding. Humans have been conditioning animals for thousands of years, rewarding the behaviour we wish to encourage and punishing that which we do not want. Control management operates on the same principle; break a task down into its components and condition a workforce to perform them. Reward the behaviours you wish to encourage. Punish or prohibit all others. Selective breeding, a more recent innovation in agricultural technology, might be said to extend the principle of conditioning by granting or withholding the ultimate genetic sanction: the right to replicate. The results in terms of agricultural productivity have been massive. Unfortunately selective breeding reduces diversity. Consider the susceptibility of modern agricultural strains to disease, and the growing global concern at the loss of the natural pool of genetic diversity from which new strains might be developed. The products of selective breeding can only survive in an artificially protected environment.

 Training, especially as often practised, or, lest we seem to malign many trainers, especially as often purchased, within the prevailing pattern, is frequently little more than an adjunct to the conditioning inherent in control management. The approach and thinking pattern, deployed when we 'train' dogs, is extended, or specified, more or less intact, to people in organisations. The repertoire of responses trained for, and the range of signals or instructions deployed, may be larger but the paradigm remains the same: repeat and reward the same task enough times and you will achieve an optimal efficiency. As a recipe for growing new capabilities it is limited. You can train a rat to run round a maze, or a young dog to perform new tricks, but the rat is still the same rat or the dog the same dog. Unfortunately, many prescriptions for bringing about a supposedly fundamental change through training are about as effective. As we argued in Chapter Three, they operate from the paradigm that a fundamental change can be achieved by applying standards and enforcing compliance, granting or withholding reward. The recipients are treated as passive, conditioned agents. Instruct the workforce that this is how it is done, with implied reward for compliance and penalty for failure and – or so the control paradigm has it – you will have a world-beating organisation. It has been seen to fail as a recipe for a lasting shift in performance in countless thousands of failed initiatives on standards, on quality, on benchmarking and on organisational development. Yet the pattern still holds the day[135].

The alternative approach to changing both organisms and organisations is genetic engineering or its equivalent, memetic cultivation. Both are still in their relative infancy but capable – if we choose – of creating far-reaching changes, and harbouring far-reaching dangers. We may deploy memetic cultivation subtly, using an understanding of the rules and thinking habits of an organisation to steer, and manipulate, a certain amount of change; or we may try to grow the capacity of organisations to change themselves and accept the loss of control that goes with true generativity. To do so we have to create the ability to see and shift limiting patterns.

This points us to the final, and perhaps most significant analogy between memetic and genetic systems. A surprising discovery of genetics is the existence of a genetic capacity for genetic engineering, a capacity that resides in strips of DNA dubbed 'transposons' or *jumping genes.*

Transposons are segments of DNA with the property of splicing and rearranging other parts of the genetic code; the equivalent of re-languaging (or editing) the genome. Geneticist Christopher Wills[136] calls them facilitative genes. They grant some genomes, some complex genetic systems, the attribute of shuffling their own genetic deck, shifting the pattern of instructions coded in particular DNA molecules. In other words, certain gene lines possess an innate ability to generate variety, an inherent facility for shifting their own patterns. Few organisations foster in their managers (or should that be leaders?) the equivalent habit of rearranging their own, or others' mental models of the world. Yet we may see the skills and practices discussed in Chapters Six and Seven as, in this context, those of memetic transposition!

Memetic transposition can be facilitated by people. That is the fifth attribute, one to which we shall shortly turn. Other forms of memetic transposon may also be built into the organisational pattern. The transposon, from a selfish gene perspective, might be considered a parasite. It gets a free ride in the replication stakes, because the genetic system of which it is part, is more evolvable. Hence an inquiry; what apparent excesses in the organisational pattern offer the same possibility?

We have argued that the organisational meme is contained in the language, behaviours, and cultural artefacts of the organisation. What would transposons in that pattern look like? Perhaps for example physical spaces, such as the drop-in rooms found in some high tech research organisations, which encourage spontaneous interaction and creativity; or perhaps breaks of pattern such as 'dress casual days'; anything in fact which offers the opportunity to break out of the 'business as usual' of a particular context. Such spaces, and breaks, make it easier for the fifth attribute to show itself, at all scales (vertical levels and scales of horizontal impact). They help pattern shifting, but are not enough.

The fifth attribute: pattern shifting leadership

With each of the preceding attributes we have drawn parallels between the genetic and memetic worlds: flexibility through minimum specification; diversity and variety; isolation and interconnection, and pattern shifting capability, all have their biological equivalents. The book has also spoken for the equivalence of replicators within the biological and cultural worlds, one genetic and the other memetic. The very idea of a replicator speaks to the ongoing nature of fixed patterns in either domain. 'Replicator' conveys sameness; the repetition or replication of patterns in life. Evolution addresses itself to change, to the change in such patterns which, over time, has led to such richness of life and living forms on earth.

It is at the juncture of the fifth attribute that we are unable to find equivalence in the natural world. We, and not the pattern and its replication, nor the vagaries of blind evolutionary processes, have the capacity to take the lead. That capacity has been granted, interestingly, by virtue of cultural evolution. As a species we, alone, have grown beyond our biological inheritance. *We can also grow beyond our cultural inheritance.*

What do we mean by pattern shifting leadership? We mean that we have the capacity, should we choose to use it, of not being led by our patterns, the capacity to neither be the victims, creations or creatures of such patterns. We have the capacity for a level of freedom that is unsurpassed, a level of freedom that is not free of patterns, but is free *with* them so that we are not led by them. This freedom grants a freedom 'to'. It is the freedom to expand upon our choice of being and to design patterns within and around us accordingly. That freedom can be gained at every level and is fundamental to a generative capacity.

If we are not led by patterns then what is it that serves to lead? It is here that the categories of language may break down, for, in the freedom to be, there is neither being led nor leading; there is only 'being'. A level of being that can shift the patterns within and around us calls for a different level of learning and promotes a different capacity and capability in the shifting of patterns.

One form of pattern shifting is from one established pattern to another, in effect replacing a pattern that is known perhaps intimately to oneself with one that is known, and presumably tested, by others. People often attempt to effect such pattern changes the more often through rational processes of knowledge transfer. But, when the pattern shifting is from what is known to something that is as yet unknown, then the pattern shift is at a deeper level. It is directed and yet uncertain. People attempt to foster a new emergence, knowing not so much the detail or pattern of that emergence, nor its precise destination, yet knowing their choice and the power of their choice in the matter. We might call this the open-ended or unknown learning that is embedded in a strong sense of purpose, compared with the more closed learning that is embedded in adopting another's pattern.

Hawkins[137] speaks of seeing learning as not only "residing in individuals"[138] to understanding that "it also resides in systemic patterns " and proceeds to comment that:

"This systemic perspective radically shifts the perspective of the organisational change agent. Instead of focusing on the parts of the organisation, they start to focus on the patterns that connect the parts; the interfaces, relationships and contacts between individuals, teams, departments and between the whole organisation and those with whom it relates... This perspective requires a new language, a language which is more analogic, metaphorical and stems from the right-brain..."

We need to be careful, for to say that learning 'resides in' is not to say that it is where learning *occurs*. It is people that learn and their learning is embedded in the cultural artefacts around them, in their relationships, in their organisations, and in the procedures, manuals, structures and ways of operating in those organisations. More accurately, it is yesterday's learning that is so embedded. These cultural artefacts are the memetic displays of the ideas and images which preceded us and which dwell within us. They are the equivalent of Argyris' thermostat, effectively a demonstration of our (collective) settings.

The thermostat can be shifted for another known, tried and tested, set of settings; for, as we have said, someone else's pattern. Or we can learn to live closer to the edge-of-chaos, in and with greater uncertainty, knowing that settings will change, that we will no longer be, so to speak, who we once were, at least in terms of our settings. This may be termed 'learning newly' or 'generative learning' – that learning which is sparked by the informal processes between people. Through processes of seeing, listening, speaking and being different new 'realities' emerge; first as new memes or meme variants, some of which are later embedded in new cultural artefacts in the world[139]. We create new orders, new manifestations in the world, from the 'chaos' of new (in the sense of different) personal and social interactions. When much of that difference is sprung or released from within, then we lessen our dependence, and can rather 'dance' interdependently with others.

Leadership, in this sense, is leading oneself beyond those patterns that have you in their grip. It is synonymous with a different sense of learning and a generative orientation to the world. It provides the possibility of developing pattern shifting at all levels; intentional transposons who make their rearranging, their re-languaging of the codes around them, more purposeful and generative. It is an attribute which can be cultivated, if not perhaps by the traditional manager, then by the new form of organisational leader, using now leadership in its more traditional sense.

Management, as a profession, grew out of the practice of supervising the manufacture, using the capital of others, of the industrial artefacts of the early twentieth century. It is perhaps no surprise that its theory and practice came to be dominated by a paradigm of design and control; a specification of how component parts shall work together and a vision of organisations as machines. Today's organisations need something different, the creation of value from ideas and knowledge, the manipulation of self-organising patterns whose rhythms resemble those of the biological world. It implies a fundamental shift in the act of 'management'. In the self-organising world the role of the 'manager' is not so much to specify and control the activities carried out by a company as it is to interpret, and rearrange when needed, the patterns that produce a given mode of self-organisation. We hear much about the challenge of managing change – but the more profound challenge is *growing the capacity of the organisation to change itself.*

Partly this is a matter of context, creating the environment and rules by which the organisation functions. Adjust them and different results follow. Partly it is a matter of 'conversation', understanding and, as necessary, seeking to create a different language by which the shared pattern of the organisation emerges, solidifies and, all too often, rules. Partly it is a matter of commitment, to chosen values and chosen results. In those three 'Cs': creating contexts (for emergence), creating conversations (different ones) and possessing as well as inviting commitment, is perhaps encapsulated an essence of leadership. We have said that such leadership can be, and needs to be, an attribute at all levels, but it is an attribute that is unlikely to develop without an example 'from the top'. An environment must be created in which the rest can happen. If it is a change from a previous environment clear signals are needed, then time for the new to emerge.

One, sometimes convenient, way to shift a pattern is to cause a shift in the physical environment. Changed environments, at all sorts of scales, often produce profound changes in the conversation of the people within them. To draw the chapter to a close consider this case, which combines the shift of physical environment with the dramatic signal: pattern shifting with a bang!

 It was the end of a typical one-day management conference in New York. I happened to be in town and dropped in to post- conference 'cocktails' to meet up with a friend who had been speaking. As the crowd thinned I fell into conversation with a guy who, at first sight, looked like another stereotyped, cautious executive but who began to speak with passion and enthusiasm of the new mood that was sweeping the company he worked for (a large food manufacturer). They had, he said with pride, just completed their ninth record quarter in a row; results driven not by lay-offs but by people thinking and behaving differently.

"How?" I said, having just spent two years living through what was shaping up to be a similar, though not so painless transformation.

"I guess" said my companion "it started with our new CEO. He's Australian. They are different."

"Too right sport" said I – giving free rein to a long subdued Sydney drawl. "What did he do?"

"Well I guess it started when he blew up the headquarters"

"What? You mean literally?"

"That's right. Ours was a company proud of our traditions. The Head Office was in the original building designed by ......(the founder) when he built the first plant. Bruce had it dynamited. He videoed the occasion and sent everyone in the company a copy. We soon got the message."

OK, so it was a dramatic use of executive power and Bruce probably did not want the building anyway. It was a symbolic act of explosive proportions, but it makes the point! What is needed is a shift in thinking, whether it be incrementally innovative or genuine breakthrough. Creativity, at least on the part of a few, must infect a host population for that population to change. The leader can render the context for that infection more or less difficult by his, or her, own patterns in the world. Unfortunately, the creative orientation is often only allowed as a reaction to circumstances. Crisis and breakdown are considered the pre-requisites of change. "People don't change until they have to."

We believe a different mindset is possible, one that is more than anticipating and adapting or coping with changes that are predicted to happen or have happened. The generative orientation is proactive and more. It sets about asking what future is wanted, and then about making that future happen. What can emerge is a future of human intention and design that has its origin in the creative act of possibility, in the human capacity to imagine something that is not already present.

What is difficult is that it requires living with less apparent certainty in the world. The self-generative system lies close to the edge-of-chaos, or from the opposite perspective only just approaches the edge-of-order. The art of managing organisations, and perhaps societies in the future, will increasingly concern not only adaptation but also generation, survival closer to the edge-of-chaos. The challenge is to learn to live with the inherent uncertainty rather than to seek refuge in false premises of predictable stability.

Summary

The chapter sought a connection between our, and others', experience and writing on generative organisation and the theory of organisations as complex adaptive systems, memetic equivalents of organisms. Out of that inquiry comes a model of interconnected attributes of the adaptive organisation. Flexibility through minimum specification, a diversity of thinking, freedom of small groups to experiment and yet connections in a pattern which encourages sharing, and a capability for genetic, or memetic, re-languaging, are properties which biological and cultural adaptive systems may be said to share. Organisations can be designed to be more adaptive. However – seeing the power of patterns, replicators, may make it easier to step beyond it. There is a human capability, frequently a dormant or latent capability, for a more generative, pattern shifting, leadership which can, if the conventional leaders permit and encourage it, enable more than mere adaptation, mere response to enforced changes of circumstance.

We find, in studies of the evolution of evolvability, powerful lessons for organisations. We also find, once intention is added, the potential to accelerate organisational evolution.

Primary Sources

The concept of the Learning Organisation informs much of this chapter. We seek however to recast those concepts within the memetic framework. Like other memes the 'Learning Organisation' is finding different, and confusing, meanings in the minds of those who use it (Price and Shaw 1996). It could be argued that the meme has now reached the bandwagon point where fashion, more than results granted, determines its spread. The sense of a Learning Organisation as generative, concerned with creating its own future and enabling individuals to create theirs, is most notably associated with Peter Senge (1990; Senge et al, 1994). We did not begin with the intention of recasting Senge's five disciplines in memetic terms, but we close by seeing a possible theoretical under-pinning for his model in our work. Senge has frequently acknowl-edged Deming (e.g. 1986) for highlighting the profound shift from management-by-fear that is required for transformation (but see also Townsend, 1970). Pascale (1991), in discussing creative tension, and being as a source of transformation, provides a background to the principles or requisite variety and their derivation from cybernetics. The desire for organisational learning which is truly generative grants a greater sense of possibility to the term than does that which sees learning as the pursuit of adaptation (e.g. Harvey-Jones 1993) or as the pursuit of training and development (e.g. much current British writing on the subject). With regard to the 'training' and 'learning' approaches to the use of standards, Hazel Price (1997) offers an example of the power of using NVQs (National Vocational Qualifica-tions) as generative tools, rather than imposed conditions.

Other writers whose work influenced this chapter were De Geus (1988) with the observation that learning is the ultimate source of competitive advantage, and (1987) with their comprehensive history and critique of conventional performance measures. Criticisms of what we would term prevalent measurement memes, and potential solutions in terms of 'balanced score-card' are offered, for example, by Kaplan and Norton (1992) and Kaplan (1994).

The biological analogies we have drawn rely on work discussed in Chapter Four, but particularly Wills (1989). Price and Evans, (1993) and Price (1994, 1995) present the early ideas which developed into this chapter. Stacey (1995), and Battram (1997) are other accessible sources concerning management and complexity. Prokesch (1997) records a conversation with the pattern shifting leader of one of the UK's largest (in financial and organisational terms) exercises of what we would term pattern shifting leadership by a CEO. Indeed it shifted organisational patterns well beyond the UK.

9

Collaborate to compete: the new strategic relationship

Two zoologists were observing the hunting behaviour of a lion when its mate appeared, obviously bent upon chasing them. "Run!", said the first. "Don't be silly" said his colleague, "you can't outrun a lion". "I don't have to", responded the first, "I just have to outrun you!"

Anon.

A company is a self-maintaining system. It is made up of individuals grouped into smaller systems and it is also an agent in one or more larger systems. It is caught up in webs of economic and cultural relationships that themselves evolve and compete with each other. Patterns operate, and interact, at each of these levels, the inter-organisational, the organisational, the inter-personal and the individual. We have explored each in turn, finishing here with strategy, and with what we term *strategic relationship*; the stance an organisation adopts towards others in its particular environment.

 We take the pattern of 'competition' as a particular example which has tended to monopolise thoughts and thinking when it comes to commercial strategies. This pattern is often perceived within the current management paradigm as the very essence of business and the irreconcilable opposite of 'collaboration'. A well-respected tradition interprets competition as part of the inevitable order of nature, the driving force, through natural selection, of biological and economic or cultural progress. The 'invisible hand' of economics or the 'blind watchmaker' of evolution, are both held to miraculously maximise the overall good. All that is required, so the pattern asserts, are a series of innately self-interested decisions. The long-term benefit of both lions and zoologists is served by the actions reported in the above anecdote.

In using competition as an example we are not trying to deny either its reality, or its benefits. We are seeking to reveal the limits, the point where competition, like any pattern, will, in replicating itself, achieve a position in which its own interest is served; where it limits rather than helps those who carry it. We could say the same thing about 'collaboration', save that it is the competition pattern that may already be limiting many Western companies and indeed some Western economies. Our argument is not that one is right and the other wrong. Patterns, like genes, are not right or wrong – they simply *are*. Our argument is, if anything, for a creative tension between competition and collaboration – a suggestion that they be perceived not as opposites but as mutually reinforcing; and, indeed, that the best way to compete within certain contexts may well be through greater collaboration. That is also, we suggest, the lesson to be drawn by looking from one class of self-maintaining systems to the other; by looking at what we may learn from nature concerning cultural and economic systems.

The comparison divides the chapter into two parts. One is an excursion into the possibilities opened by a theoretical perspective on both systems as creators and preservers of negative entropy. The second involves observations on patterns enabling, or limiting, the business partnerships. A reader with less immediate appetite for a theoretical snack might choose to fast-forward to page 345.

Looking out and locking-in

At any level in the hierarchy of memetic patterns there are always two perspectives, that of the entity carrying a particular pattern and that of the wider system in which it is operating. A company has, explicitly or implicitly, a strategy, a set of actions it takes to maintain its position in a network of transactions, economic and other relationships with customers, suppliers, competitors, partners, stakeholders, and the community. That strategy influences, and is influenced by, the actions of other agents and contributes to the wider patterns of an industrial sector, a market and a society. But those wider patterns also influence the strategy, not only by determining what will succeed and what will fail, but also by determining what is thought of and what is not.

Most thinking on the subject of strategy addresses, without questioning, the former perspective. It looks out and asks how a company accesses, and retains, a share of the 'value' created by its particular set of economic relationships. A company is implicitly assumed to be an entity competing with others. It defines, by whatever route, its strategy. There is a wealth of theory available to suggest how it should do so. One school of thought emphasises the analysis of strategic position and sources of strategic advantage and sees strategy as a rational process of planning to reduce risk and protect competitive advantage. Others argue that markets, not managers, ensure maximum profit through the process of natural selection. Evolution is nature's cost benefit analysis. As Douglas Henderson, founder of the Boston Consulting Group and inventor of the Boston Square put it[140]:

> "Classical economic theories of competition are so simplistic and sterile that they have been less contributions to understanding than obstacles. These theories postulate rational, self-interested behaviour by individuals who interact through market exchanges in a fixed and static legal system of property and contracts."

The full rigour of classical strategic analysis is, from this viewpoint, a luxury that only large firms can indulge themselves in. The majority of companies may well do better to concentrate on being 'lean-and-mean', and having several options open, in a ruthless, competitive, commercial ecology.

Other critics of the rational approach to strategy, notably Henry Mintzberg[141], have gone further and argued that strategic planning is a self-serving process, benefiting mainly the profession of strategic planners (or, one might say, the strategic planning meme). He and others have made the case that the strategy adopted by any firm is more likely to emerge, self-organise, from a compromise of human irrationality and perception, prevalent mental models and recipes, cognitive limits and micro-politics as much as be crafted through rational thought and shared purpose. In our words, this view would hold strategy-in-practice as a function of the patterns of a company rather than a matter of conscious decision and rational choice. It doesn't have to be that way: it usually is.

More recently, theory has begun to stress how the competitive position of a firm depends not only on its own capabilities and actions but also on its position in its web of relationships. Michael Rothschild, originator of the idea of bionomics, puts it well[142]: "From a bionomic perspective, organisms and organisations are nodes in networks of relationships". A company that can dominate an entire web secures a sustainable source of advantage. The personal computer industry provides a classic example. IBM's entry to the PC market provided the standard that has now locked-in 90 per cent of the industry. Unfortunately for IBM they yielded in the process, control of the key elements of that standard: the chips and the operating system, to Intel and Microsoft respectively. These two companies now dominate the network of computer makers and software writers that constitutes the industry. They control the crucial bottlenecks that determine the output of the entire system, in this case the core technology. Control of any bottleneck resource allows a company to capture the lion's share of the total value created. In other industries similar dominance has been achieved by, for example, ownership of natural resources (the oil industry), manufacturing and brand image (motor manufacture), the distribution system (modern utilities or supermarkets), or brand alone (various consumer products). In each case a particular strategic position enabled one or more companies to lock-in the competitive pattern of a particular web of relationships; to dominate the particular ecosystem.

But patterns may lock-in without the dominance of a particular company. The QWERTY keyboard or the VHS format for domestic video tapes (see Chapter Four) illustrate the point; as does the prevailing retailing system for the motor industry that is now being challenged by Daewoo (Chapter Three). In the latter case, the locking-in is not achieved through any physical standard. Rather,

it is an implicit acceptance, by all concerned, of a particular 'recipe', a particular 'mental model' of the market and of retail practice. A set of legal or accounting conventions and rituals, or accepted procurement and tendering practices can have a similar effect. Witness the recent debate on the inadequacies of traditional cost-management accounting for modern manufacturing enterprises.

Such pervasive patterns locking-in more than one industry can be part of an even wider environment, a national culture with its particular socio-political influences or professional paradigms. Richard Whittington, author of *What is Strategy and Does it Matter?* labels consideration of strategy from such a perspective 'systemic'. What distinguishes the perspective is the recognition of strategy being particular to a particular social context: "decision makers *rooted deeply* in a densely interwoven social system" (emphasis added). For 'systemists', economic behaviour is embedded in "social behaviours, nationality, professional and educational background, even religion and ethnicity". We might add, what about "even language"! Whittington offers a number of examples: the different corporate structures evolved in Taiwan, Japan and Korea, the 'Swissness' preserved in Nestlé, or the 'Dutchness' in Philips. Indeed, 'strategy' as individualistic Anglo-Saxon cultures use the term is an alien concept in other religions and languages. According to Pascale[143], Japanese has no phrase for Corporate Strategy. The very concept of orthodox strategic management, of the self-contained firm competing with the rest of the world is no more than a meme seeking to replicate itself through the interwoven structures of companies, consultants, and business schools that perpetuate it. To put it another way, "Classical strategy making cloaks managerial power in a culturally acceptable clothing of science and objectivity".[144]

It is frequently asserted that the pattern of financing of companies in Anglo-Saxon economies, a pre-eminence of equity capital and a dominant stock market, obliges managers to focus more on short-term financial performance than on the longer-term creation of either corporate value or national wealth. A higher percentage of loan finance is suggested as one source of advantage for, say, Japanese and German companies. A particular financial pattern locks-in, sets the rules of the game, for a large amount of commercial behaviour. The

Anglo-Saxon one grants, as its defenders point out, the workability of a defence against the managers of self-serving corpocracies, yet it also limits.

Faith in 'market forces'[145] is one, highly visible, symptom of the pervasive grip of the competition pattern on business in general and strategy in particular, especially in English-speaking economies. The competitive paradigm holds that the greater common good, wider economic prosperity, is thus ensured. Among the arguments frequently made in defence of this view is that competition replicates natural selection, that it is part of the natural order of the world. Darwin's theory may have constituted a fundamental challenge to an older dominant orthodoxy[146], but the new meme 'natural selection' soon found itself a niche in a different pattern, one which held what was, to the nineteenth century Englishman, the self-evident superiority of the English as, if not God's will, then clearly the inevitable, pre-ordained, outcome of nature's law of survival of the fittest. 'Evolution', provided a convenient scientific proof that self-interest served the common good and became part of the ruling pattern of competitive, laissez-faire capitalism; a pattern that made a triumphant comeback in the 1980s. Happy in the paradigm that self-interest secured, in the long run, greater wealth creation, economic and organisational theory was able to concentrate on the question of what gave the individual firm, or simply the individual, competitive advantage.

Having, it might be said, furthered the comparison by arguing the similarity of organisms and organisations, we need, before exploring the limits of the competitive pattern, to test the comparison. Does the process of 'wealth' creation in the domain of genetics support the assertion that competition is indeed the only law of nature?

Order and entropy: food and value 'chains'

Every ice-cube that melts into a glass of whisky demonstrates the second law of thermodynamics, a well-established law of physics which states that, left to themselves, systems decompose into maximum possible entropy, uniformity in the distribution of matter and energy. Given time, things fall apart. Order dissolves. On one scale, organisms and organisations defy the second law because they tap energy released by the wider thermodynamic decay of the universe to create and maintain order. Life survives on solar energy and a stock of nutrients. Human organisations tap the same energy flow and also exploit what amounts to fossil solar energy, the accumulated low-entropy of three billion year's worth of biosphere. Negative entropy created serves as a measure of the wealth generated by either system.

In the genetic system, low-entropy takes the form of biomass, carbon and associated elements converted to living tissue. Every species has a place in a food 'chain' – accessing raw materials either directly from the nutrient stock of the earth, or indirectly through eating other species. The position of a species in the chain, the means by which it accesses food and avoids being eaten, at least until its genes have had an opportunity to reproduce, constitutes its strategy. Every genetic strategy has a niche. Natural selection results in competitive exclusion. Increasing returns and 'lock-in' see to the fact that no two species occupy an identical niche.

Some genes include artefacts in the low-entropy they create.Think for example of a bird's nest. However, for all practical purposes, the memetic patterns of human organisation are unique in their ability to go beyond biomass as a store of low-entropy. They create a store of 'culturomass': one that goes by the broad name of wealth. What constitutes wealth is inextricably bound up in the prevailing patterns of a particular era, 'civilised' life and safe or moral societies. Cultural and technological artefacts, knowledge, bullion, share-holder value or consumable goods are all measures of resources converted to a form of low-entropy[147] which a particular culture values. They are highly regarded within a particular social pattern and contribute to the replication of that particular pattern and the organisations which carry it. Through their interaction, organisations both create and exchange 'wealth', the symbols and artefacts of low-entropy, much as organisms exchange food, and other 'services', to create biomass.

So what constitutes biological success? It is very easy to fall victim to anthropomorphism when answering. We are inclined, thrown by our patterns, to value predators more than prey and see species which sit at the apex of a food chain as the most successful. Most managers would prefer to see their company as a wolf, rather than as a buffalo or as grass. Yet, there is more 'wealth', more low-entropy order, in buffaloes or grass than in wolves. Wolf genes are locked in to a strategy which severely limits their numbers. Buffalo genes have been far more successful at accumulating wealth. Grass genes have been even more successful than either, in terms of their numbers; and bacteria genes yet more successful still.

From the replicator's perspective, what counts is copies, not size; low-entropy. The 'objective' is as many copies as possible, each accessing just enough energy to reproduce. Certain strains of grass could be said to have succeeded, by luring most of the human race to spend most of the last 10,000 years growing grain and keeping just enough to live on. That outcome, a marginal existence for the greatest possible numbers, is at least as plausible as an end point of unrestrained evolution as is an argument that competition automatically maximises the greater good for all concerned. It is an outcome as likely to be reached with competition as a dominant meme as it is under any other unrestrained doctrine.

The problem of judging biological 'success' also illustrates another conundrum that is met in judging what constitutes strategic success. Is creating wealth, growing the net low-entropy in a system, automatically served by all parties seeking to make money, to access and retain for their own purposes the largest available share of the going low-entropy? Does fighting over the pot always lead to growing the biggest pot? Does short-term, rational self-interest serve – regardless of distribution – longer-term wealth creation? Again it is by no means obvious that biological evidence supports the argument.

Although natural selection is driven by a fundamentally 'selfish' competition between replicators for differential selective survival, its greatest paradox is that, by the criteria of size rather than numbers, victory goes to the collaborators. As Dawkins actually makes clear[148], and the point is lost on most of his critics, even upon some other biologists, the selfish gene is a metaphor for the selfish complex of co-adapted genes. As he puts it:

"The manufacture of a body is a co-operative venture of such intricacy that it is almost impossible to disentangle the contribution of one gene from that of another."

What evolves are not individual genes so much as complex 'co-operatives' of genes that:

"...are selected not as good in isolation, but as good at working against the background of other genes in the gene-pool. A good gene must be compatible with, and complimentary to, the other genes with whom it has to share a long succession of bodies."

In other words, the action of selection on individual genes has the effect of selecting a complete genetic pattern, not an unconnected series of bits and pieces. The components of that pattern, the individual genes, are selected because it is in all their interests to belong to a successful 'cartel'. It is evolutionary suicide to break ranks. Incidentally, such mutual inter-dependence offers the likeliest explanation for the origin of multi-celled life out of symbiotic relationships between individual bacteria. By combining, individuals were able to develop biological capabilities denied to their single-celled relatives. In the process they became so inter-related that they could no longer exist independently. Organisms in which specialised organs work as a system have subsequently proven more successful at generating low-entropy than have simple eukaryotic bacteria. In terms of numbers, though, the bacteria still win. There are many trillions of them in the world and they have every chance of outlasting any other organic design. But the creativity of nature, that is everything else including our own species, depends on a degree of collaboration. If 'wealth' is the size and complexity of the low-entropy created, then collaboration pays.

An organisation is, after all, a means of achieving an end result that the individuals in the organisation could not achieve as individuals.

They have to take co-ordinated action, co-ordination that is either enforced through the control process or co-ordination which arises through some form of voluntary participation and collaboration.

The competitive pattern perceives nature, and commercial strategy, in terms of predator-prey relationships. Markets are the interactions in which a company either eats, or is eaten. What equates to food in one system is wealth, conceived of as value created, and transmitted as money, in the other. An organisation's strategic position is governed by its relative power in the exchange. The comparison is captured by the commonly cited contrast buried in the comparative metaphors of food chain and value chain. Hence Plant – Herbivore – Carnivore is contrasted with Supplier – Company – Customer. Michael Porter's Five Forces model[149] of the corporate competitive position translates to evaluating a company's power relative to the defence mechanisms employed by its prey, the power of those that would make it their prey, and the power of others seeking to take-over its economic niche.

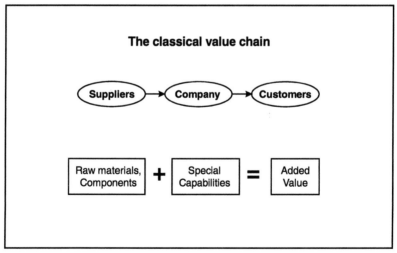

The classical value chain

Suppliers → Company → Customers

Raw materials, Components **+** Special Capabilities **=** Added Value

Figure 9.1

The standard value chain of a company, reduced to essentials. Because of the distinctive capabilities, whether it is knowledge (in many forms), processes, finance, market position or technology, a company converts materials and components into that which others will pay more for.

But the analogy fails on at least two counts. Firstly a stable ecosystem, one that has achieved an evolutionary stable state[150], is no longer comparable to a market. In any stable ecosystem each organic species has a unique niche. Two species competing head-on with the exact same strategy are in an unstable situation. One is doomed and the choice may have more to do with luck than absolute fitness. Markets will seek the same equilibrium, with the relative powers of each player similarly locked in; at which point the relationships in the market are biased in favour of certain dominant contenders. The essence of strategic success, as seen from the perspective of the single company in a free market, is biasing that market in your favour, effectively removing freedom of choice. As economists from Adam Smith onwards have pointed out, left to itself an economic system will emulate an ecosystem. Either one player will emerge as dominant, exerting monopoly control by driving competitors to extinction, or else spontaneous collaboration emerges when a cartel, oligopoly or trust maintains some fixed pattern. Like a dominant species, or ecosystem, it then stops evolving. Neither outcome can be said to be of benefit to the 'consumer'.

When any individual, company or group of companies has that power, it is then able to appropriate for its own ends any surplus wealth, any value created over and above the subsistence necessary to keep other participants active. If we choose to interpret the world in terms of predators and prey, the most successful predator does not necessarily sit at the apex of the value chain. It is the dominant 'company', the one that can retain, for its own purposes, the largest share of the net value created. And in that position, a ruling pattern is bound to seek to perpetuate its success by maintaining an established order rather than by encouraging continued innovation. Any idea taken to excess, any dominant pattern, can become parasitic. Absolute power corrupts absolutely.

The religious patterns which prevailed in medieval Europe were very successful at locking-in large amounts of low-entropy as cathedrals, monasteries and churches, artefacts which among their other attributes contributed to replication of the prevailing memome[151]. The institutions that served the dominant pattern were able to siphon off, for their own ends, a large portion of the surplus wealth created by the economic system of the day[152]. (Finally, they moved to ensure their own survival and that of their power relationships by collaboration, not competition, with the secular authorities.) Today's competitive pattern similarly thrives and co-exists with organisations that seek to appropriate for their own ends the largest possible share of the value created by their web of relationships. The parallel with medieval cathedrals can be extended to modern corporate head-offices many of which serve, intentionally or not, as aids to the replication of a particular culture and power structure, symbols of the stature of the organisation and the status, in perpetuity, of the managers who created them; in effect, corporate cathedrals. They become, in the process, maladapted, frozen into the domain of order until challenged by an equilibrium- punctuating crisis as the wider world moves on. Other rituals and other means of appropriating too much of the value created produce a similar end.

The ecology of relationship

Although we tend to view the natural order of the world as a competition between predators and prey, biology offers another distinction, that between parasite and partner, or 'symbiote'. A successful company that can dominate a web of relationships enjoys such a strong competitive position that it is tempted, within the normal competition pattern, to become a parasite appropriating for its own ends the excess value created. In the process the overall competitiveness of a wider web of relationships is frequently undermined.

If we recast the linear value chain so that any entity which takes from another a share of their low-entropy is positioned as a predator, and any entity that supplies low-entropy, whether as money, goods, or services, to a company is cast as its prey we reach the comparison shown in figure 9.2.

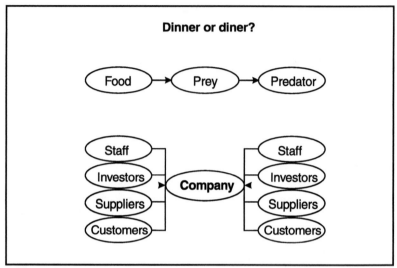

Figure 9.2

Recasting the conventional value chain to show how 'food'– low-entropy – is transferred. Viewed thus, with 'predators' defined as any organisation which receives low-entropy from another, any stakeholder can be considered to prey on a company. The relationship, as in nature, is one of reciprocal transfer of benefit and the question as to whether that transfer is symbiotic or parasitic (or both) becomes more important than the distinction of predators and prey.

 We then reach an interesting conclusion. Suppliers, customers, investors and staff – and one might add the community in which the company operates – can be both prey and predator. The economic 'food-chain' is actually a series of reciprocal, parasitic or symbiotic, relationships. The same, of course, is true of natural food chains. Recall the discussion of co-evolution in Chapter Four. Any entity which succeeds in diverting such a set of exchanges to, for all intents and purposes, its own ends is cast in the role of parasite.

That entity does not have to be a dominant company. Any organisation, any prevailing set of patterns, that can exert monopoly power ends up in the same situation. Suppliers of raw resources may achieve it. The suggestion first advanced by David Ricardo that wealth would ultimately accrue to the landlords[153] of classical economics has been instanced in more recent times by the OPEC oil cartel. A public bureaucracy such as the nomenklatura of the former Soviet Union or some old nationalised industries may likewise evolve to parasitise an economic framework, as may a trade union. The result in any instance is ultimately economic paralysis; a stasis of a dominant pattern. The short-term market economies of recent years in the USA or the UK where management action is driven by the need to ensure immediate returns to institutional shareholders, or the faith that privatisation is the cure for all economic ills, merely repeat the syndrome of the parasitic pattern.

The net effect is surprisingly similar in each case: an entire economic system under a dominant 'power group' or pattern loses generative capacity. The ruling pattern seeks its maintenance whilst it can, until ultimately it is displaced by another. Winning in a 'free' market, means distorting it. The end point is always the same; a decline in the wealth generating capacity of an entire value web. The parasitic organisation destroys the system that feeds it, and may then end up destroying itself.

The existing management paradigm first responded to those crises by learning that vertical integration did not necessarily pay. Unbundling and 'outsourcing' became the fashionable responses; recipes that many defended as proof of the virtues of competition, of the ability of markets to operate more efficiently than hierarchies. The result has been a flood of initiatives to introduce internal or external market economics back into large companies. Another 'recipe' was born and the competitive paradigm was, if anything, strengthened. Yet this response may have missed a deeper point; for what competes, in the motor industry and many others, are not networks of competitive individual firms but networks of entire supply systems or webs in which the various players depend on each other; exist in some form of symbiotic relationship. What makes one web successful in competition with another has as much to do with collaboration and shared purpose as it has to do with competition between individual firms. The deeper strategic point, now gaining wider recognition, is the observation that webs of relationships compete, webs driven by a stance that embodies a strong element of reciprocal collaboration[154]. The same tendency has been observed as contributing to the relative success of economies.

 In 1965, neither Norway nor the United Kingdom had any indigenous industrial infrastructure for offshore oil exploration and production. Both had geologists prepared to declare that North Sea Oil was impossible, and economists prepared to declare that even if it was possible it would never be a commercial proposition. Today, from a mix of government policy and private enterprise, Norway has created a number of world-class firms supporting several aspects of the offshore oil industry. The UK, despite a stronger initial base, ten years of essentially interventionist government, and fifteen years of avowedly non-interventionist government, has not. The Norwegian oil services industry evolved from nothing to become one that thrives on a web of relationships between state-owned companies, national institutions and commercial companies whose defining identity and cohesiveness is ultimately granted by the particular national and cultural tradition that is vested in the pattern of Norwegian language and society. A model that fitted neither of the classic alternatives of 'capitalism' and 'socialism', one that was simultaneously collaborative and competitive, market-led and interventionist, succeeded where both the classic alternatives failed.

When what is at issue is the competitiveness of one system, one web, with respect to another, perceiving relationships between individual firms in the web in terms of predators or prey can be limiting. It focuses the minds of managers on competition within the web rather than between webs. The distinction between predator-prey and symbiote is one of perception. Strategy is the choices a company makes, implicitly or explicitly, in its relationship to other members in its web, the stance that it takes to the world around it. Ultimately that stance is an expression of the company's intention, its purpose in the world. Stance and intention can distinguish a company exercising free choice from the organism trapped by its genes into being a victim of its past success. The company's members must however exercise that opportunity to choose. Longer-term strategy should aim to keep a web dynamic and creative. This cannot be achieved under the dominance of a parasitic pattern.

Communities of collaboration

The world of corporate strategy is gradually realising that webs of companies, companies that collaborate as well as compete with each other, are more effective at creating resources than is either a single large organisation or a network of purely competitive relationships. Surprising as it might seem, this may actually be the message evolution has actually been transmitting all along. Multi-celled organisms, including our own species, probably had their origin in the symbiotic collaboration of single-celled bacteria, collaboration which extended strategic possibility in a competitive world. Nice guys can finish first if there are enough of them. Collaboration is an emergent property, even of anarchic systems. It can be enforced – as when a leader with the appropriate technology or money commands the service, or servitude, of others. It can also be spontaneous, when selection favours symbiotic relationships to the point where those involved depend on each other for their mutual success.

 The paradox of how symbiotic collaboration can emerge from the competitive interaction of self-interested entities was answered in 1984 by a political scientist, Robert Axelrod[155]. His book, *The Evolution of Cooperation* reports the results of a computer tournament between various strategies playing the game of the Prisoners' Dilemma. The game simulates the dilemma facing two suspects being questioned, independently, on the same crime. If both collaborate, deny everything, both go free. If one defects and implicates the other the defector gets a light sentence, the other a heavy one (the real life option of a subsequent visit to the defector by the victim's friends is ruled out). If both defect, both suffer. Mutual collaboration clearly benefits each party but the risk of collaborating is too great and defect ends up being the sensible strategy for both players. The game mirrors what the competitive paradigm sees as the governing principle of transactions between organisations or individuals.

Axelrod's tournament substituted scores for sentences in the pay-off matrix. Mutual collaboration earned both players three points apiece and mutual defection one each. If one player defected and the opponent co-operated the defector won five points, the collaborator received the sucker's pay-off, nothing. Game theorists, economists, political scientists and biologists were invited to submit strategies, rules for playing the game in a series of iterations. Competing strategies played each other in various tournaments. The winner was the strategy which earned the highest score after say 200 plays. Much to many people's surprise it was the simple strategy of Tit-for-Tat (TfT) which went as follows:

- ❑ Collaborate on the first move.
- ❑ Go on collaborating until the other player defects.
- ❑ Retaliate immediately on the next turn.
- ❑ Return to collaborating immediately the other player does so (i.e., on the next turn).

TfT succeeded by building big scores whenever it met another collaborative strategy, and minimising its losses against any really nasty strategy. It also scored well against any strategy that involved learning from the opponent. Axelrod went on to simulate a second competition, one in which a cluster of entrants using one strategy were tested for their ability to invade territory belonging to another. TfT again emerged victorious. If space in the system was awarded according to results, a small cluster of TfT 'players' could displace a larger population playing fundamentally hostile strategies. Their reciprocal gains outweighed the losses incurred against hostile strategies and enabled territorial expansion. The more territory, the more gain. Increasing returns locked-in the 'market'[156].

In interpreting his results Axelrod identified four pre-conditions, rules of the game which were needed if essentially collaborative strategies were to succeed. They were:

1   A likelihood of repeated interactions. If any player knows the game is ending, or if it is reduced to a one-off contest the rewards for defection are always likely to be too great.

2   A positive-sum for the game as a whole. If the net reward for collaboration is no more than the gain to one player from defection no collaborative strategy can win.

3   A sufficient future value in collaboration. Collaborative strategies do well because they set out to lock future rounds of the game into a win-win rather than a win-lose or lose-lose equilibrium. If future reward is discounted too highly, if in effect too high an interest rate is applied to calculate the present discounted value of a future return, then sacrificing current earnings doesn't pay.

4   Swift, but not continued retaliation. TfT minimises its exposure to defectors by retaliating immediately but does not then bear a grudge provided the other player does not continue playing defect.

Axelrod also suggested examples of the spontaneous evolution of collaboration in human situations which met these conditions, among them the trenches of the First World War. Diaries from those on both sides document the spontaneous evolution of TfT strategies among front-line troops stationed opposite each other for a period. Hostilities dropped to the minimum necessary to keep visitors from headquarters satisfied that the war was being pursued. Ideally, they happened at known times so that your 'opponents' would not be provoked into breaking the unwritten equilibrium. One German is recorded as shouting across no-man's land after his side served up a more prolonged artillery barrage than 'permitted' by the tacit consensus: "Please excuse that. It is the new Prussian Gunners". It provides a fine example of the emergence, at an operational level, of unwritten rules which were very different to those intended by 'head-office'.

Whether business is seen as a win-lose, zero-sum, game or a win-win, positive-sum game is ultimately a question of the prevailing pattern of a market, a country, or set of perceivers. Evolution's success in converting the primordial soup into a complex, life sustaining, self-maintaining ecology argues for life, overall, having a positive-sum. There is more biomass, and more complex organic order, more biological wealth, in the world than there was when it started. Most would say the same about economic progress and wealth creation. The success of collaborative strategies; be they cartels, the value webs of successful industrial firms, or some economies seems also to demonstrate the point that collaboration both favours, and is favoured by, a positive-sum game. The relationship can become a virtuous circle, in which, as suggested in the next figure, collaboration promotes wealth creation, creating the positive-sum that favours collaboration.

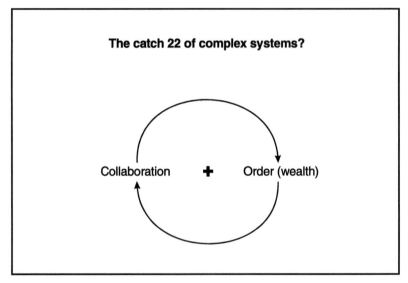

The catch 22 of complex systems?

Collaboration **+** Order (wealth)

Figure 9.3

The systematic dynamic of collaboration and wealth creation suggested from Axelrod's experiments. Each favours the other. Equally, if wealth creation is static or falling, fighting to preserve your share of the pot becomes a 'sensible' strategy – one likely to further reduce wealth creation. Any reinforcing loop can run both ways and the virtuous circle can soon turn vicious. (See Chapter Six for an explanation of the (+) systems language notation.)

In business after business, and in industry after industry, the point is being recognised with the elusive search for something called a 'partnership'. It may be a strategic alliance, a joint venture, a long-term relationship between a supplier and a customer, an attempt to complete a particular project differently, an attempt to replace an internal service with a contracted-out relationship, or simply an attempt to foster greater collaboration between two or more units of the same organisation – the isolation and interconnection of the preceding chapter. Partnership is a word that means many different things to different people, but it is a concept that a lot of businesses are realising they need. Many are frustrated by the difficulty of achieving it. Axelrod's four axioms may provide a clue as to why.

Repeated interactions

The lesson of repeated interactions is axiomatic in companies that deal directly with their customer. Most have now realised that it is easier to lose a customer than to gain a new one and cheaper to keep a customer than win a new account. Some purchasers are realising the converse, that it is less costly to stay with someone who understands your needs than to go up a new learning curve with a new supplier. When each contract is approached as a one-off deal to be negotiated through hostile tendering and where the rule for the tenderer is then "bid low and get it back on deeds of variation" – that is, win on a low price and recover profits on any changes to the original order – then one should not be surprised that spontaneous collaboration does not evolve.

If either party perceives a partnership as a limited number of interactions from which they will then exit without a subsequent encounter with the others, or if one player perceives an opportunity of gaining a permanent advantage over another, then one should not expect a partnership to succeed.

A positive-sum game

Football[157], poker, or derivatives trading are fundamentally zero-sum encounters. What one party wins, another must lose. The Golden Lifeboat Syndrome alluded to in Chapter One is another; but is, like many if not most real life zero-sum situations, a function of perception more than reality. Many businesses perceive the world as either them or us, a zero-sum game. By perceiving it that way, and operating accordingly, they are likely to have their perception strengthened. Those who act in consistency with the view that the rest of the world is out to get them, will find the rest of the world provoked into acting exactly that way. Paranoids act such that they create enemies. A business relationship, an entire supply system, an industry, or indeed an entire economy can lock itself in to a pattern where, even if it is recognised that everybody loses, at least 'we' lose less, or keep 'our' market share, and perhaps even win more in the short term. Price wars are an example[158]. The entire business system gets locked into a vicious cycle of competition, which undermines its longer-term competitiveness. The dynamic of figure 9.3 is reversed and the virtuous cycle turns vicious.

Ultimately, life is a positive-sum game. Whether or not business is seen the same way is a matter largely of paradigm, and partly, perhaps of economic cyclicality and co-evolution. A world, or an environment, in which the market is perceived as static or shrinking becomes, inevitably, a zero- or negative-sum world; one in which competition must thrive as a strategy. The danger is that, yet again, this becomes a self-fulfilling prediction. What have been described as 'abundance' or 'scarcity' mentalities create their own dynamics. If all the players see the game as having a zero- or negative-sum, their logical response is a strategy of maintaining their share through competition, adaptation and reaction. The result is a system in which, inevitably, the overall pot is reduced. Defect becomes good strategy. Cutting costs rather than creating value becomes the name of the game.

What is revealed is a Catch 22. Collaboration is fostered by wealth generation, and collaboration fosters wealth generation. Wealth destruction might be reversed by collaboration but collaboration is unlikely to evolve in a climate of wealth destruction. A market can therefore lock itself into one of two cycles of positive feedback, one a cycle of success, the other a cycle of failure. The shift from one to another is unlikely to happen spontaneously. It might be born out of crisis. Otherwise a shift of thinking, a shift of being, is required. Collaboration and commitment, or competition and control.

Sufficient future value in collaboration

By being nice first time, TfT risks a sucker's payoff. The penalty is countered by the future reward, the net gain of a string of collaborative encounters. Whether or not this is a sensible strategy depends, in Axelrod's phrase, on the shadow of the future, the discounted value of future gains; in essence, the interest rate. Too high a rate, too great an emphasis on the immediate reward, and co-operation becomes an economically stupid strategy. The dynamics of competition reinforce themselves. The less the wealth in a system is growing, or the more it is shrinking, the greater the value likely to be put on the here and now; hence, the less likely the chances of collaboration succeeding, and the more likely a system which stabilises to a state of shrinking real wealth. The shadow of the future is more than just interest rates. It embraces also, the relative value granted current consumption and future benefit by the prevailing social pattern.

Abuse followed by immediate retaliation and forgiveness

A self-organising co-operative depends on no party being able to get away with exploiting it. TfT wins because it minimises its losses against hostile strategies by retaliating. If an opponent plays defect, TfT likewise plays defect on the next turn, and goes on doing so until the opponent plays collaborate. But it remains willing to forgive. It avoids retaliation escalating. Its maximum loss is then the score for one interaction. A partnership must depend on a similar trade off. If one party is able to exploit the other, and get away with it, the relationship is sliding towards one of control and subservience. Ultimately, reciprocal collaboration implies acceptance of a balance in the rewards accruing to all participants. It also implies the ability to forget and forgive.

All of which implies that a shift in thinking may be necessary to achieve a partnership. One has to perceive a business relationship differently. The next vignette illustrates.

 ## Getting together: thinking differently about partnerships

Scene: A pub just down the road from the Headquarters building of Treadmill Inc. It's Friday evening...

Vivian: They never let you off the hook, do they Chris?

Chris: What's up Vivian?

Vivian: Another weekend gone. I've been given just six weeks to come up with a report with definite proposals for strategic alliances that will make a real difference to the business. I ask you, six weeks!; Where the .... do I start?

Chris: Come off it. You must have worked that out!

Vivian: Well, first I really need to understand what a strategic alliance is and then I guess figure out how it could fit in our context.

Chris: Do you have a sense of which of the two words 'strategic' or 'alliance' is the one to get to grips with first?

Vivian: Let's think. I suppose I'd have to answer 'strategic'. Now why is that? To me common sense dictates that the strategic rationale has to come before I consider any alliance details."

Chris: How would you know if you had a strategic rationale?

Vivian: Oh gosh, that's just too big to answer right now.

Chris: OK. So if we just talk about very general strategic direction, what sort of benefits can an alliance bring and over what

	sort of time scale?
Vivian:	That's easier. I believe it should be a long-term relationship. My gut reaction says the benefits should be related to our core business and, to make sense, the alliance would have to offer superior benefits to going it alone, either in terms of value or time.
Chris:	How does that fit with the existing strategy?
Vivian:	Well, it would have to be consistent with our mission and aims. Ideally, it would also lead to a situation which would be hard if not impossible for our competitors to follow. That way we would gain a distinct competitive advantage.
Chris:	How long do you think you need to spend on developing this strategic rationale?
Vivian:	That's not a problem. You've given me some useful ideas for rationale and I think I could have something concrete by next week. No, it is the 'alliance' question that worries me.
Chris:	Why?
Vivian:	Well I have no experience of alliances and my initial reaction to the concept is one of distrust and concern.
Chris:	Suppose you are in a working alliance, what reactions can you imagine yourself experiencing instead?
Vivian:	Definitely trust. That would also mean openness and mutual respect. I'd like some warmth, a sense of possibility, and confidence in the commitment by both parties to the common purpose. I'd also like to feel that if something went wrong there would be a friend to help and not someone else pointing the finger.
Chris:	Can you imagine yourself in any situation where you have all these reactions?
Vivian:	Well yes, but not in business. In any long-term relationship with a partner, or with a good friend, you would experience this.
Chris:	So if, for a moment, we consider a successful long-term relationship as a model, how might that apply to a business alliance?
Vivian:	That's interesting; it has triggered a whole range of ideas.

There are many different types of relationship, but the deeper ones have the qualities I described. From the business point of view we are not interested in one-night-stands or just a casual friendship. However, my experience is that it is difficult to define the precise chemistry which makes for a successful long-term relationship. My view is that there has to be a level of compatibility and a period of rapport building. Even then, things can change and people come closer together or drift apart over time.

Chris: So how could you apply that insight to forming an alliance?

Vivian: I like the model of a relationship. If we have the strategic rationale then it is as if we have agreed to go dating. The relationship is the next stage. However, there is more than one potential partner out there. Each will have different expectations and so how do we proceed? We might start by finding out the ones who have beliefs and values compatible with our own. Even then there may be problems with culture and individual chemistry.

Chris: Do you have any idea of how many potential partners you might have to consider?

Vivian: Not at this stage but probably not a lot. It doesn't matter. Even if there is not a lot of choice, the situation can be compared to an arranged marriage. I can explore the parallels from a successful arranged marriage. What's more, some of the lessons from other successful relationships would still probably be valid. Yes, the metaphor of relationships is useful and it tells me I need to understand our own culture a little bit better. I will then know the sort of partner with whom we would most likely form a harmonious, successful alliance.

Chris: Assuming you have developed the strategic rationale and identified a compatible alliance partner, how confident are you that you will guarantee success?

Vivian: Difficult to say, I'm not sure.

Chris: What's missing that could make the difference?

Vivian: Well thinking about the relationship angle I suppose. It's the day-to-day effort to make things work. There are inevitable misunderstandings in any relationship and when we are talking about two companies, not just two individuals, the chances of communication foul-ups or conflicting unsurfaced agendas are immense.

Chris: How would you like things to function on a day-to-day basis if an alliance is operating successfully?

Vivian: I'd like to imagine an alliance as two Olympic rowers. Each essential and together operating at the peak of efficiency.

Chris: What would have to happen for an alliance to achieve such performance?

Vivian: From the rowing analogy the word that comes to my mind is discipline. We would have to co-ordinate, to practise working together, to keep each other motivated and to stick by our promises. It is no good me turning up to train at 8 in the morning if you only turn up at 10. This implies we have to set some ground rules for how we are going to behave together and stick to them. They also have to be real: not a bit of paper we sign while the unwritten rule is to play around.

Chris: If you did all that, would you then be confident about the alliance?

Vivian: Pretty much. I'd want to make sure that the rules or code we followed did not become a constraint so we would have to build in future flexibility. Provided that was done, I think that the combination of good strategic rationale, compatible relationship and enabling rules would give excellent prospects for success.

Chris: How do you feel now about putting all that together in six weeks for the report?

Vivian: Much more confident. Thanks for the help.

Chris: You're welcome, but talking of partners I've a home to go to. See you Monday

The three R's of partnering

The three R's – rationale, relationship and rules – were sorted out! It sounds easy doesn't it? Whatever could go wrong? Yet in several years of working with groups trying to achieve partnerships we, and our partners, have found case after case where one or the other was missing and where grand hopes and celebration banquets to launch a new era fell foul of what everyone then perceived to be the grim realities. Behind each 'R', and indeed behind the confluence of all three, lurk the inevitable patterns.

First: Rationale

Most people use the language of partnering in a business discussion with no clear intention of meaning anything different in the matter. Consider the last time you heard the expression 'partnership'. Was one or more of the following intended?

- ❏ What we want is that you do what we say. Here is our specification for what is required of the successful partner in this tender.
- ❏ What I want is you to charge less.
- ❏ What I want is a guaranteed workload.
- ❏ What I want is flexibility of supply. People available when I need them but no longer part of my fixed costs.
- ❏ Get costs down but don't scare the unions.
- ❏ We want more of our preferred work.
- ❏ We/you want to get closer to your /my customers.
- ❏ I want you dependant on me while I am free to take my business elsewhere.

Each was said, most more than once, by one side or other, in a negotiation over a proposed partnership. The word is very common in today's business world, particularly in environments of outsourcing aspects of a business that are no longer perceived as core, and in the realm of tenders for complex projects. Both parties to a 'partnership' are frequently happy to use the language without any clarity as to what they intend, other than an attempt to shift a problem to someone else, or to profit, in the short term, from taking on that problem. The underlying rationale remains cost reduction rather than value creation, and the stance remains competitive. Partnership is a carrot to lure, or a stick to beat, another party. Then they wonder why it does not work out; or are confirmed in their self-fulfilling cynicism.

The first challenge for a partnership is to establish why it should exist. What positive-sum outcome will be realised that was not available to the individual participants on their own? All too frequently this rationale is not thought through. Very often, the different participants may see the relationship differently. One simple way of classifying partnerships is shown in figure 9.4. It asks only two questions: the type of relationship envisaged, and the time scale.

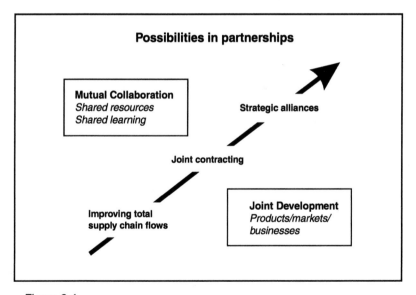

Figure 9.4

An exploration of different rationales for partnerships. Are the parties working together, sharing risk and investment, or is one supplying something to the other?

It seems simple – yet I recall one set of protracted negotiations between Firm A, who saw the deal as basically a contract, and Firm B, who saw a joint venture. Firm A wanted Firm B to be a supplier of specialist manpower and skills and had in mind a long-term contract with benefits for both parties. Firm B had a strategic vision of being close to the final customer and saw themselves as equal partners. Each was looking for an advantageous deal. Neither could appreciate the other had a different mental model of the business relationship, so firm A saw Firm B as being loath to commit itself, whilst Firm B saw Form A as protecting its own turf.

The discussion went nowhere because neither side was able to free themselves sufficiently from their existing patterns to start a real inquiry into what might be possible together. The demand for partnerships often appears in industries that, as in this case, have passed the first radiative bloom. In many cases the ability to lock-in an industrial web is favoured by the ability to create reciprocal relationships[159]. It has been argued, for example, that JVC's more open approach to licensing the VHS video format was instrumental in their securing lock-in of the domestic video pattern in competition with Sony's Beta which was retained as proprietary technology. In other instances, 'partnership' is the response of players who have failed to create a sustainable position. Putting two failures together carries the superficial rationale of reduced overheads and shared resources. It rarely works if each party continues repeating what had not already succeeded. Recall for example the numerous 'rescues' of the British motor industry by mergers. Partnership based on wishful thinking may succeed, but then so too may syndicates buying lottery tickets. Do we wish to leave it all to luck?

Second: Relationship

All the phrases given above expressing different parties' desires from partnerships were, you may have noted, expressed as 'I' or 'We' want.

Such a mode of expression easily passes unremarked in the day to day reality of an organisation. Yet it limits. It begins a conversation towards the negotiation of an agreement with the fundamental presumption that 'we' are all acting in our best interests here. The questions of what do we bring, or what could we create, begin to explore a different stance between parties to a relationship.

Where rationale refers to the context for such a thing as the increased collaboration of a partnership, relationship refers to the content, particularly to the human processes of inter-personal and inter-company arrangements. Different practices in areas such as communication, trust, contracting, conflict resolution, and being and presence require a mastery that is very different from the competitive pursuit of individual self-interest.

Batchelor and Shaw[160] have represented some of the possible differences in inter-company relationships (figure 9.5). They argue that "each quadrant suggests different perceptual and judgmental frameworks,

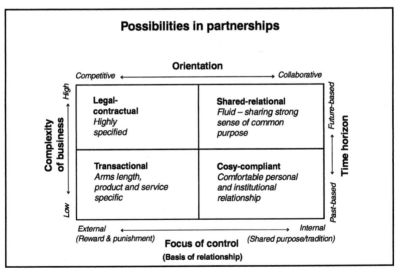

Figure 9.5

An examination of the different styles of relationship which may exist between two or more entities. Redrawn, with permission, from Batchelor and Shaw (1996).

different philosophies, different processes and practices, different rules, and, not least different skills and competencies". In short, each embraces a different pattern. The fourth quadrant, termed 'shared relational' and meant to embrace such ideas as partnership and alliance represents a discontinuity from the three other quadrants. Yet again, you cannot get 'there' from 'here'.

They refer to relationships of 'bonds' or of 'bondage': "All companies, just as all individuals, create a network of relationships around them... relationships born out of bonds or bondage. As bonds, there is in the background some sense of shared commitment out of which trust and trustworthiness is forged. As bondage, there is a sense of constraint or coercion in the relationship out of which compliance and obligation is forged."

Third: Rules

Reciprocal altruism, scratch my back and you can ride on it, promotes a partnership. If collaboration is in everyone's interest, collaboration is likely to emerge. Many partnerships start out with a fine business rationale, and even a great sense of relationship between the players, then flounder because the unwritten rules create interests and behaviour by both parties that conspire to prevent the partnership achieving that which it is capable of. We provided one example in Chapter Two. There are others:

A network of independent trainers was encouraged by the local Training and Enterprise Council to form a 'partnership', a trade association, that could jointly promote their services to local industries. Many meetings were held. There was real enthusiasm on behalf of participants, each of whom saw a possible benefit for themselves. A joint logo and a set of promotional material were designed. However, when asked, the real rules for the group were:

    ☐ "Don't give away the name and telephone number of your personal clients".

- □ "Do be sure your own contribution stands out".
- □ "Always appear busy. Don't return phone calls too promptly".
- □ "Exaggerate your fees".
- □ "Be ready to talk, but be secretive when it comes to action".

The initiative floundered, ultimately because all parties conspired to mistrust each other. the 'rules' engendered mutual distrust.

 A large technology consultancy and contract research organisation was divided into divisions, branches and projects. Theoretically projects were just that, temporary groups put together to deliver a specific objective. Top management were proud of their matrix of scientific expertise and customer focused projects. It enabled, they sincerely believed, resources from all over the organisation to collaborate on delivering a particular client solution.

In practice, competition ruled, fostered by an unstated and perhaps even unrecognised paradigm on behalf of the senior management. Project leaders got promoted by growing their projects, 'winning' not only orders, but also the annual competition for people and financial resources. For a project to actually finish; to no longer be needed, was the ultimate sign of failure on behalf of its leader. Any collaboration only followed the most labyrinthine negotiations. The whole edifice became over-capitalised, overmanned at senior levels, and over-full of work-in-progress, both physical and intellectual. Large numbers of its former staff are now redundant. Several still feel betrayed by the system that let them down.

In the language of systems thinking such examples represent the generic dynamic (explored in Chapter Six) as 'the case of accidental adversaries'[161]. The perceived interests of one party lead them to take particular actions, actions that shape how another party perceives its own interests, and therefore the actions it takes, and so on, and so on. The net result is that a desired, or intended, outcome is frustrated. Nothing changes. The only solution is to change the overall rules for each party. And behind the rules in most cases lurks a pattern; a mental model of adversarial relationships that thrives and replicates in environments in which it can maintain such relationships. A common meme infects all involved and, in so doing, conspires to limit what they can collectively achieve. Ultimately, creating organisations that can break out of that trap, that can self-organise into generative, wealth creating, positive-sum systems, demands breaking the grip of some such pattern

CRINE: a shifting industry pattern?

It is possible for the patterns which dominate an industry to shift. A current example from the oil business in the North Sea demonstrates.

 We have already made reference to the prevailing paradigms of geology and economics in the 1960s declaring the impossibility of finding, and producing, oil from the North Sea. Fortunately for the UK economy, engineers, with a little help from OPEC, proved those assertions wrong. The 1970s and 80s were, broadly speaking, a boom time for the oil industry in the North Sea. By 1990, the boom days were over. Not only was the oil price back, in real terms, to the level it had been in 1970; the largest, most easily exploited oil fields were well past their peak. Much of the resource had been produced.

What remained were two challenges; prolonging the producing life of the older fields and finding new ways to develop smaller accumulations that could not be tapped using the engineering and organisational paradigms which had evolved over the previous 20 years. Those assumptions included a fundamentally adversarial approach to the business of arranging contracts. A large oil company would discover a field and, in due course, decide what sort of installation it wanted to build to exploit it. Major contractors would be invited to tender to design the installation to the company's specification. Others would be invited to build it. Sub-contracts would be issued, and so on, and so on. Every company believed it had the best practice and stuck to its own ways of doing business. The pattern supported engineering design teams, economists, lawyers, negotiators, project managers and a myriad of other specialists, each engaged in a competition to secure, for themselves, a continuing share of a pot that was visibly shrinking; a pot constrained not just by perception but by the physical laws of the amount of fossilised low-entropy preserved in the North Sea Basin.

A cynic might say it was the threat of crisis, the impossibility of continuing with business as usual. Perhaps so, but once one or two companies discovered the potential unlocked by different language and relationship, the industry soon followed. It has succeeded in establishing a movement for Cost Reductions In the New Era (CRINE). The many players in the industry, the 'operators' (larger oil companies who finance offshore exploration and own the oil platforms) and the myriad suppliers are discovering that new relationships, and new ways of doing business benefit all concerned.

Transforming the established patterns of competition and collaboration

So, how do you proceed to transform the existing patterns of competition toward greater co-operation and collaboration where this is deemed to be beneficial?

First, there is no fixed recipe or magic formula, not even some painless process. When we are steeped in competitive ways, whether at the inter-personal or inter-company level, it first takes some unlearning before we may adopt some different practices. Adding collaborative gestures onto the familiar habits of competitive ways is at best skin deep. As Axelrod's study suggests, if we are not to degenerate into continuous TfT then we not only need the prerequisites that he outlines but also the integrity that will help us to focus on the positive-sum, win-win game and not be drawn to seek revenge and the win-lose option.

If there is no detailed recipe, is there some general high-level guidance that may be given? We suggest that a fundamental underpinning of more collaborative ways takes the form of an inside-out approach, a significant shift in the memetic patterns and ways of thinking that generally have us place collaboration in opposition to competition. We tend to interpret these concepts as though either ends of one continuum, as though opposites, from which we are forced to either select or somehow choose an appropriate balance. Treated as opposites and applying either/or thinking creates exclusive categories in which our options and choices are limited. As we have seen, collaboration can live in harmony with competition; indeed, at times, can be the only source or configuration for survival. This shift in our memetic pattern, this change to our cultural inheritance, opens up a new and different possibility through which we may perceive, interpret and interact with the world – collaboration with competition. With what were opposites now broken down, new emergent designs and practices can be developed, designs and practices which combine high collaboration with high competition.

 Based more upon 'I-in-the-picture' rather than 'I-observing-upon-the-picture' (Chapter Seven), we may then apply the interactive domains of rationale, relationship and rules to first design and then practise different ways. Let us not forget however that habits take time to change and there are frequently present strong structural forces that serve to maintain the dominant pattern of competition even when we declare that we are intent upon a more collaborative route. Past habits, in time, give way to new ways – particularly where we can expand our capacity to let go; otherwise, as ever, newcomers, not enslaved to habit, will not only have but will keep their advantage.

Crashes: the ultimate tragedies of competition?

But to what end is that greater advantage sought, that higher level of performance pursued? The CRINE case illustrates another point concerning economic success, its dependence on fossil resources. Industries and civilisations decline when all concerned are locked into what has been graphically termed the tragedy of the commons; situations where rational behaviour for everyone is to secure as much as possible of a diminishing pot, thereby hastening the over-exploitation of the pot and the ultimate demise. It is not a new phenomenon. The march of human history is replete with examples of civilisations which have over-consumed the resources which sustained them. It may be that this is the ultimate fate of any pattern which secures run-away success.

And here we meet the possibility of global limits to growth. Whether the ever-faster rate of technological innovation, and 'economic progress' can, by themselves, deliver sustainable global societies is, at best, a moot point. As a species we already access, by some accounts, 40 per cent of the net energy to the planet's biosphere. We are in the process of returning 600 million year's worth of fossil energy resources to the atmosphere in the course of some 200 years, and we live in a world of growing inequalities, within and between nations. It may be that some very deeply ingrained patterns indeed are meeting their limits. We will allude, only briefly, to some of these possibilities in the closing chapter.

Summary

We set out to examine strategy and strategic relationships in economic ecosystems; asking, what lessons might be drawn from natural selection and biological systems? Whereas most previous writers on strategy who have sought evolutionary metaphors have emphasised competition we have sought to show that nature conveys the message that reciprocal collaboration pays. It does not require an appeal to some higher principle of mutual altruism. Reciprocal collaboration between 'selfish', or self-interested entities is the source of most wealth creation.

The underlying 'wealth' of both domains is argued to be order, negative entropy, created and maintained; and the order which is valued, or successful, reflects the wider patterns of a society, or the collective genetic system of an ecology. The act of consumption in a food chain is an exchange of order, negative entropy, as is any economic transfer. Being either a supplier or a customer can both be seen as predatory acts; that is they consume part of the accumulated negative entropy of another organisation or individual. Of greater relevance to understanding strategy is the distinction between parasitic exchanges, which benefit one party, and symbiotic variants where both benefit.

Symbiosis appears as the basis for the emergence of more complex forms of natural order, and of greater economic wealth creation. It favours, and is favoured by, positive sum outcomes. Parasitic competition thrives in an environment of wealth destruction, and is reinforced by such an environment. The more deeply ingrained, the larger and harder the shift requires to get from one stance to another.

Strategic competition in the future is suggested to be between webs of related companies which will simultaneously collaborate and compete. Such webs, or partnerships, require a rationale – a positive-sum outcome – a set of relationships between the players, and a structure of rules which encourages continued mutual interaction. And finally, beyond enhanced strategic competition lies a question of competition: to what end? Are the current patterns of 'wealth creation' merely hastening the onset of a global crisis? It may be that what is killing us is trying to squeeze too much from the competition meme.

 ## Primary Sources

The literature on corporate strategy is extensive and the competing schools of thought are well reviewed by Whittington (1993), whose book secured The British Institute of Management's annual award for the best new textbook. He provides a clear summary of the role of national culture in shaping strategy. Mintzberg (1994) provides a comprehensively argued case for the perceptual and cognitive limits to classical strategic analysis. The approach to strategy that emphasises strategic position and control of a web of relationships is explored by Kay (1993) and Moore (1994). Kay makes the case for 'strategic architecture', a system of fundamentally collaborative relationships within a firm and between the firm and its suppliers and customers as a sustainable source of competitive advantage. He also presents detailed arguments concerning the use of 'strategic position' as an, often fortuitous, source of advantage. Goldratt and Cox (1989) demonstrated that bottlenecks control output and one can consider strategic position to be an extension of bottleneck theory. Moore (1994) presents the model of new markets emerging through a radiative phase followed by stabilisation. The companies which survive into stable markets lock-in a systems of relationships, a strategy for a complete web. Tylecote (1993) makes the case for the more collaborative approach underpinning the relative success of several non Anglo-Saxon economies. Different 'species' of national capitalism under different ruling 'patterns', or traditions, are examined by Hutton (1995) who makes the case of the UK getting the worst of all possible combinations. The lock-in of industry recipes, accepted and duplicated patterns of operation, is demonstrated by Spender (1989), Senge (1990) and Hamel and Prahalad (1995). Rothschild (1992) argues the comparison of ecologies and economic systems in a defence of the fully competitive view of the world, competition as a natural law, liable though to be paralysed by commercial or public parasites. His book contains many examples of the energy and entropy budgets in biological and business networks.

The comparison of economic and ecological systems as creators of low-entropy underlies an approach to steady-state economics associated in particular with Hermann Daly (e.g. 1980). Money, often confused with wealth, is strictly speaking the means by which wealth is exchanged (Crockett 1973). Added value (see: Kay 1993) is a measure of wealth created which can reflect the benefits of knowledge wealth (Nonaka and Takeuchi 1995). Lloyd (1990) explores Axelrod's (1984) work for a commercial system and argues the fundamental benefit of a collaborative stance in the creation of market and wider social value. Reader (1995) explores the background to CRINE, whilst Bibby (1995) presents an example and Green (1995) demonstrates the collaborative stance now expanding in the industry. Many modern works on strategy and change are now illustrating the benefits of, and the search for, partnerships in different industrial sectors (e.g. Kanter et al, 1992). *The Tragedy of the Commons* is explored, for example by Diamond (1992), from whom comes also the example of grass genes 'domesticating' Homo Sapiens, and Hawkin (1993).

10

When butterflies flap their wings: the shifting patterns of our time

"A company is not a machine but a living organism, and, much like an individual, it can achieve a collective sense of identity and fundamental purpose. This is the organisational equivalent of self-knowledge – a shared understanding of what the company stands for, where it is going, and what kind of world it wants to live in; and, most importantly, how it intends to make that world a reality."
Ikijiro Nonaka[162]

"How queer everything is today! And yesterday things went on just as usual. I wonder if I've been changed in the night? Let me think: Was I the same when I got up this morning? I almost think I can remember feeling a little different. But if I'm not the same, the next question is, 'Who in the world am I?' Ah, that's a great puzzle!"
Lewis Carroll [163]

 This chapter seeks to provide an end with a new beginning. The end is not a conclusion but rather an awakening, an awakening to the patterns around and within us. It may be that we end much where we began and yet see very differently. As Marcel Proust once remarked, "The real act of discovery consists not in finding new lands but in seeing with new eyes". We will explore what this new emerging view looks like: how small changes can be amplified into big effects; how organisation is born and sustained out of new, shared, patterns, and how managing in the future will be much more concerned with context and the creating or breaking of patterns, than with content and the control of fixed activity.

The illumination of pattern: a new view?

One simple proposition of this book is that, if we just expand our capacity to see patterns, we will, in turn, expand our capacity to change or shift such patterns more knowledgeably . The challenge is that much of our training has been to just see 'things', and thus see ourselves, as subjects in a world of objects. Furthermore, when we do explore patterns, we observe that many run so deep that they are hard to see, let alone move. One obvious yet profound insight is that we only see patterns in the world 'out-there' through patterns of the world 'in-here'. We gaze upon, and interact with, the world through the ideas and images which have infected our brains. Change those, and our whole gaze and interaction shifts. Part of the richer pattern, then, is our pattern of seeing. At a simple level part of this gaze, this new world view, is to see the pattern rather than be blind to it. At another level it is to see how, through the memes transported through language, we see what we are wired-up to see, what we have been taught to see. If, through acts of self-awareness, we can but 'see' our seeing, then we may expand our choice, our capacity, to either intentionally follow such patterns or to alter them. We need not, then, be slaves to our memetic inheritance.

Easily said, but to challenge the familiarity of our seeing is to challenge the very essence of our reality; a reality forged over centuries of cultural evolution; a reality embedded in the institutions of societies, and in the very thinking of human beings. Take, for example, the idea, the meme, of 'ownership'. How, and how often, that meme emerged is lost in distant history[164], yet the idea, nested in a network of associated memes such as 'property' and 'possession', has shaped behaviours over the centuries. To such an extent, indeed, is 'ownership' taken so much for granted, that it is deemed a universal 'fact' of life. It takes an alternative wisdom – the wisdom of primitive tribes – to remind us that this idea was but the creation of a particular human culture; a meme which successfully seeded itself in their language, thought and action. Its reproduction and replication has perhaps proceeded to epidemic proportions! As Chief Seattle reminds us:

"How can you buy or sell the sky, the warmth of the land? The idea is strange to us. If we do not own the freshness of the air and the sparkle of the water, how can you own them? This we know: the earth does not belong to man; man belongs to the earth. This we know: all things are connected like the blood which unites one family. All things are connected. Whatever befalls the earth befalls the sons of the earth. Man did not weave the web of life, he is merely a strand in it. Whatever he does to the web he does to himself. Continue to contaminate your bed, and you will one night suffocate in your own waste "

This is not to make the idea of ownership wrong, but rather to illustrate how it first emerged, and was then very successfully propagated across the human globe. Over the centuries, the ownership meme has been influential in shaping the conduct of human affairs. It has so infected the collective mind, and is so deeply embedded in culture, that an emergent philosophy, or way of life, materialises, namely that 'to have is to be'. People become valued, their relatedness and relationship shaped, according to their material possessions. We only see the person through their property, their material wealth. We can be so trapped in the pattern that, for example, we become a reflection of the car we drive rather than whatever drives us. This pattern of property acquisition, and the valuing of people for what they have, can serve to significantly support an economic system that emphasises material well-being: the holy grails of making money and economic growth. We are now, perhaps, becoming all too aware of the consequences of this pattern taken to excess. What chance, then, for alternative memes to replicate themselves and perhaps end or curtail the overwhelming dominance of such a pattern? Could it be that ethics, the ecology of our environment, the alienation of so many, or the search for more spiritual meaning could start to intervene in the pattern of things?

A new view and understanding of the world we live in is emerging; one that grants a new perspective on the organisations that exist in, and do so much to shape, that world. This new view, though not yet fully articulated, reflects an emergent paradigm shift, one that may lead, indeed is leading, to a different predominant world view. It is a view embodied in the realisation that less and less of the world is predictable; that the old certainties and recipes of management have reached their limits; that the pursuit of selfish interests in a world of much greater interdependencies is unsustainable; that in Kuhn's terms (see Chapter Three) the old explanations just do not work so well any more. It is a view that recognises that biology tells us as more about organisations of the future than do the more established metaphors of engineering. It is a view that arguably grounds explanations for our social structures more firmly in the process of evolution than many, including many holistic thinkers, find comfortable. It is a view that is increasingly drawing on the new sciences of Chaos and Complexity and their revelations about the behaviour of systems which are too complex to predict. It is a view that accepts that people's potential is limited when they are treated as cogs, or parts in some organisational machine.

We started the journey of this book by illustrating how organisations, technology and language co-evolve in a complex and ever-shifting system. We then went below the surface, to reveal some of the dark side of enterprise, and showed how organisations are often confounded, in their efforts to change, by the same unwritten codes that enable them to operate. We traced the origin of such codes to the shared paradigms carried within cultures and organisations. To explain the dynamics of self-organising, and self-perpetuating, systems we used the idea of 'memes'. Observations from many fields concerning apparently dysfunctional personal and organisational behaviour seem perfectly logical if one accepts organisations, and indeed human minds, as substantially a reflection of their memetic inheritance. They are, so to speak, infected by viruses; viruses whose 'purpose in life' is, without foresight, to replicate. Memes, remember, do not possess intention; they merely, blindly, copy; they simply are.

Yet by being, and perpetuating themselves, memes, interconnecting into complex shared patterns, enable no less than human culture and organisation. Without them we would have none. Yet with them, and here's the rub, we are at some stage limited; stuck, as the world around us changes, or as we aspire to create a different future, whether for ourselves or for an organisation. Memes and patterns, exist, interact and interconnect at all levels – the individual mind, the interpersonal exchange, the intra-organisational and the inter-organisational.

We then went on to explore the shifting of memes; the seeing and acting differently, that is the key to individual or organisational transformation. Seeing the memetic pattern, though critical, is not enough. Choosing to act differently is the key. Unfortunately it is personally discomfiting because, by acting differently, one risks current 'membership', and what is known and predictable, for a more uncertain future. The challenge for leaders at all scales is to create contexts – structures, spaces, and environments – in which learning and performance may occur; and to understand and enhance the conversations through which shared meanings and aspirations are created. Engaging the ideas and images in people's minds is critical to transformation. Through the seeds implanted by conversation we may help to stimulate renewal.

We then proceeded to illustrate some shifts in pattern that are possible at the company and inter-company level, how we might move from control to commitment, and how we might move from simple competition towards competitive collaboration. We argued competitive collaboration to be a major lesson from the evolutionary process.

Yet to shift the patterns when either you are riding high on success, or when you sense yourself as victim before an entrenched pattern, can seem but a theoretical stance. Whether it is the comfort of a well-worn rut, the success of the moment, the preoccupation with busyness, or the seeming impossibility of making anything other than a token difference, lock-in can severely limit your perceptual horizon. Too often we hear the complaint that people will not lift their heads, that they are too caught up in, or resigned to, what already 'is' that they cannot see beyond the present reality. Set against this tide of limited movement, where have we seen patterns start to shift?

On an international scale some movements in recent times have been phenomenal. The ending of apartheid in South Africa, the fall of the Berlin Wall and the collapse of communism, the growth of equality movements of both gender and race, are all significant shifts in pattern. All are creating some level of disorder before the emergence of a new level of order. At national levels, countries are seeing major structural shifts in their economies; with much dislocation, before possibly emerging to what have been termed 'post-industrial societies'. Many companies have produced real, rather than merely espoused, emergence towards 'empowered workforces' of 'knowledge workers', with high levels of 'involvement' and 'teamwork', to improve quality, customer service and productivity. At the personal and inter-personal level, examples of dramatic transformations serve to show what is possible once we shift some of the more deeply held patterns.

All this and more might be put down to the turbulence of our times, and for each example of movement many examples can be given of relative stuckness. Old memes die hard. Old ideas and values re-emerge in new guises. Is a new view really emerging? Is a para-digm shift actually happening?

The following table indicates some of the changes that many claim, and we agree, are taking place. These changes are radical and emergent. They are not separate; indeed they are highly intercon-nected. The world view that we are leaving behind is often termed the mechanistic view. The new one has been described by some, some-what awkwardly from our perspective, as 'post-modern'. It is a view that favours the perspectives of the life sciences, of complexity theory, and the integration of previously isolated disciplines. In an effort to avoid implying value judgement we will simply call the two views prevailing and emergent. Let us look at some of their properties.

Prevailing View	Emergent View
Thinking	
Reductionist	Systemic or holistic
Analytical	Synthesis
Rational	Intuitive
Linear	Non-linear
Exclusive; either/or, is/isn't	Inclusive, paradoxical
Perception	
Entitative	Relational
Focus on component parts	Seek to 'see' the whole in context
Premise that perception is accurately representative of what is 'out there'	Appreciation that perception is at least in part a reflection of what is 'in here'
Treated as an independent sensory phenomenon	An interdependent phenomenon – not separable from other significant human processes
Values	
Denomination and control over	Partnership and control with
Quantitative emphasis	Qualitative emphasis
Competitive win-lose	Collaborative win-win
Emphasis on growth	Emphasis on development
Evidential, requiring external proof	Internal wisdom, intuitive
Orientation	
Outside-in: people and things to be acted upon	Inside-out: people act as actors and authors pursuing processes of enactment
Control or be controlled	Co-create
Externally oriented to the world of 'things' and possessors, to having	Self-knowledge and awareness, oriented to being
Individualistic	Integrative

Exercise:

The above table is meant to be indicative rather than exhaustive. Is it reflective of a shift in paradigm? Is it your experience that such a shift is taking place?

Interestingly, much of the debate concerning these two views, even from advocates of the new, tends to become couched in terms of 'right' or 'wrong', superior or inferior. In struggling to take over the replication space of the older pattern, the newer one acquires some of its predecessor's characteristics. Those of the holist persuasion often fall into the right-or-wrong stance when they criticise reductionism. There is an alternative stance, that of seeing both views as equally valid and, rather than arguing for one pattern being superior to another, accepting the difference. In different circumstances, different explanations create different possibilities and openings for action. Beyond pattern shifting, as a single act, is seeing different patterns and their consequences and expanding choice.

Small change – big difference?

In recent years butterflies flapping their wings have come to serve as one of the defining metaphors of complex systems. No allusion to complexity is complete without the reminder that weather systems of the planet are so interconnected, so sensitive to small perturbations, that a butterfly flapping its wings, anywhere from Brazil to Borneo or Beijing, impacts a storm anywhere from New York to New South Wales. This cliché is a neat example of a small, rapidly mutating meme[165], but it nonetheless highlights the power of self-organisation, the strength of order that can emerge from chance events in a chaotic and interconnected world. It also serves to remind us that small changes in, and by, human agents may have larger, unforeseen consequences in the broader systems of which they are a part. Small actions, whether made from choice or just made, can ripple through the systems of the world. But, before rushing blindly down the path taken by others who have joined the growing fashion for using the analogy to signal the demise of rational management, let us inquire some more. What other lessons might we choose to take from the metaphor? Here are four:

☐ First, it serves as a reminder of the power of metaphors and analogies as windows onto, and potentially tools for, influencing the patterns of any situation.

☐ Second, it reminds us that the way the world is seen is a function of the perceptions of the beholder. (The analogy was first invented by complexity researchers and theorists to illustrate an observed effect).

☐ Third, it offers a powerful image of individual transformation. Can someone, through a small difference in their actions, have similar effects?

☐ And fourth, it can point the way to the equivalent unpredictability, the non-linearity, of human systems.

Metaphors and analogies are one of the powerful ways by which new memes create niches for themselves in the linguistic territory that is their habitat. They arise when individuals seek to convey and grasp some sense of shared meaning and appreciation. The communication only works when the image of the metaphor produces, in the meme-space of the recipient, a meaning close to that intended by the speaker or writer.

Thus, what the phrase 'when butterflies flap their wings' conveys, depends on a shared background of meaning. Within the community of Chaos and Complexity adherents it conveys much, including membership of a particular tribe. To much of the rest of the world it probably conveys something entirely different, perhaps some reminder of summer days and good companions! Where then does the meaning of the metaphor reside, if it is not in the pattern of words? We see again patterns within patterns, the pattern of words contains a certain superficial meaning, but the much greater meaning is in the pattern of shared experience through which the language is interpreted.

Metaphors that succeed almost cease to be recognised as such. They become part of the accepted meaning, and language, of a particular memome; as, for example, the prevalent metaphors of 'engineering' and 're-engineering' common in the unconscious assumptions of the prevailing view. Does everything have to be 'engineered'? A new vein of possibility may be opened by asking what other metaphors might serve a particular purpose, or by questioning the personal or wider patterns that lie behind a particular metaphor.

Consider, for example, the presumptions and perceptions behind 'caterpillar' and 'butterfly'. As Stephen Gould reminds, the organic self-organising system we call 'butterfly', in fact spends most of its life as caterpillar and chrysalis. 'Butterfly' is but a brief crowning glory, the sexual phase in which 'caterpillar' is genetically programmed to dress itself up for the purposes of reproducing. Yet our perceptions of maturity, development and beauty tend to value butterfly more than caterpillar. We classify the organism as a butterfly and regard the caterpillar as a garden pest. Patterns lurk everywhere!

In breaking free of its chrysalis, in metamorphosing for its moment of creative glory, the butterfly does however express what is possible, if a system frees itself from the shackles of a limiting pattern. In practice, of course, the butterfly has no choice. The caterpillar's genetic script, if it survives that long, ordains a butterfly. Humans and organisations, enabled by memes rather than genes, do have, as we have emphasised throughout this book, the freedom to choose, to discover and invent different futures. The freedom is largely latent unless some limiting pattern is seen and a revised memetic script created.

While it may be enabled by the right context, and even encouraged and helped by others, the transformation is ultimately personal. While patterns at every level interconnect – the personal, interpersonal, company and inter-company – the shift of pattern at the personal and interpersonal level is the more profound. The individual can choose to operate from a different memetic pattern, or simply to inquire into what might become possible if they were to do so. Without individuals taking that choice there is no progress. Progress "depends on the unreasonable man"[166]. The unreasonable individual who chooses to experiment with different patterns, rather than remain in the comfortable cocoon of their memetic chrysalis, may, by so doing, invite others to experiment. The invitation may open new webs of relationship, out of which new possibilities can emerge. Small ripples can have unforeseen consequences.

One butterfly, despite metaphorical fantasy, may take a risk and yet not make that much of a difference. Just as a blackbird, or a biologist, may await the butterfly that stands out from the crowd, so the world is full of metaphorical predators and dissectors poised to pounce on people and ideas who stand out from conventional reality. Whether the blackbird devours to satisfy hunger or the scientist preserves and dissects to satisfy curiosity, the would-be agent of difference is stifled. Yet butterflies persist, and, if not one, then a sufficient number flapping their wings can perturb the patterns of the future. As simulations of complex systems show, a small cluster with a different strategy can generate re-enforcing patterns that shift an entire system[167]. Any organisation can be transformed when, by default or design, its memetic pattern is altered.

That interruption, by choice or accident, is the core of 'change' and innovation, and will often meet considerable resistance. It is an act of learning and discovery, but also an act of unlearning or letting go. And here we hit patterns again. Confronted by the term 'unlearning' we have seen many, particularly those well-schooled and practised in being learned, react with shock or even denial. "One cannot unlearn", they say, "because all prior experience remains in the mind and cannot be completely forgotten." Or, say others, unlearning distinguishes nothing useful, particularly where it does not fit their own particular model of learning.

For others, especially perhaps those of a more practical bent, we have found the idea of unlearning, loosening or letting go of the attachment of a particular mental model, meme or habit, conveys a pertinent meaning. It resonates with their own experience of a personal, or organisational, transformation.

There are many routes to change and learning, many models of the learning process, and many tools, methodologies or prescriptions for managing it in individuals and organisations. We are neither out to promote another, nor to add to the store of recipes that already exists in the world of management. We have tried instead to argue for a meta-level construction; that change results from individuals seeing the patterns of which they are a part and from their choice to be in action to create alternatives.

Transformation by design involves the intentional generation of a result different to any that can be envisaged by projecting the present. There is no 'miracle recipe' for the transformation process, no quick fix that will impose a transformation on a company, for the transformation process involves the evolution of a different pattern. If a company is 'locked-in' to one prevailing pattern, one evolutionary peak, one ordered state, a transformation must represent a shift to a less predictable, less certain condition, a move towards the edge-of-chaos. The process involves seeing, and interrupting, the comfortable patterns of the previous 'order'. Those involved have to manage that shift and acquire the skill and habit of thinking differently, of fostering memetic diversity and of creating different conversations.

Transformation is a change in, not a change of, the players. It is a state of accepting the existence of choice – and its flip side, uncertainty. To put it another way, we mutually create and transform our non-equilibrium world out of our actions. Those actions are born out of either conscious choice and purpose, and the confluence of that choice and purpose with the choosing and purposing of others, or from blind response to the ideas and images that govern our minds: the alien memes within. Blind response risks keeping us stuck, at many scales, in vicious circles of decline and decay that will, without choice, only be interrupted by terminal crises.

The classic patterns of management have carried an assumption that the world is predictable. Given enough data, and sufficiently meticulous analysis, the choice can be made or the result planned and forecast. It is a comforting and secure position, but one which is increasingly untenable in today's world. Action in conditions of uncertainty displaces the search for the definitive strategic answer. Survival depends on an awareness of one's own or one's organisation's skills and capabilities, as well as the assumptions and patterns which drive them.

Why is it so often the case that there is massive expenditure to such little effect in some enterprises, with relatively little expenditure to major effect within others? We suspect that part of the more limiting pattern in terms of results (though not expenditure) is that many are locked-in to having, and thus being sold, an 'answer', one that may well not work within the deeper patterns of their enterprise. In contrast the high-leverage, 'butterfly flapping its wings' changes are found and made, in the complex patterns of organisational life, by those who put effort into discovering and making pattern changes for themselves. In short, transformation starts from within.

Slaves to, or shifters of, patterns?

We are born into patterns, we grow up in patterns, we become patterned in our ways of thinking, seeing and being. Many of these patterns are so inter-woven and interrelated that we fail to see them. For many, that's just how life 'is'. Why shift, why not simply choose to follow a given pattern?

It is when we are blind to many patterns, that default, more than choice or design, dictates that we follow them. The pattern exists, and seeks to perpetuate itself no matter what. It is as if it were a vested interest lurking in the background. We may be a beneficiary, agent or victim of a pattern. Our co-respondence may be wilful, compliant or resentful, with knowledge aforethought or ignorance. Why, then, either stay with or shift?

Reasons for staying with a pattern, whether personal or organisational, may be many. It may be that one is:

❑ blind to the pattern that exists and therefore unaware

❑ satisfied with the pattern and the results it is enabling

❑ resigned to the prevailing pattern either with the thought that this is as good as it gets and/or with a feeling of powerlessness to change

❑ receiving some form of payback from the established pattern that limits action despite dissatisfaction with the results that it is enabling

❑ preferring the security of what is known to the unknown.

Whether these sub-patterns exist at the personal or collective level, it is easy to see that, whatever the pattern of reasons, the personal has influence on the whole, as the whole has influence on the personal.

 To shift a pattern probably takes a number of additive conditions. Dissatisfaction with what is helps, at least in the sense of an awareness that something else is both possible, and is valued beyond that which the current pattern permits. A trigger can be the sight of an opening, or opportunity, to make a difference. It helps create the willingness to overcome fears and step out beyond the limits or boundaries of whatever is already experienced, namely the established pattern. It is, as Machiavelli observed (see Chapter One), the willingness to risk what is for what could be, without any assurance that what could be – a different future – will necessarily be the new pattern, or order of things, within one's immediate lifetime. What some might describe as courage, others might label as being foolish. Whatever the outcome, pattern shifters are willing to risk what is for a different level of result. Think of the pattern shifters of our time. Whether they were the prime movers of major international/ national shifts or the prime movers in, and of, their own personal transformations, each was willing to risk what was, the established pattern and its results, for something else.

Where butterflies flap their wings, people infect minds!

The butterfly, wherever its location, did not have any intention of creating a storm. It was probably more inclined to managing its species reproduction during its brief moment of crowning glory! Nevertheless, from such small actions, given the right conditions, can emerge dramatically amplified consequences. In much the same way the 'luck' of genetic variation – mutant genes – can lead to species variety. If we are not to leave pattern shifting to luck, and there will, inevitably, be random variation of patterns, then what else can be the source of a shift in pattern, no matter how grand the consequences downstream? Can we infect our own mind and the minds of others through the creation and communication of an idea?

Organisations and communities tend to become memetically sealed, immune, so to speak, from other sources of infection. The sets of nested and networked memes that serve to provide order for a particular world resist invasion, much like managers who live in the private world of their office! Over the centuries, the more obvious pattern shifts have occurred when 'new' orders have replaced old. The dominance of the new was then often justified as the natural order of things. The trend repeats itself today, as, for example, with the nature of the import of 'total quality' into some organisations (the indoctrination techniques of so-called 'sheep dipping'?). However, in the new world of our time, where the new frontier is a frontier of ideas more than physical territory or resources, new orders are more likely to be created by interconnection and emergence. Accidental or planned memetic recombination, whether in a real or virtual sense, offers more possibilities than does a simple competition for memetic dominance.

If butterflies did but know it, they might choose to flap their wings in order to create a shift in the pattern of the weather. Rumour has it that the capacity of Homo Sapiens is greater than that of the butterfly. One of our greatest capacities is language. It is not just having a language; it is the ability to language, to communicate about communication that provides an unsurpassed richness. "A vast space is opened up in which words serve as tokens for the linguistic co-ordination of actions and are also used to create the notion of objects."[168] It is through language and communication that we may so infect our own mind that we grant ourselves the mind to shift patterns and implant the will to do so in the minds of others.

Breaking out of the cocoon: existential fears to existential breakthroughs

We are simultaneously a product of, and contributor to, our patterns. When skilled and experienced in a pattern, particularly when that pattern shapes our perceptual frameworks and ways of thinking, then to think of shifting it can seem like a challenge to our very existence. We might not have the skills to grasp the competencies in the new way that we have in the old. To let go of what has helped me to at least survive to date, let alone be successful, seems like a high price to pay. But any other change is surface change.

Peter Senge captures the point well. Only after writing *The Fifth Discipline* was he to become more fully aware of the premise upon which it was written: a premise he described as "organisations work the way they work because of how *we* work"[169] (emphasis added). If you want to see any profound levels of change in an organisation you must first change how we work, that is, change must proceed at the personal and interpersonal level, in how we, and those around us, think, see and interact. Profound change demands change at the lowest unit of cultural transmission, the meme.

Change at the personal and interpersonal level may not be what many people at senior, and other, levels want to hear. Nevertheless we are all part of a pattern that simultaneously enables and limits results. To exempt ourselves from the pattern is to cast ourselves as but spectator upon the scene, no matter how well reasoned or analytical the account! It still seems to be the exception when a chief executive recognises their own contribution to the pattern, as in:

> "I know I've driven this company to where we've got to so far, and, thanks to much effort, we're doing pretty well by all the objective measures. I also know that there's a lot more potential out-there that could be released that simply won't be, if I continue to be the driver. I've got to somehow find a way that people want to do it for themselves, some way in which they are less driven and more enabled to be and do all that they can be and do. That's going to take a lot of change on my part."

The existential crisis that may befall those who are well practised in the art of dominating others – power over, rather than power with – may be converted to an existential breakthrough. Shifts in the patterns of our thinking, seeing and being open up not just new horizons of performance but also a different quality of experience, a different quality of life, in achieving those new levels. It is the shift from the dominator system to the more integrative approach.

What may be key for the existential shift is to be willing to entertain the apparent paradox of discontinuity with continuity. To maintain a deep sense of purpose, with clarity of choice in, and of, self, provides the continuity to tolerate strange new patterns, and also to actually seek discontinuities in, and of, current patterns, ones less aligned with that purpose and choice. Committing to a worthwhile purpose, while knowing that one cannot get there from here, provides for a unique blend of continuity and discontinuity, order and disorder. Entertaining this paradox often necessitates a deeper level of questioning, a level that often surfaces within existential crises. In one economist's words:

> "If knowledge is perfect and the logic of choice complete and compelling then choice disappears, nothing is left but stimulus and response. If choice is real, the future cannot be certain: if the future is certain there can be no choice."[170]

Bringing forth a world: letting the genie out of the bottle

The world for living systems is a product of what that living system is set up to see. We are, so to speak, structurally coupled with our environments. We 'see' what we are wired up to see. Thus, what one species 'sees' and responds to when compared with another is either entirely or significantly different. The world for the frog is very different from our own, but entirely normal and sufficient for the frog, to whom we are the abnormality, the undiscussable, the unknowable. Much of the wiring between species is of biological inheritance, a product of different genomes and evolution. Within the species Homo Sapiens much of the wiring is again biological but, within the scope of what has been granted biologically (and with the blessing of minimal critical specification), much of that wiring is also cultural. Thus we 'see' and respond differently given our shared and our unique cultural inheritance. Our way of knowing, our cognitive system, is patterned by our culture and provides the basis for a self-organising system, whether it be the system of a living person or a living company.

A living system, through its wiring, its structural coupling, specifies what changes in its environment will trigger changes within itself. Through such cognitive or 'knowing' processes the system 'brings forth a world'. It is a world that is clearly not independent of itself. As Fritjof Capra[171] describes it, cognition is:

"not a representation of an independently existing world, but rather a continual bringing forth of a world through the process of living. The interactions of a living system with its environment are cognitive interactions, and the process of living itself is a process of cognition. In the words of Maturana and Varela, 'to live is to know'."

Now, while we are giving short change to a fascinating new synthesis contained within *The Web of Life*, we have, we hope, travelled enough of a journey within this text for the reader to see that we not only respond to a world, but *bring forth* the world to which we respond. Much of that world, for us, is culturally inherited, through the language and institutions in which we participate.

If it is valid that we bring forth a world through what may be referred to as our 'wiring', then it is possible that we may bring forth a different world via a change in our wiring. The gift of self-awareness permits us to see patterns in our wiring and to shift them. Yet that awareness, and the capacity to both see and shift our patterns, is enabled or disabled by our mind's infection, an infection (read different wiring, cognition or knowing) that is aided by the transfer and/or creation of different ideas or memetic patterns. Among our particular species set, our peer group, it may, though, make us different.

And therein lies another pattern: what difference in us will make a difference? Can we bring forth a different world through a different wiring? And what will be the source or origin of that different wiring? The work of management has been quoted elsewhere as the creating and breaking of paradigms. It is perhaps the simpler – and more complex – to say it is the creating and breaking of patterns, patterns that, in turn, enable us to bring forth different worlds. Seen in this light, it helps to explain the difference between those companies who, for example, just *do* quality (out of compliance) and those who *are* quality (bring forth quality out of a different wiring). It is, we submit, the change in people, not of people, that serves to bring forth a different world.

The end of a beginning?

The breaking out of the cocoon, the shift from caterpillar to butterfly may appear small to many. Yet, it not only releases a crowning moment of species reproduction, but perhaps even impacts a distant weather pattern. As the ancient Chinese sage Lao Tse, whose words began this book revealed, big differences start from small changes. The paradox revealed is scale. The small shift in pattern is, from the caterpillar's perspective, indeed a metamorphosis. Does this mean that to transform results we must first transform ourselves? Can we then initiate some small changes for a potentially large difference?

To catch our mental wiring and to appreciate that it 'brings forth our world', is to no longer be a slave to the selfish pattern. We may even begin to glimpse other worlds that could be brought forth, worlds that might be not only different, but also vastly more rewarding, if we were only to shift some patterns. In doing so we may start to see that we have just begun. To begin shifting patterns, particularly at the personal level, means that we may not then be the same; and, as Alice said, "If I am not the same then who in the world am I?" And what world does that bring forth?

Who in the world do I choose to be and what world does that bring forth? To close a book is simple. To end with a new beginning is an open invitation.

Primary Sources

Much of this chapter is inspired by those who have written about the newly emerging and more holistic approach to management, and indeed society in general. We have drawn especially on Capra (1996) and Senge (1990, 1992) but acknowledge a debt to many others referenced elsewhere in the book.

It may seem strange, to many who are of the holistic or systemic persuasion, that we advocate an extension of what they would be prone to dismiss as the reductionist, or genetic determinist, view of biology. The paradox that strikes us is that it is easier to reach an appreciation of the holistic organisation, from a recognition of the systemic power of memes. As Kauffman (1995) puts it, "The proper marriage of self-organisation and selection would enlist Charles Darwin and Adam Smith to tell us who and how we are in the non-equilibrium world we mutually *create and transform*" (emphasis added). We have tried, in the scholastic journey of this book, to advance insights into that proper marriage, and the power of a world view that accepts both 'reductionism' and 'holism'. If we accept human society as more contained within the processes of the natural world, built, as Dennett (1995) would say, with sky-hooks not cranes, then we may paradoxically have more intention in creating the world we might want.

Notes

1   Pirsig (1974) Zen and the Art of Motorcycle Maintenance.

2   Keynes (1936) cited by Barber (1967) and Whittington (1993).

3   The Dutch and the Arab traders (who had sailed the Indian Ocean centuries before the Europeans 'discovered' it) monopolised the spice trade to the East Indies, the company's original objective. India was an afterthought when the original strategy proved untenable.

4   Jay (1994).

5   The system depended on some of the most rigid, unwritten codes of conduct any human society has yet created; a pattern whose grip outlived the British Empire that spawned it.

6   Thurow (1994).

7   Sakaiya (1991).

8   The result of the first global environmental crisis was the formation of the so-called Banded Iron Formations, the source today of most of our iron resources. The surplus oxygen produced by the growing population of the planet's first organisms literally rusted the planet, combining with dissolved iron to produce and precipitate insoluble ferrous oxides. Once the iron sink was used up the earth developed atmospheric oxygen, enabling all later life, but representing the first recorded global pollution event by which a species rendered its environment unable to sustain it in the future. Other similar feedbacks lie behind some – but not all – the step changes in the planet's biological record.

9   The parable concerns the frog that jumps out when placed in hot water but will slowly and happily boil to death if heated with the water.

10 The quotation is attributed to the Chairman of Taco Bell by Pfeffer (1996).

11 In most countries of the world licences to explore for hydrocarbons are offered through some variant of competitive tendering involving a combination of cash bids and work commitments. Contrary to some popular misconceptions there is no hard and fast way of knowing before drilling, how much oil will be found in a particular prospect, nor what it will be worth when it is developed. See Yergin (1991) for a fuller description. Every oil company has its legends of over-optimistic bids, and lucky failures.

12 The gender specific pronoun is deliberate. We have encountered fewer women who run companies or departments this way, which may of course reflect nothing more than sampling bias.

13 A series whose author, Anthony Jay, also numbers among his accomplishments a less well-known book, Management and Machiavelli (Jay 1994) that compares the management of many a large company with the problems of political government of a city state.

14 See Pascale (1991).

15 A 1994 survey reported to the American Strategic Planning Forum revealed Visions and Mission used by 90% of respondents, more than any other management tool.

16 Peter Scott-Morgan gives, in his book, a full description of a method for conducting such interviews and for arranging an intensive five day appraisal of a particular system of unwritten rules. It is a method honed in practice in a series of such appraisals in which I participated as the, initially sceptical, buyer.

17 See Senge et al (1994). Systems, archetype-style inquiries and unwritten rules appraisals become, in effect, interchangeable (Scott-Morgan pers. comm.). For those not familiar with Systems Thinking we include a brief summary in Chapter Six.

18 A similar underlying structure pervades the treadmill syndrome; the subject of our story earlier in the chapter. However, that case is not based on this example.

19 The US equivalent to the Daewoo example is probably Saturn which has "changed decades of tradition in the way cars are purchased". (http://www.edgeonline.com/ main/edgemag/archives/cs5.shtm) .

20 A touchdown for those inculcated in a different footballing pattern. The example is a classic case of the Fixes that Fail dynamic, the unintended consequence of a well intentioned change.

21 Brightman (1994).

22 Again those unfamiliar with Systems Thinking are referred to Chapter Six.

23 Between 1991 and 1993 IP and colleagues visited many large corporations who were implementing 'change' and improvement programmes. The vast majority had the same pattern; a committed group attached to the head office, a vision statement, a process of between four and fourteen steps, and a training package implemented via a network of 'facilitators'; one which typically started with a video of the CEO stating his commitment to the programme. Few could document the impact on their business strategy and even fewer could show how the programme was delivering different results to business as usual.

24 Goldratt (1990).

25 Or more accurately those raised as speakers and thinkers in a 'western' language. One might call it Proto-Indo European thinking (c.f. Chapter 1). .

26 Kuhn (1962).

27 Whereas he, in fact, captured and gave a different meaning to a pre-existing word.

28 Though that is precisely how many companies tried to apply it. In 1990 one major German manufacturer of luxury cars was reputedly proud of the fact that 25% of its manufacturing cost was incurred in the inspection and rework which ensured its product met its, justifiably famed, quality standards. The equivalent figure for Toyota or Nissan was under 2%. (Womak et al, 1990).

29 Ackoff (1981, 1994).

30 And it is interesting to reflect that in a world where external, geologically fixed, limits to growth are fast approaching different kinds of internal development, very fundamental shifts of pattern and paradigm may be essential for societies to stand still, that is to maintain and sustain standards and qualities of life.

31 And the huddle of expats in many a foreign community belies the inevitability of travel broadening their minds!

32 Quantum physics treats this as the problem of Schrodinger's cat. Casti (1990) explains.

33 Pascale (1991), also our source of the Matsushita quotation.

34 Belgard, Fisher, Rayner (1989).

35 Block (1991).

36 e.g. Deming (1986).

37 Many writers, educators, and commentators are now pointing to the 'Western' tradition of thinking, its strengths in terms of advances so far and its actual and potential weaknesses for the complexity of problems now confronted. We acknowledge those who have influenced our thinking at the end of the chapter.

38 DeBono (1990).

39 Ackoff (1981).

40 Kay (1993) p252.

41 See, for example, Morgan (1986) or Clancy (1989) Grant and Oswick (1996).

42 More correctly, the meme acts as if it seeks; as for that matter does the gene. We are not, repeat not, saying either has any intentionality. Replicators just are. It is just that it is much less cumbersome to write about them as if they do.

43 Darwinian evolution is a premise we are taking as given, justified in various references acknowledged elsewhere. We are drawing on many variations proposed to the basic theory, none of which conflict with the essential mechanism of natural selection.

44 And the bird 'competency' is, by day at least, rather more successful than the bat competency which has its own nocturnal niche. There is a clear parallel with the core competency approach to corporate strategy; two or more companies using different sources of advantage to compete in a given market (Hamel and Prahalad 1989; 1995). .

45   The point about strategic recipes following unconscious presumptions of past success has been made many times. Indeed, Mintzberg and colleagues have suggested perceiving corporate strategy as "a pattern in a stream of decisions" (Mintzberg and Waters 1994). Mintzberg (1994) provides an exhaustive treatment. Spender (1989) coined the idea of industry recipes. The 'recipe' industry in managerial fixes alluded to many times in this book is another manifestation of the same trend.

46   In this case The Panda's Thumb of Technology (in Gould 1991). Lest we misrepresent him we should emphasise that he highlighted the differences specifically to add weight to a case made out of a "fundamental conviction that comparisons (between biological and cultural or technological evolution) have done vastly more harm than good". We applaud the statement but are perverse enough to assert that ignoring the similarities risks perpetuating the harm.

47   It is also possible that the giraffe's long neck first evolved for some other reason entirely and was subsequently deployed for a particular diet.

48   The question of the influence of patterns on ethical and moral choices is far too complex to even try to treat here. Jane Jacobs (1993) addresses the question well, as does Dennett (1995).

49   Which, as covered in Chapter Three, is not to say that tradition is wrong, merely that it is limiting.

50   Stacey (1995).

51   'The edge of order' or 'bounded stability' would, by the way, be equally precise descriptions.

52   A pursuit which ignores feedback: the fact that, should one player in a market possess an ability to perfectly predict its behaviour, other players would have to either find alternative, and unpredictable, strategies, or stop playing. You do not play poker with someone who knows your every move before you make it.

53   And Alfred Russell Wallace.

54   A rival 'catastrophist' paradigm which honoured the nature of the geological record was French; a fact which may have influenced English opinion!.

55   Lyell (1830).

56   And even this example has now been shown to be a case of paradigm bias with the evidence observed through the wrong lens.

57   Dawkins (1989), replying to criticism of the perceived 'atomistic' approach in the first edition of The Selfish Gene.

58   Except where otherwise referenced this section relies on Hodgson (1993).

59   Among the rules thus spawned is one of giving due acknowledgement; a pattern we are seeking to honour here, and a style of academic writing in the third person that we are seeking to interrupt.

60   It can of course mislead and may strike a more academically patterned reader

as journalistic. Imitation is however the sincerest form of flattery and we acknowledge the memetic transfer in our own search for titles.

61 (op. cit.).

62 This is not intended as a criticism of Business Process Re-engineering as a business approach per se. We seek only to make the point that any pattern may enable and limit and to illustrate the propensity of the meme to go on replicating regardless of whether it continues to benefit its host.

63 See Hamel and Prahalad (1995). We return to corporate anorexia in Chapter Eight.

64 We have here the explanation of the observation that advertising is fundamentally irrational made by Kay (1993).

65 The crater is still there, as is the thin layer of iridium enriched clay that was splattered around the world. The dust thrown up from the explosion is believed to have caused a world-wide 'nuclear winter', one that the dinosaurs and many other organic designs did not survive. It is as yet only one plausible theory.

66 But gene and meme work on different time scales. The reproductive proclivities of monarchs tend to result in their genes being diluted in the larger population. 'Memetic speciation' has never succeeded in establishing a genetic equivalent.

67 Some have since showed up in other 'freak' rocks of a similar age. As a matter of curious historical coincidence I turned down a chance to be one of the students, having been convinced as an undergraduate that fossils were rather boring. Of such pre-conceptions are futures influenced!.

68 Gould (1991) and the Mavis Beacon typing manual – free with many a new PC!.

69 Arthur (1994). However, this book's editor tells another story. He claims to have found himself at a reception, sitting next to the then-Marketing Manager of Sony UK. Having a journalistic interest in the subject, he inquired politely how Sony had lost market share of the Beta system, to be told the following: three ships left Yokahama, bound for Rotterdam with a potentially market-winning cargo of Beta machines. En route, the signal was given to divert to the USA. A shift in the parity of the US dollar and the Yen was responsible, offering the prospect of instant financial reward. This however allowed JVC to slip in to the UK ahead of them – crucially, Sony had simply failed to realise that the UK market, with its major domestic TV rental component offering the prospect of bulk purchase and low-cost entry for the consumer, would be the key driver of VHS's success as the dominant domestic VCR standard forever more.

70 See Senge (1990) for the distinction of dialogue and discussion.

71 Weick (1969).

72   We follow Ackoff's (1994) use of 'mess' to refer to a complex set of interrelated elements; elements which through their systemic interaction, are not amenable to reductionism without loss of understanding. 'Mess' may also be a useful reference to the less predictable, non-linear feedback systems which characterise many human processes. To appreciate 'mess' is to appreciate that things work together in complex systems, rather than separately as if in isolated parts.

73   Dennett (1995).

74   So, by the way, do various genetically specified capabilities such as eyes or wings.

75   Our inspiration for the metaphor was DeBono's (1985) use of a deforming landscape to describe perception as a self-organising information system.

76   There is nothing wrong in this. In many instances it serves societies well. Thank goodness, for example, that in our driving practices we are schooled in and follow certain patterns.

77   Heidegger (1962).

78   Loosely, conversation is for the meme what sex is for the gene (an analogy which unfortunately ignores the reality of asexual replication).

79   Gregory (1990).

80   Unless of course the lack of a common verbal language heightens both parties' awareness of what is conveyed by the non-verbal.

81   Weick (1979).

82   More recently Gell-Mann (1994) has argued schemata are the necessary heart of any complex adaptive system. Without them no order could emerge, yet by permitting a particular order, a particular set of interactions with the world, they also limit. The only conceptual difference between schemata and memes is the concept of replication.

83   Koestler (1990).

84   Argyris (1985). Lest this next section emphasise the negative aspects of Argyris' contributions rest assured that subsequent chapters will emphasise his other contributions.

85   Argyris proceeds to contrast defensive with more productive reasoning, which has different governing values, action strategies and consequences. Chapter 7 briefly refers or see Argyris (1985).

86   On the other hand see Morgan (1986) for reviews of organisations as "psychic prisons".

87   Koestler (1990).

88   Lewin (1951).

89   Argyris (1985) op. cit.

90   DeBono (1990op. cit.).

91   Hurst (1995).

92   And by seeking to preserve for 100 years, and fighting fires, the US National Parks Service encouraged the proliferation of so much dead wood that the fires when they came in the 1980s were of a ferocity never before encountered. More recently a paradigm shift to controlled burning has occurred.

93   De Geus (1988, 1997) Schwartz (1994).

94   Argyris (1991op cit.).

95   Cited by Jay (1994).

96   Since Richard Dawkins, on whose ideas we have drawn heavily, is labelled in many such quarters as an arch-reductionist, a form of post-modernist anti-Christ. We may even find that this book is labelled as such. Anyone coming across such criticism who has not read Dawkins is recommended to the second edition of *The Selfish Gene* (1989). He is more than capable of refuting the charge.

97   We do not have space to offer here a brief primer on Systems Thinking. For more detail see Senge et al (1994). We are concerned to distinguish Systems Thinking and the more general systemic thinking..

98   Senge (1990) Senge et al (1994).

99   We will duck the discussion of whether the linear logic is hard-wired genetically, though note the evidence of 'Eastern' philosophy and different linguistic structures which casts a lot of doubt on hard line Chomskyism.

100 Compare the Business Process meme documented in Chapter Four. Systemic, Open Systems Theory, Systems Thinking, Systems Dynamics, Virtual Systems Theory are separate memes proliferating in different academic & consulting communities, often to the point of inhibiting rather than enabling shared communication between the minds they infect.

101 As an indication of the power of memetic patterns consider how positive and negative are used in this context. Many initiates to the new language experience have, at some stage, a problem describing as positive feedback a dynamic which leads to runaway 'negative' (i.e. undesired) behaviour; a vicious circle.

102 Readers who have not already had the opportunity are encouraged to become familiar with the systems archetypes introduced, especially in The Fieldbook. For four years I have been using the combination of Unwritten Rules, archetypes, and memes/emergent realities for classes of MBA students. We have accumulated documented examples and cases of every single archetype underpinned by different memetic patterns. Indeed, if one can identify the pattern at the core of the system, one may be best placed to cause a system scale shift, provided sufficient stakeholders participate in the necessary act of self-discovery.

103 Other good examples of the role of space in preserving different styles of status quo are provided by Hurst (1995).

104 Some biologists would disagree but the majority opinion would hold to the statement.

105 Smith and Rees (1997in prep.).

106 See 'Creative Tension' later in this chapter.

107 Bartlett and Ghoshal, 1994.

108 See Chapter Four.

109 Stacey (1995).

110 Pascale (1991).

111 Hamel and Prahalad (1989).

112 Issacs (1994) in Senge et al (1994).

113 We know not who first invented this term but it is a good example of a meme that seves to infect the mind, particularly when interconnected in a phrase like 'relanguaging your organisation'!.

114 Koestler (1990).

115 Heidegger, (1962).

116 Price and Shaw (1996).

117 Chia (1996) .

118 Whose company had just achieved a major growth in volume and profits of a mature product in a mature market.

118 The rise of warlords in periods of national unrest, protection rackets in modern Russia, or gang warfare in the ghettos of the USA's and Britain's inner cities are all, also, examples of the spontaneous emergence of order.

120 Hamel and Prahalad's (1995) graphic term for companies who focus only on cost cutting when facing the equation of return = profits ‚costs.

121 De Geus (1988).

122 Ackoff (1994).

123 Again practice predates theory. Recent advances in computer simulations of flocking behaviour in 'boids' have been used to generate animations such as the flocking dinosaurs of Jurassic Park, and the US Marines are reported to have 'discovered' the advantages of flexible battle strategies during the Gulf War.

124 The term 'corporate identity' is derived from a forthcoming book by Ken Baskin (1998) in which he explicitly argues for identity as the organisational gene, its DNA.

125 A recent (1997) product which exploits the processing power of genetic algorithms are computer pets. Among IT researchers the term 'memetic algorithm' is now in vogue for the next generation of 'genetic algorithms' those which will work in parallel, thus it is hoped produce even faster computing power.

126 Higher Education Institutions in the UK are a current case in point (Price and Kennie 1997).

127   The Cheetah, much admired as a symbol of efficiency, is in fact one such case. Depleted in genetic diversity it is in a dead end, cut off from the successful proliferation of the rest of the cat family. The beetle genotype has, in contrast, been extraordinarily successful at evolving. It has generated tens of thousands of species (Wills, 1989) .

128   The metaphor was used by Hamel and Prahalad (1995). Anorexia, as we noted in Chapter Four, is a true memetic disease.

129   Scott-Morgan (1994).

130   (e.g. Waldrop 1991, Kauffman 1993, 1995).

131   And if there is no synergy, the modern financial markets have proved superior to conglomerates as a way of determining investment.

132   The company is BP (see Prokesch 1997).

133   Rothschild (1992).

134   e.g. Tylecote (1993).

135   One area where the 'training pattern' is currently rampant is the system of work based vocational qualifications (NVQs in the UK and other names elsewhere). The intention is laudable; define standards based on best known practice and encourage people to demonstrate their ability to work towards them. Used as 'schema', minimum specifications which people discover their own ways of working towards, they can be enormously effective. Imposed in mass programmes of 'sheep-dipping' and 'box-ticking' and they rarely work.

136   Wills (1989).

137   Hawkins (1994).

138   And in this connection of our 'Fifth Attribute' to systems, or systemic thinking, we see also the connection to Senge's 'Fifth Discipline'. We are arguing for the use of that thinking, and indeed Systems Language (see Chapter Six) as a means to a deeper attribute, or property, that can be cultivated at any level. It is perhaps close to a combination of Systems Thinking and 'Personal Mastery'. In the pattern based conception of organisations we may begin to see why such disciplines are necessary. .

139   This is akin to Nonaka and Takeuchi's (1995) rendering of tacit knowledge explicit.

140   Henderson (1989).

141   Mintzberg (1994).

142   Rothschild (1992) page 213.

143   Pascale (1991).

144   Whittington (1993) citing Knights and Morgan (1991).

145   'The market' is another meme, one that conveys to most who are patterned by the traditions which currently dominate, a meaning far removed from the original conception of a gathering of rural traders in a small country village. .

146   As Roberts (1976) put it "Darwin's book, in combination with biblical criticism and geology made it impossible for any thoughtful man to accept - as he had still been able to do in 1800 - the Bible as literally true." .

147   On a larger scale, entropy increases in the process; an observation that is the departure point for theories concerning sustainable economies.

148   See in particular the 2nd edition of The Selfish Gene (Dawkins 1989) or a discussion by Casti (1990).

149   Porter (1980).

150   See Chapter Four for the theory.

151   An observation that is not intended to deny the artistic accomplishments of their builders or the value of the monasteries as custodians of knowledge and wisdom.

152   That ability, the extraction of low-entropy in perpetuity, is something the meme can do but the gene cannot. All genetic 'wealth' is recycled by the next generation. Memetic organisations can create enduring cultural artefacts of all kinds.

153   i.e. the owners of 'land', natural resources, rather than to the owners of capital or the providers of labour.

154   Given recent suggestions (December 1997) that the Keiretsu, in their turn, are being forced to change, or even that major Japanese firms may abandon the practice, it is interesting to speculate that another pattern became parasitic, faster than many expected.

155   In collaboration with an evolutionary biologist W. D. Hamilton.

156   Strategies which win in competition with TfT have since been discovered, as have strategies which defeat those strategies, but then lose to TfT. One is reminded of the game of stones, scissors and paper. For practical purpose however Axelrod's conclusions still seem to remain valid.

157   For an entertaining example of emergent collaboration in a situation in which a football match happened, unusually, to have a win-win outcome for the two teams involved see the end notes in Dawkins (1989).

158   And price wars may, from the consumers perspective, seem a good thing. A collaborative cartel can still become parasitic.

159   See for example, Moore's (1993) case history of Wal-mart.

160   Batchelor and Shaw (1996).

161   Compare figure 6.3.

162   Nonaka (1991).

163   From Alice in Wonderland.

164   One recent example of the emergence of the ownership meme (though the interpretation is ours) is provided by Hurst (1995). Over the last 30 years members

of the Kalahari Bushmen society have been encouraged to settle to an agricultural existence. Along with flocks of goats, malnutrition, and environmental degradation they have started to acquire material possessions. Their settlement pattern, which used to arrange itself in such a fashion that all members of an encampment could see into each others huts, has changed to one in which doors are arranged so as to provide privacy. Ownership, and hierarchy, emerge alongside wealth.

165   The 'butterfly effect' refers to the extreme sensitivity of chaotic systems to initial starting conditions, where minute changes in the system's initial state will lead over time to large-scale consequences. It has been much cited by 'New View' writers, with many different cities instanced. A small research project in memetic mutation could be undertaken.

166   And yes, Shaw, too, wrote from the pattern of his time.

167   See for example Axelrod (1984), Kauffman (1993,1995) or Waldrop (1992).

168   Capra (1996).

169   Senge (1992).

170   Loasby B. J. (1976).

171   Capra (1996).

Bibliography

Ackoff, R.L. (1981), *Creating the Corporate Future: Plan or Be Planned For*, John Wiley & Sons.

Ackoff, R.L. (1994), *The Democratic Corporation: A Radical Prescription for Recreating Corporate America and Rediscovering Success*, Oxford University Press.

Ager, D.V. (1973), *The Nature of the Stratigraphical Record*, Macmillan Press.

Allen, P.M. (1994), 'Coherence, chaos and evolution in the social context', *Futures*, 26:583-597.

Argyris, C. and Schon, D. (1978), *Organizational Learning: A Theory of Action Perspective*, Addison-Wesley.

Argyris, C. (1982), *Reasoning, Learning and Action: Individual and Organisational*, Jossey-Bass.

Argyris, C. (1985), *Strategy, Change and Defensive Routines*, Pitman Publishing

Argyris, C. (1990), *Overcoming Organizational Defences: Facilitating Organizational Learning*, Allyn and Bacon.

Argyris, C. (1991), 'Teaching smart people how to learn', *Harvard Business Review* (May-June), 99-109.

Arthur, W.B. (1994), 'Positive feedback's in the economy', *McKinsey Quarterly Journal*, 1:81-95.

Axelrod, R. (1984), *The Evolution of Co-operation*, Basic Books Inc.

Bandler, R. (1981), *Frogs into Princes: Neuro Linguistic Programming*, Real People Press.

Baskin, K. (1998) *Corporate DNA: Learning from Life*, Butterworth-Heinemann

Barker, J. (1990), *The Business of Paradigms: Discovering the Future* (video), Chart House Learning Corporation, USA.

Barlett, C.A and Ghoshal, S. (1994), *Changing the Role of Top Management: Beyond Strategy to Purpose Harvard Business Review*, (Nov.-Dec.), 79-88.

Batchelor, J. and Shaw, R. (1996), 'The shifting patterns of business: transforming purchasing for the new eras', *Proceedings of The North American Association of Purchasing Managers Annual Academic Conference*, 11-25.

Bateson, G. (1973), *Steps Towards an Evolution of the Mind*, Paladin.

Bateson, G. (1979), *Mind and Nature*, Fontana.

Battram, A. (1997), *The Learning from Complexity Pack*, Local Government Management Board, UK

Beer, M., Eisenstat, R.A. and Spector, B. (1990), 'Why change programs don't produce change', *Harvard Business Review*, (Nov.-Dec.), 158-166.

Belgard, W., Fisher, K., and Rayner, S. (1989), 'Understanding High Involvement Management: Its Theoretical Foundations', BRR Backgrounder™.

Berger, P. and Luckman, T. (1966), *The Social Construction of Reality*, Penguin.

Bibby, J.P. (1995), 'The Andrew results to date are quite simply, lower costs', *Petroleum Review*, (Jan.),14-153.

Block, P. (1991), *The Empowered Manager: Positive Political Skills at Work*, Jossey-Bass.

Brightman, J. (1994), 'Learning organizations and quality organizations: myths and realities', unpublished working paper.

Brodie, R. (1995), *Virus of the Mind: The New Science of the Meme*, Integral Press.

Brown, J.S., Collins, A. and Duguid, P. (1989). 'Situated cognition and the culture of learning', *Education Researcher*, 18, 1, 32-42.

Brown, J.S. and Duguid, P. (1991), 'Organizational learning and communities-of-practice: towards a unified view of working, learning and innovation', *Organization Science*, 2, 40-57.

Capra, F. (1996), *The Web of Life: A New Scientific Understanding of Living Systems*, Doubleday.

Casteneda, C. (1985), *Journey to Ixtlan: The Lessons of Don Juan*, Washington Square Press.

Casti, J.L. (1990), *Paradigm's Lost: Images of Man in the Mirror of Science*, Scribners.

Chandler, A.D. (1977), *The Visible Hand: The Managerial Revolution in American Business*, Harvard University Press.

Checkland, P.B.(1981), *Systems Thinking, Systems Practice*, John Wiley and Sons.

Checkland, P.B. and Scholes, J. (1990), *Soft Systems Methodology in Action*, John Wiley and Sons.

Chia, R. (1996), 'Metaphors and metaphorization in organisational analysis: Thinking beyond the thinkable', in D Grant and C. Oswick (eds.), *Methaphor and Organizations*, Sage Publications.

Clancy, J.J. (1989), *The Invisible Powers. The Language of Business*, Lexington Books.

Cohen, J. and Stewart, I. (1994), *The Collapse of Chaos: Discovering Simplicity in a Complex World*, Viking.

Cooper, D.E. (1990), *Existenialism: A Reconstruction*, Blackwell Publishing.

Covey, S.R. (1989), *The Seven Habits of Highly Effective People*, Simon and Schuster.

Crockett, A. (1973), *Money Theory, Policy and Institutions*, Nelson.

Daly, H.E. (ed.) (1980), *Economics, Ecology, Ethics: Essays Towards a Steady-state Economy*, W. H. Freeman and Company.

Darwin, C. (1859), *The Origin of the Species*, John Murray.

Dawkins, R. (1976), *The Selfish Gene*, Oxford University Press.

Dawkins, R. (1982), *The Extended Phenotype*, Oxford University Press.

Dawkins, R (1986), *The Blind Watchmaker*, Longmans.

Dawkins, R (1989), *The Selfish Gene (2nd edition)*, Oxford University Press.

DeBono, E. (1985), *Conflicts-A Better T Resolve Them*, Harrap.

DeBono, E. (1990), *I Am Right, You Are Wrong*, Viking.

DeBono, E. (1992), *Serious Creativity*, Harper Collins.

DeBono, E. (1993), *Handbook for the Positive Revolution*, Penguin.

DeBono, E. (1994), *Parallel Thinking: From Socratic to De Bono Thinking*, Viking.

De Geus, A. (1988), 'Planning as learning', *Harvard Business Review*, (March-April),70-74.

De Geus, A. (1997), *The Living Company: Growth, Learning and Longevity in Business*, Nicholas Brealey Publishing.

Deming, W.E. (1986), *Out of Crisis*, Cambridge University Press.

Dennet, D. C. (1995), *Darwin's Dangerous Idea: Evolution and The Meanings of Life*, Penguin Press.

Diamond, J. (1992), *The Third Chimpanzee: The Evolution and Future of the Human Animal*, Harper Collins.

Drucker, P. (1989), *The New Realities: in Government and Politics, in Economy and Business, in Society, and in World View*, Heinemann Professional Publishing.

Eccles, R.G., Nohria, N. and Berkley, J.D. (1992), *Beyond the Hype: Rediscovering the Essence of Management*, Harvard Business School Press.

Eldredge, N. and Gould, S.J. (1972) 'Punctuated equilibrium: an alternative to phyletic gradualism', in T.J.M. Schopf (eds.), *Models in Paleobiology*, Freeman Cooper.

Eldredge, N. (1991), *The Miner's Canary: Unravelling the Mysteries of Extinction*, Simon & Schuster.

Fairhurst, G.T. and Sarr, R.A. (1996), *The Art of Framing: Managing the Language of Leadership*, Jossey-Bass.

Ferguson, M. (1987), *The Aquarian Conspiracy: Personal and Social Transformation in the 1980's*, J.P. Tarcher.

Forrester, J. (1961), *Industrial Dynamics*, MIT Press.

Fromm, E. (1994), *The Art of being*, Continuum Publishing Group.

Fromm, E. (1996), *To Have or to Be?*, Continuum Publishing Group.

Gallwey, T. (1985), *The Inner Game of Tennis*, Pan Books.

Gell-Mann, M. (1994), *The Quark and the Jaguar: Adventures in the Simple and the Complex*, Little Brown.

Gersick, C.J. (1991), 'Punctuated equilibria as a model for organisational change', *Academy of Management Review*, 16/1:10-23.

Goldratt, E.M. and Cox, J. (1989, Revised Edition), *The Goal*, Gower, London.

Goldratt, E.M. (1990), *Theory of Constraints*, North River Press.

Gould, S.J. (1987), *Time's Arrow Time's Cycle: Myth and Metaphor in the Discovery of Geological Time*, Harvard University Press.

Gould, S.J. (1989), *Wonderful Life: The Burgess Shale and the Nature of History*, Norton.

Gould, S.J (1991), *Bully for Brontosaurus: Reflections in Natural History*, W. W. Norton & Co.

Gould, S.J (1993), 'Eight Little Piggies; *Reflections in Natural History*, Jonathan Cape.

Grant, D and C. Oswick eds., (1996) *Methaphor and Organizations*, Sage Publications

Green, R. (1995), 'A collaborative relationship does not mean a cosy relationship', *Petroleum Review* (Jan.),16-17.

Gregory, B. (1990), *Inventing Reality: Physics as Language* (Wiley Science Editions), John Wiley and Sons.

Hamel, G. and Prahalad, C.K. (1995), *Competing for the Future*, McGraw Hill.

Hamel, G. and Prahalad, C.K. (1989), 'Strategic intent', *Harvard Business Review,* (May-June), 63-76.

Handy, C. (1989), *The Age of Unreason*, Business Books Ltd.

Harthig, E. (1991), *Dawn of a Millennium. Beyond Evolution and Culture*, Penguin Books.

Harvey-Jones, J.(1993), *Managing to Survive*, Heinmann

Hawken, P. (1993), *The Ecology of Commerce. A Declaration of Sustainability*, Harper Collins.

Hawkins, P. (1994) 'The Changing View of Learning', in J. Burgoyne; M. Pedler; and T. Boydell (Eds), *Towards the Learning Company - Concepts and Practice*, McGraw Hill

Hayes, R.H., Wheelwright, S. and Clark, K.B. (1988), *Dynamic Manufacturing: Creating the Learning Organization*, Free Press.

Heidegger, M. (1962), *Being and Time*, Harper San Francisco.

Henderson, B.D. (1989), 'The origin of strategy', *Harvard Business Review*, (Nov.-Dec),139-143.

Hodgson, G.M. (1993), *Economics and Evolution: Bringing Life Back into Economics*, Polity Press.

Hosking, D. and Morley, I. (1991), *A Social Psychology of Organizing: People, Processes and Context*, Harvester Wheatsheaf.

Hull, D. (1988), *Science as a Process,* University of Chicago Press.

Hurst, D. (1995), *Crisis and Renewal: Meeting the Challenge of Organizational Change*, Harvard Business School Press.

Hutton, W. (1995), *The State We're In*, Jonathan Cape.

Isaacs, W. (1994), 'Dialogue', in P.M. Senge, C. Roberts, R. Ross, B.J. Smith and A. Kleiner (1994), *The Fifth Discipline Fieldbook: Strategies and Tools for Building a Learning Organisation*, Nicholas Brealey Publishing.

Jacobs, J. (1994), *Systems of Survival*, Hodder and Staughton.

Jay, A. (1994), *Management and Machiavelli: Discovering a New Science of Management in the Timeless Principles of Statecraft*, Prentice Hall.

Jones, S. (1993), *The Language of the Genes: Biology, History and the Evolutionary Future*, Harper Collins.

Johnson, H. and Kaplan, R.S (1987), *Relevance Lost: The Rise and Fall of Management Accounting,* Harvard University Press.

Kanter, R.M., Stein, B.A. and Jick, T.D. (1992), *The Challenge of Organisational Change: How Companies Experience It and Leaders Guide It*, The Free Press.

Kaplan, R. and Norton, D.P. (1992), 'The balanced scorecard - measures that drive performance', *Harvard Business Review* (Jan.-Feb.),71-79.

Kaplan, R.S. (1994), 'Devising a balanced scorecard matched to business strategy', *Planning Review*, (Sept./Oct.),15-19.

Kauffman, S.A. (1993), *The Origins of Order: Self Organization and Selection in Evolution*, Oxford University Press.

Kauffman, S. A. (1995), *At Home in the Universe: The Search for The Laws of Complexity*, Oxford University Press.

Kay, J. (1993), *Foundations of Corporate Success: How Business Strategies Add Value*, Oxford University Press.

Keynes, J.M. (1936), *The General Theory of Employment Interest and Money,* New York, Harcourt Brace, [cited by J.W. Barber (1967), *A History of Economic Thought*, Pelican Books, London.]

Knight, S. (1996), *NLP at Work: The Difference That Makes a Difference in Business*, Nicholas Brealey.

Koestler, A. (1990), *The Ghost in the Machine*, Arkana.

Kofman, F and Senge, P.M. (1993), 'Communities of commitment: the heart of learning organizations', *Organisational Dynamics*, Vol. 22, No. 2, 5-23.

Kuhn, T.S. (1962), *The Structure of Scientific Revolutions*, University of Chicago Press.

Lawson, P. (1993), *The East India Company: A History*, Longmans.

Lewin, K. (1951), *Field Theory in Social Science*, University of Chicago Press.

Lloyd, T. (1990), *The Nice Company*, Bloomsbury.

Loasby, B.J. (1976), *Choice, Complexity and Ignorance; An Enquiry into Economic Theory and the Practice of Decision Making*, Cambridge University Press.

Lodge, D. (1988), *Nice Work*, Secher and Warburg..

Lyell, C. (1830), *Principles of Geology*, Murray.

Lynch, A. (1996), *Thought Contagion: How Belief Spreads Through Society*, Basic Books.

Maturana, H. R. (1970), *Biology of Cognition*, reprinted in Maturana and Varela (1980).

Maturana, H.R. (1975), 'The organisation of the living: a theory of the living organisation, *International Journal of Man-Machine Studies*, 7:313-332.

Maturana, H.R. and Varela F. (1980) *Autopoiesis and Cognition: The Realization of the Living*, Reidel, Dirdrecht.

Matzdorf, F., Dale, M., Green, M. and Kennie, T.R.M. (1997), *Learning to Succeed: Organisational Learning in the Surveying Profession*, London, Royal Institution of Chartered Surveyors.

Maslow, A.H. (1954), *Motivation and Personality*, Harper and Row.

Maynard Smith, J. (1989), *Evolutionary Genetics*, Oxford University Press.

McCarthy, I.P., Lessure, M., Ridgeway, K. and Fielder, M. (1997), 'Building a Manufacturing Cladogram', Int. J. Technology Management, 1/3:269-286.

McGovern, P. (1995), 'Learning from the guru's: Managers' responses to the unwritten rules of the game', *Business Strategy Review*, 6/3:13-25.

Mingers, J. (1994), *Self-Producing Systems: Implications and Applications of Autopoiesis*, Plenum Press.

Mintzberg, H. (1994), *The Rise and Fall of Strategic Planning*, The Free Press.

Mintzberg, H. and Waters, J.A. (1994), 'Of strategies, deliberate and emergent', in H. Tsoukas (ed.), *New Thinking in Organizational Behaviour*, Butterworth Heinemann.

Mitroff, I. (1987), *Business Not as Usual: Rethinking Our Individual, Corporate, and Industrial Strategies for Global Competition*, Jossey-Bass.

Mitroff, I. and Linstone, H. (1996), *The Unbounded Mind: Breaking the Chains of Traditional Business Thinking*, Oxford University Press.

Moore, J.F. (1993), 'Predators and prey: a new ecology of competition', *Harvard Business Review*, (May-June),75-86.

Morgan, G. (1986), *Images of Organization,* Sage Publications.

Mumford, A. (1993), *How Managers can Develop Managers*, Gower.

Nelson, R.R. and Winter, S.G. (1982), *An Evolutionary Theory of Economic Change*, Harvard University Press.

Nonaka, I. (1991), 'The knowledge creating company', *Harvard Business Review*, (Nov.-Dec.), 96-104.

Nonaka, I. and Takeuchi, H. (1995), *The Knowledge Creating Company: How Japanese Companies Create the Dynamism of Innovation*, Oxford University Press.

Parker, D. and Stacey, R.D. (1994), *Chaos Management and Economics*, London Institute of Economic Affairs.

Pascale, R.T. (1991), *Managing on the Edge*, Simon & Schuster.

Payton C. E. (1977), *Seismic Stratigraphy - Applications to Hydrocarbon Exploration*, AAPG Tulsa.

Peters, T.J. and Waterman, R.H. (1982), *In Search of Excellence*, Harper and Row.

Pfeffer, J. (1996), *Competitive Advantage Through People: Unleashing the Power of the Workforce*, McGraw-Hill.

Pirsig, R.M. (1974), *Zen and the Art of Motorcycle Maintenance: An Inquiry into Values (10th Edition)*, William Morrow and Company.

Popper, K.R. and Eccles, J.C. (1977), *The Self and Its Brain*, Springer Verlag.

Porter, M.E. (1980), *Competitive Strategy: Techniques for Analyzing Industries and Competitors*, The Free Press..

Porter, M.E. (1985) *Competitive Strategy: Creating and Sustaining Superior Performance,* The Free Press..

Porter, M.E. (1990), *The Competitive Advantage Of Nations*, The Free Press.

Price , H. (1997), 'Annie's Case: Using NVQ Standards to Generate Learning in a Small Company' In T.L. Campbell (ed.) *Proceedings of the Fourth Conference of the European Consortium for the Learning Organisation*, La Hulpe.

Price I. (1993), 'Aligning people and processes during business focused change in BP Exploration', *Prism*, 4:15-31.

Price, I. and Evans, L. (1993), 'Punctuated equilibrium: an organic metaphor for the learning organisation', *European Forum for Management Development Quarterly Review*, 93/1:33-35.

Price, I. (1994), 'The genetics of the learning organisation' in P. DePotter, and T.L.

Campbell (eds.), *Proceedings of the First Conference of the European Consortium for the Learning Organisation*, Gower, London.

Price, I. (1995),'Organisational memetics?: organisational learning as a selection process', *Management Learning*, 299-318

Price, I. and Shaw, R. (1996), 'Parrots, patterns and performance – The learning organisation meme: emergence of a new management replicator', in T.L. Campbell (ed.), *Proceedings of the Third Conference of the European Consortium for the Learning Organisation*, Copenhagen.

Price , I. and Kennie, T.R.M. (1997), *Punctuated Strategic Equilibrium and Some Leadership Challenges for University 2000*, 2nd International Dynamics of Strategy Conference, SEMS Guildford

Prokesch, S.E. (1997) 'Unleashing the Power of Learning: An Interview with British Petroleum's John Browne', *Harvard Business Review*, (Sep-Oct),16pp.

Raup, D. (1986), *Extinction: Bad Genes or Bad Luck?*, Oxford University Press.

Reader, C. (1995), 'The general consensus is that CRINE pays', *Petroleum Review*, (Jan.),12-13.

Ricoeur, P., Blamey, K. and Thopson, J.B. (1991), *From Text to Action: Essays in Hermeneutics*, Northwestern University Press.

Roberts, J.M. (1976), *The History of the World*, Hutchison.

Rothschild, M. (1992), *Bionomics: The Inevitability of Capitalism*, Futura.

Sakai, T. (1991), *The Knowledge-Value Revolution or a History of the Future*, Kodansha.

Schaffer, R.H. and Thompson, H.A., (1992), 'Successful change programs begin with results', *Harvard Business Review*, (Jan.-Feb), 80-89.

Schapiro, E. (1995), *Fad Surfing In The Boardroom*, John Wiley and Sons.

Schein, E.H. (1993), 'On dialogue, culture, and organisational learning', *Organizational Dynamics*, 22, No. 2.

Schwartz, P. (1991), *The Art of the Long View*, Doubleday.

Scott-Morgan, P.B. (1993), 'Removing barriers to change: the Unwritten Rules of the Game', *Prism* Q4, 5-18.

Scott-Morgan, P. (1994), *The Unwritten Rules of the Game*, McGraw Hill.

Scott Morton, M.S. (1991), *The Corporation of the 1990's: Information Technology and Organizational Transformation*, Oxford University Press.

Senge, P.M. (1990), *The Fifth Discipline. The Art and Practice of the Learning Organisation*, Doubleday.

Senge, P.M., Meen, D. and Keough, M (1992), 'Creating the learning organisation: an interview with Peter Senge', *The Mckinsey Quarterly*, No. 1.

Senge, P. M., Roberts, C., Ross, R., Smith, B. J. and Kleiner, A. (1994), *The Fifth Discipline Fieldbook: Strategies and Tools for Building a Learning Organisation*, Nicholas Brealey Publishing.

Smith, L.J. and Rees, D. (1997), *Comparative Assessments and Process Benchmarking Portering Services*, Facilities Management Graduate Centre, Sheffield Hallam University, UK.

Somit, A. and Peterson, S.A. (1992), *The Dynamics of Evolution: The Punctuated Equilibrium Debate in the Natural and Social Sciences*, Cornell University Press.

Spender, J.C. (1989), *Industry Recipes*, Blackwell.

Stacey, R.D. (1993a), *Strategic Management and Organisational Dynamics. London*, Pitman.

Stacey, R.D. (1993b), 'Strategy as order emerging from chaos', *Long Range Planning*, 26:10-17.

Stacey, R. D. (1995), 'The science of complexity: an alternative perspective for strategic change processes', *Strategic Management Journal*, 16:477-495.

Stacey, R. D. (1996), *Complexity and Creativity in Organizations*, Berrett-Koehler.

Thurbin, P.J. (1994), *Implementing the Learning Organisation: The 17-Day Programme*, Financial Times & Pitman Publishing.

Thurow, L, (1994), 'New game, new rules, new strategies', *RSA Journal*, 50-56.

Townsend, R.L. (1970), *Up The Organisation. How to Stop the Company Stifling People and Strangling Profits*, Hodder Fawcett Ltd.

Tushman, M.L., Newman, W.H. and Romanelli, E. (1986), 'Convergence and upheaval: managing the unsteady pace of organisational evolution', *California Management Review*, 29/1, (fall): 29-44.

Tylecote, A. (1993), *The Long Wave*, Routledge.

Waldrop, M.M. (1992), *Complexity: The Emerging Science at the Edge of Order and Chaos*, Simon and Schuster.

Walton, R.E. (1985), 'From control to commitment in the workplace', *Harvard Business Review*, (Mar.-Apr.), 77-84.

Waterman jr., R.H. (1987), *The Renewal Factor: How the Best Get and Keep the Competitive Edge*, Bantam Doubleday Dell Publishing.

Weick, K.E. (1991), 'The non-traditional quality of organizational learning', *Organization Science*, 2,2.

Weick, K.E. (1969), *The Social Psychology of Organizing*, Addison-Wesley

Weick, K. E (1979), 'Cognitive processes in organizations', *Research in Organizational Behaviour*, 1, 41-74

Whittington, R. (1993), *What is Strategy and Does it Matter?*, Routledge.

Wills, C. (1989), *The Wisdom of the Genes, New Pathways in Evolution*, Oxford University Press.

Wilson, C. (1990), *Access to Inner Worlds: The Story of Brad Absetz*, Celestial Arts.

Winograd, T. and Flores, F. (1987), *Understanding Computers and Cognition: A New Foundation for Design*, Ablex Corp.

Womack, J.P, Jones, D.T and Roos, D. (1990), *The Machine that Changed the World*, Rawson Associates.

Yergin, D. (1991), *The Prize*, Simon and Schuster.

Index